FUNK THE CLOCK

FUNK THE CLOCK

Transgressing Time While Young, Perceptive, and Black

Rahsaan Mahadeo

CORNELL UNIVERSITY PRESS   ITHACA AND LONDON

Copyright © 2024 by Rahsaan Mahadeo

All rights reserved. Except for brief quotations in a review, this book, or parts thereof, must not be reproduced in any form without permission in writing from the publisher. For information, address Cornell University Press, Sage House, 512 East State Street, Ithaca, New York 14850. Visit our website at cornellpress.cornell.edu.

First published 2024 by Cornell University Press

Library of Congress Cataloging-in-Publication Data
Names: Mahadeo, Rahsaan, 1982– author.
Title: Funk the clock : transgressing time while young, perceptive, and
   black / Rahsaan Mahadeo.
Description: Ithaca [New York] : Cornell University Press, 2024. | Includes
   bibliographical references and index.
Identifiers: LCCN 2023032512 (print) | LCCN 2023032513 (ebook) | ISBN
   9781501774201 (hardcover) | ISBN 9781501774218 (paperback) | ISBN
   9781501774232 (epub) | ISBN 9781501774225 (pdf)
Subjects: LCSH: Time—Social aspects. | Racism in the social sciences. |
   Youth, Black—Social conditions. | Time perception—Social aspects. |
   Race—Social aspects. | Racism.
Classification: LCC HM656 .M245 2024 (print) | LCC HM656 (ebook) | DDC
   304.2/37—dc23/eng/20230724
LC record available at https://lccn.loc.gov/2023032512
LC ebook record available at https://lccn.loc.gov/2023032513

For Ana and Asani

Contents

Acknowledgments	ix
Introduction	1
1. Whose Time Is It?	29
2. *Teefing* Time	59
3. The Makings of a "Maybe Environment"	89
4. "Keisha Doesn't Get the Call before Kimberly"	110
5. *Tabanca* Time	125
6. Transgressing Time in the Fast Life	137
7. Why Is the Time Always Right for White and Wrong for Us?	146
8. Prescience within Present Orientations	167
Conclusion	199
Methodological Appendix: Interview Schedule	207
Notes	213
Selected Bibliography	255
Index	271

Acknowledgments

When I was an undergraduate, a sociology professor invited our seminar class to his house for an end-of-year gathering. During what was supposed to be a relaxed evening of reflections and takeaways, the professor somehow felt compelled to discuss my writing with the rest of the class and said, "You should write the way you talk." This was code for, "Why are you trying to sound intelligent?"

The professor was referring to a twang familiar to many kids who came up through the Providence public schools. I think within some perverse realm of whiteness, the professor had convinced himself that he was doing me a favor by helping me "find my voice" and alleviate the pressure of assimilating to Western logic and writing conventions. Still, what he failed to appreciate was that he had already suspended me in his own version of the "ethnographic present." I was frozen in an urban sociological fantasy that pathologizes racialized students from poor, urbanized space as incapable of keeping pace with the rigors of the academy. The professor's words were a reminder that I was living, learning, and laboring in a system that was designed without me and so many others in mind. Thus, it was not possible for me to engage with complex theories and concepts without sacrificing my voice.

I imagine the professor assured himself that what he said was not racist (at least not as racist as another one of his sociology colleagues, who accused me of plagiarism by telling me that "undergraduates do not write like this"). But he failed to recognize how maddening it is for a first-generation college student to be told he doesn't have to conform to the same wretched system that demands he do so in order to achieve at least a modicum of "academic success." At the time, I didn't have an expression to describe such behavior. Today we might call it "gaslighting." The problem was not that I needed to find my voice—it was that the academic-industrial complex had already rendered my voice unintelligible. Insofar as my words were comprehensible, I would need to be ventriloquized by a reputable representative of the university. Given my antagonistic relationship to the university, I have come to appreciate the need to write the way I speak. Thank you to everyone who has encouraged me to do more code sticking and less code switching.

Anything I can offer through this book is a product of what I've been given. Material support goes a long way to making books like this possible. Still, without the care and generosity of so many friends, colleagues, mentors, and youths, this

x   ACKNOWLEDGMENTS

book would not exist. The magnitude of my gratitude cannot be contained in words. To that end, I hope my appreciation is and has been felt as much as it is read or understood.

I am immensely grateful to the youths who contributed to this book. It is no coincidence that some of the most radical and transformational movements emerge from the willful energy of younger generations. Experience may come with age, but so does resignation to the status quo. Youths' unadulterated and unadulted imaginations have serious counterhegemonic potential because they are not afraid to ask questions. They ask these questions while letting their visions for another world run wild. So many youths who contributed to this book had a unique ability to imagine a not-yet-here beyond and outside the current space-time. If transformative change starts at the *radix*, or the root, then it only makes sense to center the sprouts.

This book is based on research I conducted in the Department of Sociology at the University of Minnesota. Thank you to my mentors: David Naguib Pellow, Joyce M. Bell, Rose M. Brewer, and Jeylan Mortimer. Thank you, David and Joyce, for nurturing my urge to maintain an antagonistic and fugitive relationship to sociology. Your genuine care and fierce advocacy let me know you had my back. Though illegible to the university, I recognize and appreciate the inordinate amount of labor you perform inside and outside the classroom. Thank you, Rose Brewer, for your mentorship and guidance and for modeling what it means to be committed to struggles beyond the academy. Thank you to Jeylan Mortimer for helping me to think about how to situate my work within various subfields in sociology, even when I found it most comfortable to be outside those fields.

Much of the writing of this book occurred during my experiences at Georgetown University. Thank you to Kathleen Guidroz, Becky Yang Hsu, Yuki Kato, Brian J. McCabe, Kristin Perkins, and Sarah Stiles for reviewing early book proposal drafts and providing such thoughtful feedback. Special thank you to Carole Sargent, director of the Office of Scholarly Publications at Georgetown, for transforming my diffidence over the book into a sense of possibility and wonderment. Finally, thank you to my mentor, Corey D. Fields. Your guidance, brilliance, and sense of humor only made my experience even more gratifying. You went out of your way to check in personally and professionally. I left each of our meetings with greater enthusiasm than when I entered. Even when the COVID-19 pandemic struck, your support did not waver. How you managed to so effortlessly be both conscientious and visionary in such a place like the academy remains hard to fathom. Still, I am grateful for all you do.

It is difficult to write a book about time while feeling the pressure to be punctual with my prose. My nonlinear writing process consists of pauses, stops, reversals, detours, misdirection, disorientation, ambivalence, ambiguity, wanderings, and wonderings. Thank you to Jim Lance, Clare Jones, Mary Kate Murphy, and the entire editorial staff at Cornell University Press for extending such grace when it came to deadlines. I would be lying if I said that I was intentionally funking the clock. The truth is, each second, minute, hour, day, and week I was not able to complete this manuscript increased what already felt like an unbearable weight. Jim, your enthusiasm for this book affirmed my excitement in what was at the time still just a hope. I am grateful for our many email jam sessions and idea shares in the very early stages of the pandemic. I never expected an editor's vision to be so aligned with my own. Thank you for trusting my voice and vision.

I was fortunate enough to host a manuscript development workshop that included a stellar list of scholars, including La Marr Jurelle Bruce, Lisa Marie Cacho, Corey D. Fields, Freeden Blume Oeur, L. H. Stallings, and Terrion Williamson. What an honor it was to be in the company (albeit virtually) of so many scholars whose work has significantly informed my own.

Many thanks to past and present members of the Critical Race and Ethnic Studies (CRES) interdisciplinary writing group at the University of Minnesota. Countless members of CRES read drafts of nearly every chapter and helped sharpen my analyses in ways that exceed the conceptual boundaries of a single discipline, especially sociology. The imprint of their generous feedback and thoughtful engagement can be found throughout most chapters in this book. This brilliant group of scholars includes Bodunrin Banwo, Ana Cláudia dos Santos São Bernardo, Sayan Bhattacharya, Kidiocus Carroll, Diana Chandara, Chip Chang, René Esparza, Tia-Simone Gardner, Roy Guzman, Elena Hristova, Ezekiel Joubert III, Dewitt King, Brittany Lewis, Brian Lozenski, Emily Mitamura, Joanna Núñez, Naimah Pétigny, Kong Pha, Beaudelaine Pierre, José Manuel Santillana Blanco, Rashad Williams, Colin Wingate, and AK Wright. I'm grateful to you all for creating a meaningful space for study and fostering the type of fellowship that requires no competition. Thank you for modeling what it means to be beholden to one another rather than to the systems and conventions we are seeking to dismantle. When it comes to being good friends, you all have mad skills.

There are so many others who have helped to make this book possible by being generous readers, thought partners, mentors, and friends. This list includes Felicia Arriaga, Ahmad Azzahir, Elder Atum Azzahir, Freeden Blume Oeur, Eduardo Bonilla-Silva, Naomi Macalalad Bragin, David Brunsma, Raphael Coffey, monét cooper, David Embrick, Freda L. Fair, Rod Ferguson, Denise Ferreira da Silva, Carrie Freshour, Pallavi Gupta, Troy Harden, Theresa Hice-Fromille, Anthony Jimenez, Lauren Elizabeth Reine Johnson, Phil Kretsedemas, Cedric De Leon, May Lin, Jodi Melamed, Corey Miles, Melissa Milkie, Avarigi Miller, Victor Ray, Dylan Rodríguez, Michael Rodríguez-Muñiz, Marcell Saliba-Coffey, Uriel Serrano, Pramila Vasudevan, and Michelle M. Wright. Special thank you to Ruha

Benjamin for the invitation to serve as a co-organizer for the two-part "Time for Black Studies" symposium sponsored by Princeton University. Ruha, your prescient vision for a more just and sustainable world is truly inspiring.

Most of the ideas for this book were cultivated during my time at the University of Minnesota. Without the support of friends and colleagues, I would have lost much of my energy to keep on keeping on. Thank you to Matthew Aguilar-Champeau, Karin Aguilar-San Juan, Eden Almasude, Tanja Andic, De Andre Beadle, Matthew Boynton, Javaris Bradford, Kriti Budhiraja, Edgar Campos, Teri Caraway, Corey Culver, Hana Dinku, Carl Elliott, Gunercindo Espinoza, Jennifer Etienne, Courtney Gildersleeve, Lisa Gulya, Kristin Haltinner, Amber Hamilton, Cassandra Hendricks, Choua Her, Erin Hoekstra, Zenzele Isoke, Siddharth Iyengar, Anthony Jimenez, Annie Jollymore, Amber Jones, Yagmur Karakaya, Meg Krausch, Snigdha Kumar, Wenjie Liao, Alex Manning, María José Méndez, Natasha Moore, Devika Narayan, Mario Obando, Yuichiro Onishi, Karla Padrón, Lena Palacios, Lisa Sun-Hee Park, Soham Patel, Miray Philips, Victoria Piehowski, Mary Pogatshnik, Amber Joy Powell, Anuradha Sajjanhar, jim saliba, Malak Shahin, Wahutu Siguru, Emily Springer, Catherine Squires, Stephen Suh, Joe Svec, Jasmine Tang, Farrah Tek, Shakita Thomas, Edén Torres, Aisha Upton, Alexandra Vagac, Madison Van Oort, Aria Weatherspoon, Rob Wilson, and Atosha Zerbine. Respect due to mi bredren Christopher "Junior" Williams. You were my only East Coast–Midwest connection, but I did not know it until I moved to the Twin Cities. Apprecilove star. Special thanks to Anthony Jimenez. I feel incredibly fortunate for the many experiences we've shared that have allowed me to call you a friend, comrade, and brother.

At Providence College, I've had the pleasure of being supported by some amazing colleagues. Special thanks to Zophia Edwards and Trina Vithayathil for their guidance and advocacy, and their fierce resistance to Civilization and the institutions that cultivate it.

There is an iterative connection between my scholarship and activism. As I think about how racialized violence takes time, I cannot help but recall the inordinate amount of time I and so many other comrades spent fighting court cases, challenging student conduct charges, performing "community service," and contending against other repressive tactics used to quell dissent. Most of the fieldwork for this book was conducted while we were actively engaged in struggles on and off campus. So thank you to Irina Barrera, Marco Cruz Blanco, Fathi Fae, Natalie Goodwin, Tori Hong, Hoda Isak, Melinda Lee, Katie Levin, Nadio Linoo, David Melendez, Joanna Núñez, Zack Pierson, Leah Prudent, Idalia Robles de León, Meron Tebeje, Duaba Unenra, and Khin Warkhaung. I remain in communion with those freedom fighters who have made the transition to another spacetime, including Jesús Estrada Pérez, Rose Freeman Massey, Mel Reeves, Ms. Anna Stanley, and Tor.

ACKNOWLEDGMENTS xiii

Thank you to Terrion Williamson and the entire Black Midwest Initiative for mapping presence in presumed absence. The many Black artists, activists, scholars, and other community-connected folk in the Midwest are a reminder that Blackness defies longitudinal and latitudinal coordinates.

I cannot ignore the many nourishing spaces outside the university that protected me from the desiccating elements of the university. Before beginning my fieldwork, I had already established ties with a few youth groups in St. Paul and North Minneapolis, including Urban 4-H, and I began volunteering with two groups of high school youths. Some of my fondest memories are of weekly meetings and several events that were truly youth oriented, youth driven, and youth led. I left each meeting awestruck at how all the youths were light years ahead of where I was at their age. Their prescience gave me tremendous hope for what was and what could be. So thank you to Samantha Compean, Dani Rae Gorman, Ryoko Grosbusch, Adriana Leal, Gao Lee Brandy Matute, Danna Morales, Soukie Nantharath, Frank Rypa, Ka Thao, and Miesee Xiong. And of course, thank you to our incredible coordinator, Kathryn Sharpe. Each of you will forever hold a special place in my heart.

Thank you to all my organizing pals with the Social Justice Education Movement (SJEM): Cory Cochrane, Sadie Cox, Sarah Garton, Liya Gebremariam, Max Hoiland, Ro Lin, Tracy Pham, Madeleine Pinkerton, Abigail Rombalski, Kurt RuKim, and Sarah Zalanga. Reflecting on our many visioning sessions and the love, care, and joy infused into the Social Justice Education Fair still brings a smile to my face. It was my organizing with SJEM that opened the door for me to become a part of Free Minds, Free People. Much love to the entire Free Minds, Free People family.

During my time in the Twin Cities, I had the good fortune to organize with and learn from a range of brilliant organizers. Love and solidarity to Jose Avilar, Stephanie B., David Boehnke, Monique Cullars-Doty, Alaina DeSalvo, Rahhel Haile, Isuru Herath, Nazir Khan, Ricardo Levins-Morales, mk nguyen, Nick O., Peter Rachleff, Alisha Roopchand, Anna Stitt, TK, Duaba Unenra, Robin Wonsley, and Ladan Yusuf. Thank you to one of my closest connections to sweet, sweet T&T in the Twin Cities, Marla Jadoonanan—D' original "Trinisotan." Many of us know you as "Ma" because of the warm and welcoming atmosphere of the best restaurant in Minnesota. You nourished more than just our bellies. You also fed our spirits and souls.

During my brief time in DC, I was fortunate enough to connect with some of the sharpest organizing minds in the DC, Maryland, Virginia (DMV) region. Thank you to all my comrades with the DC Incarcerated Workers Organizing Committee (IWOC) and Free Them All VA for modeling a community of care and accountability to make prisons and other systems of captivity obsolete. My organizing was so intimately linked to the topic of race and time that it became the premise for the opening to the conclusion of this book. Special shout-out to the Behind the Walls committee in Providence, Rhode Island. Since leaving the East Coast to begin work in Minnesota, I experienced some serious strain over engaging in meaningful struggles in communities that welcomed me but that I could still not necessarily call home. Returning to Providence and joining Behind the Walls helped to alleviate a lot of these tensions. Sending health, strength, and ease to comrades behind and beyond the wall. Please know that when we make the call to "free them all," we don't place an asterisk or footnote next to "all." "All" means all. There is no qualification for liberation. This is solidarity, not charity, and we show it without expectation for reciprocity.

I strive to write with and for those without extra initials behind their name, especially those who have taught me more than most people with degrees. So I was quite honored when my father's key partner, Isaac, told me that he read a draft of chapter 2. Isaac said that he had not given a lot of thought to the phrase "*teefing* time," but he acknowledged that we must *teef* time "because time is Babylon own."

Family remains a site of so much warmth, nourishment, and love. Thank you to all my aunties, uncles, and cousins everywhere. Love and eternal gratitude to my mother and father. Your embrace nourishes me. Your words affirm me. Your love sustains me. Thank you for nurturing my desire for connection and a sense of solidarity. Thank you for letting my imagination run wild and for accompanying me in my travels. Thank you for helping me recognize that schools were not the only site of knowledge, knowledge production, and knowledge producers. My biography informs my scholarship, and my story would not be complete without my siblings—Jawara, Amina, Jordan, and Noah. Our upbringings were together and apart. Still, love kept us close, and we continue to come through for one another when hard times hit. I love you all.

I cannot imagine having completed this manuscript without the love and support of my partner, Ana Cláudia dos Santos São Bernardo. Your kindness, patience, and grace are virtues I admire and cherish. Eu te amo. As we embark on our new journey as parents, I am eager to continue learning with and from you. Asani is extremely lucky to have a mother who showers him with so much love and care every day. Thank you, Asani, for helping me to see the world through your eyes. Because of you, I embrace the opportunity to learn and unlearn every day. Daddy loves you.

An earlier version of chapter 7 was published as the following article: "Why Is the Time Always Right for White and Wrong for Us? How Racialized Youth Make Sense of Whiteness and Temporal Inequality," *Sociology of Race and Ethnicity* 5 no. 2 (2019): 186–99, © American Sociological Association, 2018.

INTRODUCTION

Asking "What time is it?" orients one to time and space. The banality of the question, though, should not excuse what are arguably serious onto-epistemological limitations.[1] Rather than using an adjective (i.e., "what"), it is more generative to use a determiner (e.g., "whose"). Asking "Whose time is it?" exposes the possibility that some may own time, while others can only owe it. Not only does the question help distinguish between time's owners and borrowers, but it opens up space for explanations of temporal exploitation and violence. What if being on time meant that others were always off time or late and thus penalized? To what extent does possession of time require dispossession? Posing these kinds of questions upends mutually agreed-on conceptions of time and creates space to problematize universal logics that legitimate the temporalization of race, ontology, and the human.

Funk the Clock is about those who are said to be emblematic of the future yet are denied a place in it. To that end, I aim to illustrate how Black youth reckon with time. I specifically study how race, racialization, and racism condition the time perspectives of Black youth in urbanized space.[2] Their accounts expose fissures between those who have time and those who are bound by it. Their stories highlight a distinction between the possessors and dispossessed within existing temporal orders. Reframing the question from "What time is it?" to "Whose time is it?" creates desperately needed theoretical space to trouble time and critique its capacity to possess those who possess it. The title of this book is a response to the question of "Whose time is it?" Thus, *Funk the Clock* is also both an invitation and provocation to let Black youth give the finger to the hands of time, while inviting readers to follow their lead. By funking (with) the clock, Black youth refuse to inhabit the white, middle-class, and heteropatriarchal dimensions of time. Because the time they use may not be their own, Black youth recognize the need to funk the clock and thus funk with time. When I asked JT, a seventeen-year-old mixed, transmasculine youth, whether he believes in lateness, he had this to say:

> See, here's the thing. . . . Like sometimes I think about this when I'm up way too late, but the whole time is a human concept and an illusion and whatever, is something that I take probably too seriously. But it's true, animals don't really rely on time. Plants don't really rely on time. It's really only people that do. The only way that I can see animals relying on time is when the seasons start to change and then they need to move. But that's only four times when the seasons change. But the time is constantly changing for us. We have twelve-hour clocks and we have twenty-four-hour clocks and there's different time zones and . . . yeah, it's weird. If I were to answer, "Are you late to school?" Yes. All the time. But if we're gonna get existential, like, no one's ever late. You know?

Identifying time as a "human concept" suggests that JT recognizes the importance of asking "Whose time is it?" before asking "What time is it?" Ironically, JT uses nature to denaturalize time and funk with what Elizabeth Freeman calls the "forms of temporal experience that seem natural to those they privilege."[3] JT's curiosities leave him up "way too late" wondering what makes people, but not plants and animals, so dependent on time. Why are humans, but not nature, subject to the temporal discipline of the clock? It's unclear whether JT has ever received a satisfactory answer to his question. But he remains emphatic that no one is ever late.

In *Funk the Erotic: Transaesthetics and Black Sexual Cultures*, L. H. Stallings conceives of funk as "a multisensory and multidimensional philosophy" linked to "the erotic, eroticism, and black erotica."[4] According to Stallings, funk shapes "film, performance, sound, food, technology, drugs, energy, time, and the seeds of revolutionary ideas for various black movements."[5] Thus, "funk" is perceptible through a variety of senses. We may see someone who looks blue and assume they are "in a funk." Some may smell a funk or foul odor. "Funk" is also transmitted through sound. Funk is not only a genre of music but also a style (e.g., a funky beat). Though the meaning of "funk" is contingent on time and space, it is also located squarely within Black social life. To "make it funky" is a directive to make the imperceptible perceptible. Asking an artist to "put some stank on it" is a request to make the track so funky that you can smell it. The funk may be pungent enough that you must hold your nose and nod in rhythmic agreement to the beat—"stank face." "Making it funky" is also to make the intangible tangible. You "feel the funk" and your body moves accordingly. You "let the rhythm hit" and despite the musical blow, you "feel no pain."

"Funk" also represents a euphemism for "fuck." The contributions I make lie not necessarily in fucking time but in fucking/funking *with* time. To be "fucked with" is to be teased, troubled, and/or tormented. Hence, "I'm just fuckin' with you." Those who are consistently fucked with know that "I'm just fuckin' with you" is not *just* a "just." Getting fucked with can leave someone fucked up. In fucking with time, my aim is to do such irreparable damage that I leave it completely fucked up. When things are "funked up," they are usually not right or out of order. To be out of order, though, is not always a bad thing. In *The Undercommons: Fugitive Planning and Black Study*, Stefano Harney and Fred Moten draw on Frantz Fanon's use of *lyse*, or lysis, and in doing so, put forth "a call to disorder, to complete lysis."[6] To funk the clock is to resist the call to order, the call to coevalness, the call to capital accumulation, and the call to remain synchronized with the whiteness and heteronormativity of time. Hence, it is worth asking whether a function of funk is to queer. This book presents several stories of youth funking the clock, queering the clock, and refusing a call to (temporal) order, including punctuality. For Dominique, a sixteen-year-old Black, trans, and "gender fluent" youth, it mattered less whether someone was late.[7] What was most important was having the opportunity to "re-feel" what happened: "Lateness? When somebody . . . when you needed something at a certain time but you're about to do something else and that thing is late. But I feel like there's no such thing as lateness as long as you showed up and you can re-feel what happened. You know? I don't think people should be marked tardy if they can catch up on what happened already. You know?"

Dominique rejects temporal protocols for punctuality, while envisioning a world where lateness does not apply. By suggesting that there is "no such thing as lateness" because people can complete what has already been done, Dominique illustrates an iterative and perhaps nonlinear relationship to the past, present, and future.[8] Within Dominique's analysis is the possibility of reconciling the past with the present, while acknowledging the presence of the past in the present. To what extent is Dominique speaking to the way in which systematic forms of racialized violence leave many Black people and other racialized persons always already outside conventional opportunity structures and behind white time? Not only can people, in Dominique's world, materially make up what was left undone, but Dominique's emphasis on how people can "re-feel" what happened reflects their connection to the experiential dimensions of social time so often lost within *chronos* and white time.

4   **INTRODUCTION**

Dominique's analysis signals the inextricable connection between space and time. By privileging presence over punctuality, Dominique creates the necessary space to eliminate the strictures of time. Perhaps Dominique is engaging with what M. Jacqui Alexander describes as "the embodiment of the Sacred." Like CP Time, the Sacred dislocates "linear time,"[9] while centering transformative and transgressive temporalities that exceed the conceptual boundaries of the "West," modernity, and progress. I imagine Dominique would agree with Alexander's claim that "linear time does not exist because energy simply does not obey the human idiom."[10] For instance, while someone may arrive at a particular function an hour late, to the perceived latecomer they are right on, or perhaps off, time.

To accept Dominique's claim that lateness does not exist requires an appreciation of ambiguity and funk. I see funk as upholding a key tenet of Black studies: namely, to rewrite knowledge as we know it. Sylvia Wynter reminds readers of an essay written in 1984, when she proposed that "the task of Black Studies, together with those of all other New Studies that entered academia in the wake of the Sixties uprisings, should be that of rewriting knowledge."[11] Stallings's meditations on funk signal a deep and abiding commitment to not only rewriting knowledge but also thinking about other genres of the human beyond/other than what Wynter calls "descriptive statements" of "Man1" and "Man2."[12] "Funk," Stallings writes, "produces alternative orders of knowledge about the body and imagination that originate in a sensorium predating empires of knowledge."[13] Thus, Stallings takes up another central task of Black studies, as articulated by Alexander Weheliye—"the definition of the human itself."[14]

Aims of the Book

This book is more than just a tome on time. In turning to the experiences of Black youth, it reveals why conventional sociological theories of time are both empirically and theoretically unsustainable and, more importantly, why they need to be funked with. As an application of ethnographic observation and in-depth interviews, this book departs from conventional sociological theories of time and representations of Black youth within urban sociology. My aim is to wean sociology off vapid approaches to operationalizing time by revealing how time is racialized, how race is temporalized, and the consequences of owing versus owning time. Through these young people's stories, we come to see that by borrowing time, Black youth could be criminalized by anyone—salespeople, teachers, police, and deputized whites.[15] The charge? Using time and space that does not belong to them. Despite the stigma of time theft, the Black youth I study openly rebel against punctuality and time's call to order. Youth funk up the clock while also funking with whiteness. Assailed by the onslaught of schedules, tardiness, deadlines, curfews, and other technologies of temporal discipline, Black youth have no other choice but to fight back in order to free themselves from time. By redefining start and end times and resisting liberal futurities predicated on "equal" opportunities, Black youth become key moderators of time and temporality. Funking the clock proves to be a site of generation. Each chapter in this book, then, is filled with vivid examples of youth constructing alternative temporalities that center their lived experiences and ensure their worldviews, tastes, and culture are most relevant and up to date. In their stories exists the potential to stretch the sociological imagination to make the familiar (i.e., time) strange. Through such an exercise, fissures and fractures emerge, revealing why existing theories within a sociology of time are untenable. In sum, this book forges new directions in the study of race and time, upending what we think we know about time and centering Black youths as key collaborators in attending to the task of rewriting knowledge as we know it.

Whose Youth Are the Future?

Embodying innocence, vulnerability, and boundless potential, children and youths are synonymous with future possibilities. Adults treat children as having the freedom to explore a world that promises protection and security. Investments in the future begin when we invest in children, or so they say. In short, "save the children" is also a call to save the future. The impetus behind this project does not rest in a shared belief that "the children are the future." What concerns me, rather, are the children already relegated to an antifuture and thus out of and outside time. These are the children deemed always already expendable within time. Teachers are more likely to fail these youths because they "aren't going to amount to anything" and hence remain noninvestments in the venture-capitalist future.[16] Doctors are more likely to ignore these children's symptoms because they "mature faster" than their peers, thus making them less susceptible to "childhood illness." Police are more likely to kill these youths because they look like "demons" with the strength of "Hulk Hogan." I am concerned about those youths consistently warned that they will likely end up either dead or in jail. In short, I am concerned with those who exceed containment within the category of "youth" because the innocence, vulnerability, and boundless potential of the Child function as exclusionary criteria.[17]

In *No Future: Queer Theory and the Death Drive*, Lee Edelman describes the "Child" as the "perpetual horizon of every acknowledged politics, the fantasmatic beneficiary of every political intervention."[18] It is the innocence of the Child that "solicits our defense."[19] What concerns Edelman is the potential of the

Child to render the queer outside time and thus the future. As Edelman notes, "The sacralization of the Child thus necessitates the sacrifice of the queer."[20] As compelling as Edelman's argument is, I am left wondering about the eligibility criteria required to access the category of the Child and whether all children are capable of "sacralization." We might then ask, Whose children are the future?

I argue that in prefiguring the Child as white, sociology is left with a narrow conception of youth development. Insofar as the Child is emblematic of futurity, the queer cannot exist. That is to say, within the logics of "reproductive futurisms," the queer, according to Edelman, must be sacrificed in order to save the Child.[21] Within one elision, however, exists many more. What concerns me are those left unprotected and largely outside the category of the Child. I am referring not only to racialized youth but also to queer and trans children of color. If, as Edelman argues, the queer exemplifies a threat to "reproductive futurism" and the Child is "the obligatory token of futurity," where and when does this leave Black youths, particularly Black queer and trans youths like Dominique and JT?[22] My research attends to their experiences. For example, how do Black youths fit into the "future," when racialized and structural violence squeezes them out? How do Black youths read themselves into the future, when the future is so illiterate that it equates "child" with whiteness? As I wrestle with these questions, I wrest the "Child" from the clutches of whiteness and "Man" and show just how indispensable Black and other racialized youths are to what was, what is, and what is to be.[23]

This is what Nina Simone means when she sings, "To Be Young, Gifted and Black." The world that is "waiting" for Black youths may look quite different from the one they currently inhabit. As the subtitle of this book suggests, I aim to add a dose of funk (as tactfully as possible) to Simone's classic by substituting "perceptive" for "gifted." Several of the youths I worked with at Run-a-Way knew there was another world waiting for them because they could see it. But just because another world may have been waiting for Black youths does not mean they were going to wait for it. Hence, Black youths funked the clock in order to inhabit that world today.

The intersection of race and time is still a largely unexplored topic within sociology, while any examination of the temporalities of racialized youth remains unprecedented.[24] Because of this empirical void within sociology, an undertaking of this magnitude is most fruitful when engaging with a range of disciplines. Hence, in addition to sociology, this research is informed by a variety of fields including Black studies, queer theory, ethnic studies, critical anthropology, cultural studies, American studies, critical geography, history, and English. I place these various disciplines in conversation to describe how time is racialized, how race is temporalized, and how racialized violence shapes youths' perspectives on time.

Johannes Fabian refers to "temporalization" as "the various means a language has to express time relations": "Semiotically, it designates the constitution of sign relations with temporal referents. Ideologically, temporalization has the effect of putting an object of discourse into a cosmological frame such that the temporal relation becomes central and topical (e.g., over and against spatial relations)."[25] Fabian critiques anthropology's approach to locating its object within time while making clear that temporalization is wrought with power relations. Fabian is specifically concerned with social scientists' refusal to allow "the other," or the exoticized object of social research, to inhabit the same (modern) space and time as the researcher. By contrast, this book acknowledges that Black youths are ahead of ~~their~~ time.[26] I also show respect for youths' power to defy the "here and now" in favor of what José Esteban Muñoz describes as a "then and there."[27] The intimate connection between space and time warrants some discussion of the context in which I study the temporalities of Black youth.

Run-a-Way

In December 2014, my interest in studying the relationships between race, time, and youth brought me to Run-a-Way—a multiservice center in Minneapolis, Minnesota, providing support to youth in crisis, and where most of this story takes place. "Run-a-Way" is a pseudonym, as well as a play on existing constructions of youth "deviance," delinquency, and the consequences of being unhoused. I liken this prescience to Cedric Robinson's notion of the "Black Radical Tradition." Robinson makes a similar point when distinguishing between a "runaway" and "fugitive status": "At some point when I was writing *Black Marxism*, I came across the notion of the 'runaway.' Most historians talk about runaways, write about runaways. But I became convinced that that language contained and persisted in the notion that slave agency was childlike. Children run away, but what these people were doing was achieving fugitive status."[28]

Robinson's critique of "runaways," while mostly on point and on time, overlooks the capacity of Black children to achieve a fugitive status. Perhaps Robinson sees the "child" as always already white, thus making Black youths exempt from critique. Still, having worked in paid and unpaid youthwork positions for nearly a decade, I know that youths do not simply "run away." Many are, in fact, running *a* way. In other words, they are running with a vision and with prescience.

I volunteered at Run-a-Way as a direct-care worker for fifteen months. Run-a-Way sought to set itself apart from what youths may be accustomed to seeing in similar programs such as group homes, residential programs, hospitals, youth jails, and other restrictive settings. Unlike in most of these programs, youths are not mandated to remain at Run-a-Way. During my time there, I worked with over one hundred youths but limited my research to thirty, including twenty-one who identified as Black or African American, seven mixed-race youths (most of whom have one African American/Black parent), one Native youth, and one youth who identified as "Hispanic." Nine youths who identified as Black or African American also identified as Native American, making the connections between Blackness and Indigeneity an integral part of this story. With heteronormativity and maleness indexing "natural history," nation making, empire building, and youth development, queer and trans youth generally, and Black queer and trans youth in particular, remain largely ignored within studies of time.[29] My interviewees included fifteen boys, fourteen girls, and one nonbinary youth.[30]

The group was consistent with the overall demographics of youth served at Run-a-Way, 67 percent of whom are between the ages of fifteen and seventeen, while 30 percent are between twelve and fourteen, 2 percent between ten and twelve, and 1 percent age eighteen. While there is a similar ratio of white to nonwhite among staff, volunteers, and interns, most of the youth served are nonwhite, with a significant overrepresentation of Black/African American youth. The racial and ethnic demographics of Run-a-Way youth are as follows: 50 percent Black/African American; 22 percent white; 16 percent "biracial"; 4 percent Native American; 2 percent Hispanic; 2 percent Asian; and 4 percent other. Girls have a slight majority (55 percent) over boys (44 percent) at Run-a-Way. In 2018, Run-a-Way served 833 youths (15 percent of the total number served) who identified as LGBTQ. The overrepresentation of queer and trans youth at Run-a-Way was consistent with previous statistics on youth homelessness in Minnesota.[31]

Funk the Formula

This book is based on "mixed methods" research. The strict limits on what constitutes mixed methods research in sociology makes such a claim debatable. To be more specific, sociology tends to privilege a combination of quantitative and qualitative research methods as the only mix that counts. Despite its emphasis on time, this book has little to do with numbers or quantitative statistics. How do we quantify qualitatively distinct experiences? What are the consequences of reducing lived realities to coefficients and asterisks? In short, what is lost in statistical translation? I am funking the literal formula required in quantitative analyses and the methodological formula that seeks to quantify the unquantifiable and demonstrate a regression from a mean that does not mean much to those rendered illegible within the mean itself.

In addition to my use of in-depth interviews and ethnographic observation, I rely on less conventional approaches that in many ways exceed the methodological capacity of "qualitative" or "quantitative" research. This book is part autoethnography and memoir, which makes memory work integral to my method. My biography informs my scholarship in important ways. Still, I'm hesitant to reduce my story to "data." I am not seeking to claim generalizability or representativeness based on the way my life has unfolded. Instead, I acknowledge the way in which particular events in my life course shape the way I theorize connections between time and race.

My biography also informs my writing style. As a youth, sidewalks, stoops, corners, bus stops, basketball courts, school hallways, cafeterias, auditoriums, and the classroom all looked and sounded a lot like the "Can You Use That Word in a Sentence?" contest that Kiese Laymon describes in *Long Division*.[32] Like City and LaVander Peeler—two of the novel's central characters—if you wanted clout, you had to be nice with words. Wordplay was both an offensive and defensive strategy. In other cases, the goal was more simple: funk the grammar. So when the pressures of the university demand conformity to the formulaic prose saturating sociology, I think about the utility of greater code sticking and less code switching. My hope is that readers engage with this book as they would a favorite song—through feeling more than listening or reading.

It would be disingenuous of me to suggest that I am striving to make *Funk the Clock* accessible to all Black youths. First, it is worth considering that any attempt to make academic writing and knowledge "more accessible to a wider audience" presupposes the idea that there is something that the university has to offer to this wider audience in the first place. Such presuppositions only further privilege the university as a gatekeeper of knowledge, while disregarding the many contributions of knowledge producers outside the academy. Second, there is a need to appreciate difference within already differentiated groups and refrain from what Michelle M. Wright describes as a "qualitative collapse" (of Blackness).[33] Though Black youths recognized the way their fates were linked to other Black people, they also recognized that Blackness and Black people are not singular but plural. Several Black queer and trans youths, for example, exposed the multidimensionality of Blackness. Hence, these stories may resonate with some Black youths but not others.

Sociology, as a discipline, has left me averse to prescribed ways of thinking, learning, and knowing. I remain skeptical of sociological claims and subtitles that begin with "How to . . ." Perhaps sociology could benefit from fewer answers and more wonderings and/or questions, including self-inquiry and self-critique. For example, how are sociologists complicit in concealing what they claim to be hidden in plain sight? Is sociology capable of making space for more knowledge destruction and less knowledge production? There is no question that other sociologists find themselves in a similarly antagonistic relationship to the discipline. Sociology and "its others" have work to do.[34] The goal is not to save the discipline, but rather to decide on the appropriate ways for sociology and sociologists to be held accountable for creating the same systems of power and domination they seek to dismantle. If this is not possible, then perhaps the goal is to make the current enterprise of sociology untenable.

My research began with ethnographic observation, and a significant amount of my time at Run-a-Way was spent observing how the youths spent "their" time. I volunteered four days a week for approximately six hours a day, usually from three in the afternoon until nine or ten o'clock at night. I spent much of my initial ethnographic work observing the youths' comportment to personal and programmatic schedules. I paid close attention to their punctuality, comparing their physical deportment in meetings with staff to their demeanor with peers. Jottings helped capture how they responded to programmatic benchmarks such as chores, job applications, and medical appointments.

Rather than feed into the empirical obsession with coherence and intelligibility, I situate my participant observation within the subfield of cubist ethnography. Within cubist ethnography, according to Javier Auyero and Débora Alejandra Swistun, "the essence of an object is captured only by showing it simultaneously from multiple points of view."[35] Attempting to understand how Black youths reckon with time requires a similar willingness to embrace the heterogeneity, inconsistencies, and contradictions of temporality. I spent approximately three to four hours after each shift at Run-a-Way translating my jottings into ethnographic fieldnotes. After approximately six months of ethnographic observation, I began conducting in-depth interviews. Still, as I describe my attempts to funk the formula, I cannot help but heed Katherine McKittrick's caution: "Description is not liberation."[36] And contrary to the claims of both conventional and critical sociologists, neither is prescription.[37] Conventional sociological research methods courses emphasize four types of social research: (1) descriptive, (2) exploratory, (3) explanatory, and (4) evaluative. To this end, it is worth reminding sociologists that just as description is not liberation, neither is exploration, explanation, or evaluation, particularly when it comes to understanding Black life, Black sociality, and Black people.

With permission from each youth, all interviews were audio recorded. Interviews ranged from forty-five minutes to one hour and forty-five minutes, with most averaging about one hour. Interview locations varied depending on available space and the youths' preferences. Most interviews took place in a private conference room, usually reserved for evening groups on subjects such as "healthy relationships" and "chemical health." The interview schedule contained a series of questions related to (1) opportunity structures; (2) perceptions of time and space; (3) race, racialization, and racism; and (4) life course transitions and trajectories. In return for their participation, each youth received a ten-dollar gift card. At the end of each interview, the youths completed a one-page sheet with several demographic questions related to race, ethnicity, school, and eligibility for free or reduced lunch at school.

During my orientation to Run-a-Way, most staff and volunteers were encouraged to "meet youth where they are at." To refrain from reproducing the violent temporalizing logics of the "ethnographic present," I strived to meet them both where and *when* they were at.[38] As I argue in chapter 7, several youths at Run-a-Way were not only ahead of their time but ahead of time itself. For example, a number of Black youths engaged in a sort of self-synchronization by linking their own tastes and worldviews with the latest trends in music, fashion, and social media. Youths taught me what was "lit" and "litty." Sometimes I had to learn the hard way. For example, during a game of foosball, before each score or mere attempt to score, one youth would taunt me by saying, "Look at the flicka da wrist."[39] I was familiar with the verse's connotation and was impressed with the youth's wit and skill in turning a reference to cooking crack into some effective trash talking—so effective, in fact, that the score was something like eleven to one. Admittedly, I had not yet heard this song. So later that evening, I found myself doing my homework on YouTube. Being an effective youthworker requires you to be a quick learner, especially when it comes to youth slang. Those who cannot keep up will be left in the discursive dust, precisely because many Black youth wield a "high-tech dialect you ain't catch yet."[40]

My aim in this project was to theorize with youth, rather than using them as evidence. First, I took note of Renato Rosaldo's serious, yet sincere, reminder that "the objects of social analysis are also analyzing subjects whose perceptions must be taken nearly as seriously as 'we' take our own."[41] Upon entering Run-a-Way, most youth began creating their own research agendas, and both staff and volunteers were objects of their analysis. Their data often included personal information about staff and volunteers (e.g., age, marital status, and racial/ethnic background). My own racial identity proved to be of great interest to a number of youths. As a mixed-race person, I received the usual "What are you?" question.[42] If staff were present and overheard such a question, they sometimes intervened by treating the youths as if they had just cursed. It is quite common in youthwork for staff to evade questions about their personal lives by saying something like, "We are not here to talk about me. Let's focus on you and how we can work together to help you reach your goals so you can get out of here." Alternatively, some workers are taught to answer youths' questions with a question of their own: "Why does my race interest you?" While such questions are offered with

12   INTRODUCTION

the purported goal of protecting both the youth and the worker, they inevitably intensify existing asymmetrical power relations.

Most youths were proficient at observing while being observed. They peeped the scene, the program, and the staff using what Steve Mann describes as "sousveillance": "observing and recording by an entity not in a position of power or authority over the subject of the veillance."[43] Simone Browne goes on to advance the concept of "dark sousveillance":

> a way to situate the tactics employed to render one's self out of sight, and strategies used in the flight to freedom from slavery as necessarily ones of undersight. . . . I plot dark sousveillance as an imaginative place from which to mobilize a critique of racializing surveillance, a critique that takes form in antisurveillance, countersurveillance, and other freedom practices. Dark sousveillance, then, plots imaginaries that are oppositional and that are hopeful for another way of being. Dark sousveillance is a site of critique, as it speaks to black epistemologies of contending with antiblack surveillance, where the tools of social control in plantation surveillance or lantern laws in city spaces and beyond were appropriated, co-opted, repurposed, and challenged in order to facilitate survival and escape.[44]

Black youths at Run-a-Way were adept at dodging cameras when returning to the program after curfew or simply evading staff during the day. There were approximately five television monitors located in the main office on the first floor that relayed video feeds from the cameras. I never saw any staff reviewing old footage, though it no doubt happened. I sensed that many staff members reckoned with the tension of needing to perform carework within the context of a paternalistic power structure that treats youths as liabilities.

At Run-a-Way, youths learn to be deferential to a number of adults whom they may have known for only a few days, weeks, or months. Some of the younger staff, particularly college interns, pointed out that adults' expectations that youths remain deferent was an extension of hegemonic power and made youths, particularly racialized youths, vulnerable to authoritative manipulation and control. Generally, there were few staff members who maintained a "by-the-book" approach to the work. Most staff, particularly staff of color, tended to strike a balance between sharing some aspects of their personal lives and keeping other parts private. When asked about my own racial identity, I tended to respond by describing my parents' racial identities. I informed youths that I was "mixed race" and that my mother is white and my father is from Trinidad and is of Indian (South Asian) descent. My father identifies as Black and Indian. But I did not expect youths to read me as Black. In fact, several assumed I was Latino.

Regardless of whether you are a caseworker, teacher, doctor, or other professional, interviewing youths is not an easily adaptable skill. My experience as a former youthworker and social worker reminded me that many youths have legitimate reasons to remain tight-lipped around adults.[45] Most youths at Run-a-Way had already shared their stories with multiple staff members at Run-a-Way alone, including intake workers, caseworkers, and therapists, and even with their peers during groups. During interviews, I did not ask about "turning points" or "transitions" in the life course, but rather gave youths the space and time to contribute in whatever way made them most comfortable. In my experience, social workers, family regulation/child welfare workers, and even some youthworkers are experts at reading a child's biography through a lens of "intergenerational transmission" of dysfunction. Several youths shared intimate aspects of their biography both during and outside interviews. The fact that many of these disclosures were volunteered, rather than extracted, signaled at least partial trust in my role as a volunteer staff. While my interview schedule did not include many sensitive questions related to family or personal experiences with various forms of trauma, an abstract topic like time is not a popular conversation starter. But the lack of empirical evidence about the temporalities of Black youth is precisely why this research is not only warranted but desperately needed.

Interviews presented the opportunity for youths to elaborate on what is so often obscured in quantitative research methods: namely, the incommensurability between white and nonwhite experiences and the false equivalence between control variables and racialized reality. Youths were eager for the opportunity to make experiences routinely rendered illegible within quantitative data legible, such as racialized bias in schools or at Run-a-Way, whiteness, and police violence. Still, I left ample room for them to deviate from the methodological path of the interview. They did not always answer the questions I asked. Instead they sometimes inverted the terms and conditions of the interview by turning questions on their head. In turn, Black youths at Run-a-Way expanded the breadth of our collective theorizations on time.

I draw inspiration from Yarimar Bonilla's research on contemporary labor activism in Guadeloupe, the overseas department of France. In aiming to place Guadeloupean labor movements within the context of broader Caribbean postcolonial politics, Bonilla is careful not to ventriloquize her interlocutors. Rather, the goal is to "not just 'face the native' but *theorize with them*" (emphasis in the original).[46] Bonilla's aim aligns with my broader commitment toward decentering the university as a gatekeeper of knowledge and the primary site of knowledge production. I respect the intellectual capacity of those without extra initials behind their names to sabotage research agendas, demolish cherished theoretical frameworks, and effortlessly extinguish scholars with caustic quips like, "Who

INTRODUCTION

lied to you and said it was a good idea for you to become a professor?" or "Your scholarship smells like scholarshit."

Apart from locked facilities (i.e., detention centers and residential treatment programs) and actual homes, there are few places like Run-a-Way where youths live, learn, and labor. Among its many services, Run-a-Way offers access to a twenty-four-hour crisis hotline, an emergency shelter program, a transitional living program for sixteen- and seventeen-year-olds, individual and family counseling, community education and outreach, and weekly support groups for boys, girls, and queer and trans youths. Youths at Run-a-Way are there "voluntarily," though many are brought by parents, social workers, or other referral sources. Most attend public school outside the program and spend a fair amount of time in their communities. Leaving the program without permission, however, places a youth at risk of "losing their bed," or being barred from returning without staff approval. The combination of research methods, procedures, and sampling strategy produced rich findings and contributions to the sociology of time, urban ethnography, and the life course perspective. From morning wake-up calls to evening curfews, I and other staff members at Run-a-Way remained embedded in an environment where Black youths' temporalities manifest.

Funk the Spot

Run-a-Way is in a bustling, commercial district in the Twin Cities comprising yuppies, hipsters, college students, and older homeowners, most of whom are white. All of Run-a-Way's services are housed in a three-story brick building. I spent most of my time at Run-a-Way in the emergency shelter program, located on the second floor. For most youth, there is only one way in and one way out of the emergency shelter program—a large door at the top of the second-floor stairwell with a small rectangular windowpane on the upper half of the door. Upon entry, youths are greeted by a vibrant mural filled with colorful trees, a cornucopia of fruit, inviting messages like "Peace" and "Welcome," and a palette of painted people. In the middle of the wall, there is an elevator used by staff and youths with disabilities. The elevator is located in a spacious living room with a worn shag carpet, several pieces of furniture, and a large shelving unit for books, board games, and a large flat-screen TV. When not in use, the TV was locked behind two cupboard doors. Staff members maintaining more austere approaches to their work treated television watching as a way of skirting the challenge of engaging youths in more generative activities or conversations. To avoid the risk of placating them with television, staff encouraged them to spend their free time playing cards, drawing, playing foosball, and, when possible, listening to music in the annex space attached to the living room.

Typically, there were also approximately three to four working desktop computer stations, where youths could do homework, apply for jobs, or perform other tasks that aligned with Run-a-Way's expectations for "progress." Across from the activity room is a long hallway leading to a laundry room and four to five bedrooms, most of which were gendered. From what I observed, queer and trans youths were usually allowed to reside in rooms matching their gender identity.[47] There were two beds in each room, some of which were bunked. Each room shared a bathroom with neighbors in the next room over. Next to the beds was ample storage space for clothes, shoes, school supplies, and so on. There was also shared desk space facing large windows overlooking the street below.

Windows were a key benefit of the activity room and bedrooms. Not only did they provide sunlight and fresh air, but they also served as important portals to the outside world, which was largely a world of whiteness. Youths delighted in mocking the local residents out for a stroll, a casual run around a local lake, or other activities they saw as reserved mostly for the white and wealthy. Black and other racialized youths held little to no reservations about yelling out the windows to ask local passersby, "How come you dress like you ain't got money?" Playing pretend poor was, in the words of many youths, "not cute." In fact, most of them were insulted by local hipsters who appeared unfazed by any expectations to prove they were not poor. Unlike Run-a-Way's neighbors, Black and other racialized youths could not inhabit a whiteness that, in Sara Ahmed's words, "allows bodies to move with comfort through space, and to inhabit the world as if it were home."[48] Many racialized youths, particularly Black youths, knew that the sense of safety and security that local residents maintained required the construction of unsafety in their communities, including Minneapolis's Northside.[49] It was this recognition that motivated one youth to ask a white man walking by the program's courtyard, "That's you with that gas?"[50] This was his attempt to get the white man to admit to smoking weed. The youth knew the answer to his own question but still found it amusing watching white people try to decipher slang. More importantly, all the youths outside that day enjoyed the sight of upper-middle-class whites questioning their own spatio-temporal location and proprietorship, while wondering whether they could still move through the world like they owned it. Making fun of local residents, though, was nothing compared to the youths' being made to feel as though they inhabit a different space and time, despite residing next door.

When outside the program, youths saw firsthand what George Lipsitz terms "the possessive investment in whiteness" and protectionist stances over white spacetime.[51] Based on their experiences in the upscale community surrounding Run-a-Way, many youths were not under any illusion that "Minnesota nice" would protect them. Even before "social distancing" was a thing, local white residents would cross the street to avoid racialized youths. I watched white people clutch their purses, just as tightly as they held their children, as we made our routine treks around a local lake. Even if they received an occasional fake smile, the youths knew that this was more indicative of Minnesota polite than Minnesota nice. At six or seven in the evening, it was far too late for our ragtag group of youths and adults to be out on a field trip. I would not have been surprised if some neighborhood parents used youths at Run-a-Way as scare tactics, warning their children to behave themselves unless they wanted to end up like "those kids." Apparently, white habitats were integral to constructing what Eduardo Bonilla-Silva calls "white habitus."[52]

During most shifts, there were approximately two to three staff members on the floor, though it was not uncommon to find at least one of them in the office completing paperwork or having a one-on-one conversation with a youth about their progress in the program and long-term goals. At nine thirty at night, after a day filled with recreational activities, homework help, and meals, youth and staff gathered in the living room of the shelter program to do "end-of-the-day check-ins" and our group closing. A staff member would initiate the conversation by asking for a volunteer to say their name and report a "high and low"—a positive and negative part of the youth's day. After each youth checked in, staff asked about their needs and preferences for the next day's morning activity. Youths took turns informing the group of their school's start time, the time they wished to be woken up, whether they would take a shower in the morning or evening, and whether they had any current medication needs. During most circles, those who were enrolled in school left a half-hour window between the time they woke up and the first bell. Most students, especially those relying on public transportation, would inevitably be late to school. Staff often challenged a youth's desired wake-up time by writing an earlier time in the shift report. Still, there were countless instances of youths refusing to wake up any earlier than their requested time. Whether they were arriving fashionably late to a party or making their presence felt by disrupting existing schedules, Black youths at Run-a-Way asserted their positions as temporal conductors and demonstrated a unique ability to funk the clock, whether at school or at Run-a-Way.

The daily structure for youths at Run-a-Way varied by program. Those in the emergency shelter program spent more time with one another compared to those in the independent living program located one floor above. Mealtimes, however, were one exception. Every evening, youths in the independent living program and emergency shelter program gathered on the third floor to break bread. Usually at least one staff member and one youth helped prepare the evening's meal together. Before each meal, staff and youths would gather in a circle and each say one thing they were thankful for. Most staff expressed being thankful that the youths at Run-a-Way were somewhere safe and that they had an opportunity to share a meal together. Responses from youths struck a similar tone, with most expressing gratitude to friends and staff from Run-a-Way. On weekends and nonschool days, youths from both programs also had breakfast and lunch together. Still, there were marked distinctions between the emergency shelter program and the independent living program.

Though several youths from the emergency shelter program regularly petitioned staff to transfer to the independent living program, only a select few would be chosen to "step up." Located on the highest floor of the building, the independent living program is designed to signal progression from a lower level or stage of youth development. Eligible youths must demonstrate a certain level of "maturity." Many make the transition from the emergency shelter after showing compliance with the program structure. Most had to be at least sixteen years old and be actively searching for a job and/or their own apartment. While many youths stayed in the emergency shelter program only for a couple of weeks, those in the independent living program had the option of staying up to one year, with some staying longer due to extenuating circumstances.[53] For example, during their time in the program, some youths lost jobs, got "got" by shady landlords, or faced challenges in reunifying with their families. Still, most who transitioned from one floor below were happy to no longer be among the "little kids" in the emergency shelter program.

Most youths in the independent-living program had greater freedom, including later curfews, which meant the floor tended to be quieter than the shelter program. There were also some slight differences in the physical design of the program. For example, in place of the large living room was an industrial-size kitchen with ample cafeteria-style seating. There was a tacit understanding that the kitchen was contested terrain. Because youths in the independent living program could buy their own food to keep in the program, there were occasional quarrels over food that went missing. This was one of the many reasons why staff pleaded with youths to label their food with the stickers provided. Youths took pride in being able to buy and cook their own food, which they would prepare after coming home from school or work. Overall, staff held greater expectations for youths in independent living, in hopes of strengthening their preparedness to find a steady job and/or an apartment once they left Run-a-Way.

Most other space at Run-a-Way was reserved for administration, case management, conference rooms, activities, and storage. The case management office, health clinic/medicine room, individual and family therapist offices, and several rooms used to conduct intakes with new youths, were located on the ground floor. There was also a wing of the ground floor housing additional office space, accessible only by staff. The basement held a conference room, which functioned as an activity space in the evening. As part of their contractual agreements, several local youth-based organizations visited Run-a-Way to facilitate weekly workshops and activities in the conference room. Youths participated in pet therapy with dogs, made art with graffiti artists, rehearsed roles with performance artists, practiced meditation, and competed in the occasional video game tournament. The basement also housed a makeshift gym, with minimally operable machines that most youths were reluctant to use out of fear of being spotted using janky equipment and getting injured while doing so. Connected to the gym was a donation closet. Youths who arrived at Run-a-Way without sufficient clothes, shoes, coats, or hygiene products were able to take whatever they needed from shelves of new and used items. Most of the food for breakfast, lunch, and dinner came from the food pantry, large walk-in refrigerator, and freezer in the basement. Only staff were permitted to access the food pantry and fridge, but youths would occasionally finagle their way in and gather a stash of snacks for personal and possibly collective use. In warmer weather, youths spent recreation time in the backyard, where they had the option of playing basketball using a portable hoop on a small concrete patio similar in size to two parking spaces. Those that opted out usually spent time hanging out together at a picnic table on a small grassy area in the backyard. When in the program, youths made the rounds through all these spaces, but they spent most of their time in the emergency shelter program and/or the transitional living program.

RACIALIZATION AND TEMPORALIZATION OF YOUTHS IN URBANIZED SPACE

Based on self-identifying information acquired during intake processes,[54] I use the term "racialized youths" to refer to youths of color. I do not use "Black youths" and "racialized youths" interchangeably. Instead, "racialized youths" is meant to be inclusive of the few youths in this book who may not identify as Black but are nonetheless racialized. Black and other racialized youths experience similar consternation over being told they are "the future" while watching their futures foreclosed by structural violence. My aim, though, centers the experiences of Black youths, including several who identify as Black and Indigenous. I occasionally use "racialized youths" rather than "youths of color" to avoid euphemizing a dynamic, hybrid, and heterogeneous group of racially marginalized persons. "Youths of color" and "people of color" are both rooted in a politicized consciousness and awareness of the collective strength and self-determination of racially oppressed groups.

What concerns me, though, is the potential for "people of color" to flatten difference in service of mutuality, equilibrium, equivalence, commensurability, and consistency. In such cases, "people of color" obscures the incommensurability of

INTRODUCTION   19

different forms of racialized violence and the need for those disproportionately harmed to disproportionately benefit. Attention to such complexities upholds key principles of intersectional analysis. As Grace Hong writes, "what *intersectionality* inherently means is the recognition of difference rather than a demand for uniformity."[55] This book resists demands to sacrifice incommensurability in favor of similarity. Instead, each youth's story remains grounded in nuanced understandings of their unique relation to racialized violence and the disproportionate impact of temporal alterity.

Too great an emphasis on "people of color" conceals the way in which anti-Blackness and colonization exceed the available meanings and grammars linked to "discrimination" or even "racism." This is in part why Dylan Rodríguez aims to distinguish white supremacy from both anti-Blackness and racial-colonial power. "The latter forms of dominance," Rodríguez argues, are "not fundamentally aspirational, but the long existing, *pre-aspirational* conditions through which white supremacy is made fathomable and coherent."[56] As hauntings, the afterlives of slavery and conquest condition Black and Indigenous persons' life chances and chances at life.[57] By differential "chances at life," I am referring to the role of educational enclosures, the penal-legal system, police terror, and starvation wage work in contributing to the premature deaths of those attempting to survive in spaces not meant for living. A central contribution of this book is to illustrate the role of racialization and racialized violence in taking time from Black youth. Not only do I make clear how time is racialized, but I also argue that racialization itself takes time.

To better operationalize how racialization takes time, I draw on Steve Martinot's conceptualization of racialization as a cultural structure—a structure of social categorizations of people.[58] Racialization, Martinot writes, has "nothing to do with blood or the inheritance of appearance. It is a social status that is imposed on people through political definition."[59]

> It [racialization] derives from the verb "to racialize." It refers not to the social status of people (of different colors) that produces itself culturally in this society (as Omi and Winant 1994 use the term), but rather to what is done socially and culturally to people for which personal derogation and alien status are part of the outcome. It is a transitive verb. "Race" is something that one group of people does to others. In the hierarchy of "race," one group racializes another by thrusting them down to subordinate levels in a dehumanizing processes. . . . [R]ace is something that Europeans, in the course of colonization of other people, have done to those people. "To racialize" and "to humanize" stand opposite each other, in contradiction.[60]

Racialization, according to Martinot, occurs within three distinct yet mutually constitutive dimensions: (1) individual, (2) institutional, and (3) cultural. At the individual level, racialization involves what Frantz Fanon describes as "epidermalization"[61]—the inscription of race on the body. It is a process of being, as Fanon so eloquently notes, "overdetermined from the outside."[62] Racialization commands racialized subjects to reckon with the experience of being marked as temporally, spatially, and ontologically other. Racialization requires the construction of a threat to produce and protect the purity of whiteness. Once overdetermined as inferior and thus a "threat," racialized subjects are at an even greater risk of violence.

Racialization, however, is not limited to microlevel interactions but is part of the standard operating procedure of virtually all social institutions. Racialization has no fixed spatial, temporal, or institutional location. Schools, hospitals, the penal-legal system, poor urbanized space, wealthy suburbanized space, and the state are among the many institutions in which racialization resides.[63] *Funk the Clock* examines how many of these institutions remain complicit in ensuring that racialized youth begin from temporal deficits. For example, the equation of the ghetto and barrios with anachronistic space ensures that Black youth will remain suspended in time and rendered illegible within progress narratives linked to modernity.[64]

Finally, at the cultural level, racialization takes form in what Martinot describes as the "white para-political state, its periodic white vigilantism, the general support for police harassment and brutality against black and brown people, and support for U.S. interventionism."[65] It is within the cultural level that deputized whites deny Black youth coevalness, or the capacity to inhabit a similar spacetime. Lacking contemporaneity within white logic made it possible for many Black youths at Run-a-Way to have consistently been in the wrong place at the wrong time. At all three levels, racialization constitutes whiteness. In other words, white people need racialized others to know they are white and thus not (negatively) racialized. Racialization also affirms white people's status as modern and antithetical to the atavistic status of their negatively racialized counterparts.

Racialization is further complicated by Nandita Sharma's reference to "negatively racialized persons."[66] Sharma allows the term to stand on its own without conceptualization, but she seems to suggest that racialization is integral to the construction of an ontological order through selective ascription of value and humanness. Though "negative" reinforces an absolute state of abjection, if left alone "racialization" possesses a universal application across all racialized groups. While "positive racialization" may sound absurd, there remains a need to recognize differences among those within an already differentiated category.

Racialization involves more than what Michael Omi and Howard Winant describe as the institutionalization of particular groups into "a politically organized racial system."[67] It also, they argue, exceeds "the extension of racial meaning to a previously racially unclassified social relationship, social practice or group."[68] Countering existing ideas within the sociology of race and ethnicity as well as critical race theory, this research does not entertain the common sociological claim that white people must also be included within the category of "racialized." Such claims teeter on a precipice above white liberal humanisms and relentless pursuits of commensurability. I cannot, though, be an apologist for whiteness.[69] Neither will I massage its contours to help white people feel included as "other" or "them," when they are in fact "it" and "us." To further substantiate my position, I draw on Helen Ngo's instructive conceptualization of "racialization":

> Throughout this book, "racialization" designates the process by which one is deemed to have "race." In the context of the West, this invariably means the process by which people of color are assigned a racial identity, whereas people of Caucasian description are not; racialization is about the production of a racialized "other" and a concurrent non-naming, normalizing, and centering of the white "I." . . . Racialization, then, is almost always a form of racism. . . . Moreover, I use separate terms also to draw attention to the way racialization—the process of assigning a racial identity to a person of color with all its associated meanings and trappings—forms the basis of racism understood in its narrower sense.[70]

According to Ngo, the banality of the white "I" is what disqualifies it from racialization. Sylvia Wynter might describe this as the "overrepresentation of Man as human." Whiteness is as much of a sociohistorical construct as other racial formations, but in reality, whiteness proceeds as if it were race neutral and ahistorical. This is why scholars describe whiteness as a "hidden ethnicity" and white people as "cultureless."[71] Renato Rosaldo makes this point exceptionally clear when distinguishing between the white, Western self and the nonwhite other: "As the Other becomes more culturally visible, the self becomes correspondingly less so."[72]

White people understand themselves as the default racial group yet still without race. While some white people recognize the construction of whiteness and what Nell Irvin Painter describes as "the history of white people," most understand themselves to be the default.[73] So as much as we can agree that white people are not race neutral, I believe there exists an important need to distinguish between what is and what ought to be the case.

22   **INTRODUCTION**

This is especially important given the success of the Trump administration in weaponizing whiteness while also constructing it as under threat. For example, Mike King's theorization of "aggrieved whiteness" reveals a perverse logic that leaves an overwhelming number of white men "in their feelings."[74] They are reminded that there is no need to apologize for being white. To the extent that white people are connected to racialization, they are, according to Denise Ferreira da Silva, products of raciality that manufactures the "transparent I" in the form of a "post-Enlightenment" European subject and the racialized, subaltern, and affectable "Other."[75] While some critical race theorists petition for white inclusion in the category of the "racialized," this book thwarts such attempts in favor of a more nuanced and critical assessment of racialization.[76]

Because racialization is itself a value-making process, the racialization of time reinforces a dichotomy of "deviance" and decency, whereby white people reap rewards for remaining on (white) time and nonwhite people pay the price for remaining off it. Racialization is a process of ontological ordering in which life value is guaranteed for some, ascribed to a select few, and denied to others. Racialization is also relational. Thus, differential racialization occurs within an uneven biopolitical distribution, whereby specific categories of the human gain value through the devaluation of others. Racialization and racialized violence ensure that Black and other racialized youth remain asynchronous and out of step with temporal progress. Perhaps time's march onward is predicated on racialized youth remaining stuck in place.[77]

The temporalizing capacity of racialization is clear. What is less evident is racialized youth's capacity to resist temporalization. *Funk the Clock* tells the story of Black youths reckoning with time and producing liberatory temporalities to free themselves from essentialist representations and narratives not their own.[78] Black youths can no longer be told the time. The firsthand accounts making up this text suggest that Black youths have a lot to say not only to time but also to those who claim to be able to tell it.

My aim, then, is to trouble time through ethnographic observation and first-person interviews far too rich and theoretically dense for interpretation within existing sociological paradigms. To this end, youths at Run-a-Way present a preview of what it looks like to live asynchronously with the temporal logics of whiteness, anti-Blackness, conquest, heteronormativity, and capitalism. Rather than being punctual, meeting deadlines, and abiding by curfews, Black youths at Run-a-Way prefer to get there when they get there. Instead of being future oriented, they remain present oriented yet remarkably prescient. At Run-a-Way, whiteness does not serve as a reference to gauge who or what was most enlightened or modern. Instead, Black youths cast whiteness into a played-out past, declaring their sociality most relevant and up to date, while taking the title of avant-garde. This is what it means to funk the clock.

Book Overview

This book makes several independent interventions and collectively facilitates a paradigmatic shift toward a new sociology of time. Chapter 1 opens with an acknowledgment of the undeniable role that time plays in orienting everyday life. From the moment a person wakes until the time they retire to rest, time orients eating patterns, leisure activities, hygiene, and work schedules. Paradoxically, it is time's banality that obscures its significance as a central organizing principle used to distinguish between the owners and owed within time. In order to make the mundane matter, I illustrate how time is racialized and how race is temporalized by troubling normative conceptions of time within classical and contemporary sociology. Drawing on previous literature within the sociology of time, I argue that "social time" renders racialized persons illegible within time. Social time requires the systemic marginalization of racialized subjects from the existing temporal order and the social itself. The "social" in "social time," I argue, belies unity, equivalence, equilibrium, mutuality, and any possibility of creating a time shared by all. Instead, white time prefigures social time. "White time," for example, represents a site of exploitation and extraction of nonwhite life. Similarly, "racial time" is premised on enslavement, dispossession, and death. Given that time is money, it makes sense that white time and racial time remain the products of racial debt. In the wake of emancipation exists "slavery's afterlife" and a racial debt that continues to mount because racialized exploitation and violence lack a deadline and defy location within a linear timeline.[79]

Yet still, resistance is central to this story. The brutality of white time led many youth at Run-a-Way to challenge temporal conventions and mock the clock. For example, despite the enforcement of strict bedtime curfews, one member of the night staff at Run-a-Way admitted, "No one ever goes to bed by nine thirty." I leverage the concept of "CP Time," or "Colored People's Time," to illustrate the power of temporal subversion. How might CP Time serve as an internally functional metric to cope with the timelessness of racialized violence?[80] CP Time aids Black people and other racialized persons in their efforts to contend with what Eduardo Bonilla-Silva calls "racialized social systems,"[81] which take "their" time. Several youths found ways to violate white, Western, linear time, predicated on a past, present, and future. Having acknowledged the incompatibility between their lived experiences and racialized temporality, the youths at Run-a-Way subverted white time through what I call *transgressive temporalities* and *insurgent time.* By arriving to school late, missing curfew, or skipping work, Black youths violated that which consistently violates them.

The impetus behind the second chapter comes from a warning. Once the state terminated my father's time in this country and forcibly removed him, he would make the following demand of all his children: "All yuh must *teef* time and come nah man."[82] My father never asked us to "find time" or "make time." Instead the goal was to thief it. Thus, in chapter 2, I describe the consequences of transgressing time while young, prescient, and Black. This chapter answers a straightforward yet understudied question: What does it mean to use time that does not belong to you? As youths transgressed time and space, they were charged with "walking up to no good" because they "fit the description." In distinguishing those who own time from those who owe it, this chapter expands the breadth of life course scholarship and time use studies. The American Time Use Survey (ATUS), for example, lacks any adequate measures of either racialization or racism. If the ATUS cannot account for the time that youths spend processing acts of racialization or racism, then it is inevitably capturing but a fraction of this group's purported "time use." Racialized violence, however, is incommensurable with routine activities such as the time youths spend on personal hygiene or chores. Experiences with racialization and racism remain unquantifiable. They literally and figuratively do not count. To racialized persons, and Black youths in particular, acts of racialization and racism will always count because they are *countless.*

Space is the mutually constitutive counterpart to time and a vital part of this story. Chapter 3 begins with two starkly different representations of the Twin Cities from a 2015 issue of *The Atlantic.* Both articles were published shortly after I began my fieldwork with youths at Run-a-Way. In "The Miracle of Minneapolis," Derek Thompson describes a "rising tide" of Fortune 500 wealth benefiting all Twin Cities residents. According to Thompson, the significant number of Fortune 500 companies in the Twin Cities helped subsidize "the Minneapolis miracle" through the redistribution of commercial tax revenues to "enrich some of the region's poorest communities." In a response, Jessica Nickrand takes Thompson to task for perpetuating "Minneapolis's White Lie" and using white people as a reference category for assessing the economic status of all others. Nickrand references several studies suggesting that the "Minneapolis Miracle" has disproportionately benefited the city's white population and resulted in some of the greatest employment and educational disparities between whites and non-whites in the nation.[83]

What the United States owes Black and Indigenous youth exceeds the available vocabularies associated with "debt." The history of "Mnisota" (the Dakota Sioux name for "Minnesota")—unceded indigenous territory—is one of violated treaties, conquest, genocide, and racial capitalism, making Blackness and Indigeneity important parts of this story. Youths who identified as Black and Native resisted what Mark Rifkin calls "settler time,"[84] while maintaining psychic connections to relatives and ancestors. Racialized violence, however, is never past but present. Hence, I explore how systematic neglect, underdevelopment, and divestment of majority-Black communities in the Twin Cities is key to the construction of what fifteen-year-old Devon describes as a "maybe environment." Devon's phrase provokes further exploration into the saying "I heard a white man's yes is a Black maybe." "Black maybe" signals a double standard wherein what is guaranteed to whites is but a possibility for Black people. The use of "maybe" does not only function as a discursive tool. There is a materiality to "maybe." As Devon states, "It's very, very hard to raise a kid in a maybe environment. Maybe I'll get a job. Maybe there'll be money coming in and maybe we'll have an apartment." What are common markers of life course transitions and trajectories proved to be a maybe for many of the youths at Run-a-Way.

The experiences of youth attempting to survive within "maybe environments" and make sense of educational and work opportunities nearing obsolescence is well documented in sociology, particularly urban ethnography. Less attention is devoted to what it means for Black youths to work twice as hard to get half as far as their white counterparts. In chapter 4, I argue that such incommensurable labor-time inevitably results in Black youths having far less time than their white peers. The combination of compressed time and foreclosed opportunities abbreviates aspirations for the life course. The time that Black youths spend searching for work is protracted not only because of delays in callbacks but also due to the psychic labor required to make sense of the ease with which white youths find jobs. Lamont, who was sixteen years old, recalled a saying from his mother that succinctly describes this problem: "Keisha doesn't get the call before Kimberly." Racialization and racism, I argue, exceed the conceptual capacity of transitions and trajectories and instead function as life course constants for Black youths. In naming racialization and racism "life course constants," I make the case that working twice as hard to be twice as good means that racialized youths are consistently forced to do more with less (time).

I use chapter 5 as a temporal break or caesura to linger in a previous spacetime and enduring funk. I consider the temporality of this book and strive to resist any literary urge to reach the conclusion by privileging what has felt like an endless pause over progress. I invite the reader to "hold up" and "wait a minute," as I perform additional memory work and enter what I call *tabanca* time. In Trinidad and Tobago, *tabanca* refers to an agonizing feeling often induced by an unrequited love or longing for a person or thing. Signaling the book's overall musicality, I think of this chapter as an interlude and an opportunity to think about the book's overall pacing, tone, sound, and general relationship with time and space. My father funked the clock in a variety of ways, but the "fast life" proved to be his chosen transgressive temporality. He never described what he did as "crime." In fact, he said he was doing what he had to do to survive. This mattered little, though, because time had a tenacious revenge impulse. As a form of payback, time teamed up with space. I soon learned that this temporal-spatial collaboration would deny my father and all his children any opportunity to share another minute of coevalness. As a consequence of his temporal transgression, my father was deported. "Postdeportation," I argue, is a misnomer, precisely because deportation is a process, not an event. My father may no longer be incarcerated, but he is still doing time. It is a time that can never be done and a time that can never claim to heal the same harm it caused. For my father and many others, the opportunity to make in one week what many people make in a month is a compelling proposition when you have to work twice as hard to get half as far.

In chapter 6, youths make clear that the urge to transgress time is not isolated to my father's generation. Prepared to begin a long and hard road filled with roadblocks at every conceivable level of opportunity, some Black youths in urbanized space learn various shortcuts and detours along the life course. The dilatory payoff associated with (s)low-wage labor and schooling prompted some youths to seek expedited pathways to make money and funk the clock, including the "fast life." When I asked eighteen-year-old Finesse to characterize those involved in the fast life, he responded by saying, "People that really got no other choice. I never heard nobody gettin' into [the] trap that wanted to be in the trap [a site of drug dealing]. You know? Nobody wakes up and is like, 'Hey, I'm gonna go sell some crack.'" Finesse's perceptive response is a reminder that the "trap" is just that—a trap. Still, when forced to choose whether one will "trap or die," it becomes clear that some must hustle to live.

Black youths recognize that working twice as hard to get half as far means that they will inevitably have less time than their white counterparts. Thus, chapter 7 investigates how Black youths interpret time in relation to whiteness and their assessments of white youths. Independently, the study of whiteness and the study of time are important interventions in sociology. A solid foundation for any empirical investigation of the relationship between whiteness and the time perspectives of Black and other racialized youths, however, has yet to be set. Despite the temporal inequalities between them and their white counterparts, youths at Run-a-Way discovered ways to invert the terms of temporality to ensure that their culture was always most relevant and "up to date" and never late.

In spite of whiteness's links to modernity and that which is future oriented, Black youths viewed their white counterparts as behind time, "lame," or just plain wack.[85] Being up to date or up on the latest trends was gauged not by whiteness but by being in tune with Blackness. Birkenstocks and socks may be constantly trending according to white time, but within the context of Run-a-Way, Black youths declared such fashions wack on arrival. Run-a-Way became the site for experimenting in alternate spatial and temporal realities, where and when Black youths' styles, trends, and tastes were most relevant while whiteness was cast into a played-out past. In exposing the wackness of whiteness, Black youths discovered ways to mock the clock and further funk with time. By turning the fundamental principles of whiteness on their head, they reconfigured the terms and conditions of modernity to locate whiteness and white people within anachronistic space. Making whiteness wack also signaled the youths' recognition that being most up to date was more a matter of being off white time than on it.

With greater attention to climate change, pandemics, and the future of the planet comes renewed attention to the future and those emblematic of it. Hence, in chapter 8, I ask whose children are the future and whose children are relegated to the "ethnographic present." It is what Nancy Lesko describes as the "evolutionary supremacy of the West" that keeps Black and other racialized youths lingering in temporal suspension:

> *Adolescence is an emblem of modernity, and time is its defining mode....* In my view, adolescence enacts modernity in its central characterization as *developing* or becoming—youth cannot live in the present; they live in the future, that is, they exist only in the discourse of "growing up." Adolescence reenacts the evolutionary supremacy of the West over primitive others in its pathologized (internalized) progress from (primitive) concrete operational stages to (advanced) abstract ones. Adolescence continuously enacts Western progress carried in the oppositional positions of past and present and ever points to even greater futures. (emphasis in the original)[86]

As Lesko notes, whiteness, maleness, and future orientations were key characteristics in the making of adolescents. This particular genre of adolescents, in turn, came to be part of the foundational logics of nation and empire building. The construction of white youths as future oriented required nonwhite peoples to remain suspended in time. I make the case, however, that urban ethnographic representations of Black youth in poor urbanized space as "present oriented" elide their prescience. Having a preview of the multiplicative forms of oppression yet to come over the life course, Black youths retain a unique ability to foretell their futures.

With limited life chances and limited chances at life, youths at Run-a-Way saw the future as fugitive. It is, then, not as though Black youth have not thought about the future. It is precisely because they have cogitated so deeply over their futures that they reject what is constantly on the run—"equal opportunity" within a highly unequal world. Their choice not to entertain liberal futurities directed toward "freedoms" associated with whiteness and a "postracial era" does not make them present oriented. It makes them prepared. Interpreting time as an iterative process incapable of being isolated to a finite past, present, or future allows Black youth to construct their own spatial imaginaries where they interpellate themselves in answers to "Whose time is it?" by responding, "It's we o'clock."

What forms of time exist beyond a time that is always right for white and whiteness and wrong for the racialized and rightless? In chapter 8, I return to the core questions driving this book and push them further to consider the implications of upsetting time as we know it and perhaps moving toward a teleos of time itself. I take stock of the theoretical contributions that emerge from this story of Black youths reckoning with time and funking up the clock. It is through their experiences that the shift from "What time is it?" to "Whose time is it?" not only makes sense but maintains grammatical coherence and correctness. As youth shift time, they create the necessary "temporal caesura" to imagine alternative temporalities and futurities that exceed the limitations of white, androcentric, straight, and linear time.[87]

Black youth's temporalities are not only transgressive but transformative. Transgressive temporalities are conducive to the production of a nowness situated outside the past, present, and future. Youth not only see foreclosed futures in the present but also imagine a "then and there" of Black sociality free from white time and racialized violence. I contend that the residence of slavery's "afterlife" in the present leads many youth to imagine the "not-yet-here." As Black youth both funk the clock and queer the clock, they place the direction of time under their discretion.

1

WHOSE TIME IS IT?

Within the sociology of time, the overrepresentation of white time as time itself exceeds the problem of "measurement error."[1] Because, as Barbara Fields notes, "whiteness leads to no conclusions it does not begin with as assumptions," white time is simultaneously *telos* and *logos*.[2] In other words, it represents an answer planted in the question; a conclusion rooted in an introduction; the punchline in the joke. How, then, do we take sociology-of-time scholarship seriously?

It is inaccurate and irresponsible to ask, "What is time?" or even "What time is it?" More precise lines of inquiry are required. For example, how is time racialized? How is race temporalized? Who is legible within time? Who can claim ownership over time? Who can only *owe* time? What happens when you use time that doesn't belong to you? What happens when your "time use" is read as time theft? Can time heal the same wounds it inflicts? How do we account for the time expended to process racialized violence? Who benefits from such processing of time? Who is harmed by it? What forms of time exist beyond a time that is always right for white and whiteness and wrong for the racialized and rightless?

In this book, Black youth offer answers to these questions by showing us how they reckon with time. In documenting their experiences, my aim is not to help an "underrepresented category" go from dysselected to selected within the sociology of time.[3] It is not as though the sociology of time underrepresents Black and other racialized youth. It is that white time itself precludes their selection as modern subjects. Hence, this book is as much about wrecking as it is about reckoning. I specifically seek to "catch wreck" on the sociology of time and what Adrienne Rich describes as "white solipsism,"[4] a sort of "tunnel vision" where there is only one time—white time. All other conceptions of time remain asynchronous and thus temporally other.

Without critically questioning the prefiguration of time as white, sociologists retain license to treat time as an undervalued and underutilized factor in social research. To "make amends" for sociology's dismissive stance toward time, the keepers of the canon suggest that (white) time is in crisis and in need of recuperation, resuscitation, and recentering. As John Hassard puts it, "The dominant research paradigm has been one favouring 'slice-through-time' investigations, and in particular studies whose conclusions are based on one-shot statistical correlations. In short, time has tended to be excluded as an explanatory variable, or else introduced only in post hoc justification."[5]

In bemoaning time's exclusion as an explanatory variable, Hassard effectively makes what is overrepresented appear underrepresented and thus worthy of recognition. In other words, whiteness and (white) time are supposedly at risk of empirical neglect and in need of protection. Without serious reflexion over the racialization of time and the temporalization of race,[6] sociologists increase the likelihood of creating larger empirical voids than those they are attempting to fill. Calling attention to the "marginalization" of time is but one of the many ways in which sociologists ignore the possibility of negation within a negated category. In other words, as marginal as time may be within sociology, it retains a powerful capacity to not just marginalize but disappear temporal others.

The study of "social time" aims to fulfill "the sociological imagination" by linking individual experiences to broader social structures.[7] Émile Durkheim, for example, distinguishes between "the complex of sensations and images that serve to orient us in duration and the category of time" and social time[8]—qualitatively different interpretations of time based on shared group beliefs. Durkheim's distinction between modern time based on clocks and calendars and social time invokes the Greek notions of *chronos* and *kairós*. *Chronos* corresponds with linear, androcentric interpretations of time.[9] As such, *chronos* becomes synonymous with clock time. Conversely, experiential dimensions of time are better interpreted through *kairós*, or what Hassard describes as "existential-time."[10] Antonio Negri makes a similar distinction between "internal" and "external time."[11] The historian Vanessa Ogle describes social time as "notions of how to use and pass one's time in daily life and in interactions with others."[12]

As John Hassard notes, "For Durkheim all members of a society share a common temporal consciousness: time is a social category of thought, a product of society."[13] Favoring homogenous conceptions of time, however, erodes qualitatively disparate temporal experiences.[14] Hence, Durkheim's universal conceptions of time are more selective than collective. Countless scholars carry on Durkheim's tradition of subsuming the particular within the universal by endorsing social time while ignoring those denied access to the "social" itself.

In their analysis of social time, Pitirim Sorokin and Robert Merton note, "The system of time varies with the social structure."[15] The issue, though, is not a matter of acknowledging temporal heterogeneity and how "social structure" shapes time, but rather how time functions as a tool of ontological and racialized violence. Absent from Sorokin and Merton's acknowledgment of the importance of "social structure" is any mention of race or racialized violence. The authors speak to the potential uneven distribution of time when they write, "Quantitatively equal periods of time are rendered socially unequal and unequal periods are socially equalized."[16] But "socially unequal" periods of time obscure the role of time as a source of inequality. In other words, time is not a universal element capable of being used or misused to produce unequal periods. Rather, as an instrument of oppression, time is integral to the maintenance of a sociogenetic order,[17] in which racialization determines the extent to which life value is guaranteed to some, conditionally granted to a few, and completely denied to many others.

Eviatar Zerubavel emphasizes the need to extend Durkheim's ideas by investigating the "social aspects of temporal reference."[18] "Temporal coordination," according to Zerubavel, is integral to the standardization of time: "Social life as we know it would probably be impossible were we to rely entirely on time units at least one day long when temporally coordinating ourselves with others."[19] "Temporal coordination," however, is yet another euphemism sociologists use to signal a sort of mutualism, cohesion, and equivalence that does not exist. What might it mean to consider the possibility that temporal coordination is orchestrated through extraction, dispossession, gratuitous violence, and impunity?

It is interesting to think about how Zerubavel's emphasis on the importance of temporal coordination to social life substantiates key critiques of time, temporality, and social life/death within Afro-pessimism. Consider Frank Wilderson's argument that time and space are irredeemable to "the Black":

> The capacity to redeem time and space is foreclosed to the Black because redemption requires "heritage" of temporality and spatiality, rather than a past of boundless time and indeterminate space. Also, a "general deprivation of affect" cannot be calculated by the Black. Temporally, the Black would have to be able to say when Blackness and the deprivation of affect were not coterminous. Onto this five-hundred-year obliteration of subjectivity it would be difficult, if not obscene, to try to graft a narrative which imagines, from the Black position, the essence of "ontological malady" as an "exile from affect."[20]

Here, Wilderson calls attention to the continuity of enslavement and the negation of Black personhood within anything that could be considered "social life." Zerubavel's emphasis on temporal coordination cannot be felt by those who are consistently subject to the ongoing brutality and coordinated violence of time itself. In short, there can be no talk of temporal coordination without first discussing the coordination required to make an anti-Black world. This is not an argument in favor of temporal order, in part because so often the cause is always already the effect.[21]

Modernity and the Enlightenment helped not only mark time but also temporalize nonwhite people as temporal deviants and/or degenerates.[22] In *Time Binds: Queer Temporalities, Queer Histories*, Elizabeth Freeman makes clear that, by definition, modernity and the Enlightenment required the construction of racialized others as suspended in time or completely evacuated from any temporal experience at all: "As anachronism's emblem, racialized Blackness seems to secure the present's modernity, its difference from rather than interpenetration with earlier moments: wherever 'race' is, there modernity supposedly can't be, *yet*" (emphasis in the original).[23]

Sociologists perpetuated the temporalization of race by conflating whiteness with progress and nonwhiteness with present orientations and inertia. Lewis Coser and Rose Coser, for example, distinguish between the "future orientations" of the West and the "chiliastic" or "hedonist" characteristics of "deviant time perspectives."[24] Not surprisingly, "deviant time perspectives" are racialized: "One is more likely to find a tendency to accept passive chiliastic visions, for example, among the peasants of the European Middle Ages and Negroes in the *antebellum* South."[25] The authors juxtapose "passive chiliastic visions" to "dominant, active, individualistic" time perspectives associated with the progress narratives of "Western" culture.[26] Constructing Black people as passive millenarians legitimates the construction of poor urbanized space, particularly Black ghettos throughout the United States, as anachronistic and present oriented.

The equation of whiteness with progress leaves many racialized subjects both out of and outside time. "Those who reject the activistic future orientation of the dominant culture," according to Coser and Coser, maintain "deviant time perspectives."[27] Similar to criminologists, sociologists of time construct "deviants" and "deviance" as nonwhite. Present orientations, lateness, delay, and an audacious disregard for white time are defining characteristics of temporal deviance and deviants.

There is, however, a cruel irony to constructing millenarian visions of the future in direct opposition to Western culture. The same "Western culture" Coser and Coser privilege as future oriented is what John Mbiti blames for political instability in many African nations:

> Partly because of Christian missionary teaching, partly because of western type education, together with the invasion of modern technology with all it involves, African peoples are discovering the future dimension of time. On the secular level this leads to national planning for economic growth, political independence, extension of education facilities and so on. But the change from the structure built around the traditional concept of time, to one which should accommodate this new discovery of the future dimension, is not a smooth one and may well be at the root of, among other things, the political instability of our nations. In Church life this discovery seems to create a strong expectation of the millennium. This makes many Christians escape from facing the challenges of this life into the state of merely hoping and waiting for the life of paradise.[28]

As Mbiti demonstrates, Africans on the continent and across the diaspora remain in a no-win situation. They are punished for envisioning the future and for thinking in the present. Though Coser and Coser seek to establish a correlation between "Utopian orientations" and those "alienated from the prevailing cultural values," they ignore how such orientations remain rooted in the past and present.[29]

Within Coser and Coser's typology of "dominant" and "deviant" time perspectives, the race of the "dominant culture" goes unnamed, precluding inquiry into the relationship between whiteness and future orientations. For example, why is whiteness so preoccupied with the future? Perhaps the residency of conquest and "slavery's afterlife" in the present leads many white people to relocate to a less burdensome and more abstract spacetime called the "future."[30] Black and other racialized subjects do not have the luxury of entertaining a future eviscerated through captivity within a punitive welfare state, economic dispossession, and routinized racialized violence. As I demonstrate in chapter 8, Black youth reject both whiteness and "liberal futurities" predicated on false promises of "equal opportunity" and neoliberal "freedoms."[31]

Are racialized time perspectives "deviant" or defense strategies? White time is a violent time—one that sets the tempo for conquest, enslavement, and what Walter Mignolo calls the "geopolitics of economy,"[32] in order to distinguish those who own time from those who can only be owned by it. Similarly, "modernity," "progress," and "development" function as euphemisms for temporal violence. Paul Gilroy holds that "racial subordination is integral to the processes of development and social and technological progress known as modernisation. It can therefore propel into modernity some of the very people it helps to dominate."[33] Gilroy makes clear that development, and by extension time, requires subjugation. To the racialized and dispossessed, the violence of time is clear. To those who maintain a "possessive investment" in time, such violence is naturalized and legitimate, based on what Clarissa Hayward calls "good stories," which, she argues, "are not objectively good" but rather "politically powerful" in that they convince white storytellers and listeners that what they own is a product of a strong, individualistic work ethic independent of the privileges afforded to them based on their race.[34]

How white people, particularly those in the United States, tell "good stories" while actively ignoring the presence of the past (i.e., "slavery's afterlife" and conquest) is symptomatic of what Zerubavel calls "mnemonic myopia."[35] Similarly Renato Rosaldo might classify this phenomenon as a form of "imperialist nostalgia," whereby social scientists long "for what they have destroyed."[36] Given its emphasis on progress, linear time complements such myopic thought. As Denise Ferreira da Silva notes, "Linear temporality, as a rendering of separability and determinacy, accounts for the obscuration of how the colonial participates in the creation of capital."[37] In other words, linear time relies on progress narratives to conceal the role of the primitive accumulation required for capitalist modes of production.

Zerubavel suggests that being a part of a "mnemonic community" allows members to share interpretations of historical events.[38] The extent to which ongoing racialized violence factors into collective memories within mnemonic communities, however, goes unexplored and unmapped in Zerubavel's *Time Maps*. By his own admission, his "ultimate goal in this book, therefore, is not to explain mnemonic variation, but to identify the common generic underpinnings of the social structure of memory."[39] Where Zerubavel takes a greater interest in "common generic underpinnings," I question the extent to which "common" is overrepresented as white. Hence, I direct my attention to the "uncommon," or more specifically those denied access to the concept of "common" and coevalness.

Zerubavel's interventions in studies of collective memory and time have also found their way into scholarship on race and racism. For example, in *Resurrecting Slavery: Racial Legacies and White Supremacy in France*, Crystal Fleming advances the concept of racial temporality to refer to social actors' "claims about the content of the racial past, present and future as well as the relationship among racial categories, relations and processes in these different time periods."[40] Fleming's focus on temporal representations of race and the elision of white supremacy from French narratives about slavery makes important interventions in research on collective memory and constructions of the past.

For Fleming, time becomes a racial concept based on individual identities and associated with particular periods. This is but one of several points of my departure from such theorizations about time and temporality. Before racialized temporalities there is what Michael Hanchard calls "racial time."[41] This is a system of (ontological) measurement that is predicated on progress (and which is thus asymmetrical) and the extraction and exploitation of racialized life. Hence, how do you resurrect that which is still living?[42] It is worth asking whether examinations of temporal perspectives, collective memory, and historical elisions actually naturalize time itself as a system of measurement rather than a tool of ontological (dis)assembly, asymmetrical violence, and racializing assemblages. While I am also interested in temporality, I am reluctant to legitimate a key instrument in the anti-Black project of world making.

Conventional theories within the sociology of time reveal more than they conceal. Invested in a "white habitus,"[43] and absorbed in "white solipsism," the prospective gatekeepers of a sociology of time cannot behold the power structures to which they are beholden. Differing time perspectives can exist only when there is something to be different from. White time remains the central reference category for most sociological analyses of time. Prefiguring time as white arrests racialized subjects in an anachronistic realm of foreclosed life chances and chances at life.

Black youths at Run-a-Way refused to be located in anterior time. Instead they resisted white time while becoming innovators of temporalities with greater latitudinal breadth to encompass the entirety of their identities. Discrete notions of the past, present, and future did not apply because time felt more recursive than progressive. Having acknowledged the incompatibility between their lived experiences and linear time, Black youths funked the clock in theory and in practice. I think of these subversions in two distinct yet related ways. First, *transgressive temporalities* signify disorientations to white time, modernity, and liberal futurities, all of which deny Black youth a place in time. To isolate transgressive temporalities to the realm of thought, however, is to ignore their role as catalysts. To that end, *insurgent time* represents the everyday tactics youth use to remain off rather than on time. Within this asynchronous relationship, time is measured not in seconds, minutes, and hours, but in degrees of resistance and self-determination. In this sense, the Black youths at Run-a-Way located themselves outside white time and anachronistic space. Instead, mocking the clock made these youths ahead of both their time and time itself. By arriving at school late, missing curfew, not showing up for work, skipping court dates, and/or distracting or redirecting others during meetings, Black youths violated that which consistently violates them, while creating new temporal modes of being. For example, JT illustrates a transgressive temporality marked by a liberation from lateness and time itself.

36   CHAPTER 1

When it came to school attendance, he made it clear that punctuality was not a priority. I asked him how often he got to places "on time." He replied,

> Um, usually I can get there at about the time that I say I'm going to get there. To be completely honest, my only problem is school. It's just because getting up that early for something that I don't enjoy or don't want to do, I don't like. But I was able to get to a friend's house at four in the morning because I told them that I'd be able to and I did.

Insurgent time is what transgressive temporalities look like in practice. JT's willingness to meet up with a friend at four o'clock in the morning but not to make it to school by eight o'clock is not simply an affront or transgression. Rather, he funks the clock and resists the temporal strictures of schooling through what James Scott calls "infrapolitics"—"resistance that avoids any open declaration of its intentions."[44]

JT's thoughts on lateness, though, remain at odds with those of many adults, including Vice President Kamala Harris. In her role as San Francisco district attorney from 2004 to 2011, Harris issued citations to parents whose children missed more than fifty days of school. She described truancy as a public safety issue, suggesting that high school dropouts were at increased risk of becoming victims or perpetrators of crime. Each year, she sent a letter to every San Francisco parent of public school students, warning them of potential prosecution for truancy. As she recounted in a speech in 2010,

> I believe a child going without an education is tantamount to a crime, so I decided I was going to start prosecuting parents for truancy. . . . I said, "Look. I'm done. This is a serious issue, and I've got a little political capital and I'm going to spend some of it." And this is what we did. We recognized that, in that [anti-truancy] initiative, as a prosecutor and law enforcement [official], I have a huge stick, the school district has got a carrot—let's work in tandem around our collective objective and goal, which is to get those kids in school.[45]

What Harris and others may describe as "truancy" may in fact be signs of fugitivity[46]—something very much warranted under the callousness of white time and its synchronized systems. How might we begin to think of tardiness and truancy less as an example of wrongdoing and more as a means of escape? JT's antagonistic relationship with school was indicative of his vexing relationship to time. Why would he or other youths be in a rush to do something they "don't enjoy or don't want to do"? JT's tardiness was not unique, and as I will show, Black youths did not entertain the possibility that liberal opportunity structures, such as school and work, could ever be a site of liberation. Rather, this chapter is filled with instances of Black youths defying space and time while producing transgressive and transformative temporalities.

CP Time: Never on Schedule but Always on Time

Relegated to anachronistic space or erased from time and history altogether, Black and other racialized persons maintain a unique relationship to time. Rather than serve as an orienting force, time symbolizes a source of tremendous agony and pain. As white people amassed time through colonization and enslavement, Black and Indigenous people bore witness to the oppression of progress. In analyzing temporality within the African diaspora, Michael Hanchard describes time as a vehicle for "British racism and imperialism" in Ghana. Time helped expedite the extraction of capital, resources, and surplus value while slowing "the educational development of Ghanaian children and the training of teachers."[47]

Hanchard shows how time is not only constructed but also managed and manipulated. Temporal concepts such as "duration, pace, trajectory and cycles," as identified by Ronald Aminzade,[48] are calibrated to white time, white people, and whiteness. Hanchard makes clear that when the hands of time resemble the hands of white people, Black people do not exist. To the extent that Black people can be temporally interpellated, they are cast into an anachronistic time and thus made vulnerable to dispossession, debt, and death. Hanchard, though, sees "Afro-modernity" as an important site of Black resistance to the violence of colonial time. Afro-modernity, he observes, "consists of the selective incorporation of technologies, discourses, and institutions of the modern West within the cultural and political practices of African-derived peoples to create a form of relatively autonomous modernity distinct from its counterparts of Western Europe and North America."[49]

In conversation with Gilroy's *The Black Atlantic*, Hanchard emphasizes the importance of Afro-modernity as "a counterculture of modernity." At its core, Afro-modernity negates the notion that Black people are the antithesis of modernity.[50] The antagonistic relationship between Western time and Afro-modernity is what Hanchard calls "racial time," which he says "is defined as the inequalities of temporality that result from power relations between racially dominant and subordinate groups. Unequal relationships between dominant and subordinate groups produce unequal temporal access to institutions, goods, services, resources, power, and knowledge, which members of both groups recognize."[51]

Social time was and still is racial time. Racial time demands that racialized violence remain in full effect and that affectable subjects be most harmed.[52] Racial time took on a distinct cultural meaning for Black people living in the United States. If capital was a metonym for Black, how could Black people claim ownership over time when time was/is also money?[53] Disavowed from the social and from social time, Black people sought to unsettle and expose the intimate relationship between time and power. Many saw the potential to eke out openings for resistance within routinized economic exploitation and defied the logics of capital accumulation in favor of transformative temporalities such as CP Time (Colored People's Time). CP Time derives from the incommensurable relationship between time and Black people's racialized realities, which literally and figuratively don't count within categories of seconds, minutes, hours, and so on. CP Time is not simply an appreciation of lateness, but a byproduct of the tension over expecting punctuality, when racialized social structures ensure that Black life chances are habitually late or absent.

As a transformative temporality, CP Time belies uniformity and is not indicative of how all racialized persons use time. More specifically, not all Black people use CP Time or use it in the same way. Nevertheless, CP Time remains an important cultural construct to understand how power works, and specifically how white time *works on* racialized persons. As an orientation constructed against white time, CP Time functions as a counterframe to white time and whiteness.[54] Ronald Walcott explains why CP Time (or CPT) occupies a unique niche in Black popular culture and parlance:[55]

> Black people always seem to be late and, in fact, have been late so often and so predictably that they themselves have coined a term for it: CP Time, Colored People's time. CP Time is usually spoken of in tones of the profoundest dismay (by Blacks who lament their brothers' "irresponsibility that will hold us all back") or of outraged complacency (by whites who see this habitual lateness as yet further instance of our don't-give-a-damn-attitude, "but really, what can you expect?") or of amused tolerance (by the rest of us who are so accustomed to it we hardly notice it). *CP Time actually is an example of Black people's effort to evade, frustrate and ridicule the value-reinforcing strictures of punctuality that so well serve this coldly impersonal technological society. Time is the very condition of Western civilization that oppresses so brutally.* (emphasis added)[56]

Not only was time wielded as one of many tools of racialized violence during slavery, but as Walcott ably demonstrates, time also became a catalyst for Black resistance and fugitivity from what Fred Moten describes as "structures of subjection . . . that overdetermine freedom."[57] In *Black Time: Fiction of Africa, the Caribbean, and the United States*, Bonnie J. Barthold helps answer a central question orienting this chapter:

> The slave owner became the archetypal owner of time. As an owner of time, he could own slaves, upon whom he imposed both the concept

and the consequences of ownership but to whom he denied the right of ownership. His physical enslavement of the slave was axiomatically equivalent to his enslavement of time. Had the slave master had his way, the result would have been the imposition of timelessness on all his slaves—not in the sense of Western transcendence but in the sense of total dispossession, as in the pennilessness of bankruptcy.[58]

The Industrial Revolution and the rise in technology brought forth opportunities for slave owners to confer temporal regulation on the timepiece. One of many "structures of subjection" during enslavement was the clock. Mark Smith's work on slavery in the US South details how time (via clocks) was used to "regulate labor both socially and economically" while reinforcing the equation of whiteness as modern.[59] In short, time does not only regulate labor but also organizes racial orders. To the slave denied ontological value within the racial order, the "whip" and "watch" were synonymous.[60] Henry James Trentham's testimony is one of over two thousand former slave narratives in George Rawick's *American Slave: A Composite Autobiography*. Here, Trentham exemplifies why time is such an oppressive force for enslaved people: "We hated to see the sun rise in slavery time, 'cause it meant another hard day."[61] In short, time gives a licking and keeps on ticking. To the enslaved and dispossessed, time symbolized relentless brutality and suffering. As Smith writes,

> [African Americans] accommodated and resisted their masters' attempts to inculcate a modern clock-based time sensibility during slavery. . . . African Americans can adjust to white time sensibilities, which stress punctuality and are future oriented, but they can also reject these same sensibilities as a form of protest against democratic capitalism, generally white bourgeois sensibilities specifically, by eschewing the authority of the clock and adopting presentist and naturally defined notions of time, a tendency that sociologists and the public alike have come to call Colored People's Time, or CPT.[62]

Smith's conception of CP Time coincides with Walcott's in that both recognize a shared analysis of white time among Black people and both emphasize the importance of violating a violent system. Renato Rosaldo takes up the concept of CP Time to illustrate efforts to resist incompatible standards of white time and temporal "Otherness":

> Those in our society who fail to conform to the painfully imposed "time-discipline" are commonly described as living by C.P.T. (colored people's time), Indian Time, or Mexican Time. . . . "We" have "time-discipline," and "they" have, well, something else (or, as we say these

days, "Otherness"). The former quality of time can be described in relation to cultural artifacts such as clocks, calendars, appointment books, and the like. More significantly, it can be understood in connection with capitalists' desire to discipline and synchronize the labor force, rationalizing production and maximizing profits, but probably not enhancing the quality of life.[63]

I use the concept of CP Time not as an example of how time is racialized, but as an example of resistance to racializing time (i.e., white time). Though some research exists on Black resistance to time pre- and postemancipation,[64] less attention is paid to the way Black youth carry on tradition to transgress time today. I argue that Black youth, similar to earlier generations, apply revised versions of CP Time to strain, agitate, and mock the higher temporal worth and status granted to white time. It is not enough, though, to simply highlight the incompatibility between white time and the temporal realities of Black youth in urbanized space. Without illustrating the importance of creativity to challenging systems of power and domination, analyses of resistance remain incomplete. As innovative knowledge producers and culturesmiths, Black youth, especially those in urbanized space, rely on nonnormative temporalities not only as forms of resistance to power and domination, but also to ridicule the time as a racist, sexist, and capitalist construct. In doing so, youths at Run-a-Way bring new meaning to the phrase, "See you late(r)."

Contemporary forms of "infrapolitics" are situated within legacies of resistance. The historian Robin D. G. Kelley, for example, illustrates how Black workers in the early twentieth century resisted workplace exploitation through a variety of tactics including "wigging" (the use of company time and materials for personal reasons), "pan-toting" (the practice of taking home leftovers, excess food, and utensils by domestic workers), foot-dragging, feigning illness, absenteeism, and rigging company clocks to "steal time."[65] In using such tactics, Black workers helped further expose the discordant relationship between Black labor and white time. The sense of empowerment that may accompany acts of "industrial sabotage," should not, however, diminish the significance of subsequent retaliation and punishment. In referencing Joe Trotter's study of African Americans in West Virginia, Kelley states that "theft, sabotage, and slowdowns were two-edged swords that, more often than not, reinforced the subordinate position of Black coal miners in a racially determined occupational hierarchy."[66]

Though CP Time represents a generative site for social movement scholars seeking to explore relations of power and resistance, investigations of Black youth's relation to CP Time remain underdeveloped. Perhaps CP Time's appreciation of ambiguity and contradiction makes it antithetical to positivist sociology's relentless and ruthless quest for "truth." The neglect of CP Time generally has left sociology in need of a more complete analysis of the socialities and temporalities of racialized youth, and Black youth in particular. Sociologists of time may benefit from exercising their own "sociological imaginations" in order to make the familiar (i.e., white time) strange and make the mundane (i.e., whiteness) matter.

Based on my interviews at Run-a-Way, it was clear that CP Time does not hold as much cultural relevancy among most youth today as it did for Generations X or Y. Most of the youths I interviewed were unfamiliar with either term, but a few likened it to what they called "Black people time" and "POC time." During my interviews, the "CP" in "CP Time" usually required some unpacking. To make CP Time a bit more relevant, I offered the following prompt: "If I say that there's a party going down tomorrow at ten p.m., but we're on CP Time, what time do you think the party will start?" Most youths picked up on this hint and figured out that the party would start later. We also talked about why the term "colored people" was and still is racist, while also examining the false equivalence between "colored people" and "people of color." I wondered whether the youths' limited understanding of the historical connotations of "colored" was symptomatic of white, linear, progressive time's capacity to conceal a racialized violence that is not only past but present. When the past is always present for Black youth, knowledge of history is also knowledge of now.

I'll Get There When I Get There

To be Black in a state of white supremacy exemplifies a contradictory experience. Many youths at Run-a-Way recognized the contradiction of claiming to be on time when they were consistently beginning from behind or beginning from deficits. When I asked Devon about the purpose of CP Time, he said, "I mean, honestly, I feel like that was the best way to stick it to the man then." At the time of the interview, fifteen-year-old Devon attended an alternative high school for aspiring musicians. Devon's dream was, as he put it, to "transform the world through [his] music." "Sticking it to the man" was Devon's way of showing how CP Time becomes a route to resistance through ridicule. According to Devon, CP Time relies on humor to remind "the man" of Black people's (temporal) self-determination. CP Time may be best summed up as "lateness with (or without) a smile." Some join in the amusement, remaining unperturbed by the lack of respect for time. Others, including "the man," experience intense consternation over the contradiction between lateness and punctuality.

Whether used to redefine or rupture existing relationships to white time, CP Time functions as a kind of transformative transgression among Black people and other racialized subjects. To be used by time, as opposed to using it, exposes an exploitative side of time concealed within universalist frames of social time. In fact, to some, social time may look a lot like carceral time. Before learning the meaning of CP Time, Devon inferred that it was a way to distinguish between Black and white time use:

> For us, like, growing up it was how Black people spent their time compared to how white people spent their time. . . . There's a really big difference. I grew up knowing that Black people time was what we do within our day and how different. . . . Because we spend our time . . . a lot of us spend our time in jail, some of us spend our time taking care of kids, single parents taking care of kids. White people take their kids to daycare and all that, which is how different it was.

Devon recognizes the structural factors that result in such qualitatively distinct experiences between Black and white people. But he also subscribes to some of the racialized scripts created by urban sociologists, political scientists, criminologists, and others invested in carceral curricula. By suggesting that a lot of Black people spend time in jail, Devon constructs the prison-industrial complex as a primary site of time use for both prisoners and nonprisoners. Devon does not, however, use the term "mass incarceration" to describe the significant number of Black people in jails and prisons.

As Dylan Rodríguez notes, critiquing "mass incarceration" as an issue affecting all is insufficient, when the "masses" are not being incarcerated.[67] In fact, the prison-industrial complex is intent on containing those already captive while exonerating the key architects of "white reconstruction."[68] "Mass incarceration" is also not merely an issue of too many people being incarcerated. The word "mass" summons calls to "reform" the prison-industrial complex by reducing the number of currently incarcerated people or sending fewer people to jails and prisons. The problem with these proposals is that they naturalize the prison-industrial complex. According to Rodríguez, "mass incarceration narrativity" makes "incarceration" not only theoretically possible, but legitimate.[69]

The equation of Blackness and "criminality" is a form of not only racialization but also temporalization. Jared Sexton helps illustrate this point when reciting a scene from the 1967 film *In the Heat of the Night*. In the scene, Virgil Tibbs, played by Sidney Poitier, tells Mama Caleba, played by Beah Richards, "There's white time in jail, and there's colored time in jail. The worst kind of time you can do is colored time." Sexton goes on to describe "colored time" as "interminable, perhaps even incalculable, stalled time."[70] Similar to an event horizon—the region of no escape within a black hole—the prison-industrial complex represents a spacetime that thwarts opportunities for exit and obstructs observation from the outside. Devon identifies the prison-industrial complex as a site of significant time use for Black people in the United States. In short, carceral space both stalls time and steals it from Black prisoners, while making escape virtually impossible. Consequently, racialized youth, and Black youth in particular, are forced to do time more than use it. In referencing single parenthood, Devon also alludes to the disproportionate impact of incarceration on Black families, making clear that time is racialized and gendered.

Devon and Sexton make clear that white time constructs disparate life chances between white and nonwhite people. The manipulation of white time ensures that opportunity structures are accessible to some and denied to others. White time disavows nonwhite coevalness. For example, because schools are calibrated to white time, it is no surprise that students of color are tracked into "remedial" or "slow" classes. As anachronistic educational space, "special" or "remedial" classrooms come to naturalize educational inequalities, including the unequal distribution of resources between "mainstream" classes and classrooms designated for students with disabilities. As I demonstrate in chapter 2, white time requires Black youth to use a time that does not belong to them and to risk being charged with time theft. White time then ensures that the probability that Black youth will be arrested and incarcerated is always greater than their white counterparts. Though Devon's conceptualization of CP Time differs from its conventional meaning, he still manages to help us consider why white people use time while Black people remain used by it.

Expecting Black people to be punctual when white time guarantees they will remain "behind schedule" as a result of ongoing forms of exploitation, dispossession, and structural violence is asinine.[71] CP Time reflects a temporal orientation that resists confinement within a binary of on-off time. Rather, CP Time embraces contradiction, ambiguity, and a multitude of cultural meanings. Its association with delay and being behind the clock seems, on the face of things, to reinforce stereotypical associations between race and time. Lost within such representations is, to paraphrase Gayatri Chakravorty Spivak, the capacity of the "subaltern to speak."[72]

"I'll get there when I get there" is a familiar refrain to followers of CP Time. The phrase reflects an active effort to unsettle expectations of punctuality by resisting coherent meanings and intelligible standards of time. In short, Black people are going to take their time because their time is always already taken (by white time). To "get there when I get there," then, is a call for greater appreciation of ambiguity and irony, which tends to frustrate white time and white people. In short, CP Time threatens the stability and regularity of white time while affording Black people some degree of temporal liberation.

44   CHAPTER 1

Pierre Bourdieu holds that access to time is contingent on "power and the objective chances open to it."[73] Thus, "temporal power" signifies the "power to perpetuate or transform the distributions of various forms of capital by maintaining or transforming the principles of redistribution."[74] With little control over the means of production, how much temporal power do racialized and dispossessed people hold? How might CP Time serve as a tactic used to not only disrupt temporal power but create new modes and owners of production? And what role does CP Time play in efforts to abolish capitalism when time is money?

Claiming ownership of time takes a variety of forms. "Absolute power," Bourdieu notes, "is the power to make oneself unpredictable and deny other people any reasonable anticipation, to place them in total uncertainty by offering no scope for their capacity to predict."[75] CP Time forces those with the greatest temporal power to wait in submission, as those cast into temporal alterity funk the clock. CP Time, thus, helps provide some semblance of freedom and a belief in a collective power to resist temporal discipline, in favor of ambiguity. In doing so, Black people express a refusal to be bound within a temporal system that eviscerates the potential for self-determination or collective well-being. As suggested, however, CP Time need not be understood only as a form of agency and/or resistance, especially given the many consequences of following CP Time (e.g., school detention, work termination, stigmatization). Rather, CP Time is functional for those who must contend with institutionalized oppressions that deny them both time and space.

As a strategy of resistance to existing forms of temporal power, CP Time involves the power of persuasion—particularly persuading others to wait. "Waiting," as Bourdieu asserts,

> implies submission: the interested aiming at something greatly desired durably—that is to say, for the whole duration of the expectancy—modifies the behavior of the person who "hangs," as we say, on the awaited decision. It follows that the art of "taking one's time," of "letting time take its time," as Cervantes put it, of making people wait, of delaying without destroying hope, of adjourning without totally disappointing, which would have the effect of killing the waiting itself, is an integral part of the exercise of power.[76]

CP Time promotes indeterminacy of presence/attendance, allowing Black people to control their schedules and those of others. For many Black youths at Run-a-Way, it was only a matter of time before their time mattered, and for fourteen-year-old Quincy, Black time already mattered most:

> RM: So if I said there's a party and it's goin' down at ten, but we're on Black people time, what time does the party actually start?

QUINCY: Party start when the Black people get there.... Whatever time we get there, that's when the party start. Like, Black people ... if you tell them to do something, like, Black people, 'cuz it's our history, we don't like listening 'cuz we've been like, you know, tortured so much and we have to do stuff. Like, most Black people be like, "I'm gonna do what I want and see how that goes." Yeah ... Black people don't listen. That's just not us. We don't listen. We ... we listen all our lives, how about we *don't* listen anymore? And that's why you see most Black people out there doin' what they doin' now 'cuz they don't wanna listen anymore. 'Cuz they're tired of listening. So yeah. They're tired of listening.

In Quincy's response, we find several rich elements of CP Time, including ambiguity, resistance, and transformation. Quincy is adamantly opposed to abiding by a time that doesn't abide by him and other Black people. The party may start at ten, but it goes until Black people say "when." The cumulative impact of and unfolding chronicle of Black captivity, dispossession, debt, and death obviate any expectation for Black deference to white time. Quincy demonstrates the possibility of creating while defying. The ambiguity of what can be produced does not deter Quincy from resisting. Rather, ambiguity is a source of momentum, because while the pathway to liberation may not be clear, the chance to be free from enslavement and "slavery's afterlife" is better than no chance at all.

But what other powers does CP Time hold beyond resistance and ridicule? Upon closer examination of Quincy's words, we are reminded of Walcott's earlier conceptualization of time as "the very condition of Western civilization that oppresses so brutally." CP Time is, then, also an opportunity for Black people, including Black youth, to heal from temporal violence and the violence of white time. Quincy's refusal to listen is part of that healing process. Quincy is refusing the directives of not only the slave driver, the overseer, the officer, the missionary, and the teacher, but also the clock orienting them all.

CP Time and other racial temporalities need not only exist as responses to dominant narratives. In some instances, what may be read as "oppositional" may be experiments in alternative socialities centering spontaneity and a sort of coordinated unpredictability. For example, the anthropological linguist Susan Phillips reveals how the rhythm of daily life among the Ilongot tribe creates ways to be beholden to one another as opposed to time:

They [non-Indians] try to learn from Indians at what time the event will begin. Often the person questioned will say he doesn't know, but if pressed, he may give a specific time—e.g., 8 P.M. or "some time after 9."

The non-Indians will arrive at that time, only to find that "nothing is happening" yet, and no one seems to know when something will happen. They wait anywhere from twenty minutes to several hours before the event begins."[77]

In his analysis, Rosaldo argues,

Far from being devoid of positive content (presumably because of not being rule-governed), indeterminacy allows the emergence of a culturally valued quality of human relations where one can follow impulses, change directions, and coordinate with other people. In other words, social unpredictability has its distinctive tempo, and it permits people to develop timing, coordination, and a knack for responding to contingencies. The qualities constitute social grace, which in turn enables an attentive person to be effective in the interpersonal politics of everyday life. . . . [A]mong the Ilongots zones of indeterminacy, particularly in social visits, promote a human capacity for improvisation in response to the unexpected, and this very capacity can be celebrated as a cultural value."[78]

Does improvisation or the celebration of "cultural value" constitute "temporal power" or something else? Black people throughout the diaspora recognize that CP Time is both an inside joke and an acknowledgment of Black people's capacity to remain in physical, psychic, and emotional communion with one another, despite their "stranger" status and geographic boundaries.[79] While CP Time forces adherents of white time to wait, it proves less consternating for Black people, who respond with what Walcott calls "amused tolerance."[80] "I'll get there when I get there" also means "I'll see you when I see you." When encountering one another, most Black people know that if it is "good to see you!" then it is also "good to be seen." Though only sixteen, Sean has apprehended the importance of Black temporal traditions and demonstrates his proficiency in our discussion of what he calls "Black people time": "I dunno, I think it's called Black people time. I don't know what that CP thing is. I know what Black people time is. So Black people time is you a couple . . . you a *little* late."

Sean punctuates his remarks with a dose of humor that both ridicules and resists white time—the inside joke being that "a *little* late" to Black folk actually meant *a lot* late to others. Sean's personality always brought life to our one-on-one conversations and radiated throughout the milieu of the program. During free time, Sean commandeered the center's small boom box, tuned into whatever station was "the Twin Cities' Home for Hip Hop and R&B" at the time, raised the volume high enough for all on the second floor to hear, and proceeded to "cut a rug"—the literal one in the center of the living room of the emergency shelter program. Sean invited both peers and staff to join, but most seemed too shy to participate. Humor and performance characterize both Sean's personality and CP Time or "Black people time." Just as Sean took center stage to show off his dance moves in front of peers and staff, CP Time is a pronouncement of one's arrival before familiar and unfamiliar audiences.

Others may arrive late, seeking less fanfare and without much expression at all. Yet all are expected to appreciate ambiguity and not act "brand new" when someone is, as Sean puts it, "a little late." Ambiguity proved to be an orienting theme for many youths at Run-a-Way. Some, like sixteen-year-old Lamont, offered less explanation for following CP Time:

> RM: Would you say that you're someone that follows CP Time?
> LAMONT: Yeah, I would.
> RM: Yeah, OK. Is there a reason or is it . . . ?
> LAMONT: No, I just . . . it just happen like that.

Lamont's remarks are dense as much as they are terse, and they capture an important feature of CP Time—it is best to "get there when you get there." By suggesting that his lateness "just happen like that," Lamont conveys a refusal to remain bound within temporal parameters and allows his life to unfold organically according to his own idiosyncratic schedule. When asked whether he has a personal schedule, Lamont's response was, "No. I just go by the day." At the time of our interview, he was in the independent living program and had just applied to Job Corps after being expelled from school for fighting.[81] Lamont's idiosyncratic schedule is versatile and conducive to improvisation and shifting plans based on impulse. When one's schedule is as flexible as Lamont's, time itself bends in a variety of ways. Lacking access to consistent meals, shelter, medical care, and income warrants some degree of flexibility in one's schedule.

Staff at Run-a-Way often described the program as an interim placement for youths "in limbo"—a transition phase before moving to a more permanent placement such as a home, a foster home, a group home, residential placement, a hospital, or a juvenile detention center. Youths were in limbo because many lacked clarity regarding where they would go after Run-a-Way. Some, especially those without a home to return to, did not learn about their next placement until just a few days before they moved. Most, however, came to Run-a-Way because of family challenges and planned to return home after meeting program expectations, including taking part in group activities and setting educational goals, as well as participating in individual and family therapy.

Transience made it difficult for youths to develop lasting relationships with staff. There were, however, some exceptions. Finesse, who was eighteen years old at the time of our interview, moved up the ranks from the emergency shelter program to independent living, establishing enduring relationships with numerous staff members and youths at Run-a-Way. The independent living program, located on the third floor of the building, was where older youths could focus on improving activities of daily living (ADLs) in order to eventually find their own apartment. Because the independent living program allows youths to stay there for up to one year (and in some cases longer), Finesse was one of a select number of youths whom I saw regularly during my time at Run-a-Way.

Finesse identified himself as "Jamaican and Irish" and described himself as having "white skin with Black features." He and I bonded over similar racialized biographies and our mutual love of hip hop. At the time, Finesse was an aspiring rapper who was shot in the leg just before coming to Run-a-Way, while hanging out with a group of friends. He does not believe he was the intended target of the shooting, but he admitted to having ties to the Crips, which sometimes led to tension with other youths at Run-a-Way. It was not Finesse's first time at Run-a-Way. Before being shot, he volunteered as an informal personal trainer for several youths in the emergency shelter program. Like many of his peers, Finesse returned to the program after continued challenges at home. When I met him, he was confined to a wheelchair and was unable to leave the program due to safety concerns. Within five months, however, Finesse was getting around with crutches while his injured leg remained protected by a cast. Despite not finishing high school, he had a good-paying job at the Mayo Clinic. His boss kept his position secure until he was able to return after the shooting. Still, Finesse lost a significant amount of time at work and went months without pay. He had a passion for his job and thrived as a trainer. He even tried to share some of his personal-trainer knowledge with his younger peers at Run-a-Way. In their eyes, Finesse was a "real cool dude," partly because his job involved working with the Minnesota Timberwolves.

Finesse was also known for his sense of humor, as demonstrated in our conversation about CP Time. Before I could provide an example, Finesse said, "I know what you're talkin' about. You're talkin' about how . . . maybe it's different than what you were gonna say, but when I hear that what I'm thinkin' is like Black people are always late type shit. . . . 'I'm around the corner' but they really be like forty-five minutes away. . . . That's what I was thinkin' of. When you first said 'CPT' I thought you were talkin' about the buses in Chicago."

Finesse possessed a magnetizing sense of humor and a tacit awareness of the importance of ambiguity to CP Time. Ambiguity is also integral to fully capturing what Michelle M. Wright describes as "the multidimensionality of Blackness."[82]

"*In any moment in which we are reading/analyzing Blackness,*" she argues, "*we should assume that its valences will likely vary from those of a previous moment.*"[83] Her book *Physics of Blackness* is Wright's provocation to ask not only "What is blackness?" but also "Where and when is blackness?"[84] Based on Finesse's calculation and according to CPT, Blackness, and more specifically Black people, is both "around the corner" and "forty-five minutes" late. To suggest, however, that all Black people abide by CP Time would undermine Wright's emphasis on heterogeneity and contradiction. Rather, my aim is to challenge misreadings of CP Time based on the incompatible metrics of white time.

According to Wright, "linear progress narratives" are highly "allergic" to contradictions.[85] Given the connection between linear progress narratives and whiteness, this makes a great deal of sense. Seldom does whiteness accept ambiguity as an answer because, like linear progress narratives, it yearns for coherence and remains intolerant of contradiction, making it antithetical to women-of-color and queer-of-color epistemologies. Existing as a nonwhite, racialized subject within whiteness is itself a contradiction—one that frustrates and strains yearnings for intelligibility. Similarly, Wright's emphasis on the heterogeneity of Blackness belies coherence and linearity.

It is ironic that whiteness is so intolerant of ambiguity and contradiction when, as W. E. B. Du Bois observed, slavery and colonialism contradict white America's putative commitment to liberal, democratic, and universalist virtues.[86] As Wright notes, "In *Souls [of Black Folk]*, although the Negro American is not reconciled, split, he is not contradictory: his desire, according to Du Bois, is perfectly logical. Instead the (racist) white American is being contradictory."[87] Du Bois believed that to the extent that Black people lead contradictory lives, they do so in part because white America has violated its own claims to universal rights and freedoms.[88] Hence, Du Bois consistently inverted whiteness and centered Black sociality, while making white time contradictory to Afro-modernity and CP Time. I have so far demonstrated how attuned youth are to the pace, cycles, and rhythms of CP Time. To what extent, though, do Black youth actually move to the beat of CPT?

CP Time as Praxis

Here, I focus on what youths do to remain off white time rather than on it. Abiding by CP Time signifies a shift from external conceptions of time (*chronos*) to an internal/experiential dimension (*kairós*). The notion of "time-as-thing," according to Bourdieu, "is the product of a scholastic point of view."[89] Shifting to the experiential dimension of time, Bourdieu adds, "Practice is not *in* time but *makes*

50   CHAPTER 1

time (human time, as opposed to biological or astronomical time.)"[90] As noted earlier, CP Time is as transformative as it is transgressive, and Black youths at Run-a-Way were adept at making time while also destroying it.

Though few were familiar with the phrase, many youths at Run-a-Way had some experience applying the basic principles of CP Time. Gerard, a sixteen-year-old in the emergency shelter program, was somewhat reserved but also quite charismatic and capable of seizing any opportunity to be the center of attention. Having a darker complexion meant that Gerard was often mistaken for Somali, but he self-identified as Black and Native. I asked him what time the party would kick off if it allegedly started at 10 p.m. CPT. After I clarified the difference between CP Time (CPT) and central standard time (CST), Gerard said, "Colored People time, like . . . it's gonna be [pause] when you say it's at." Gerard helps expand conceptualizations of CP Time by reminding us of the importance of self-definition and self-determination. While clock time, linear time, modern time, and other indicators of white time may organize most forms of social life, CP Time creates the temporal caesurae that Black people require to control not only time but the pace of social life in any given setting.

I met Gerard on two different occasions at Run-a-Way. Our first meeting was characteristic of his stay in the program: transitory. Gerard returned home within a couple days of our first meeting. He spent a significantly longer period of time during his second stay. We built enough of a rapport that Gerard's mother gave me permission to conduct our interview at their home in Near North, a majority-Black community in Minneapolis still under intense police occupation, socially and economically dispossessed, and defiantly vibrant. Further along in our interview, Gerard admitted to following CP Time, while legitimating lateness as personal opposition to that which was "lame"—punctuality. I asked him whether he identified as a follower of CP Time. He replied, "Absolutely. . . . 'Cuz I always . . . I always end up at parties really late. I like doing that, I don't know. I don't . . . I never go somewhere early, that's lame."

According to Gerard, lateness prevents "lameness." Having the latest fashions may not mean much unless one's outfit includes being "fashionably late" as an accessory. To Gerard, being fashionably early is *not* a thing. Being "fashionably late," though, is fairly conventional conduct for parties. So it is somewhat disingenuous to suggest that Gerard's taste for lateness is that unusual. But Gerard did not just transgress the social time of parties. In fact, his relationship to school and work was marked by an unwavering commitment to insurgent time:

> RM: Do you care about being late?
> Gerard: Nuh uh. I don't really care. School-wise, I still don't care. . . .
>   'Cuz you'll get there eventually. . . . Being late, something I always

do. . . . Work wise, I dunno, sometimes I actually go to work late. It doesn't really matter.

RM: How important is it for you to be on time?

GERARD: I wouldn't say it is important. Like, if you're wasting my time by rambling or something. School-wise, say you're teaching me something I already know, that would be wasting my time.

When white time is the dominant metric in work and schooling, it is clear that Gerard's penchant for lateness cannot be divorced from space and place. Many Black youths in urbanized space recognize that they often learn, labor, and live in spaces designed without them in mind.[91] Gerard's remarks are reminiscent of Damien Sojoyner's conceptualization of school as an "educational enclosure" that *suspends* Black youth in time.[92] School, for example, is not simply incompatible because of a biased curriculum or the mismatch between students of color and the teachers they learn from. Instead Gerard sees school as a waste of time because, as he states, "You're teaching me something I already know." Not only is time wasted, but in Gerard's case, time is appropriated by the educational system. What does it mean to attend school on time, only to learn that you aren't going to learn anything at all?

Punctuality was also not a priority for sixteen-year-old Shanté. Money, however, was:

I'm always late though. I'm never on time to nothin', even when I had to go pick up and drop off [drugs]. I was never on time. And that was bad though. They [other dealers] used to be so mad. "What are you late for? You takin' all day." I was doin' other stuff, gettin' other money. You ain't there when you supposed to be, even though you know you supposed to be there. I knew but I wasn't there. . . . I was like, they ain't goin' nowhere 'cuz they need *my* money.

Shanté's history with the "family regulation system" made her one of the savviest youths at Run-a-Way and clearly ahead of her time.[93] Shanté was so prescient and well versed in the logics of capitalism that she regularly endorsed the notion that "time is money."[94] Compared to some of her peers who may "act out," Shanté usually chose to "cool out." Shanté's "cool pose," however, belied androcentric assumptions about young Black men coming of age. Not only was Shanté capable of anticipating and preempting racialized violence, but as a young Black woman, her "multiple consciousness" provided a standpoint on and analysis of Black women's and femmes' resistance to simultaneous and multiplicative oppressions.[95]

CHAPTER 1

Shanté was one of approximately ten youths at Run-a-Way with experience in the "fast life."[96] While more male-identified youths than Black girls and femmes disclosed selling drugs, Shanté's accounts suggest that she was as experienced as boys at Run-a-Way, if not more so. Despite the high risk of arrest and the potential of violence from peers, customers, and police, Shanté appeared to march to the tick of her own clock and transgress time. She was not, however, naive, acknowledging that "dudes are quick to shoot a girl." Yet still, she mustered the courage to take her and other people's time and make "other money." To Benjamin Franklin and others moved by the "spirit" of capitalism, Shanté's disregard for time reads as one of the highest forms of temporal treason. As Franklin observed, "After industry and frugality, nothing contributes more to the raising of a young man in the world than punctuality and justice in all his dealings; therefore, never keep borrowed money an hour beyond the time you promised, lest a disappointment shut up your friend's purse forever."[97]

To the extent that time is money, Shanté is indeed keeping "borrowed money," albeit in the form of seconds, minutes, and hours. But she expressed little concern about her customers shutting their purses because, in her words, "they ain't goin' nowhere 'cuz they need *my* money." Examining Shanté's relationship to time while living the fast life is reminiscent of Kemi Adeyemi's work on slowness as a practice among Black queer women in the neoliberal city. Adeyemi writes, "The question of slowness as a racialized queer aesthetic or practice may very well open the door for more, and more critical, reviews of how economic and cultural capital govern belonging in and to the neoliberal city, but also deeper understanding of how Black queer subjectivities within, and Black queer people's attachments to, the neoliberal city are staged through specific negotiations of temporal orders."[98]

What does it mean for Shanté to practice slowness while living the fast life? For Benjamin Franklin, practicing slowness may inch closer and closer to the profane, but for Shanté, her time is sacred. Tarrying may be antithetical to the logics of capital accumulation, but Shanté proves that in taking her time, she is in fact taking the time of others in order to make more money. As a burgeoning entrepreneur, Shanté needs little instruction on the relationship between supply and demand. To those forced to wait all day, their time is spent. But for Shanté, her ability to make "other money" on top of what she is about to earn makes her right on time. Slow money may be better than no money, but taking time while collecting fast money is an irresistibly lucrative prospect for Black youth targeted for temporal dispossession over the life course.

Shanté is not only negotiating the temporal orders of the neoliberal city but asserting her role as a moderator of time. Not only does she funk the clock, but she also queers it. Though Shanté identifies as "straight," her relationship to time does align with what J. Jack Halberstam describes as alternative temporalities among queer subcultures. As Halberstam writes, "Queer subcultures produce alternative temporalities by allowing their participants to believe that their futures can be imagined according to the logics that lie outside of those paradigmatic markers of life experience—namely birth, marriage, reproduction, and death."[99] Halberstam calls attention to the potential of queer and trans persons to transgress boundaries and dichotomies that fail or refuse to affirm the fullness of their identities. Similarly, Kara Keeling describes how queerness appears "as a structural antagonism of the social," including social time.[100] Shanté refuses social time and what Halberstam calls the "temporal frames of bourgeois reproduction and family, longevity, risk/safety, and inheritance" in favor of a queer time: namely, the fast life.[101] Abiding by queer time, though, increases the risk of the criminal legal system converting, and perhaps queering, survival strategies, including selling drugs, into "crime."

In *Social Death: Racialized Rightlessness and the Criminalization of the Unprotected*, Lisa Cacho recounts the death of her cousin Brandon and his refusal/failure to follow conventional pathways to the "American Dream":

> In some ways Brandon lived in a "queer time and place," and in others he might even be considered a "queer subject." Even though his experiences weren't necessarily comparable or similar to other queers of color, a queer of color analysis "makes some sense" of his life without condemning or celebrating who he was or who he could have been. . . . For Brandon, the failure to meet heteronormative and neoliberal expectations (and his reluctance to even try to attain them) was compounded by his racial background as Chicano/Mexican American. He was not just a lazy kid without a high school diploma who drank too much and lived off his parents. When Brandon defied normative investments in heteropatriarchy and American enterprise, he gave credence to racial stereotypes, which is partly why he also could not be fully valued through a politics of racial normativity.[102]

As I will demonstrate in chapter 6, the fast life is queer insofar as it refuses compliance with conventional life course transitions and trajectories and liberal futurities predicated on freedoms and rights that backfire when asserted by Black youth.

Youths' support for queering time, however, varied. While many shunned punctuality, others had little patience for lateness. As stated earlier, not all Black people follow CP Time, and as Remy notes, consistency and punctuality take precedence over being "fashionably late." I asked Remy to define lateness.

REMY: Lateness. Um, if I tell you to be somewhere at a certain time and bring this and bring that, but you come five hours late and you didn't bring a goddamn thing I told your ass to bring! You are late.

RM: Yeah. And do you believe that lateness is a real thing?

REMY: Personally, yes. 'Cuz we all livin' on our own timeframe. So on my side, yes, to me you are late. Maybe you're not late to you, but to *me* you are late.

RM: How important is it for you to be on time?

REMY: Super important, 'cuz I got anxiety like a muthafucka. I don't like bein' late.

As a sixteen-year-old Black and Native gender-nonbinary youth with an abiding commitment to transformative justice work, Remy was deeply connected to their community. Our connection extended beyond our time at Run-a-Way through our mutual involvement in antioppressive organizing. Remy's consideration of how other people perceive time suggests their broader awareness of relationality and the subjective dimensions of time. Remy's claim that "we all livin' on our own timeframe" helps us further distinguish between *chronos* and *kairós*, or institutionalized time—organized around clocks and calendars—and personal "timeframes." With Remy's emphatic call for punctuality, it seems only right (and perhaps right on time) to put them in conversation with Shanté.

Despite living the fast life, Shanté's habitual lateness suggests that she is comfortable "getting there when she gets there." In a scenario where Remy is waiting on Shanté, the potential for tension seems great. It is possible that if their paths were to cross under different circumstances, Shanté could be the person to whom Remy refers when speaking about expecting a delivery. In this situation, Shanté may not see herself as late, but as Remy suggests, she undoubtedly is.

CP Time as a "Hidden Transcript"

How might we shift understandings of lateness from a defiance of deadlines to a byproduct of oppressive protocols that continue to discipline Black youth, including Black girls and femmes? In my work, racialized and gendered standards of beauty, particularly hairstyle, proved to be a significant concern and source of time use among many Black girls. The following fieldnote from August 6, 2015, offers an example of how two sixteen-year-old girls, Shanté and Tasha, resist white time while also producing a spacetime that centers aspects of Black womanhood:

> I arrived at 3 p.m. The staff met in the activity room to review the "pass-ons."[103] There were "no new updates" for most of the youth. However, the pass-ons note that Shanté and Tasha stayed up until 2:30 a.m. doing hair. Tasha, who wears her own hair in a small afro, spent the night giving Shanté [a] new weave.

Staff did not impose any consequences for the "curfew violation." Time, however, remains a tool used to uphold racialized and gendered standards and regulate Black girlhood. The expectation to "look presentable" holds a specific meaning for Black girls, and as a man with straight hair, my knowledge on the subject of Black women's hair is not experiential or rooted in any standpoint. Instead I can only speak from a position of abstraction based on the little I learn from Black girls and women themselves. Black girls and women, though, remind me that the expectation to look presentable does in fact take time. The amount of time Black girls spend sitting in a single position getting their hair done/did is a process. Brushing, detangling, stretching, sewing, braiding, and the use of products not only takes time but takes significant physical and emotional strength. To construct Shanté and Tasha as passive temporal subjects, however, obscures their capacity to transform punitive standards of beauty into a potentially enjoyable activity. By doing hair, both girls establish an important bond while exploring the potential of desire and pleasure as sites of resistance. While enjoying each other's company, they join in the co-construction of insurgent time. They take pleasure in beautifying each other and defying white time because of its failure to affirm Black girlhood.

Black women's hair remains an intimate part of their identity. Like double consciousness, Black women's hair care is a physically, psychically, and emotionally expending activity. Shanté and Tasha may know they are not their hair, but they also know that misogynoir fails to make this important distinction. In response to onerous expectations for "presentability," a number of Black girls at Run-a-Way kept their hair wrapped or covered in a shower cap during the day. Aware of the many racialized and gendered expectations for hair presentation, Black girls like Shanté and Tasha found it necessary to escape to their bedrooms—one of the few sites at Run-a-Way where Black girls found solidarity with one another through mutualism—to expose their hair. Negotiating the pressures of "good hair," Eurocentric standards of beauty, and misogynoir *take* time. My aim here is not to debate the extent to which Tasha and Shanté resist racialized and gendered protocols, but to reveal how the girls resist temporal strictures by both femming and funking the clock.

Resistance, though, is a part of many Black girls' repertoires, and Shanté and Tasha may be rehearsing their own version of "infrapolitics." They are well aware of the risk of being "written up" (penalized) for staying up past curfew, yet they still recite a "hidden transcript" or "offstage" discourse to challenge "public transcripts"—"the open interaction between subordinates and those who dominate," in the words of Erving Goffman.[104] As "weapons of the weak," hidden transcript literacy rates tend to be higher among poor, racialized persons.[105] Consequently, hidden transcripts present the greatest threat to dominant groups. In violating curfew, the girls carve out space and time within the broader context of an impatient white, androcentric time that consistently spurns Black girlhood.

The consequences of violating "public transcripts," including the program curfew, varied among staff. Dwayne, for example, is one of several Black staff members in the independent living program, and he describes himself as "laid back" when it comes to curfew violation: "No one ever abides by the nine thirty [weeknight] bedtime." Youths in the independent living program adhere to a "plus-minus" system determining privileges and penalties. If they break curfew, they receive a "minus" on weekly progress sheets, resulting in a deduction in their weekly allowance. Abiding by curfew, though, gives them a "plus," thus increasing their chances of receiving their entire allowance. Some youths expected staff to show some sympathy for their tardiness by offering an occasional grace period. Such favors, however, were not so easy to grant. With cameras located on every floor and in various locations outside the building, both youths' and staff members' movements were consistently monitored.

There was also the issue of "consistency." White staff called for consistency as a show of fealty to "order" in the program. Staff framed consistency as being in the best interest of the youths. They expressed concern over sending mixed messages and being accused of bias or favoritism. With most of the administrative and managerial staff being white, Black direct-care workers were careful about letting some youths slide for curfew violations. Dwayne, however, would occasionally make an exception for youths he saw as "doing the best they can." Dwayne negotiated with youths, bargained with staff, and, at the same time, funked the clock. But youths often struck a deal that required them to perform an additional chore or study for one hour longer in order to get paid. Thus, Dwayne's advocacy may have funked up the clock only so much. While successful in deferring and averting the threat of punishment, such negotiations still demanded time from racialized youths. With time being money, it is no surprise that youths fulfilled their half of the bargain by *spending* time in service of capital (i.e., their weekly allowance). Though the temporal parameters regulating curfew hampered a sense of freedom and discretion, both Black staff and Black youths worked together to challenge "public transcripts" by regularly rehearsing "hidden" ones.

It's Me/We O'Clock

As I have argued, inclusion into social time, by definition, requires exclusion. Based on an appreciation of subjective/experiential interpretations of time, "social time" signals inclusion within a collective that shares temporal benefits. Upon further analysis, however, the construction of the "social" belies unity, equivalence, equilibrium, mutuality and any possibility of creating a time enjoyed by all. The synchronicity between social time and white time requires the systemic marginalization of racialized subjects from the existing temporal order and the social itself. The neglect of racialized time perspectives within a sociology of time results in major empirical delays and shortcomings.

What concerns me as a scholar of race, time, and critical theory is a serious dilemma within the sociology of time: the overrepresentation of white time as time itself.[106] What good is seeking to understand the temporal perspectives of the "other" when white time remains the central reference category? When temporal conventions are synchronized to white time, racialized subjects will inevitably be late, precisely because they are always already constructed as behind time or outside time altogether. Moreover, white time requires the exploitation and extraction of nonwhite life in order to function. By paying unconditional deference to white time, social scientists legitimate the elision of race, racialization, and racialized subjects from analyses of time and temporality.

Black youth reckon with white time in a variety of ways. JT, for example, is capable of meeting a friend at four o'clock in the morning but is less invested in getting to school on time because, in his words, "no one's ever late." Sean is also not that worried about being a little late, even if "a little late" is actually a lot late. For Gerard, being late holds weight and is key to maintaining a particular level of cool. Others, like Shanté, recognize the need to maximize their time while reducing the time of others. Youths like Remy, however, abhor lateness and demand punctuality. In Quincy's case, time is contingent on Black people's presence. In short, the party and, to some extent, time itself do not start until Black people say "go." Regardless of whether youths I spoke with knew the definition of CP Time, most appreciated the need to transgress time and funk the clock.

What makes CP Time and other transgressive temporalities generative and functional is a collective appreciation of lateness. While it's a source of consternation and agony for some, lateness is an acceptable and functional part of racialized temporalities. Exhausted by the many social institutions synchronized to white time, Black youth find relief in spaces where lateness is not only acceptable but appreciated and endorsed. I argue that transgressive temporalities and insurgent time are functional precisely because they allow Black youth to maintain in school, at work, and in other spaces predicated on the detention and suspension of both time and personhood. Transgressive temporalities and insurgent time help free Black people from white time and the torment of lateness. In this sense, CP Time and other transgressive temporalities hold the power for Black people to heal from temporal violence. When adherence to white time requires Black exclusion, dispossession, and social death, Black people recognize that being on time may involve just as many consequences, if not more, as being late. Black youth, like many other racialized subjects, are in no hurry to be exploited. Hence, they will take their time, while potentially taking the time of others.

Abiding by CP Time is an opportunity to shake, break, make, and take time. In short, CP Time is subversive and productive. By transgressing white time, youth also produce new socialities not dependent on antagonism. They are adept at controlling and manipulating time according to their schedules. In short, time cannot proceed without their permission. Regardless of the second, minute, and/or hour, the timepieces of Black youth are all set to the same dial: "me/we o'clock."

Though sociologists have had ample time to consider the role of race, racialization, and racism in analyses of social time, existing scholarship suggests that, ironically, they remain at an impasse and thus behind their own chronotopic clock. This chapter cannot make up for the time lost within such empirical voids. It does, however, bring the discipline of sociology up to date with racialized temporalities of those consistently "at risk" of academic racism and neglect within white time.

2

TEEFING **TIME**

My dad does not live in this country. He didn't leave of his own volition, though. Because he did what he had to do to survive in spaces where social life and social death coexist, compete, and sometimes share a symbiotic relationship, making them one and the same,[1] he was forcibly removed and sent to Trinidad. Before my family learned about international phone cards, most of our communication was limited to handwritten letters. Our "kites" were routinely intercepted and tampered with before they ever reached their destination. Eventually we got put on to phone cards, but static interfered in more ways than one. Most of our conversations are still largely sporadic, anarchic, errant, and unintelligible—just the way my father likes them. He knew there were always some special uninvited guests who just crept in on the "other" line and were constantly monitoring our conversations. His suspicions, though, were not without merit. Many calls literally put the "tap" in "phone tap." In some cases, we could actually hear others in the background. To this day, my father's signature goodbye is ironically an introduction to his partner "Tone" (i.e., dial tone).

Initially I was hurt by these abrupt hang-ups, until I realized that he was simply trying to avoid doing charity work for the feds. Still, there are always a few indelible jewels that my father drops during our chats. Once he was back in "sweet, sweet T&T," my father expressed his desire to see his kids by making the following demand of all of us: "All yuh must *teef* time and come nah man." At the time, I was working as a social worker in Boston and still struggling to create some semblance of this elusive "time management" that so many of my coworkers spoke of. From their perspective, time management involved "finding," "making," or "creating." None of my colleagues ever encouraged me to thief time. I am left to wonder whether becoming a manager of time requires policing time's teefs. Reflecting on my father's admonition, I wonder who he thought we were thieving time from. See, because before time can be "teefed," it must be owned. So who owned the time we had to teef? It was only as I began writing this book that I realized that I and many Black and other racialized subjects have to teef time because we are using time that does not belong to us.

Still, there are consequences for using things that do not belong to you. A parent may reprimand their child who takes a toy from another child's hand during a play date, because you need permission before using someone else's toy. A housemate may call a house meeting to find out who took the leftovers that went missing overnight. If the meeting produces no clues and only more questions, the housemate is likely to become less trusting and more possessive. Generally, we act as if the consequences of using another person's property are clear. You take someone's toy, you get in trouble. You take someone's leftovers, you have to accept responsibility. But what are the consequences for using what is allegedly available to and owned by all?

This chapter is driven by this straightforward yet understudied question. The youths at Run-a-Way make clear that the answer to it is not the same for everyone. We think of time as available to and owned by all, yet for the youths at Run-a-Way, their use of time is both determined and policed by racism. For them, "time use" is read as "time theft" and thus criminalized. Furthermore, the relationship between time and racism, according to the youths I interviewed, is subtractive. In other words, the labor involved in processing racialized violence *takes* time. According to financial models, the earlier subtraction of time makes it hard to turn any remaining time into money. Not only does processing racism take time, but time is *taken* from Black youth forced to perform an inordinate amount of physical, psychic, and emotional labor to reckon with what Johannes Fabian calls the "denial of coevalness."[2]

Youths at Run-a-Way report being criminalized by salespeople, teachers, police, and many deputized whites.[3] The charge? Using time and space that does not belong to them. The evidence is always already stacked against them. "Walking up to no good" and "fitting the description" mark the transmutation of time use into time theft. The aim of this chapter is to expose the extractive and exploitative character of racialization and time. Investigating this form of temporal "accumulation by dispossession," as David Harvey puts it,[4] reveals that time is not equally available to all. Rather, there are stark differences between the owners of time and its borrowers.

Presenting a racial critique of time and alleged time use itself opens up epistemological space to explore the material effects of what Pierre Bourdieu calls "temporal power"—the "power to perpetuate or transform the distributions of various forms of capital by maintaining or transforming the principles of redistribution." According to Bourdieu, access to time is contingent on power: "The extreme dispossession of the subproletarian—whether of working age or still in that ill-defined zone between schooling and unemployment or underemployment in which many working-class adolescents are kept, often for a rather long time—brings to light self-evidence of the relationship between time and power . . . in which the experience of time is generated, depends on power and the objective chances it opens."[5]

Bourdieu, however, neglects the racial and ontological dimensions of "temporal power," or what Michael Hanchard calls "racial time." Racial time, Hanchard argues, thrives off the power relations between the racially dominant and subordinate, thus unsettling the indivisibility of the "social" within "social time" (see chapter 1). "Unequal temporal access to institutions, goods, services, resources, power and knowledge," he says, guarantee that the racially dominant will keep pace with time, while the racially subordinate will lag behind.[6] In short, social time was and still is racial time.

Not only is all time racial time, but according to Charles Mills, time is also white. "White time," he observes, is a "'sociomental' representation of temporality shaped by the interests and experience of the White 'mnemonic community.'" White time, like racial time, requires dispossession of the already dispossessed. Mills makes the case that, as a social construct, race cannot be divorced from the social: "Race does not ontologically preexist the social; race is ontologically dependent on the social."[7] Just as race is dependent on social construction, racial time, according to Mills, requires the "representational production of white time" by the social.[8]

As I demonstrate throughout this chapter, white time is calibrated according to the exploitation, dispossession, criminalization of, and routinized violence against Black youth. In recounting multiple experiences with police, salespersons, and white people on the street, youths at Run-a-Way brought to light the subtractive relationship between time and racism. They spent time questioning why they were continuously monitored while shopping. They questioned why they were harassed by the police. And they spent additional time questioning whether racialized social systems and individuals would treat white youth the same way. I conceptualize this inordinate amount of physical, emotional, and psychic energy as *processing time*—the time spent reckoning with racialized violence. Processing times and the labor time they necessitate, however, remain unquantifiable. This labor consumes a significant amount of time that remains largely incalculable because the time required to process racialized violence literally and figuratively does not count.[9] To racialized persons, however, experiences with systems of racialized violence will always count, because they are countless.

62   CHAPTER 2

Racism *Takes* Time

Attempting to quantify the time-consuming experience of racism is a largely futile quest. Living with racism involves careful reflection on and analysis of racist acts. Racism is not something that people get used to or forget. Processing acts of racialized violence is psychic, physical, and emotional labor—labor that many perform just to get by, maintain, and survive. The length of time required to process an act of racialized violence cannot obscure the qualitative experience with the act itself.

Racialization and racism resulted in significant time loss for many youths at Run-a-Way. It is during adolescence that many racialized youth report their first encounter with racism.[10] Most youths were poised to speak on the issue of racism, and when I asked fifteen-year-old Kendra if she had ever been targeted because of her race, she responded without hesitation:

> Yes. All the time. . . . Say I'm on the bus going to school and this guy or girl . . . [of] a different race than I am starts yelling or getting mad because I'm Black. . . . And then I have to crack him in his face and then they . . . cause me not to be able to get to school on time. . . . So it always takes up time to actually cuss them out or something.

Kendra's sense of being the target of racism and anti-Blackness "all the time" exemplifies the time-consuming nature of racialized violence. She also reveals the psychic and cognitive labor required to address racist acts. This labor, however, seems largely ignored by teachers and administrators at school. In short, Kendra's lateness is inexcusable, despite the undeniability of anti-Blackness. I asked Kendra about the time required to perform these forms of labor in response to racialized violence:

> KENDRA: I guess it takes up your time 'cuz you're always thinkin' about what people think and what they say. You're always thinkin' about how you look to other people. So if you're getting bad looks you're wondering, "OK, what am I doing wrong?"
>
> RM: When you have these negative experiences does it cause you to have to think about it more often after the altercation has occurred?
>
> KENDRA: Yeah, it does. Because it's like, I thought slavery and all that racism crap was over. And it's like, having to live in a world where . . . [*pause*] You can't be judged by the color of your skin and we still live in a world like that today. It's just petty.

Not all youths have to ask, "What am I doing wrong?" Kendra, though, seems to ponder this question regularly. And yet, time is unforgiving. When it comes to the time expended to reckon with racialized violence, time has a no-return policy, especially if you're a "teef." Kendra invokes several aspects of Du Boisian thought to illustrate what it means to live with racism. In asking herself, "OK, what am I doing wrong?" she echoes Du Bois's memorable question, "How does it feel to be a problem?" By acknowledging racism as a source of time consumption, she recognizes that "the Negro Problem" is a problem of white America's response to Black life.[11] Under a white racial gaze, Black youth are forced to question their own integrity because, as Kendra's remarks suggest, their integrity remains an open question to others. When I asked Kendra how often she thinks about racism, she responded by saying, "Every time I'm around a white person. To be honest," and she chuckled.

In detailing the importance of a "double consciousness" to Black sociality, to what extent did Du Bois consider this "peculiar sensation" a form of time use? Does a doubling (of consciousness) necessitate a fractioning (of time)? Du Bois may not have set out to quantify the physical, emotional, and psychic labor associated with a double consciousness. To suggest, however, that he had not considered what is lost/taken by "always looking at one's self through the eyes of others" would be a specious assumption. Evidence of Du Bois's prescience can be found in this passage from the essay "On the Faith of the Fathers": "Such a double life, with double thoughts, double duties, and double social classes, must give rise to double words and double ideals, and tempt the mind to pretense or revolt, to hypocrisy or radicalism."[12]

This statement exemplifies a phrase familiar to many Black people: "You have to work twice as hard to get half as far." By definition, working twice as hard to be half as good means that the halves have significantly less time to accomplish their goals than their more temporally advantaged counterparts—the haves. Without an appreciation of the ways that racialization and racism condition the time perspectives of racialized persons, sociologists construct time use as a homogenous and routine activity familiar to all. Such universalisms, however, ignore the significance of *processing time*—the time expended on the infinite and incommensurable process of reckoning with racialized violence. Remy, a sixteen-year-old, Black, nonbinary youth, recognizes that teaching biases are deeply racialized and, in the end, major learning impediments for Black students:

> White kids simply got it easy. They doin' somethin' for two seconds and it's over.... Let's say we all get asked the same thing and the white people do everything that they were asked to do and they get to go. Even though the Black person did the same thing but maybe the professor wants to push them because they care or they wanna see if they can work a little bit harder.... I feel like ... when I raise my hand I get ignored, [but when] the white kid raises their hand, the teacher goes to them. So I'm

spendin' more time on my work because I'm struggling and because the teacher not helping me. And so it's taking me more time to get work done and to learn stuff, so it's slowing me down in school 'cuz I have so little time to learn what the teacher's teaching us every day.

Remy reveals the temporal impact of working twice as hard to get half as far as their white counterparts while in a learning environment predicated on "equal opportunity." The number of hours in a school day is the same for all students in a particular school. Remy's account, however, reveals that while all students may have quantitatively similar amounts of time in school, Black students' temporal experiences are qualitatively distinct. Processing times are not compartmentalized into scheduled intervals of the day or placed on anyone's to-do list. Rather, processing racialized violence spills over into each and every part of a youth's daily routine. These spillover effects result in a smothering and layering of already densely packed temporal experiences. What is supposed to be scheduled learning time for all students is, for Remy, processing time. Questioning whether racialized bias is responsible for differential treatment in the classroom compresses Remy's time to learn. For Remy, the classroom is a site of multiple forms of time theft. Remy sees white students' education subsidized by the systemic neglect of Black students. As white teachers privilege white students, Black youths like Remy find themselves constantly beginning from behind. As racism interferes with regularly scheduled activities, Remy and countless other Black youths are asked to do more with less (time).

Processing racialized violence while learning cannot be reduced to mere "multitasking." Remy is doing much more than simply comprehending while reading aloud. It is unrealistic to expect that Black youth will never have to think about racism and racialization. But it is also unrealistic to expect these youth to allocate a specific amount of time to process racialized violence. For many students, an extended ringing bell signifies the end of the school day. For racialized youth, the same bell ring marks a recalibration of processing time as they make their way out of school and into the streets. When asked about things that take up their time but not that of their white counterparts, Remy offered this cogent response:

> Walkin' alone home at night. Makin' sure people not watchin' you, especially white people 'cuz they love to call the police for no fuckin' reason. I have to worry about not making white people uncomfortable 'cuz . . . if they feel in danger, *we can get hurt.* 'Cuz I know that from the moment I wake up to the moment that I go to sleep, I am being targeted as a Black person, as a person of color. . . . So I'm doing extra stuff to make sure that I'm safe and I'm getting treated fairly and equally and I'm working harder. . . . And so it's literally just taking up my time.

When around white people, Remy is forced to worry about being the target of racialized and sexualized violence. Through Remy's experiences we come to see that both white fragility and the threat of racialized violence (e.g., being targeted by police) *take* an inordinate amount of time. To what extent does white fragility center white people while ignoring those that are actually vulnerable to racialized violence? Remy is aware that when that which is fragile breaks, nonwhite people get hurt. Not only is Remy subject to the threat of whiteness and its shards, but they are also forced to accept that whiteness inflicts harm with impunity. What worries Remy and many other Black people, however, is not simply the impunity of whiteness but an understanding that white people are emboldened by this impunity to unleash anti-Black terror in everyday life.

As both an involuntary activity and a survival strategy, double consciousness is a vital part of Black sociality. As August Wilson affirms, "Blacks know more about whites in white culture and white life than whites know about blacks. We *have* to know because our survival depends on it. White people's survival does not depend on knowing blacks" (emphasis in the original).[13] As Remy shows, their survival depends on knowing whites. This is what makes racialization, according to Helen Ngo, a "non-event":

> In experiencing one's body schema as inherently unsettled or at any moment "unsettleable," the racialized body not only becomes accustomed to but indeed *anticipates* these moments of unravelling.... That is to say, racialized bodies, by virtue of the common experience of racism, learn to anticipate and be "on guard" for such occurrences.... The experience of being constantly marked by others' racialized perceptions and responses becomes incorporated into the body schema such that one comes to anticipate, based on frequent experience, that this identity will once more get called into question.... Moreover, the question of anticipation also draws us back into the discussion of temporality, where in the moment of anticipation and defense, one never quite lives in the present, but always ahead of one's self and situation (in a similar but different way to how disappointment recalls one away from the futuricity of intentional being).[14]

Failure to make white people feel comfortable places Remy and other Black people at risk of getting hurt. Remy alludes to the very real possibility that a white person could harm a Black person for unauthorized use of both time and space. In anticipating the threat of racialized violence, Remy struggles to be fully (in the) present. Instead, they are forced to think ahead of themself and think ahead of white people. Remy's future orientation contradicts representations of Black youth in poor urbanized space as present oriented and capable only of living in

66   CHAPTER 2

the moment. The mental, emotional, and physical preparation Remy performs out of concern for "making white people uncomfortable" *is* labor—labor that remains unquantifiable yet time consuming.

I conceptualize *unquantifiable time* as the time corresponding to the physical, emotional, and psychic labor performed by racialized persons as a means of survival. The exhausting exercise of having to think not only for yourself but also for others is not measurable within conventional time-use categories. Thinking about racialized violence intersectionally requires an appreciation of the simultaneity, interaction, exponentiation, and layering of multiple forms of oppression that belie additive models of seconds, minutes, and hours. This is what makes attempts to quantify time expended to process racialized violence so paradoxical. Highlighting the unquantifiability of racism is not an attempt to account for or compensate for stolen time. Exposing racialized violence as a form of time theft stands as an intervention in and of itself. But who, might we ask, consumes the time of racialized persons, particularly Black youths?

Thinking for both themself and white people requires Remy to perform a significant amount of labor that exceeds temporal and compensatory boundaries. Racialized persons are not paid to process their experiences with racism. In fact, they are more likely to foot the bill from licensed mental health counselors after individual therapy sessions. In turn, the racialized violence of white time remains largely subsidized by nonwhite labor. My interview with sixteen-year-old Cedric makes this point exceptionally clear:

> CEDRIC: The other day, it was a month ago. Me and my brother was walkin' down the street to the library and we started wrestling. Then this white guy drove past and was like, "I hope you kill each other." I was like, what do you do? We stopped and was wondering is it because we was play fighting and he thought it was serious? But it was like a hundred other people around but nobody said nothin' but him. So we was kinda thrown off by it.
> RM: And what did you all do after?
> CEDRIC: We talked about it for like an hour as we was walkin'.

Within what Sara Ahmed describes as the "phenomenology of whiteness," the white male driver in Cedric's account could "move with comfort through space" and "inhabit the world as if it were home."[15] Synchronized to space and time, whiteness worked, in this case, to deny Cedric and his brother a place in time. The white man cast both boys into an anti-Black climate that rendered them disposable and expendable. To process the racist act, Cedric spent an hour speaking to his brother. Just as race is relational, so are time and time loss in one space or place accompanied by temporal gains somewhere else. In other words, Cedric and his brother did not just lose time; their time was mined by the "white guy" driving by. The man thus profited off the unquantifiable time and labor Cedric and his brother used to make sense of the violent act. By "profit" I am referring to the way in which this man reaped what Du Bois calls a "public and psychological wage" at the expense of Cedric and his brother. The wage was public because Cedric and his brother were performing unpaid labor to reckon with whiteness in a crowd of one hundred people. On top of the white man's temporal earnings, he was also emboldened by whiteness's psychological wage—a wage paid by Cedric and his brother that evidentially granted him license to commit further acts of racialized violence without consequence. There are no wages to be earned by the targets of racialized violence. Cedric and his brother cannot recoup this time or labor, which instead are added to a growing number of hours, minutes, and seconds spent living within "slavery's afterlife" and settler colonialism. Being both Black and Native in urbanized space, Cedric must wrestle with settler-colonial logic predicated on the need for Native peoples to vanish and the desire to keep Black people captive postemancipation. The boys' experience is a reminder that the afterlife of slavery and ongoing forms of settler colonialism are incommensurable with a paycheck. What the United States owes Black and Indigenous youth exceeds the conceptual capacity of "debt."

When time is stolen from one place, it amasses somewhere else. Cedric's and his brother's time was likely transferred to white time. Charles Mills writes,

> Assuming that, with reference to the appropriate stochastic counterfactuals, we could conclude that the life expectancy of Blacks (for instance) has been diminished by these temporal deprivations, we can then say that the time they would have had has been removed. . . . Where has it gone? Could we speak, perhaps fancifully, of its having been transmuted into White time, and posit a set of intra- and intercontinental equations that could be shown to balance through increments of White time on one side matching decreases of non-White time on the other, shortened life-spans over here extending life-spans over there? If so, then metaphysically these processes, these regimes of temporal exploitation and temporal accumulation, would not just be taking time—as, trivially, all processes, exploitative and non-exploitative, do—but transferring time from one set of lives to another.[16]

Mills makes clear that, within the context of white time, nonwhite time is not simply taken but excavated and transferred. The white man in Cedric's account exploited the two youths, resulting in temporal accumulation and temporal deficits. The moment the white man opened his mouth and spewed such vileness marked the start of the temporal reallocation process. The event initiated a gradual transfer of time from Cedric and his brother to the white man. Each minute of processing time corresponded to further temporal accumulation for the white man. As a form of time mining, racialized violence generates time and wealth for white people. As a measurement of racial capitalism and Black debt, white time subsidizes white life while depreciating the value of Black life. In other words, white wealth is a product of Black and other racialized debts.[17] Truncated life expectancies among Black people are in fact *lowered*, not lower. Capitalism, the legal system, carceral schooling, the nonprofit-industrial complex, racialized medicine, and the state all ensure that existing as a poor racialized subject in the United States means you have to wait.[18] Wait for service. Wait for a visit. Wait to be educated. Wait on your caseworker. Wait to be seen. Wait to be made unseeable. Wait on whiteness because whiteness takes its/your time. Perhaps the problem of quantifying racialized youth's time use is not solely a product of the countless seconds, minutes, and hours spent processing racialized violence. Maybe racialized youth are living on time that is not their own—what we could conceive of as borrowed time.

Taken Time and Unsettleable Debts

While most work is performed in the service of productivity and with the expectation of compensation, the labor required to process racialized violence cannot be paid because it represents an unsettleable debt. I liken unsettleable debt to Denise Ferreira da Silva's concept of "unpayable debt."[19] Both debts are incapable of being settled because what is done cannot be undone. In fact, what is done is liable to a redoing. Slavery's afterlife and settler-colonial violence signify not only continued "accumulation by dispossession,"[20] but the degree to which time, for racialized persons, is nonlinear.

Recurring forms of racialized violence bely linear time and teleological assessments of race and racism, ensuring that some debts can never be settled.[21] Rather than ending, racism is extending, yet the labor required to process racialized violence exceeds the compensation limits of overtime and double-time pay because both rely on a false pay scale balance between workers. What to many whites is a wage is, for racialized subjects, an unsettleable and incommensurable debt. Incommensurability, however, does not preclude responsibility.[22]

Though processing acts of racialized violence offers little financial return for laborers, this work is highly generative for racial capitalism.[23] Here, I detail how police, salespersons, deputized whites, and those invested in maintaining what Eduardo Bonilla-Silva calls "racialized social systems" accumulate time through racialized violence (i.e., surveillance, harassment, and racist attacks).[24]

This section attends to the synchronization of white time and racial dispossession. I use the notion of "time mining" to illustrate the extractive and exploitative potential of racialized violence. Given that time is money, mining time is a lucrative enterprise. I argue that racialized violence produces significant debt and dispossession, which in turn subsidize white time. In addition to bolstering the relational role of white wealth and Black debt, racialized social systems convert the time that racialized persons spend reckoning with racialized violence into profit. The subsidies gained through time mining and racialized violence perpetuate existing forms of temporal power and discipline.

To further examine the temporal costs of racialized violence, I asked youths about their experiences as consumers. Most described exerting significant time and energy to participate in what most of their white counterparts describe as a leisurely activity. To better understand what made these experiences so temporally taxing, I asked the youths to describe how they expect to be treated when entering businesses. Fourteen-year-old Cherise, for example, had this to say: "It's different in each store, but they'll keep an eye on you, 'cuz they think you're gonna steal something. And like, they'll follow you around the store just to make sure you don't." Jerome (sixteen years old) picked up where Cherise left off by describing an experience of being profiled and then followed: "Mm, sometimes I think they treat me different 'cuz I'm Black so they think I'm gonna steal something. . . . 'Cuz I was in Marshall's . . . I was looking at something and one of the managers was like, 'Do you need help?' And I said no. And then she act like she was workin' over there and she kept asking me 'Do you need help with something.' I kept saying no."

In her account, sixteen-year-old Tasha provided a vivid example of how her double consciousness remains in full effect while shopping:

> Like . . . you know those white people at the store . . . those white people that be workin', like cops or whatever who be lookin' at you in the store? They be always thinkin' you're stealing, just because you're Black. Like, I got my own stuff! I got money! Yeah, I just think that's like really rude. Just because I'm Black. I'm coming in the store with a bag, doesn't mean I'm gonna steal. Not every Black people steal stuff. They should know that. Like, white people steal! Asian people steal!

Similarly, Kendra showed how a purse goes from fashion accessory to accessory to theft when worn by Black girls: "They're, oh my goodness, they're always staring. I carry a purse, so they're always watching me or following me or asking me, 'Do you need help?' every five minutes because I'm Black and they think I'm going to steal. And it's not true. I have money so I don't have to steal. Not every Black girl or girls of color steal."

70   **CHAPTER 2**

Beyond having to think for others, each youth articulated the physiology of racialization, what Frantz Fanon calls "epidermalization."[25] Epidermalization, or the inscription of race on the body, takes time. The white child who screams, "Look, a Negro!" subjects Fanon to psychic labor. This gesture further ostracizes Fanon from white spacetime. Just as Fanon is "overdetermined from the outside," each youth's time use became interpreted by the exterior as criminal.[26] The "outside" is similar to what Denise Ferreira da Silva describes as the "stage of exteriority" on which "the racial" is signified and marked as "other."[27] It is on this stage that racializing logics mutate youths' time use into time theft.

The twin process of epidermalizing and criminalizing racialized youth engenders new forms of what Simone Browne terms "racializing surveillance": "a technology of social control where surveillance practices, policies, and performances concern the production of norms pertaining to race and exercise a 'power to define what is out of place.'"[28] Browne studies Blackness as "metaphor and as lived materiality," with particular attention to the way Blackness becomes an object of surveillance.[29] The racializing power of epidermalization defines not only a person's degree of humanness but also their spatial and temporal location. As Cherise, Jerome, Tasha, and Kendra illustrate, the white gaze is especially vigilant in stores. In retail spaces, the gaze functions as a data-mining tool and tracking device, locating each youth as out of place and out of time. Within retail stores exist certain temporal eligibility criteria that Black youths seem to rarely meet. Salespersons relegate Black youths to a state of temporal alterity upon entry. Beholden to the white gaze, salespersons refuse to entertain the possibility that Black youths have enough money to shop in the store. The thought is too preposterous, given that structural violence keeps Black youths suspended in poor urbanized space devoid of coevalness.

As the gaze tracks youths from the ghetto to the store, we also see how salespersons fully invest in seeing and recognizing criminality. Salespersons, white and nonwhite alike, then capitalize on the opportunity to read Black people. The time youths *spend* processing racializing surveillance increases investments in white time and other time-saving technologies. Cherise, Jerome, Tasha, and Kendra each reveal that racialized algorithms inform protocols for responding to Black youths. The physical, emotional, and psychic labor resulting from racialized violence forced many youths at Run-a-Way to think not only for themselves but for others. Notice the youths' use of the phrase "they think" to describe the vigilance of store clerks. "They think" was a recurring phrase throughout most of our conversations about racism. In claiming to know how they are perceived by salespersons, youths exercise their double consciousness to move through space and time. In addition to noting the "epidermalization of inferiority," Fanon writes, "I was responsible not only for my body, but for my race and my ancestors.

I cast an objective gaze over myself, discovered my blackness, my ethnic features; deafened by cannibalism, backwardness, fetishism, racial stigmas, slaver traders, and above all, yes, the grinning *Y a bon Banania*."[30]

Here, Fanon ably demonstrates the psychic labor associated with a double consciousness. Psychic energy activates key synapses in order to connect with racialized histories while establishing connections across space and time. Epidermalization is accompanied by physiological responses, and as youths were "overdetermined from the outside," they comported themselves differently in space and time. In anticipation of being misrecognized by salespersons, Remy feels the pressure to buy or bounce (leave):

> REMY: They be actin' real scared. Like I'm just about to walk up in there and start hurtin' people or I'm gonna take things from their store. Sometimes I do, 'cuz I feel like if you gonna treat me like I am, I might as well. Whether I did it or not, if you feel like I did, you gonna call the police and I'm gonna go to jail. Even if I didn't do nothin'. So I might as well. You know? When I walk up to the cash register, they stand back a little bit. You know? They look at me like they studyin' me like they ain't never seen a Black person before in their life. Like they just so scared like I'm gonna do something to them. And that's hard 'cuz I feel . . . I just feel so alienated. Like . . . that's the one thing your racism where I feel like I'll never get used to.
>
> RM: And . . . is that a very time-consuming thing for you too?
>
> REMY: Yes.
>
> RM: Can you say a little bit more about how it wastes your time?
>
> REMY: It doesn't . . . really waste my time, it more speeds it up. 'Cuz when I go into the store, I don't even go into a store unless I know exactly what I'm finna' to get, exactly where I'm finna' to get it from 'cuz I'm trying to be in and out. And if I ain't ever been in that store before, I'm not goin' unless I'm goin' with one of my white friends. 'Cuz the anxiety is like . . . I don't want people to be followin' me around. Like when I walk into a store I never been to before then they really lookin' at you like, "Why it's takin' them so long to find what they need in my store? What they doin'? They doin' somethin' else." You know? So it's like it's really . . . it just gives me a lot of anxiety 'cuz it's taking me more time to look for what I need.

In Remy's words, they are not only seen or perceived by a white person—they are studied. As a Black, nonbinary youth, Remy performs an inordinate amount of labor (none of which is compensated; rather, it is incommensurable) simply to cope with the anxiety of being studied and mined by white salespersons working in straight economies of time.[31] In stores, Remy is overdetermined by their Blackness and queerness. The white gaze is also gendered and sexualized and seeks to sync Remy with heteronormative protocols and "biological time."

As a nonbinary youth, Remy is also funking the biological clock that demands they identify themself within a gender binary. Perhaps Remy is thinking and being within the context of what Tavia Nyong'o calls "non-binary blackness: a blackness that asserts another temporality than that which is enforced within straight time."[32] Remy feels the weight of being overdetermined by the white, cisheteronormative gaze. Still, they embody a temporal orientation that refuses the onward pace of gendered progress narratives. Remy does not entertain "chrononormative" logics endorsing the accomplishment of a singular, specific gender identity.[33] Instead they force surveilling eyes to reckon with their refusal to be pigeonholed into a specific spatial-temporal location that belies their subjective coordinates. Nor will Remy be bound by developmental deadlines. When it comes to locating themself on the gender spectrum, it is not a matter of Remy getting there when they get there. Instead Remy acknowledges that they are always already where they need to be. The problem lies not with Remy but with those consternated by incoherence, incongruity, and inconsistency and allergic to ambiguity. Remy, though, is no stranger to infrapolitics, as demonstrated by their use of a white friend to funk the clock and maneuver through space. The white peer is meant to act as a buffer against racialized violence by deflecting the white gaze to other "potential suspects." Though their friend may help Remy pass (temporally and temporarily) into and through white spacetime, the pass expires once outside the store.

White people read Fanon and Remy in a way similar to how Katherine McKittrick describes Black people in Canada: as "surprises."[34] Remy's Blackness and queerness invoke wonder while simultaneously alerting technologies of racializing surveillance. In transgressing gender norms and roles, Remy is also transgressing time, particularly the "self-naturalizing" character of straight time.[35] They are resisting the progressive nature of linear time and any supposed accomplishments related to identity within existing strictures of gender and sexuality. In addition to the phenomenological effects of racializing surveillance, there are the consequences of temporalization. Here I am referring to the ways in which queer and trans people are consistently imagined as underdeveloped or overdeveloped. Black queer and trans youths, in particular, are consistently adultified and hypersexualized. Remy knows that being studied means they are simultaneously racialized, sexualized, and gendered. Consequently, Remy is rendered illegible within the category of the Child.

Cherise, Jerome, Tasha, Kendra, and Remy all described how their Blackness is surveilled and ontologically located as out of place and time. Each explained what it means to be seen while seeing oneself. For example, just as the time expended to reckon with racialized violence is unquantifiable, so too is the time Remy spends processing the intersections of Blackness and queerness. Within their accounts lies the convergence of Du Bois's "double consciousness" and Fanon's concept of "sociogenesis," or what Sylvia Wynter calls the "sociogenic principle": "The concept of sociogenesis underlines that: I am who I am in relation to the other who sees me as such; and, in a society structured upon racial hierarchies, becoming black is bound up with being perceived as black by a white person (as Fanon understood that we *was* black, according to the child's and the mother's eyes)."[36]

Shopping as a racialized subject is a sociogenetic process—one that mines time while supporting racial capitalism. Sensing the anti-Blackness of capital and what Steve Martinot calls "capitalization," Remy hastens their shopping, revealing the effectiveness of surveillance technologies within racial capitalism.[37] The quicker the purchase, the faster the profit. The time white salespersons *take* to surveil and profile Remy and countless other racialized youths yields tremendous profits in time, money, and intel. According to a 2017 article in *The Economist*, "The world's most valuable resource is no longer oil, but data."[38] Increasing investments in home security systems, such as Amazon's Ring, have intensified concerns over racial profiling. Racializing surveillance generates racialized data, which are used to equate criminality with nonwhiteness, and Blackness in particular. As Ruha Benjamin reminds us, "Anti-blackness is no glitch" but a "form of evidence" within the New Jim Code.[39] Consequently, youths like Remy must work physically, emotionally, and psychically to reckon with what it means to "fit the description." In return, racial capitalism offers no compensation, only further exploitation. Racializing surveillance thus represents an illicit investment in "seeing" and "recognizing" nonwhite criminality.

Black youths demonstrate that shopping is hardly a leisure activity, because epidermalization, criminalization, racialized surveillance, and other sociogenetic processes prove to be the greatest consumers (of time) in any store. Taking their time in stores makes Black youths vulnerable to having their time taken. Taken time is a product of exploitation and extraction through racialized violence and surveillance. The physical, emotional, and psychic labor required to reckon with racialized violence remains unpaid, producing an unsettleable debt. Despite this debt, it is racialized youths who are more likely to owe, rather than own, time. Hence, youths provide additional answers to the central question orienting chapter 1: Whose time is it? Racialized surveillance and the labor required to think not only for themselves but for whiteness and white life are sources of dispossession

74 CHAPTER 2

but also a reminder that time is not their own. Hence, racialized youths' alleged "time use" remains a misnomer.

The Temporal Arithmetic of Misogynoir

While this chapter brings greater attention to the way that racialization and racism function as sites of systemic temporal dispossession and violence, ignoring the way in which sexism, patriarchy, misogynoir, and sexualized violence take time risks flattening difference while foreclosing discussions of incommensurability. Hence, this section attends to the unique ways that Black girls and one nonbinary youth at Run-a-Way reckon with the time taken by symbolic and structural violence. Arithmetically, we might describe this particular operation (i.e., taking time) as subtraction. What may not be as apparent is the way in which racialized and sexualized violence also add time, divide time, multiply time, or even exponentiate time.

Feminist scholars,[40] queer theorists, and cultural studies scholars have made significant inroads toward understanding the gendered and sexualized dimensions of time.[41] The association between whiteness and linear time (see chapter 7) is indicative of androcentric logics that demand progress regardless of those trampled in its path. Adherence to linear time makes people "forgetful" not only of conquest, genocide, and slavery, but also of the way that androcentrism remains indelibly etched in each. Progressive time dismisses the time taken from women within the context of reproductive labor, patriarchy, and the psychic expenses paid to process sexualized violence and the epistemic brutality of what La Marr Jurelle Bruce describes as the "aegis of Reason": "a proper noun denoting a positivist, secularist, Enlightenment-rooted episteme purported to uphold objective 'truth' while mapping and mastering the world."[42] The feminist scholar Elizabeth Deeds Ermath argues that women never had any ownership of time to begin with: "The phrase 'women's time' is a contradiction in terms. If, as I believe, our conventional definitions of it are rooted in patriarchy, then women's time *qua* time does not exist at all: except as an exile or an absence of time as it is conceived in patriarchal conventions, that is, as what Julia Kristeva calls 'linear time, the time of project and history.'"[43]

"Women's time," as Ermath sees it, cannot exist when interpellated through patriarchal logics and projects. History itself is a project that, according to Ermath, requires the exclusion and repression of women.[44] Patricia Hill Collins makes a similar, yet more nuanced, argument about Black women's relationship to time: "Women did not retain authority over their time, technology, workmates, or type or amount of work they performed. In essence, their forced incorporation into a capitalist political economy as slaves meant that West African women became economically exploited, politically powerless units of labor."[45] Though white women were often rendered invisible within the context of history, such elision necessitated the construction of Black women as surrogates and/or empty vessels. While Ermath and other feminists depict time as a negative value for women generally, Collins and other Black feminists remind white feminists that white women, while temporally marginalized, have historically benefited from the extraction of Black women's time and labor.[46] In short, white women's dispossession of time first required the fungibility of Blackness, the ungendering of Black women, their dysselection from womanhood and femininity, and their selection into the category of what Joy James calls "Captive Maternals."[47] Constructed as "politically powerless units of labor," Black women became units of time and targets of its dispossession.

In *Black Time: Fiction of Africa, the Caribbean, and the United States*, Bonnie Barthold describes how Western constructions of "illegitimacy" ensured that Black children could make no claims to time. Barthold writes, "The child not 'owned' by a father has no legitimate relationship to time or to society; he is born into a fallen state."[48] While Barthold privileges the severed filial bond between a father and son, Hortense Spillers critiques the way the flesh and blood of Black women is "ejected from 'the Female Body in Western Culture'":[49]

> Even though we are not even talking about any of the matriarchal features of social production/reproduction—matrifocality, matrilinearity, matriarchy—when we speak of the enslaved person, we perceive that the dominant culture, in a fatal misunderstanding, assigns a matriarchist value where it does not belong; actually *misnames* the power of the female regarding the enslaved community. Such naming is false because the female could not, in fact, claim her child, and false, once again, because "motherhood" is not perceived in the prevailing social climate as a legitimate procedure of cultural inheritance. (emphasis in the original)[50]

The purpose of this section is to identify some sources of temporal dispossession and division specific to Black girls, as well as Black queer and nonbinary youths. Interviews with Black girls, femmes, and nonbinary youths reveal several other time-structuring factors that compound the temporal tax of racialization and racism, including misogynoir and transmisogynoir. Appreciating the time-consuming experience of exercising a double consciousness should not eclipse the impact of what Deborah King describes as Black women's "multiple consciousness":

> The triple jeopardy of racism, sexism, and classism is now widely accepted and used as the conceptualization of black women's status.

However, while advancing our understanding beyond the erasure of black women within the confines of race-sex analogy, it does not yet fully convey the dynamics of multiple forms of discrimination. Unfortunately, most applications of the concepts of double and triple jeopardy have been overly simplistic in assuming that the relationships among various discriminations are merely additive. . . . The modifier "multiple" refers not only to several, simultaneous oppressions but to the multiplicative relationships among them as well.[51]

King reveals the problem with using an additive model to make sense of the race-gender analogy. Misogynoir is not simply a product of the simultaneity or synchronization of oppression against Black women. These oppressions are also interactive. The equation of Blackness with maleness, and femininity or womanhood with whiteness, renders Black girls, femmes, and nonbinary youths invisible. As King notes, "It is mistakenly taken for granted that either there is no difference in being black and female from being generically black (i.e., male) or generically female (i.e., white)."[52] In short, racial realities cannot be divorced from gendered realities. Looking at either as separate perpetuates additive models of social difference that are ultimately anti-intersectional.

To extend my analysis of the time-consuming aspects of racism, I asked Black girls and one youth who identifies as Black and nonbinary about the unique experiences that consume their time, compared to boys. Tanisha, who was seventeen years old and two months pregnant with her first child at the time of our interview, described one of many controlling images that regulate her time and sense of self: "Mm, being called a ho. Boys don't have to think about [that]. Well, if they were called one, they wouldn't care. But girls do." Compared to boys of color (and white boys), Tanisha reveals the multiplicative relationship between her Blackness, gender, and sexuality. She must reckon with the fungibility of Black femmeness while simultaneously, and perhaps subconsciously, accounting for the time required to navigate social space. Multiplicative forms of oppression demand simultaneity—questioning whether responses to your hair, Blackness, and femininity will invite interrogation over what you choose to do with your body. At the same time, the relationship between sexism and time, like that between racism and time, is subtractive and divisive. Still, Tanisha was intent on reclaiming her time and pursuing her aspirations of becoming a lawyer, nurse, attending a musical arts college, and/or studying real estate.

Tanisha knew that as a Black woman, her life chances were significantly different from those of her white counterparts. I asked her and other Black girls about things that consume their time but not the time of white girls. Several Black girls explained why having to think about standards of beauty is a form of cognitive labor—labor that should not negate the physical labor associated with actually fulfilling these standards. I asked Tanisha to think of some things she must worry about that white girls can ignore:

> TANISHA: Their hair. . . . Well, they don't really care. I don't think they care about how they look. 'Cuz they say . . . they say sometimes if you're wealthy, wealthy people don't really dress like . . . I don't know. They don't really care how they dress. . . . Yeah, that's how rich people is. Most of them . . . I think they just spend money on better things than clothes and shoes. Hair and all that.
>
> RM: How about being a young Black woman, how do you think other . . . how do you think non-Black girls, meaning Latino girls, Asian girls, girls who aren't Black, what do you think you still have to think about as a Black woman that they don't have to think about?
>
> TANISHA: Being called bald headed.

Tanisha's remarks signal an awareness of how easy it is for others to hold her body and various parts of her body captive, while projecting their own desire onto her. To construct Tanisha's concern over being called "bald headed" as a product of self-consciousness ignores her multiple consciousness that requires an accounting of the perceptions and the ever-present threat of misogynoir. Chris Rock may not have intended to harm Jada Pinkett Smith when comparing her to the title character in *G.I. Jane* during the 2022 Oscars. Still, the joke had a distinct sting when added to and multiplied by the open and public wounds associated with controlling images, discursive violence, expectations for "good hair," and Pinkett Smith's public disclosures about her personal struggle with alopecia. Speaking to the intimate connection between discourse and action (i.e., power), Spillers writes, "We might concede, at the very least, that sticks and bricks *might* break our bones, but words most certainly *will* kill us."[53] Tanisha's multiple consciousness reminds her that being called "bald headed" is a threat not simply to her self-esteem but to her life as well. This form of optical dissection is what legitimates the separation of "flesh" from "body."[54]

When divided by misogynoir, the time of Black girls lacks a remainder. The inordinate seconds, minutes, and hours girls spend processing and resisting misogyny, patriarchy, and gender violence are seldom accounted for in urban sociology and ethnography. I asked all the youths who or what controls their time. In response, sixteen-year-old Shanice said "boys" and "friends" at school. I asked her how people show respect for her time:

SHANICE: They don't. They think, you know, when you're busy they think they can just control it. They think that they can just do whatever they want 'cuz they don't have nothin' to do and they try to stop you from doin' what you really need to do.

RM: What do they [boys] usually do that shows a disrespect for your time?

SHANICE: Boys, they'll touch all over you, you know, come here and, you know, hug you and then our friends will be like, "Come on, come with me. Walk me to this place. Walk me to that place." And . . .

Misogynoir subtracts and divides spacetime while multiplying and exponentiating oppressions. Offering us another way of conceptualizing the spacetime continuum, Shanice shows how boys disrespect her time by violating her space. There are important racialized and gendered dimensions of space and time grounded in philosophical tradition. According to Denise Ferreira da Silva, Immanuel Kant successfully negates exteriority (spatiality) by locating the subject of scientific knowledge within the interior (mind) and thus time: "Although he postulates that space is the condition of possibility for representing external (exterior) things, the objects of knowledge, Kant further renders knowledge an effect of interiority when he places all phenomena in time."[55]

Though Ferreira da Silva may not explicitly describe the link between exteriority and gender, there remains an intimate connection between space, femininity, and Blackness. Interiority is a key attribute of what Ferreira da Silva describes as the "Transparent I," which exists within time and the "scene or representation." By contrast, the "affectable other" is marked by exteriority or space and is thus subject to the "scene of regulation." Black girls, femmes, and nonbinary youths help constitute the category of the "affectable other." Thus, colonizing space is an integral part of the colonization of (Black) women's bodies. In controlling Shanice's time, boys are also enacting phenomenological violence—a violence that requires emotional, physical, and psychic labor while mining both time and space from Black girls. When I asked Shanté about things she must worry about that are not of similar concern for boys of color, she responded with the following:

It's like the protection. They gotta worry about beef and rivals, but we gotta . . . I gotta worry about when I'm walkin' down the street if a dude finna' to kidnap me, he about to grab me and try to rape me, if he gonna try to hit on me. Then if I don't have no protection or no weapon on me, then my life is in danger 'cuz my . . . I can fight but my fist is not gonna hit no grown man and he might not hit the floor as quick as I think he gonna and then it's my life in danger.

Shanté recognizes that violence against her and Black boys is not contingent on transgression. But she is also acutely aware of the capacity of anti-Blackness, as a structure and concept, to overwhelm the distinct impact of misogynoir. The times boys feel comfortable going out in public may be different from those when Shanté does. For Shanté, boys and girls have different levels of violability. While boys may be subject to violence at the hands of other boys, they are less likely to be the targets of the gendered and sexualized violence that Shanté must account for each time she leaves home.

I also asked Remy whether there are things they have to worry about that are of less concern for boys of color. They replied,

> Yes. Now, I don't identify as female. I identify as nonbinary agender. So when people look at me, they see a feminine female. And people like to target females on the street, you know, lots of sexual harassment. So open, so ain't nobody tryin' to hide it no more, nothing's discreet about it. They just out in the open, just sayin' whatever they wanna say. They feel like they can just touch you wherever they wanna touch you no matter what. No matter what time of day it is. And definitely get paid less, especially as a Black female of color. We automatically get paid like, what, sixty-five cents out of the seventy-five cents that a white woman makes.

Remy covers several components of a multiple consciousness. From their vantage point, cisheteronormativity, sexualized violence, and the gender-racial wage gap are always already interacting in ways to place them and other Black girls and femmes in multiple jeopardy. Just as time consumed by racialization and racism remains unquantifiable, there is no way to fully account for the time and energy that Black girls, femmes, and nonbinary youths spend negotiating (trans)misogynoir. Through their stories, Black girls, femmes, and nonbinary youths prompt us to question whether the time spent reckoning with patriarchy—including sexual harassment, misogynoir, and racialized standards of beauty, as well as heteronormative and chrononormative logics—can be classified as time use.

Time Use or Time Theft?

What does it mean to use time that doesn't belong to you? To youths at Run-a-Way, it means that police and nonstate actors deny Black coevalness by targeting youths for being out of place and "up to no good." In turn, the youths are more likely to be used by time than to use it for themselves. In distinguishing those who own time from those who owe it, I expand the breadth of youth development

80   CHAPTER 2

and time use studies. The American Time Use Survey (ATUS), for example, lacks any adequate measures of either racialization or racism. While time-use charts clearly delineate chores, homework time, and recreational activities, in what category does the time spent processing racialized violence fit? Seconds, minutes, and hours as units of measure mean little when one cannot claim ownership over time. If the ATUS cannot account for the time youths spend processing acts of racialization or racism, then it is inevitably capturing but a fraction of this group's purported time use. Racialized violence, however, remains incommensurable with routine activities such as the time youths spend on personal hygiene or chores. When Black youths are routinely used by time, studying their "time use" patterns is an empirical error.

According to Marx, the transmutation of a thing into private property begins with the use of that thing: "Private property has made us so stupid and one-sided that an object is only *ours* when we have it, when it exists for us as capital or when we directly possess, eat, drink, wear, inhabit it, etc., in short, when we *use* it."[56] It is unclear, however, whether Marx considered the extent to which time itself was already private property. Both white time and whiteness are the property of whites.[57] For Black youth, white time represents a time they owe rather than own. Consequently, they must first borrow time before using it. Neferti X. M. Tadiar describes how most migrant domestic workers go into debt as a result of "mortgaging" their time to find work outside their home countries. This debt, as Tadiar affirms, constitutes a "life they owe rather than own."[58] Since time is money, it makes sense that poor, racialized youth owe rather than own time.

We need no other evidence that time is in fact money than the banality of temporal sayings. Consider, for example, the adage that "time waits for no one." Just as time does not wait, neither does capitalism. Time and capital accumulation are predicated on future orientations, speculative investments, and other progress narratives. It makes sense that those who attempt to *take* "their" time are punished for slowing down time, money, production, and progress. Still, the impatience of time and money warrant resistance. This book illustrates the ways in which Black youth, dispossessed of time-money, practice a form of temporal sabotage by throwing a wrench into the gears of white time and reversing linear progress narratives. Based on their experiences with past and present racialized violence, as well as projections of future harm, Black youth prohibit time from proceeding without being accountable to those targeted for temporal exploitation.

Racialization and racism *take* time while also seizing what Tadiar calls lifetime: "the overlooked productivity of social practices of life making that seem to lie outside contemporary modes of exploitation of life as living labor."[59] Time is taken by "processing" racialized violence and continuously questioning one's placement in existing onto-epistemological orders. Racialized youths at Run-a-Way described countless experiences with police terror. Shanté, who is sixteen years old, described the following encounter with police outside another youth program:

> One time I was outside at like three in the morning, right outside the shelter I was stayin' at. The cops pulled up and arrested me, put me in the back of the car 'cuz it was [after] curfew. And . . . they like, "Do you have any tattoos? Where's your ID? What's your name?" and they like, "OK, you need to stop with the attitude." I was like, "I don't have an attitude. This is how I talk." They're like, "Oh, well, keep on with that attitude and you're 'bout to go downtown." And I was like, "This is how I talk. First of all, I'm irritated 'cuz you just put me in the back of a cop car." And then there was bottles outside and he like, "Have you been drinking?" and got the flashing light in my eyes. I was like, "You can do a breathalyzer. I'm clearly sober." . . . I don't take authority well. They just disrespect us so quickly.

Shanté explains why racialized youth are more likely to be used (and abused) by time than to use it themselves. Curfews are products of both temporal and spatial relations. "Juvenile curfew laws" remain heavily enforced in communities of color, disproportionately targeting Black youth.[60] Time thus makes theoretically possible that a curfew can be violated, and that police terror is necessary. In short, time creates "crime." What is legible as "crime" is contingent on space. As Jodi Rios demonstrates in *Black Lives and Spatial Matters: Policing Blackness and Practicing Freedom in Suburban St. Louis*, police create "crime" by issuing citations for cosmetic matters, including a resident not painting the front and back door of her own house.[61] Such predatory tactics of law enforcement are what Rios describes as "policing for revenue."[62] What does it mean, though, to make a living off life-taking systems?

When poor urbanized space is equated with anachronism, Black youths like Shanté become temporal and spatial interlopers infringing on white time and space. While violating curfew constitutes a temporal transgression, Shanté is always already read as transgressive, which means police read her alleged "time use" as criminal conduct. In addition to violating curfew, Shanté also violates white time—a time that denies Black people coevalness within modernity. Shanté's encounter with police is not random. When womanhood and femininity are read as white, Black women, Indigenous women, and women of color have few protections from police terror.[63]

My conversation with Melissa makes this point exceptionally clear. Melissa was a high school senior and maintained a towering presence even when not in

82   **CHAPTER 2**

school. She had a powerful voice—the kind you heard before seeing her. Perhaps her use of her outside voice indoors came from her avid soccer skills. As she often reminded me and most others at Run-a-Way, "Soccer is life." During our interview, I asked Melissa how she interacts with people in positions of authority.

> MELISSA: Not well . . . 'cuz . . . for instance, police. I feel like some of them are racist. Like they automatically assume . . . I'm finna' to pull out a weapon or something. And how they react to movement.
>
> RM: Can you say more about that?
>
> MELISSA: Like, if I just take my hands out of my pocket then they think I have something or something. You know what I mean?
>
> RM: Yeah. Have you had any particular experiences like that that you could share?
>
> MELISSA: Yeah, like when I was at a foster home and I was just sitting there and he [the police officer] was like, "Why do you look like you have an attitude?" And I'm like, "What? I don't have an attitude." . . . And then . . . he's gonna touch me and I was like, "Don't touch me!" And then he's gonna try to tackle me to the ground for no reason. I wasn't even doing anything.

Melissa's account, like Shanté's, reveals what in fact may be the violent origins of "tone policing." Questions seemingly absurd to many white youths are not only discerning but vital to the safety and survival of Black and other racialized youths. Do I have to keep my hands out of my pockets? Do I keep my hands in my pockets? What happens when I take my hands out of my pockets? Will they think I'll be pulling out something more powerful than a wallet? Will I be accused of stealing? Will I be searched? Will I be arrested? Will I be sexually abused? Will I be next? The processing time of each of these questions literally and figuratively does not count. Read as a transgression, Melissa need not do anything to be the target of police terror. In other words, state violence against Black youth is not contingent but, as Frank Wilderson notes, "gratuitous."[64]

Still, Melissa was quite charismatic, and her sense of humor kept me laughing during most shifts. Despite the program's efforts to eliminate any distinction between staff and volunteers, some youths still knew I was different. Melissa was one of them, and she was keen on learning what made me tick. She was quite nice at flipping the script and finding ways to interview me. I was partly responsible for inviting such questions, in part due to my own apprehension over "exercising authority." The following jotting from July 2, 2015, the day Melissa and a thirteen-year-old named Emory arrived at Run-a-Way, helps capture my usual response to youth resistance:

> During today's trip to the museum, I walked with several youth including 13-year-old Emory and 16-year-old Melissa. Melissa plays soccer. At the start of our walk, Emory asked me to remind him of my name. When I did, he mocked my name, calling me "croissant."[65] Jokingly, I told Emory that his comments were re-traumatizing as I grew up being teased by that name. Melissa found the name hilarious.

Melissa found the name I shall not mention to be so amusing that she adopted it as my nickname for the rest of her time at Run-a-Way. Almost a year after meeting Melissa, I was on the Northside for two popular events taking place on the same day: "Flow," an annual art crawl, and "Carifest," an annual Caribbean music festival. I was walking through a parking lot on one of the main streets when I heard that familiar voice yell, "Croissant!" I turned around to see Melissa and some of her peers with a staff member from another program. We caught up for a little bit before the staff member redirected Melissa and her friends back to their weekend outing. As we parted ways, it remained unclear whether Melissa and her friends would be able to enjoy the weekend festivities without being targeted for teefing time.

The time Shanté, Melissa, and other Black youths spend thinking not only for themselves but for police as well illustrates the relationality of racialized violence. Processing racialized violence is in and of itself a research process. Black youths at Run-a-Way regularly collected data, analyzed and interpreted that data, and then drew conclusions about their relation systems of power and domination, specifically racialized social systems. Interpreting one's position through what Du Bois calls the "revelation of the other world" takes time.[66] Though one's consciousness may double, time does not. In fact, this sort of doubling requires fractioning. Kendra exposes the divisibility of time when she uses her "own personal time" to wonder why police construct her and other Black youths as "up to no good":

> Say that you're going to just go out and have a good time with your friends or something. Like, my own personal time and you've gotta worry about being targeted by the police because they see a group of Black kids all together. So it's like, "What are they doing? They're probably up to no good." Just because of the color of our skin. But if you see a group of white kids you ride past them like they're not doing anything.

A gathering of white people is a "social," while, according to Kendra, a gathering of Black people is a threat to the social. Presumed guilty until proven less guilty, Black youth understand the consequences of being seen together by police. In vivid detail, Kendra not only describes what she and other Black youth have to think about when it comes to police encounters, but also narrates the police's response to Blackness and Black youth. Such a description requires a sort of racial metamorphosis, whereby Kendra enters the mind of a police officer in order to confirm what Calvin Warren observes: that the "ontological problem of blackness is not yet resolved."[67] Not only is "not doing anything" (mis)read as "doing something," but according to police, Kendra and other Black youth must be "doing *something criminal*." Kendra's remarks echo those of the many Black girls featured in Saidiya Hartman's *Wayward Lives, Beautiful Experiments: Intimate Histories of Social Upheaval*. Regardless of whether public assembly is a site of affirmation and defense for many Black youth, "what mattered was not what you had done, but the prophetic power of the police to predict the future, and anticipate the mug shot."[68] Perhaps the "prophetic power of the police" is a product of the future orientations of whiteness. Whiteness, white people, and especially white police are so future oriented that they have already forecasted the futures of Black youth, and according to each, the future for Black youth is always already criminal. Thus, under the guise of "stopping crime" or "preventing" it, the police Kendra pictures have license to harass Black youth for being currently, if not eventually, "up to no good." Police have already predicted that, instead of being destined to shine, Black youth are destined for crime or destined to "do time." Still, for many Black youth, no prediction was necessary, because they were always already charged with using time that does not belong to them.

My interviews suggest that police read Black youth as agentic insofar as they are "criminally culpable."[69] "Up to no good" was a recurring theme the youths at Run-a-Way used to describe reckoning with racialized violence. Sixteen-year-old Lamont, for example, described the criminalization of his time use for walking around:

> One day I was just walkin' down the street and I was with ... I got white friends too so I was with one of the white friends, right. And he was walkin' on the other side of the street, and the police pulled me over and gave me a ticket. They said it was like ... walking up to no good. Like walkin' around up to no good and robbin' and stealin'. Somethin' like that. I forget the real name they put for it, but that was the definition of it. You know what I'm sayin'? Walkin' around up to no good, and I was just walkin' by myself. And he [Lamont's friend] was still walkin' across the street, he didn't get stopped for nothin'. I got stopped. He was like, "What'd they stop you for?" Like, I don't know. ... They think you're walkin' up to no good, they stop you. ... They didn't stop the white

dude. I was kinda mad. . . . I felt like it was kinda racist. 'Cuz I told them I was with the dude across the street and they just let him keep walkin', you know what I'm sayin'. Then he finally came across the street once he realized they were finna' to let me go, you know what I'm sayin'. He was like, "No, he's with me," you know what I'm sayin'. And after he told them that, you know what I'm sayin', like they got cool and like, "Oh, I'm just gonna write him [Lamont] a ticket . . ."

In addition to the inordinate amount of time consumed by racialized violence, the charge of "walking up to no good" exemplifies the criminalization of racialized youth's time use. As a Black youth from a low-income community, Lamont is not legible to police and many others as "good." Hence, he must rely on his friendship with a white youth to buffer his encounters with police. Once Lamont's white friend steps on the scene, the police suddenly "got cool." It is as if Lamont's white friend's own legibility within time underwrites Lamont's existence as a temporal subject.

Though he could not immediately recall the charge, through some clarifying questions Lamont remembered the police describing his behavior as "loitering." Should such a charge be that surprising within the context of what Stephanie Donald and Cristoph Lindner call the "inert city"?[70] When whiteness is equated with active forward motion and Blackness treated as stagnant,[71] police read racialized youths like Lamont as "loiterers." Tragically, while activeness or activity may protect racialized youths from a loitering charge, it is no defense from the criminalization of agency. It is important that we not ignore that in charging Black youths with loitering, police are actually charging Black youths with being.

Some might find it convenient to describe Lamont as being the wrong race at the wrong/white time. But Lamont was walking through a majority-Black community in North Minneapolis, not far from where his cousin, Jamar Clark, was killed by police on November 15, 2015—one month before our interview. Within racialized enclosures such as the ghetto, police officers serve as "watchmen" and moderate the tempo of anti-Blackness, in accordance with white time. The spatialization of Blackness suggests Lamont was exactly where he was supposed to be—enclosed and trapped. Any attempt to deviate from the enclosure meant that the police would arrive not just on time but early to greet him with racialized terror. "Predictive policing" does not predict crime. It predicts/creates "criminals." How can police predict already established outcomes? No predictions are necessary when you create the same problems you claim to solve.

For police and white civilians turned deputies, "up to no good" functions as probable cause and motive. On February 26, 2012, George Zimmerman used "up to no good" as a license to kill seventeen-year-old Trayvon Martin:

DISPATCHER: Sanford Police Department. . . .

ZIMMERMAN: Hey we've had some break-ins in my neighborhood, and there's a real suspicious guy, uh, [near] Retreat View Circle, um, the best address I can give you is 111 Retreat View Circle. This guy looks like he's up to no good, or he's on drugs or something. It's raining and he's just walking around, looking about.[72]

Already a watchman, Zimmerman required no deputization. Emboldened by the notion that white people are not just protected by the police but *are the police*, Zimmerman read Martin's agency as criminality and ensured that his time at life would not exceed another minute. The "blameworthiness of the free individual," as Hartman puts it, highlights the continuum between freedom and slavery.[73] With "emancipation" came new forms of punishing Black people and Black sociality. Lamont's repeated reference to being read as "up to no good" harks back to the period of Reconstruction, when "vagrancy laws" legitimated the capture and arrest of Black people found without a labor contract. These and other "Black Codes" marked a seminal phase in slavery's afterlife. As fugitives of white time, Black youth were not only on the run; they were wanted for attempting to use time that did not belong to them. Black youths like Lamont were charged with "walking up to no good" while walking *down* the street in their own neighborhood. Lamont's encounter with police reveals the transmutation from time use to time theft, while illustrating how racialized violence takes time.

When the time is always right for white and wrong for nonwhite, is it even possible for Black youths to use time? According to my father, time use was not an option. Instead he urged us to "teef" it. Though Black youths at Run-a-Way may not have perceived their time use as time theft, they were acutely aware that completing schoolwork, playing, shopping, hanging out with friends, or even simply walking came with clear consequences.

Youths' unauthorized use of time was read as time theft and thus criminalized by salespersons and the police, as well as deputized whites. If youths were not stealing time, it was clear that time could only be borrowed. While their white counterparts could own time, racialized youths at Run-a-Way could only owe it. We need only look to the many systems that hold Black youths captive to understand what it looks like to owe time. When Black youths are late for school, they must report to detention and pay back the clock and the keepers of time (i.e., teachers and administrators). Detentions, suspensions, and expulsions are not simply academic consequences but forms of temporal violence. Repeated disregard for the academic clock may bring Black youths to the attention of truancy court, placing them at greater risk of entering carceral space. Contrary to popular belief, Black youths held captive in jail are paying a debt not to society but to time and its regulators.

Spending time processing racialized violence ensured that the youths' time was not their own. Rather, whiteness, white people, and racialized violence infiltrated their psyches to demand more labor time. Remy, for example, went to extreme lengths to protect themself, knowing that their *actual* safety was predicated on white people's *sense* of safety. Youths like Cedric and his brother had to spend time making sense of a white man's anti-Blackness. Shanté and Melissa had to wonder whether they would have been tone policed by actual police if they were not young Black women. Finally, youths like Lamont could not help but wonder why, according to police, he was "walking up to no good," while his white friend was just walking.

Each of these accounts raises the question: if Black youths did not have to perform such involuntary labor processing racialized violence, how else might they use their time? What might Cedric and his brother have done instead of talking about a white man's violent actions for over an hour? How might Remy spend their time if white people's safety did not supersede the safety of all others? How might the time youths spend shopping change if they did not have to think about how they are viewed by salespersons every time they enter a store? It matters less how youths choose to spend their time, so long as it is theirs. Herein lies the problem of racialized time. It is the product of exploitation and extraction. Consequently, Black youths remain in debt, owing both time and explanations. They must explain why they entered a store and did not immediately make a purchase, why they are walking, why they are out at night, and why they are together. In short, Black and other racialized youths must make the case for why they are using time that does not belong to them.

During my time in the Twin Cities, I had the privilege of collaborating with the renowned, Minneapolis-based movement artist Ricardo Levins Morales. Ricardo is known for literally "drawing the line for social justice" in brilliant artwork. Most people who have had an opportunity to share physical and mental space with Ricardo know that "artist" is but one of many titles he holds. He is also a brilliant activist who does not shy away from the messiness of organizing, but instead finds creative ways to, in his words, "ask bigger questions," in the spirit of solidarity. I, like many other organizers in the Twin Cities and beyond, still consider Ricardo a one-of-a-kind friend and mentor. One of the first posters I bought from Ricardo was a piece titled *Firsts*. In the poster, Ricardo depicts a white person in a suit, carrying a briefcase, walking away from a crowd of mostly nonwhite people, with the following message sketched between both parties: "What if nobody could have seconds until everyone had gotten firsts? Could I be sent to jail for asking that?" Ricardo's use of "seconds" likely referred to second helpings of food. Still, I could not help but consider the temporal use of "seconds." In reframing/rephrasing this question temporally, we might ask, "What if nobody could have seconds, minutes, or hours, until everyone had time? Could I be forced to do time for asking about it?"

Throughout this chapter, each youth has provided further evidence that both time and space subsidize white life while amassing an incommensurable debt to Black youth. The instances of racialized violence I have presented here are not meant to cast readers as voyeurs. Rather, each account strains mutual conceptions of time. These Black youths were consistently used by white time and white space. They demonstrate why the concept of time use lacks measurement validity—the extent to which a concept measures what it intends to measure. Given that Black youths' time use was routinely surveilled and criminalized, it appears that they were renting time rather than using it.

3

THE MAKINGS OF A "MAYBE ENVIRONMENT"

What was once a destination for many during the Great Migration is now the basis for a good-old fashioned talking to. "Why are you moving to the Midwest? Are there *any* people of color there?" These were just some of the questions I got from friends and family after they learned of my decision to pursue a PhD in Minnesota. Truth be told, I asked myself the same questions. Coming from mostly Black and Latinx neighborhoods in Boston and Providence, I sensed that a move to the Midwest would require some serious adjustment. My limited knowledge of US geography left me with provincial conceptions of states outside the Northeast. Before moving to Minnesota, my perceptions of the Midwest were restricted to fields and whiteness, which regularly mixed to form fields *of* whiteness.

Observing a whiter and whiter demographic at each rest stop, gas station, hotel, and supermarket during the drive from Providence to Minneapolis only reinforced my earlier assumptions about whiteness and space. If what Sara Ahmed calls a "phenomenology of whiteness" helps us to see how "whiteness allows bodies to move with comfort through space, and to inhabit the world as if it were home,"[1] I wonder to what extent a phenomenology of whiteness infringes on the phenomenology of Blackness. I learned that my rendering of Minnesota was not inaccurate save for some parts of Minneapolis and St. Paul and sections of surrounding suburbs. Good Samaritans warned about venturing too far beyond Twin Cities lines, as the contrast between white and nonwhite grew more ostensible. But even making light of the overwhelming whiteness of the Twin Cities in the absence of snow risks participating in settler-colonial logic and obscuring Indigeneity and the Black Midwest.[2] Studying Black youth in the Twin

Cities is, then, not only an attempt to bring attention to presence in presumed absence. Just as I aim to funk the clock, this work attempts to funk with settler time as well as white spatial and temporal imaginaries.[3]

Even the term "Midwest" itself implies that this region had yet to fulfill a sort of Orientalist fantasy predicated on asinine logic that suggests there can be an "East" and "West" on a sphere called "Earth." The "Midwest," though, is not some inchoate space or merely an amalgamation of East and West Coast culture. Rather, the Midwest, and the Black Midwest more specifically, remains a rich site of intellectual and cultural production that must be taken on its own terms. The Twin Cities, for example, represents a site of both funk and flava—a funk drawn with purple, not green, stank lines and a flava that tastes like "Hot Cheetos and Takis."[4]

Based on the overwhelming amount of urban ethnographic research throughout the late twentieth century, it is easy to see why some still conflate Chicago with the entire Midwest. Social scientists, particularly sociologists from the Chicago School, cornered the market on urban ethnographic research and set up shop in the Windy City. But the Midwest is more than Chicago. Even before the murder of George Floyd, plenty of Minnesotans were calling for greater attention to systemic racism, anti-Blackness, and settler-colonial violence that disappears Indigeneity into whiteness.[5] Why did social scientists not listen? Perhaps Black life and Black sociality remained unintelligible unless first filtered through the logics of crisis, abjection, and metaphor.[6] Terrion Williamson makes this point exceptionally clear when describing the impetus behind the Black Midwest Initiative:[7]

> The conditions under which black people live are, and historically have been, in stark contrast to the experiences of many other residents of those same cities. You might argue, pretty credibly in fact, that there is nothing particularly particular to the Midwest in this—that black life is conditioned by precarity wherever it is lived. But what is distinct about black Midwesterners is the extent to which our lives fail to register collectively as worthy of sustained attention except, of course, in moments of crisis when the national spotlight hones in just long enough to use us as fodder for the expediencies of political outrage—think Chicago, Flint, Detroit, Ferguson.[8]

When the Twin Cities erupted after the murder of George Floyd, the national spotlight was once again on Minneapolis and St. Paul. That spotlight shined brightly on those targeted and arrested for the destruction of destructive property but conveniently dimmed when organizers, activists, artists, and other communities in the Twin Cities mobilized mutual aid and healing justice collectives. The spotlight lessened further during scenes of asymmetrical warfare between police and protesters. Still, explicit forms of police terror can easily mask the symbolic and structural violence that remains less salient yet equally, if not more, pernicious. As Saidiya Hartman writes, "The most invasive forms of slavery's violence lie not in these exhibitions of 'extreme' suffering or in what we see but in what we don't see."[9] Perhaps some of what is unseen is in fact hidden, sanitized, and/or romanticized.

In March 2015, approximately four months after I began volunteering at Run-a-Way, *The Atlantic* published an article by Derek Thompson titled "The Miracle of Minneapolis." Increasing incomes, affordable public transit, low unemployment, and high college-graduation rates were just a few of the indices Thompson used to gauge the quality of life in the Twin Cities:

> Only three large metros where at least half the homes are within reach for young middle-class families also finish in the top 10 in the Harvard-Berkeley mobility study: Salt Lake City, Pittsburgh, and Minneapolis–St. Paul. The last is particularly remarkable. The Minneapolis–St. Paul metro area is richer by median household income than Pittsburgh or Salt Lake City (or New York, or Chicago, or Los Angeles). Among residents under 35, the Twin Cities place in the top 10 for highest college-graduation rate, highest median earnings, and lowest poverty rate, according to the most recent census figures. And yet, according to the Center for Housing Policy, low-income families can rent a home and commute to work more affordably in Minneapolis–St. Paul than in all but one other major metro area (Washington, D.C.). Perhaps most impressive, the Twin Cities have the highest employment rate for 18-to-34-year-olds in the country.[10]

Readers quickly recognize that the "miracle" Thompson refers to is an economic one. The Twin Cities are home to nineteen Fortune 500 companies, which, according to Thompson, helped subsidize "the Minneapolis miracle" through the redistribution of commercial tax revenues to "enrich some of the region's poorest communities." The miraculous portrait Thompson creates, however, is what Jessica Nickrand, in a response also published in *The Atlantic*, calls "Minneapolis's White Lie." Nickrand challenges Thompson's claim that the programs for sharing commercial property taxes would "lift all boats," including low-income communities of color:

> The policies that Thompson cites as responsible for keeping "the poorest areas from falling too far behind" were designed for a population that looks very different from what Minnesota looks like in 2015. The Minnesota Miracle Plan of 1971, which was mentioned in Thompson's

article, required all municipalities in the metropolitan Twin Cities area "to contribute almost half their growth in their commercial tax revenues" to a fund that would be invested directly back into the community. This served the area well until 2002, when the Minnesota Legislature revised its property- and income-tax systems. This resulted in a nearly 10 percent decrease in revenue-raising capacity between 1999 and 2002. Since 2002, 90 percent of municipalities in Minnesota have seen their tax revenues drop another nine percent. Even with these cuts the Twin Cities still experience lower overall rates of poverty than other cities around the country. But poverty is increasing, and it is largely centralized in the Twin Cities' communities of color.[11]

Nickrand suggests that part of Thompson's white lie involves the use of white people as a reference category. Thus, it is irresponsible to entertain Thompson's romanticized picture of the Twin Cities, when Minnesota maintains the lowest rankings in the nation on key indicators of social welfare. Nickrand references a WalletHub study that ranked Minnesota third in terms of the highest poverty-rate gap (296%), just below North Dakota (328%) and Connecticut (340%).[12] Nickrand warns, "If racial inequalities are not addressed, Minneapolis could find itself as one of the nation's poorest cities when it comes to racial politics and urban decline."[13]

It is no surprise that, in a piece published on November 16, 2018, *USA Today* ranked the Twin Cities fourth among the "15 worst cities for black Americans."[14] How miraculous, then, is the "Minneapolis Miracle" for Black and other racialized youths at Run-a-Way? When did guarantees (for white people) become "miracles"? What role do white spatial imaginaries and white temporal imaginaries play in constructing suburbanized and urbanized space? What is the difference between staying and living in poor urbanized space? What are the makings of a "maybe environment"? To answer these questions and others, I present this analysis of race, space, and time in the Midwest.

Recounting the narratives of Marie-Joseph Angélique, the Portuguese-born slave accused of burning down most of Montreal, Katherine McKittrick describes Angélique and other Black people in Canada as "surprises."[15] What, then, does it mean to be Black in the Midwest? Does it mean believing in those deemed unbelievable? Perhaps engagement with Black life in the Midwest requires an engagement with wonder. What wonder could possibly exist in a region of mostly "flyover states"? In flying over the Midwest, what is overlooked? Blackness? Indigeneity? Black people? Indigenous people? If Black people are a surprise in the Midwest, are Indigenous people similarly astonishing? Blackness and Indigeneity both defy latitudinal and longitudinal coordinates and exceed containment within a specific region. As Richard Iton writes, "Moreover, beyond the cataloguing of geographical presences and genealogical connections, there is the possibility of approaching Black identifications conceptually: as a matter of indexing a related set of sensibilities that resist quantification, physical or temporal classifications, and corporeal boundaries."[16] Blackness, specifically, "anarranges" linear logic and what Michelle M. Wright calls "middle passage epistemologies."[17] McKittrick describes Black geographies as "unhinged from territory and its attendant juridical requirements" and thus in defiance of racial-cartographical coordinates.[18] What makes Black people such a surprise to Canadians is not that they exist, but that they exist in the midst of whiteness.

According to demographic data from the American Community Survey (ACS), at the time of my research the Twin Cities was approximately 62.2 percent white; 17.3 percent Black or African American; 9.6 percent Asian; and 10 percent Hispanic or Latino. Native Americans and Alaskan Natives made up 1.6 percent of the total population of the Twin Cities. Because whiteness remains the central reference category for white sociality, a single nonwhite person has an incredible capacity to turn a predominantly white space into a hyperbolized nonwhite space. The magnification of nonwhiteness leads many white people to conclude that the sprinkling of a few faces of color shields them from any claims of discrimination or racism. "Minnesota Nice" is an added line of defense brandished by many white people when confronted by accusations of racialized violence. Minnesota Nice requires reciprocity, mutuality, coherence, consistency, and a false equivalence between the experiences of white and nonwhite people. In theory, Minnesota Nice is universally accepted and practiced. In reality, it legitimates some of the cruelest forms of violence against racialized persons precisely because the established discursive parameters prohibit the potential to be mean, angry, or enraged. In other words, the emphasis on "nice" summarily dismisses the potential to be anything but kind. Minnesota Nice may be nice for whites, but it is beyond a nightmare for many Black folks.

Perhaps there is room to think about the temporal dimension of Minnesota Nice and what it requires of Black youths. How might the expectations associated with Minnesota Nice actually come to harm Black youths in the Midwest? Does Minnesota Nice ask them to remain patient in school, when education comes slowly or not at all? Does Minnesota Nice demand that Black youths smile when a police officer stops them for "walking up to no good"—a charge that always already precludes the possibility of Black youths being nice? Minnesota Nice might demand patience and remind Black youths that opportunity will come "in due time," without acknowledging the time that is long (over)due. We might also consider, as the previous chapter suggests, that racialized violence results in an inordinate amount of time taken and thus due to Black youths.

A 2013 report produced by the Council of Minnesotans of African Heritage (formerly the Council on Black Minnesotans) reveals qualitatively different educational experiences between Black and white students. For example, while 75 percent of all students in Minnesota graduate on time, only 55 percent of students of color do so. According to the report, less than half of all Black third graders achieved expected reading proficiency for their grade level, compared to approximately 84 percent of their white counterparts.[19] Prospects for employment and escaping impoverishment are additional sites of struggle for Black Minnesotans. According to the 2017 American Community Survey's five-year (2013–17) estimates, the unemployment rate for people sixteen years and older was 4.3 percent. While only 3.6 percent of whites were unemployed during this period, the Black unemployment rate was 11 percent. While Black people make up just 6 percent of all Minnesotans, they made up 28.2 percent of those living below poverty. By contrast, whites make up 83.7 percent of the state population but only 7.2 percent of people below poverty.[20] Though both Minnesota and the Twin Cities are majority white, it remains essential to analyze racialized peoples in relation to one another and not just in relation to whiteness.

Blackness and Indigeneity in the Midwest

Settler colonialism and anti-Blackness both remain in full effect across Minnesota. Some scholars emphasize the incommensurability of slavery and settler colonialism, while more recent scholarship suggest that there is possibility within this sort of impasse.[21] As Tiffany Lethabo King, Jenell Navarro, and Andrea Smith argue, the "stuckness" of incommensurability is itself a form of relationality between Black and Native peoples.[22] The "stuckness" the authors describe derives from analyses and critiques of sovereignty, land, labor, and questions of the Human. For example, in critiquing Native studies scholars who misrecognize slavery as a form of "deculturalization" or "loss of sovereignty," Jared Sexton writes, "Slavery is not a loss that the self experiences—of language, lineage, land, or labor—but rather the loss of any self that could experience such a loss. Any politics based on resurgence or recovery is bound to regard the slaves as the 'position of the unthought' (Hartman and Wilderson 2003)."[23] There is a temporal order to Sexton's critique that suggests that before there can be a loss of "language, lineage, land, or labor," there has to be a self to lose such things. For Sexton, enslavement precludes the possibility of such personhood, thus rendering Black people to the "unthought."

In response to Sexton's critique of "sovereignty," Andrea Smith states, "While Sexton holds that Black peoples occupy the 'unthought of sovereignty,' colonization itself makes alternative conceptions of reality unthinkable."[24] Here Smith is attempting to push back on Sexton's claim that "colonization is not a necessary condition of enslavement."[25] Still, Smith is wary of "sovereignty" as an endpoint and instead describes the pursuit of sovereignty itself as "deferred genocide."[26] Frank Wilderson also critiques sovereignty as a tool that perpetuates "savage" negrophobia in film.[27] The range of such debates exceeds the scope of this book but nonetheless informs my thinking about Blackness and Indigeneity in Minnesota and the living histories of both groups.

The inextricable connection between space and time reveals not only the logic of *terra nullius* (land belonging to no one) but, as Helen Ngo argues, the concomitant violence of *tempus nullius*: "On this view, Australia was not just 'founded' on the basis of terra nullius, but also tempus nullius—uninhabited time, time not utilised or made use of, time that therefore does not register as such."[28] Thus, conquest left Native peoples devoid of space and time. Manifest destiny, the Doctrine of Discovery, and violated treaties upheld the twin logics of *terra* and *tempus nullius*. The Treaty of Traverse des Sioux and the Treaty of Mendota, for example, legitimated occupation of Dakota lands by both settlers and Anishinaabe peoples.[29] As the Wahpetunwan Dakota professor Waziyatawin writes, settlers coerced Native people into signing treaties by "withholding rations (theoretically guaranteed from previous treaties)" or threatening to take lands by force without any compensation.[30] Adding to the cumulative settler-colonial violence, settlers passed new legislation that unilaterally abrogated earlier treaties, while providing white settlers with Dakota treaty annuities and ushering in a US-military-led operation of evisceration.

The limited number of Native youths in youth programming is a direct result of attempts to decimate Nations while diminishing and disappearing settler violence. Though Native adults make up just 1 percent of the total population in Minnesota, they make up 12 percent of the state's unhoused population.[31] Among the youths who contributed to this research, one identified as Native, while nine identified as Black and Native. Though Native youths represented one of the smallest populations served at Run-a-Way, to not convey the presence of supposedly past settler-colonial violence would be tantamount to reinforcing settler logic that holds that Native peoples should not only disappear "but must always be disappearing," as Andrea Smith puts it.[32]

Smith describes how courts in Virginia during the early eighteenth century "ascribed Native slaves with the same status as Black slavers." In 1806, the Supreme Court, in *Hudgins v. Wright*, removed Native peoples from the category of Blackness and declared them "FREE."[33] Smith's broader critique is that Native people must disappear into "whiteness (civilization) or Blackness (extermination) in which Indigenous disappearance itself disappears. . . . However,

96   **CHAPTER 3**

the threat of disappearance into Blackness makes disappearance into whiteness appear as both survival and a choice rather than deferred genocide."[34] In short, assimilation is death.

Despite the "stuckness" some find themselves in when thinking through questions of Blackness and Indigeneity, youths I spoke with who identified as both Black and Native formed their racial identities in relation to multiple parts of their biographies, as well as space and time. When asked about the importance of their past, nearly every Black, mixed Black, and Black and Native youth talked about enslavement, colonization, or both. Among them was Sean, a sixteen-year-old Black and Native, queer youth. Sean responded to my question about the importance of his cultural past in this way: "Yeah, I talk about the past. What I've experienced. For us, slavery or Indians, when white people came over and took America from us. Yeah."

It is not uncommon for parents, local elders, and other members of the chronologically gifted class to remind younger activists, "You don't know where you are going unless you know where you are coming from." Despite being confined to linear progress narratives, this phrase seemed to resonate with many youths at Run-a-Way. For example, Gerard completed ancestry tests to learn about his family's Indigenous history. When I asked Gerard about the importance of his cultural past, he offered,

> It's very important to see how it's shaped the society we have today. I think that it's all very important because if you didn't have that history knowledge then that'd be Bad News Bears for you. . . . Actually, one of my ancestry things [referring to ancestry tests]. Have you ever did that? Your ancestry? . . . I had like a lot of Natives. Like, Native Americans. I was from a Winnebago tribe or whatever. That's really interesting.

Sites of Relational Racial Identity Formation

Both family and school serve as important sites of relational racial identity formation. Seventeen-year-old Adam was the only Native youth who did not also identify as Black. Adam identified as Native but, in his words, could pass for white, Asian, and/or Mexican. Adam described himself as quite different from his brother, who was eager to learn "traditional things," including how to make fry bread, how to play drums, and how to make dresses for powwows. Adam attributed his brother's penchant for learning Native traditions to his close relationship with their grandmother.

Adam's distant relationship with tradition and family was different from that of some of the youths who identified as Black and Native. One such youth was

Cedric, who was sixteen at the time of our interview. I also asked him about the importance of the past.

> I feel like it's very important. Like, my Grandma is Native so what I do is I smudge . . . every other day if I can or every day. 'Cuz . . . sage is used to cleanse your body and cleanse your house for thirty days. Whenever I'm sick I go smudge and the next day I'm perfectly fine or the next couple of hours I just start to come back. So I feel like it's very important.

Though only sixteen years old, Cedric smudged not only to cleanse but also to remain in communion with many of his elders and ancestors. Cedric's observance of Native tradition signaled a deep connection to the past and present. When I asked Tanisha whether she talked about her cultural history with her family, she described her grandmother as a beacon of historical knowledge:

> I try to with my grandma. . . . Well, she told me that we have a Native in our family. And the only person that we knew or that was still alive that was Native in our family, like fully Native, was her grandpa. And she told me that he didn't like colored . . . the colored people in our family, which was kind of weird to me 'cuz he's Native. Not white. So kinda shocked me.

In "Uncle Tom Was an Indian: Tracing the Red in Black Slavery," Tiya Miles describes how African Americans invoked Native ancestry as a tactic to destabilize fixed and essentialist constructions of Blackness.[35] To what extent did Black youths' Indigeneity also destabilize single-origin stories? Studying the multiple dimensions of Black and Native youths' biographical histories side by side rather than in isolation reveals the importance of relationality within racial formation.[36]

Reckoning with distinct identities and mutually constitutive histories extended beyond the family. Many youths learned what Black and Native history was by learning what it was not. They recognized that much of their schooling was synchronized to "settler time." Such synchronization necessitated the violent erasure of Black and Native history, leaving many youths disenchanted with their schooling. For example, Remy, a sixteen-year-old Black and Native, nonbinary youth, explained why they were so turned off by their educational experiences:

> Standardized tests. Those teachers who tell you, oh, well, when you walk in and they're like, "Oh, you have an hour to finish this pop quiz." And you get a real-life grade on it but then they ask you to write a paper and they expect you to write a five-page paper in two minutes. And just the expectation. And the privilege, just the white privilege. I just don't like the fact that I have to learn about my culture as an elective and how us

learning about white people be the main thing. It's like there's really no excuse for it. It's not like they're saying, "Oh, we're learning about what happened in America." 'Cuz even if they were saying that, then we shouldn't be learning about white people at all, to be honest. So I don't like that. Because white people aren't even from America. They couldn't even stand they own continent. Like, come on now. This is the Native Americans' country. White people love taking things from other people. That's they favorite thing to do, I promise you. Love takin' stuff that ain't theirs.

As with youths who identified as Black and/or African American, the significance of the cultural past to Black and Native youth was integral to shaping their present realities. Most youths who identified as Black or African American invoked the civil rights movement and resistance during slavery to signal the connection with the past. Their connection to their cultural pasts recognized the mutually constitutive nature of settler colonialism and enslavement. Despite the "stuckness" brought about by conceptions of slavery and settler colonialism as incommensurable, Black and Native youths found ways to reconcile both within the context of their own relational identity formation.

Though I have so far centered Black and Native life in Minnesota, I would be remiss to ignore other racialized groups that constitute the distinct demographics of the Twin Cities in particular. A number of migrant groups have come to call the Twin Cities home. Consider that the largest number of Somali migrants and refugees in the United States reside in Minnesota. St. Paul is also home to the largest Hmong American community in the United States. While scholarship on Asian racialization continues to grow, the experiences of Southeast Asians, particularly Hmong, Cambodians, Laos, Karen, and Vietnamese, warrant further research.[37] Still, it may be worth refraining from settler equivalence and considering the experiences of the unsettled settlers, or, as Nandita Sharma describes them, "those who are rendered as always-already oppositional others."[38] Free trade agreements, deregulation, speculative capitalism, privatized land, ecological violence, the destruction of local economies, and the paternalistic role of the International Monetary Fund and the World Bank in increasing a debt that should be owned by developed, as opposed to developing, nations is all further evidence of the role of geopolitics in spurring migration.[39]

Reducing analyses of race, racialization, and racism to a settler-Native binary risks obscuring the importance of relationality to processes of racial formation.[40] In some cases, the absence of racialized groups from sociological research may serve as a generative site of inquiry as opposed to strictly an opportunity for critique. For example, the absence of youths who identify as Native, Latinx, and Asian and Pacific Islander at Run-a-Way is due in large part to their population numbers within shelter programs. According to findings from the 2015 Minnesota Homeless Study, only 11 percent of unhoused youth in the state identify as Hispanic; 9 percent identify as American Indian, and only 2 percent identify as Asian.[41] Though existing demographics limited the opportunity to be more inclusive of other racialized youths, this book brings greater attention to what it means to be Black in the Midwest.

Minnesota Maybe

The racialization of space is inextricably linked to the racialization of time and the temporalization of race. For Charles Mills, ownership of space is contingent on ownership of time and vice versa: "Whose space it is depends in part on whose time it is, on which temporality, which version of time, can be established as hegemonic."[42] The naturalization of time zones, for example, conveniently obscures the role of capitalism and colonialism.[43] So although time differs depending on the space and region of the world we inhabit, what happens when people within the same alleged time zone are read as temporally distinct? For example, how might prisoners "doing time" in the same region as their loved ones remain in what Richard Wright calls a "No Man's Land"—"a shadowy region . . . the ground that separated the white world from the black"?[44] Can time actually be "done" when carceral logics (e.g., law, "crime," "deviance," and policing) serve as timekeepers outside carceral space (i.e., prisons)? Analyzing themes of time in the writings of Black novelists, Barthold likens "No Man's Land" to a "state of timeless estrangement": "For Bigger, as for the other residents of this landscape, living in No Man's Land is tantamount to spiritual and/or physical death, where the isolation in time coincides with an isolation from the human community."[45]

In *Time and the Other*, Johannes Fabian makes a compelling case that social scientists prohibit "the other," or the exoticized object of social research, from inhabiting the same space and time as the researcher: "The history of our discipline [anthropology] reveals that such use of Time almost invariably is made for the purposes of distancing those who are observed from the Time of the observer."[46] Sociology is not immune from denying empirical subjects the opportunity to inhabit the same space and time as researchers. Despite the discipline's emphasis on the iterative relationship between the individual and the social, sociologists look more like psychologists when privileging individual behavior, morals, and values over systems and institutions. William Julius Wilson, for example, uses limited access to "social capital" as grounds for denying poor Black families coevalness (i.e., a place in time):

> Inner-city social isolation also generates behavior not conducive to good work histories. The patterns of behavior that are associated with a life of casual work (tardiness and absenteeism) are quite different from those that accompany a life of regular or steady work (e.g., the habit of waking up early in the morning to a ringing alarm clock). In neighborhoods in which nearly every family has at least one person who is steadily employed, the norms and behavior patterns that emanate from a life of regularized employment become part of the community gestalt. On the other hand, in neighborhoods in which most families do not have a steadily employed breadwinner, the norms and behavior patterns associated with steady work compete with those associated with casual and infrequent work. Accordingly, the less frequent the regular contact with those who have steady and full-time employment (that is, the greater degree of social isolation), the more likely that initial job performance will be characterized by tardiness, absenteeism, and, thereby, low retention. In other words, a person's patterns and norms of behavior tend to be shaped by those with which he or she has had the most frequent or sustained contact and interaction. Moreover, since the jobs that are available to the inner-city poor are the very ones that alienate even persons with long and stable work histories, the combination of unattractive jobs and lack of community norms to reinforce work increases the likelihood that individuals will turn to either underground illegal activity or idleness or both.[47]

Wilson makes clear that "social isolation" is less of a choice and more indicative of structural economic changes. But by representing Black people in urbanized space as trapped within a degenerative and regenerative system of social, cultural, economic, and temporal regression, Wilson displaces an emphasis on structure in favor of a psychosocial analysis. Wilson, though, is not unique. Many urban sociologists complicit in the reproduction of temporal stigmas are simply doing their job. As a discipline predicated on interpreting the iterative relationship between individual and social structures and linking biography to history, sociology prides itself on its unique capacity to reveal what is hidden in plain sight.[48] Unfortunately, few seem to question how sociology can honestly work toward such a goal when it remains complicit in *hiding* what is hidden.

Here, I aim to complicate existing sociological analyses of the relationship between poor urbanized space and time. I argue that in limiting their analyses to the interplay between culture and structure, urban sociologists have constructed inadequate representations of the temporal orientations of people residing in poor urbanized space. How do Black youths at Run-a-Way view their communities in relation to time? To what extent do they reckon with the temporal stigmatization of their communities? What are the implications of constructing people within the same time zone as "behind" and "ahead of" time? To answer these and other questions, I privilege a conversation with fifteen-year-old Devon. I asked all of the youths how outsiders view their community.

> DEVON: Old, run down. We are not very up to date. I mean, a lot of us are still wearing Jheri curls. Yeah. I feel like . . . we're definitely described as being behind or not very up to date.
>
> RM: Why would you say that is?
>
> DEVON: Because . . . there's nothing that's really pushing us into the modern time. We live in crappy buildings, we get treated crappy. And so there's no real reason to push forward, so we just remain in this same type of . . . we just remain behind. There's nothing pushing us forward.
>
> RM: How do you think white people view you as an individual in relation to time?
>
> DEVON: . . . I don't like to assume, but I know some of them view me as being slow, lazy, not hardworking, not using my time the right way.
>
> RM: Any reason why you think that?
>
> DEVON: I think that's because of my skin. Because that's what they see so many of my people doing, they assume that when they see me that I do the same thing as them.

Devon reveals a corporeal dimension to the temporalization and racialization of space. Once white people epidermally define and spatially locate Devon through racializing surveillance, they place him outside white time.[49] Key to racialization is the ascription of value and worth. In Devon's case, white people rely on space as an indicator of individual value and worth. Devaluing space, in turn, justifies devaluing those within that space. For example, "crappy buildings" legitimate "crappy" treatment of residents. Devon's reference to Jheri curls is not an attempt to put down other members of his community. Perhaps he is struggling to reconcile the relevance of Jheri curls within the context of white time. Jheri curls, then, are not a product of "cultural lag" or indicative of life in an "urban jungle."[50] Is there room to appreciate the possibility that old heads might rock a Jheri curl to transgress time and defy linear progress narratives by embodying the timelessness of Rick James and N.W.A.? Toward the end of our interview, I asked Devon at what age he believed people should have children. In his response lies a provocative analysis of race, space, and time:

> Oh, I feel like it should be when you're out of college and you have a good job, and everything is stable. Because it's very, very hard to raise a kid. I know this from personal experience. It's very, very hard to raise a kid in a maybe environment. Maybe I'll get a job. Maybe there'll be money coming in and maybe we'll have an apartment. I feel like if you're gonna have a kid it should be in a very stable, very for-sure environment. I'm not saying you have to be rich and own a big house, but you should have a form of income coming in, you should have a house at least, whether it's just an apartment or whatever, but it should be a very for-sure environment.

When Common begins "U, Black Maybe" by distinguishing between a "white man's yes" and a "black maybe," the rapper signals a double standard wherein what is guaranteed to whites is but a possibility for Black people.[51] As Devon suggests, the use of "maybe" does not function only as a discursive tool. There is a materiality to "maybe." The construction of the ghetto, for example, required uncertainty about how residents would survive ("Maybe they'll make it out. Maybe they won't"). Ambiguity and, more specifically, the production of ambiguous life chances through the construction of space and opportunity structures make certain aspects of Black life a "maybe." Devon pointed out a striking difference between raising a child in a "maybe environment" and a "very for-sure environment." According to him, the overwhelming sense of uncertainty in "maybe environments" hamper efforts at time management. I asked Devon who or what is responsible for creating "maybe environments":

> DEVON: I feel like it's . . . shared between people who have not really worked towards making it a for-sure environment so it stays a maybe environment. I also feel like it is a system. The government and the police and all the people we're supposed to trust have also made this maybe environment a bigger even maybe. Because they're not giving us jobs. But at the same time they're taking our money and they're sending us out to war. But they're not feeding us. They're not protecting us. And so it's made it an even worse environment because of the lack of responsibility that they've put into our community.
>
> RM: Can you say more about how systems like police, governments, make it a maybe environment?
>
> DEVON: I'm not saying all social workers are like this, but in the Black community many, many families are torn apart by social workers

THE MAKINGS OF A "MAYBE ENVIRONMENT"   103

> because you take the, what do you call it. The . . . child protection
> services. A lot of them come in because it's a single mother and she's
> been raising her kids on her own and this social worker comes in and
> she one by one divides and conquers the family. She stops in all the
> time, she interviews the kids equally, and a lot of them just basically
> put the stress on the family and eventually the stress just breaks the
> rope and the family falls apart. And then the social workers come
> in and they divide up a family. And it makes the community worse
> because of the pain that that inflicts on the community.

Though part of this response seems to reinforce urban sociology's emphasis on ambiguity as an inherent part of life in poor urbanized space, Devon offers a structural analysis of the makings of a "maybe environment" and a broader atmosphere of uncertainty.[52] According to Devon, "the government and the police" are largely responsible for *making* so many things a "maybe" for racialized and dispossessed persons in urbanized space. As products of systematic racialized violence, "maybe environments" occupy a unique space within and outside white time. Insofar as "maybe environments" are held to standards and expectations of white time, they remain within white time. Wilson, for example, maps "maybe environments" onto standards of white time including heteronormative family formation, "breadwinners," norms, punctuality, and stable work histories. It is not that racialized people do not know how to conform to white time; it is that white time requires the exploitation and extraction of nonwhite life. Hence, white time limits a racialized person's potential to find "stable work" because it takes their time through exploitation.

Consider the experience of a single mother who has to wake up at four o'clock in the morning to get her daughter ready for day care before going to her own job. At five o'clock, the mother and daughter are on a bus headed toward the day care. After dropping the child off at day care at six, the mother is back on a bus headed to work. The trip, however, involves two different buses, and the mother arrives late to work. If time is in fact money, much of the mother's time spent preparing for work remains uncompensated for by her employer. The employer legitimates its wage theft under the guise of white time, literally making gains (i.e., capital) at the mother's expense.

Similar examples of such time theft have been well documented since the early twentieth century. Drawing on archival data, Evelyn Nakano Glenn describes the sacrifices Black women made when performing reproductive labor for white families: "A black child nurse reported in 1912 that she worked fourteen to sixteen hours a day caring for her mistress's four children. . . . She reported that she was allowed to go home 'only once in every two weeks, every other Sunday

104   CHAPTER 3

afternoon. . . . I see my own children only when they happen to see me on the streets.'"[53] Here we see that Black women's estranged relationships with their children is but a reflection of their estranged relationships to time. Glenn reveals one of many sources of the mounting debt held by those who are likely to owe, rather than own, time. E. P. Thompson helps illustrate this point when distinguishing between an employer's time and the alleged "time" of a worker: "Those who are employed experience a distinction between their employer's time and their 'own' time. And the employer must *use* the time of his labour, and see it is not wasted: not the task but the value of time when reduced to money is dominant. Time is now currency: it is not passed but spent."[54]

Such temporal extraction and filial estrangement are key to the production of "maybe environments." Maybe a Black mother working for a white family will be able to see her children. Maybe she won't. Though a Black mother may live in the same city as the white family that employs her, she does not have access to the resources of what Devon calls a "for-sure environment." "Maybe environments" remain outside white time and a white habitus by dint of their racialized composition. The temporalization of urbanized space, according to Anne McClintock, required that Black people be cast into a temporal alterity, diametrically opposed to modernity:

> The urban slums were depicted as epistemological problems—as anachronistic worlds of deprivation and unreality, zones without language, history, or reason that could be described only by negative analogy in terms of what they were not. . . . Like colonial landscapes, the slums were figured as inhabiting an anachronistic space, representing a temporal regression within industrial modernity to a time beyond the recall of memory.[55]

As McClintock illustrates, poor urbanized space is a site of temporal stigma marking poor people as inherently regressive. Sociologists and urban ethnographers, in particular, are complicit in making poor urbanized space asynchronous and temporally "deviant" (a point I return to in greater detail in chapter 8). Opportunities to improve life chances in "maybe environments" are habitually late or absent. The certainty of ambiguity requires residents of those communities to maintain a unique relationship with time. Many of the youths I interviewed came from two notable "maybe environments" in the Twin Cities: the Rondo neighborhood in St. Paul, and North Minneapolis.

The Presence of the Past in Rondo and North Minneapolis

From 1956 to 1968, under the guise of "urban renewal," or what James Baldwin once called "Negro removal,"[56] more than five hundred families were uprooted as construction of the I-94 freeway rammed through the heart of St. Paul's Black community. Urban renewal effectively destroyed several sites of Black sociality, including homes, businesses, churches, and social houses. Racial segregation, and more specifically anti-Blackness, made many of these sites vital to promoting a sense of safety and affinity among Black people. Today, Black residents of St. Paul still remember the process of urban renewal in part because the past for Black people and many other racialized subjects is always present. Each year in mid-July, many residents of Rondo and the broader Twin Cities gather to celebrate "Rondo Days"—a weekend festival commemorating the vibrant social life of the historically Black community. On July 17, 2015, the then mayor, Chris Coleman, declared July 17 "Rondo Remembrance Day," saying, "Today we acknowledge the sins of our past. . . . We regret the stain of racism that allowed so callous a decision as the one that led to families being dragged from their homes creating a diaspora of the African-American community in the City of Saint Paul." Coleman then went on to issue a formal apology to past and present residents: "Today as Mayor of Saint Paul, I apologize, on behalf of the city, to all who call Rondo home, for the acts and decisions that destroyed this once vibrant community."[57]

Like many other forms of racial violence, removing sites of Black sociality, Blackness, and Black people in service of capitalism and what George Lipsitz, in the title of his book, calls "the possessive investment in whiteness" represents an incommensurable debt. It is unclear whether Coleman was apologizing for a continual undoing of Black social life or for what the mayor treated as an isolated case of racism relegated to a specific historical spacetime. To ensure that the past remains a present part of the Black community in St. Paul, Rondo residents proposed the creation of the Rondo Commemorative Plaza. Unveiled on July 14, 2018, the plaza offers "a space for education, contemplation, inspiration, and community building."[58]

Traveling far enough west on I-94 (the same highway that divided Rondo) will bring out-of-towners to another predominantly Black community: North Minneapolis, otherwise known as the Northside, North, and sometimes Near North. According to a geographic profile by Minnesota Compass, Blacks or African Americans make up 55 percent of the Near North community, while whites make up only 14 percent.[59] North Minneapolis is, according to the Center for Urban and Regional Affairs, a site of ongoing "strategic disinvestment and racial segregation."[60] "White flight" and the shift from public to private investments resulted in decades of economic decline and undervalued housing stock. Consequently, the Northside is increasingly becoming the target of gentrification. As the population of young white families grows in North Minneapolis, many responses to key questions about Black people's future in the community begin with a "maybe": "Maybe I'll graduate." "Maybe I'll find a job." "Maybe I'll have to move." "Maybe I'll survive."

The makings of the Northside and other "maybe environments" reflect the makings of what Douglas Massey and Nancy Denton describe as "the underclass."[61] Racialized violence, "rapid economic growth and growing spatial deconcentrating," white suburbanization, the withdrawal of commercial institutions from the inner city, "urban renewal," institutionalized racism in housing markets and federal housing authorities, failed public policy, restrictive enforcement of antidiscrimination legislation, and geographic and political isolation are integral to the construction of poor urbanized space and the "underclass." The authors go on to note that "segregation, not middle-class outmigration, is the key factor responsible for the creation and perpetuation of communities characterized by persistent and spatially concentrated poverty."[62] The *making* of "maybe environments" implies an ongoing construction ensuring that racialized histories are rarely past. Instead, subprime mortgages, gentrification, and "accumulation by dispossession" have become the standard operating procedures for what Paula Chakravartty and Denise Ferreira da Silva call "the racial logic of global capitalism."[63]

Despite their contributions, however, the extent to which Massey and Denton intervene in conventional social scientific understandings of poor racialized persons is debatable. For example, while the authors acknowledge that the construction and persistence of the ghetto is a product of systemic racism and discrimination, their explanation for the perpetuation of the "underclass" reifies socially constructed conditions of the ghetto itself. Ultimately, through their own structural explanations of segregation, Massey and Denton pin themselves into a familiar culture-of-poverty trap. Take, for instance, the use of the term "underclass." The "under" in "underclass" implies subordination. Not only is the "underclass" subordinate to all other socioeconomic classes, but it is also temporally inferior. In turn, the ghetto becomes a key emblem of anachronistic space marked as backward, behind time, and devoid of coevalness. By definition, the "underclass" is "under" other classes. Hence, social scientists can make sense of "underclass" only through a paternalistic and deficit ideology that requires what is "under" to advance through racial progress and uplift. Remaining true to conventional social science, Massey and Denton turn to public policy and state-expansionist strategies to address ongoing racial segregation,[64] while ignoring that poor urbanized space remains underwritten by a possessive investment in whiteness and, more specifically, white space and time.

White Spatial and Temporal Imaginaries

In the 1972 hit song "Across 110th Street," Bobby Womack sings, "The family on the other side of town would catch hell without a ghetto around."[65] Here,

Womack refers to the mutually constitutive relationship between the ghetto and the suburbs. He makes clear that suburban maintenance requires both the systemic construction and destruction of the ghetto. The "family on the other side of town" requires uncertainty within "maybe environments" as proof of their residency in "very for-sure environments." Certainty is backed by a possessive investment in whiteness and white habitus.

It is no coincidence that "white habitus" is just a couple of letters short of "white habitats." Where white people live shapes their worldviews and orientations. Existing sociological research reminds us that "maybe environments" exist in relation to the guaranteed privileges of "very for-sure environments." The blueprints of many white habitats form within what Lipsitz calls the "white spatial imaginary":

> This imaginary does not emerge simply or directly from the embodied identities of people who are white. It is inscribed in the physical contours or the places where we live, work and play and it is bolstered by financial rewards for whiteness. Not all whites benefit from the white spatial imaginary, and some Blacks embrace it and profit from it. Yet every white person benefits from the association of white places with privilege, from the neighborhood race effects that create unequal and unjust geographies of opportunity.[66]

The solipsistic design of many white habitats leaves little space for analysis of the structured advantages woven into whiteness. Instead, personal success is naturalized and detached from the institutionalization of whiteness in education, employment, housing, the penal-legal system, and public policy. Expanding on Lipsitz's white spatial imaginary, Charles Mills calls for a corresponding "white temporal imaginary," to consider the role of white time in shaping social cognition. Mills argues that a "white temporal imaginary" is key to "structuring social affect as well as social cognition, and helping to constitute exclusionary gated moral communities protected by temporal, no less than spatial, walls."[67] Spatial and temporal walls extend beyond gated communities.

The walls of whiteness require the construction of other impenetrable barriers difficult to break from the outside. I am referring to mutually constitutive relationships between gated communities and the ghetto, project, hood, trap, and/or barrio.[68] I wonder what it might look like if youths like Devon had an opportunity to speak back to the many white homeowners who accuse him and other Black youths of being "up to no good." Maybe Devon might remind them that "everything you got is because other people got got." For those unfamiliar, to "get got" is to get tricked, duped, fleeced, hoodwinked, bamboozled, and/or fooled. During my upbringing, my hood had what are called "getters." A getter is a person who might "get you" for your chain, wallet, pocketbook, and so on.

Some might describe such actions as "crime." Getters call it "survival." And what many may never understand is that, in most cases, it is survival.

In this hypothetical scenario, though, Devon is confronting getters that live beyond the boundaries of the ghetto. Those that live within a white habitus and white habitats have what they have because Black, brown, and Indigenous people got more than just got. What many middle-to-upper-middle-class white people have is the product of debt, dispossession, and death. Redlining, restrictive covenants, highway construction, blockbusting, deindustrialization, and the pathologization and punishment of those living in poor urbanized space secure whiteness and protect white space. The Twin Cities' own history of racist real estate policies, specifically restrictive covenants, became the subject of a 2018 PBS documentary titled *Jim Crow of the North*.[69] Devon's conception of a "maybe environment" signals his awareness that white people's safety is predicated on nonwhite people's unsafety. The space that many white people call home cannot exist without the ghetto. "Urbanized" space is just a few letters short of "suburbanized" space. Some stay in one or more of these locations because, as Saidiya Hartman notes, they are places not meant for living in:

> We stay there, but we don't live there. Ghettos aren't designed for living. The debris awash in the streets, the broken windows, the stench of urine in project elevators and stairwells are the signs of bare life. "The insistent, maddening, claustrophobic pounding in the skull that comes from trying to breathe in a very small room with all the windows shut," writes James Baldwin, daily assaults the residents of the ghetto, the quarters, the 'hood. It produces the need to "destroy tirelessly" or "to smash something," which appears the most obvious path of salvation. As C.L.R. James observes about the San Domingo masses, they destroyed "what they knew was the cause of their sufferings; and if they destroyed much it was because they had suffered much."[70]

Spaces "not designed for living," however, are not devoid of life. As gated communities strive to protect whiteness and wealth, insurgency brews among temporally dispossessed and racialized peoples in urbanized space. The brew will eventually spill over into an urge toward destroying that which is destructive. In other words, when segregated by the walls of wealth and whiteness, poor, racialized people remain intent on razing what is raised and rising. The asynchronous temporalities of "maybe environments" and "very for-sure environments" must recalibrate according to standards not set by white time but by Black resistance.

Calibrated according to white spatial and temporal imaginaries, "The Miracle of Minneapolis" offers a future-oriented portrait of two cities haunted by a present past that disproportionately harms racialized and Indigenous peoples. Derek

Thompson credits top-down economic theory (i.e., the maintenance of capitalism) with the preservation of the "American dream." Thompson's universal claims offer further evidence of the use of white life as a reference category to make sense of the life chances of all Twin Cities residents, including nonwhite ones.

"The Miracle of Minneapolis" is more than a "white lie." It is a form of journalistic perjury overrepresenting white life as life itself while rendering the Black Midwest invisible. There is a difference between a "miracle" and guaranteed success at every conceivable level of measurable success. For those with the complexion for the protection, however, "miracles" and "guarantees" are apparently interchangeable. Perhaps the real "miracle" of Minneapolis and greater Minnesota lies within the capacity of Black and Indigenous people to continue to resist and rage against ongoing forms of racialized violence.

The systematic neglect, underdevelopment, and divestment of majority-Black communities in the Twin Cities is key to the construction of "maybe environments." What is guaranteed to many white youths is more likely a "maybe" to Black youths, particularly those residing in poor urbanized space. Despite representations of poor urbanized space as inherently uncertain, I argue that Black youths retain an acute awareness of the future, making them more prescient than "present oriented." When the response to a yes-or-no question is "maybe," most youths know to be prepared to wait. For racialized youths in urbanized space, however, a "maybe" is not only a potential response to ordinary questions but also a default decision on their life chances. Black youths at Run-a-Way interpret maybes as the product of structural violence that offers some people guarantees and others gimmicks. The promises made to white youths cannot be understood without the false promises made to those not white. Relying on "maybe" to gauge their life chances, Black youths can hope for the best, but they are accustomed to preparing for the worst. In other words, what was once a maybe becomes an unequivocal no for Black youths.

Beyond the conventional deficit-based perspectives used in the makings of a "maybe environment," there exists a more liberating framework. It is one less concerned with the imposition of uncertainty on poor racialized communities through a top-down dynamic and more attentive to "radical" resistance that, remaining true to the etymology of the term (*radix*, the Latin word for "root"), comes from the ground up. It is a paradigm that refuses to be contained by the fixity of "yes" and "certainly," one that is deliberately elusive, fluid, dynamic, and fugitive in order to escape the rigid confines of dominant modes of thought, discourse, and action. So when someone asks a Black youth, "Can we count on you to behave? Be on time? Do what we tell you to do? And follow the rules?" the most dignified, self-determined, affirming, and life-preserving reply might just be, "Maybe."

4

"KEISHA DOESN'T GET THE CALL BEFORE KIMBERLY"

White time cannot guide, let alone measure, the racialized life course of youths whose past is always present and whose future is *made* habitually truant. An always present past and fugitive future require a transgressive relationship with time. Living a life along a "straight and narrow" path is conducive to those whose life course unfolds seamlessly in white time. Completing school and finding a job represent common benchmarks along the life course and key indicators of the transition to adulthood.[1] Still, many youths begin their pursuit of a high school diploma from a deficit. When I asked sixteen-year-old Terrell whether he feels he has more or less time than white youths, he shared this:

> OK, so like me. . . . I'm not financially good, you know. . . . So I really don't have no time. So I gotta do what I gotta do. But people always say white people, "They rich. They have money." When their kids just bein' born they already have money in the bank for them [to have access to] when they turn eighteen. Before they even be one years old [the money is in the bank]. So you think about it like this—white people, they never started from the bottom. Like, I could say every Black person I done seen started from the bottom. So, when a white person tell me, "You're doin' no good," I feel like, "You can't say nothin'. Everything been handed to you your whole life."

Even at sixteen, Terrell knows that time is money and that not being "financially good" means he is without both. Compare Terrell's situation to the white youths he sees as the beneficiaries of parental wealth. Regardless of whether every white kid has a trust fund, Black youths share Terrell's perspective, particularly those who know what it means to work twice as hard to get half as far. So we need not be surprised when Black youths feel some type of way when white people claim to have started from the bottom. In Terrell's mind, white youths started not from the bottom but from the intergenerational transmission of racialized wealth. In airing out white people's dirty laundry, Terrell is also exercising his double consciousness. He opens a window to whiteness and invites others to look inside. Double consciousness, however, is more than just a "second sight." It is an ontological orientation and assessment.

Terrell knows how his existence as a young Black male is interpellated though a lens of subordination and abjection. He understands that he and other Black youths are read as "doin' no good." But he also makes clear that he is prepared to check white people on their anti-Blackness by reminding them, "You can't say nothin'." In other words, white people can't tell Terrell nothin' because their wealth and whiteness already speak volumes. Terrell refuses to let white people put him down because he already knows how they reached the top: it was not by dint of sheer hard work but through racialized dispossession, debt, and death. Hence, any white person attempting to shame Terrell for "doin' no good" runs the risk of being silenced not just by Black youths themselves, but also by the piercing reverberations of slavery's afterlife, settler colonialism, and other sources of temporal accumulation.

How might we think about Terrell's description of the intergenerational transmission of wealth as also an intergenerational transmission of time? In what ways do temporal inheritances cumulate for white youths over the life course, and how do such accruals occur at the expense of Black youths? Terrell's response helps explain why many white youths have a head start in life and thus a head start at life chances. This chapter acknowledges that the private realm of the family is but one of many sources of temporal inequality between white and nonwhite youths over the life course. Not only do white youths start off with more money in the bank than Black youths, but they are also more likely to remain temporally advanced in school and in the labor force.

My conversations with youths at Run-a-Way suggest that structural racism and anti-Blackness protract Black youths' learning experiences and opportunities to find work. At school, teachers and administrators temporalize Black youths as "behind," and white time ensures that there will always be a "behind" for some children to be "left." As they searched for jobs, the Black youths I spoke with quickly learned how racist hiring practices required them to work twice as hard to get half as far (as their white counterparts). Even when they did find a job, they knew Black people were the last hired and the first fired—yet another reminder that time was not on their side. Delays due to racism in schooling and

112   **CHAPTER 4**

the labor force were further evidence that many nonwhite youths at Run-a-Way could not abide by the same timetables as their white counterparts.

Most youths I interviewed expressed feeling greater temporal constraints compared to what they saw as relaxed life course transitions and trajectories among white youths. They described time loss as a product of increased physical, emotional, and psychic labor. Having not yet attended college, sixteen-year-old Remy was still able to project what they believed to be a likely length of time based on the experiences of relatives. I asked Remy how long it takes someone from their community to complete college:

> REMY: Um, I know it took my auntie like ten years 'cuz she kept dropping out and then she would go back and she would have to finish.
>
> RM: Why do you think it took her a little longer?
>
> REMY: She told me that she personally felt like she had to work hard . . . like, harder than the other kids, but what she meant by that was she felt like it was a race. . . . She said she felt like a field slave. So like maybe if you work this hard you can get close to the master, you can get close to the teacher. So maybe if you do this right then you'll get this in return even though everyone else is doing it but you've just gotta work harder for it 'cuz I want you to show me the difference. . . . It just gave her a lot of anxiety and she wasn't comfortable with that.
>
> RM: Do you feel like you and even maybe your auntie usually have to work twice as hard as white people to get certain things?
>
> REMY: Most definitely. . . . Yes, 'cuz I feel like I'm doing extra stuff. . . . I don't wanna do their job 'cuz I feel like I'm doing two jobs at once. I don't wanna do extra stuff 'cuz then that's taking up time. It takes time to do extra stuff. If we both got the same amount of time but we got two different things to do and that one person has one thing to do, then that means that I have less time.

Remy's auntie's intermittent education belies linear progress narratives and linear time. Racialized students in colleges and universities do not just drop out—they are pushed out. Remy's auntie's academic struggles are not due to a lack of effort or limited academic preparedness. Instead, racialized bias, whiteness, and the awareness of having to work significantly harder than most of her counterparts consume her time. Having to constantly think in such relational terms is, according to Remy, like "doing two jobs at once" and hence a waste of time. How do we account for less traveled life courses, particularly the life courses of Black youths forced to work twice as hard to get half as far?

For Black and other racialized persons, including Remy's auntie, timetables rarely feel relaxed. In fact, she had little opportunity to "explore" college. Instead, college felt like an anxiety-provoking race that consistently left her behind, academically and temporally. Having taken ten years to complete college is indicative of what it means for Black youths to work twice as hard to get half as far. Nonlinear life courses, such as Remy's auntie's, are products of routine subjugation necessitating "one step forward, two steps backward." Incommensurability is an important theme of this chapter, given Black youths' claims of having to work twice as hard to go half as far as their white counterparts in school. Believing that educational opportunities came late or not at all, many Black youths at Run-a-Way concluded that school was largely a waste of time *and* space.

"Saved" or Imperiled by the Bell?

When in school, youths orient themselves to time and space through a variety of mechanisms. Some may use the current class period to assess what remains in the school day. Others might make a mental note of a teacher's beverage (e.g., coffee or water) to gauge where they are at in the day. Still others may try to find a window to locate the sun. Students in private school might be reminded of the time of day based on the wear of their peers' uniforms. But there remains one temporal device guaranteed to prompt responses from students, teachers, and staff no matter the time of day: the school bell. Start and end times in school are calibrated according to the buzz, beep, or ringing of the bell. Classes, lunch, recess, and school itself all begin and end at the bell's command. The perfunctory nature of the school bell, however, does not exculpate it from the charge of temporal violence. Defying the bell places students at risk of punishment, such as detention, suspension, or expulsion. It is then worth asking, who is saved by the bell and who is imperiled by it?[2]

The bell, however, is but one of many technologies that make some Black students averse to schooling. Biological racism, a colonized curriculum, and racialized discipline are key ingredients in a compost of punitive pedagogies required to keep students more captive than captivated in the classroom. In turn, the prospect of education being a life course transition remains debatable given that so many Black students, Indigenous students, and other students of color are lingering in school and thus *suspended* in time. With white time and "Western civilization" indexing what constitutes knowledge production, opportunities for curricular coevalness remained off limits to the Black students I interviewed. When

114   CHAPTER 4

I asked Dominique about how they used their time in school, they emphasized the importance of not thinking about time at all:

> I try to forget about time at school too because it's a lot of busywork and I hate busywork. And . . . I hate being told to do an assignment without, like, you know, having structure. You know? Like, I can't do a class without structured notes. I passed my government class with ninety-nine percent because he had structured notes. . . . I like classes when it's like that. Structured, I can actually look back. I actually learn better that way. And that helps it pass the time. But in, like, normal class when you're just reciting a textbook, memorizing that section of the textbook and then taking a test. And then you're gonna forget about it. And then you're gonna bring it up at the end of the semester, take that test, and then walk away. But some of the stuff that we learn is irrelevant. Like, I really do not care about Alexander the Great. That is not going to shape my future. I feel . . . we should study more current events, stuff that actually affects us now, stuff that we can have a conversation about. 'Cuz normal people *do not* talk about Alexander the Great or Cleopatra or King Tut.

Being "held back," "left back," and/or forced to repeat a grade is one of the many ways schooling temporalizes Black and Indigenous students and other racialized students and increases their temporal debt. Though many racialized youths remain targeted for being "slow learners" or in need of segregated education, Dominique points out that it is in fact their curriculum that is not only outdated but potentially responsible for keeping them behind in school. In addition to being designed without particular students in mind, many schools were also designed to fail. "Normal" classes, according to Dominique, rely on rote memory and arbitrary learning measures that disproportionately harm Black youths. Students like Shanté yearn for not just answers but analysis of contemporary social problems. The institutionalization of rote learning and biased curricula in schools, however, remind Black youths that racism remains a life course constant. As Shanté states,

> Even in school they don't . . . in the textbook maybe a half a page on slavery and all they do is talk about cotton. Like, they don't teach you nothin' about the past, all that we been through. All they teach you about is the world problems. Like, don't nobody care about that. We wanna know is why our people was gettin' hanged and beaten and havin' to slave in a field from sunup to sundown. Why y'all still treatin' us like we work for y'all every day?

Can centuries worth of content on enslavement fit on "half a page"? What does "half a page" of such content convert to in terms of time? The answer, according to Shanté, is not enough. She critiques her school's curriculum for neglecting slavery while denying students an understanding of the continuity of racialized violence over the life course and from past to present. She concludes with a stunning reference to what Saidiya Hartman might describe as "slavery's afterlife."[3] For Shanté, slavery extended, rather than ended. At the same time, the school curriculum precludes the possibility of exploring slavery's afterlife when its actual life is ignored. Expecting students to be on the cutting edge of visionary goals for building a more just and sustainable world means little if schools are not providing students with an accurate representation of what is most unjust and unsustainable. Though Devon knew he had the potential to succeed in school, he saw himself "changing the world" through a future career in music. Because the subject of racism was consistently suppressed inside the classroom, Devon felt it was imperative to use his talents as an aspiring rapper to speak on the topic through his rhymes:

> In school . . . when we talk about the civil rights movement and slavery, it's a very short subject. . . . And I feel like not enough time was being put into it and I thought where we lived, people were being beat up by police every day and there was nothing on it about . . . there was nothing in it in the news. And I felt like it was just not being identified enough. And so I took it upon myself to identify it in my music and to say this is actually happening whether you'd like to admit it or not.

Devon went on to intimate why teachers and administrators neglect Black history in school curricula:

> Because a lot of Black culture is not necessarily violent, but there's been a lot of fighting for what we believe belongs to us. And some of it has been through marching and peaceful and that's what they teach you about, because it's peaceful. The reason they don't teach us about Malcolm X is because Malcolm X believed in "by any means necessary." You should get your freedom no matter what it takes. And that's not what they wanna teach kids.

Devon describes how schools are more inclined to interpellate Black culture through a lens of violence, except when violence functions as a catalyst for liberation. Beyond an emphasis on teaching and learning, school is also a site of discipline, and as Devon suggests, schools will not teach students what is necessary

116   **CHAPTER 4**

to experience freedom. His remarks amplify the advice of many revolutionaries committed to Black liberation, including Assata Shakur, who affirms,

> The schools we go to are a reflection of the society that created them. Nobody is going to give you the education you need to overthrow them. Nobody is going to teach you your true history, teach you your true heroes, if they know that that knowledge will help set you free. Schools in amerika are interested in brainwashing people with amerikanism, giving them a little bit of education, and training them in skills needed to fill the positions the capitalist system requires. As long as we expect amerika's schools to educate us, we will remain ignorant.[4]

Rather than accepting the popular logic that "education is the key," Shakur sees schooling in the United States as a way to lock Black people into a life course devoid of resistance and self-determination. The education she describes is one defined by hegemony—whereby coercion, consent, and common sense ensure the social reproduction of racial and economic stratification. Shanté's perceptions of school did not deviate far from Shakur's critique. When I asked Shanté if and when she ever felt that people showed a lack of respect for her time, she replied, "Yeah, in school. All . . . they want you to do is just sit there and read books and fill out papers. Like, you wastin' my time literally. 'Cuz I could be doin' that somewhere else or I could be doin' somethin' better. 'Cuz fillin' out books is not helpin' me put food in my mouth or clothes on my back."

According to Shanté, schools offer few opportunities to help students survive, let alone be free. Rather than being a key to success, school was, in Shanté's opinion, limiting her life chances. Encouraging students to view education as an investment in future employment opportunities in the life course means little when exigent material needs, including food and shelter, pressure the present. Perhaps schools are synchronized to white time—a time that supports a structurally advantaged life course precluding the need to seek assistance from state services, including housing and food assistance programs. Shanté cannot help but view school as a space to waste valuable time, leaving Black youths feeling as if they are consistently beginning from behind.

Classic work in the sociology of education makes clear that schools have a greater capacity to stratify students along racial and class lines than they do to educate. In *Learning to Labor*, Paul Willis explores the divergent life course trajectories of two groups of youths in the United Kingdom from the early to midtwentieth century—the lads and the "ear'oles." Willis details processes of social reproduction in schools and the workforce, ultimately showing "how working class kids get working class jobs." What I find most intriguing is Willis's attention to the two groups of youths' distinct relationships to time:

> If one wishes to contact them, it is much more important to know and understand their own rhythms and patterns of movement. These rhythms reject the obvious purposes of the timetable and their implicit notions of time. The common complaint about "the lads" from staff and the "ear'oles" is that they "waste valuable time." Time for "the lads" is not something you carefully husband and thoughtfully spend on the achievement of desired objectivity in the future. For "the lads" time is something they want to claim for themselves now as an aspect of their immediate identity and self-direction. Time is used for the preservation of a state—being with "the lads"—not for the achievement of a goal—qualifications.[5]

While the "ear'oles" treat schooling as a key opportunity to improve their qualifications through neoliberal logics of self-discipline and future projections of an entrepreneurial self, the "lads" are in no rush to be exploited by a system that demands conformity and suppresses dissent. Notwithstanding these contributions, Willis misses an important opportunity to explore why reasons for rejecting the "timetable" may differ between Afro-Caribbean youths and their white counterparts. Without examining how time is racialized and attending to particularities of anti-Blackness, Willis ignores the inordinate amount of time Black youths spend reckoning with racist teachers, peers, and curriculum.

For Black youths learning and laboring in "enclosures," an education feels more like a lock than the key. Damien Sojoyner adopts Clyde Woods's use of "enclosures" to describe the "historical contestations over power, resources, and ways of life that have ushered us to the present."[6] Sojoyner emphasizes that enclosures, like temporal orientations, are contingent on history and not static. Racialized subjection in schooling is indicative of the fact that many of the early "architects of Black education" were not Black.[7] It is, then, no surprise that many youths at Run-a-Way recounted disparate treatment of Black and white students by teachers. When I asked him to think about examples of racism, Marcus, who is sixteen, described teachers' preferential treatment of white students:

> In school sometimes with some teachers . . . they favor or they have more patience with the white students than with the Blacks. Maybe based on their beliefs towards the culture, but I definitely see that in the school systems.

Though educational enclosures may not be static, racialized bias within schooling is a constant. In showing greater patience with white students than

Black students, Marcus's teachers cooperate to maintain an unequal system of time. These teachers do not, however, simply distribute time unevenly between white and Black students. Rather, they are responsible for robbing Black students of time while donating it to their white counterparts. Less patience means less time for Black students and more time for their white peers. In expanding vast temporal inequalities, racialized bias in schooling also adds to what Gloria Ladson-Billings describes as massive "education debt"—a product of the unequal distribution of schooling resources between white and nonwhite students, as well as "historical, economic, sociopolitical, and moral decisions and policies."[8] The convergence of mounting education debt, racial time, and racialized bias within schools requires Black students to work twice as hard to get half as far as their white counterparts. If we consider the time taken through school discipline and punishment, the education and temporal debt owed to Black and Indigenous students and other racialized students exponentially increases.

As teachers and administrators issue suspensions and expulsions to nonwhite students at disproportionately higher rates than their white counterparts, questions remain concerning how students of color come to terms with lost/stolen time. Can we actually expect educational transitions in the life course to occur "on time," when Black youths are constantly beginning from behind?[9] Bringing attention to the role of racialization and racism in taking time away from youth compels teachers and social workers to critically examine seemingly race-neutral policies. Race and racism make education policy, and at the same time, educational policy makes race. Consider the disproportionate harm of zero-tolerance policies to students of color. Nancy Lesko's critique of zero-tolerance policies proves instructive for considering the disparate experiences between students with the luxury of time and those targeted for temporal dispossession: "Zero tolerance policies are appealing because they suggest a return to learning-centered and orderly schools, but they impose a punitive and arbitrary juvenile justice system mentality and cannot take into consideration students' understandings of safe and unsafe zones, both in school and between home and school. Zero tolerance means that the moratorium of adolescence will be greatly shortened for some, while others still have time to accumulate credits in the leisure curriculum."[10] As the primary targets of zero-tolerance policies, it is no surprise that Black and Indigenous students and other racialized students are left with zero time. As Anne Arnett Ferguson writes, "Time in the school dungeon means time lost from classroom learning; suspension, at school or at home, has a direct and lasting negative effect on the continuing growth of a child."[11]

Temporal debts in schooling are the result of racialized discipline, anachronistic curricula, and the time taken by Black students working twice as hard to get half as far as their white counterparts. Despite liberal universalisms of shared success among all students regardless of race, racial time in education ensures that many children will in fact be left behind, not just in school but in time as well. Planned obsolescent education requires earnest consideration of the concept of failure in schools. What does it mean for students to "flunk" in systems designed to fail? It means Black students will be "held back," not just in a grade but in time. While Black youths often begin their educational journeys from deficits, their white counterparts begin with bonus time (i.e., the time impatient and neglectful teachers take from Black students). Schooling is but one of many examples of how white youths obtain temporal benefits at the expense of an increasing education debt owed to Black and other racialized students.

The "Temporal Order" of Race and Opportunity

Employment is a common life course transition that complies with the mandates of linear, progressive time. Whether it is a part-time or full-time job in high school or seasonal work, employment represents an opportunity for greater autonomy and financial independence. The school-to-work transition is not, however, a seamless one. I asked youths at Run-a-Way to estimate how long it takes to find a job in their community. Estimates ranged from a week to a year. Youths attributed protracted searches for work to racialization and racism in hiring practices. Most believed that Black and Indigenous youths and other racialized youths would inevitably spend more time trying to find a job than their white counterparts.

Black youths did not just "lose time" during their prolonged search for work. Instead, structural racism in hiring processes dispossessed them of time. Temporal dispossession involves the twin process of theft and accumulation. Similar to temporal theft, temporal dispossession involves temporal gains elsewhere. Racialized social systems reconstitute such gains, exacerbating temporal inequalities between the rich and the poor. In response to my question about how long a job search in her community would take, Shanté offered this:

> SHANTÉ: That? Man, a long time! Like, I think it'd be like three months, maybe even longer. I know my brother been lookin' for a job for the past year.
>
> RM: Wow. What causes it to take so long?
>
> SHANTÉ: First it's 'cuz we Black. They thinkin' we gonna steal from their store and then we ... most Black people out here use drugs and they drug test at most companies now, so the drug test really get people

off 'cuz if you can't pass your drug test you not gonna be able to get no job. The process is way longer.

RM: And would you say that's a lot different for white folks when they look for jobs?

SHANTÉ: Yeah . . . like, a lot of my white friends, we apply for the same job and they got the call the next day and I never got called.

Shanté's account of searching for work as a Black youth provokes an important question: Who is stealing from whom? Shanté claims that store owners racially profile her and other Black youths as possible thieves. To what extent, though, are employers taking Black applicants' time through countless hurdles including drug tests, unnecessary background checks, personality tests, and other dilatory tactics, all of which is uncompensated time? Before Shanté's time is taken, it must first be devalued in relation to the time of her white counterparts. Shanté's time, however, is not worthless but highly lucrative to employers who require Black and other racialized youths to generate a "diverse group of candidates" from which to reject or selectively recognize in order to fulfill their neoliberal multiculturalist agenda. In the words of Michael Hardt and Antonio Negri, "Every difference is opportunity."[12]

Whether three months is an average estimate for finding work is beside the point. Shanté sees opportunities for Black youths to achieve key life course transitions as significantly different from those of white youths. When employment discrimination lengthens the time that youths spend searching for work, time itself does not increase. As the time to find work lengthens, deadlines to meet basic needs shorten. In other words, racialization and racism not only take time but compress it. In the following exchange, Devon illustrates the material consequences of temporal dispossession for members of his community. I also asked him how long it takes someone his age to find work in his community:

DEVON: In my community it can take up to a couple weeks up to a month.

RM: Would you say that's a long time?

DEVON: Yeah. I mean, definitely . . . yeah. It's definitely a long time. . . . Because, well, people in my community, the reason why kids in my community get jobs is because their family life is struggling. And so if you're waiting a few weeks to a month, by the time you even get your job your lights could be off, your . . . you could be evicted . . .

As Devon shows, with each unit increase in the time spent seeking work, there is a significant decrease in the remaining time to meet basic needs for survival.

There is then a concomitant increase in the possibility of greater suffering among those already economically and temporally dispossessed. For many families living in poor urbanized space, financial and temporal dispossession is not a new, but a persistent, situation marked by several situational imperatives. Devon's answer illustrates how electric bills and rent payments cannot wait even though opportunities for employment take their time and whatever time poor families allegedly "have."

Constructions of Black people in urbanized space as languishing in time due to a lack of motivation and orientation to the future ignore the presence of dispossessing forces. Whether waiting on a job, waiting on an education, or waiting for service, "racial time" and "white time" are designed to wear Black people down. Several youths described disparate experiences between white and Black youths in their search for a job. After recounting what happened when she and her white foster sister applied for the same job at Dairy Queen, Kendra estimated that it takes Black youths about two months to find a job.

> RM: Does that seem like a long time?
> Kendra: Sort of. Because I . . . have a foster sister and she's white and . . . we both got an application to Dairy Queen and I put mine in and she put hers in, but she's the only one that got an interview back. So I guess it also depends on what color you are.
> RM: I'm sorry to hear that. Did this happen just recently? Did she get the job too?
> Kendra: Yeah, she got it.

Kendra expresses dismay knowing she must work significantly harder than her white counterparts to get half as far. While it is unclear why Dairy Queen chose to hire Kendra's white foster sister over her, other youths found themselves in similar situations. Lamont, for example, shared a way of testing for racialized bias when searching for work with white friends. I asked him whether he ever feels racially profiled.

> Lamont: Yeah, by the police and in jobs.
> RM: And how so?
> Lamont: Like . . . like every day, really. You know what I'm sayin'? If I was to walk down the street at nighttime, like ten or eleven o'clock, pretty sure I'd be gettin' pulled over again sayin', "Walkin' up to no good." You go to a job, you know what I'm sayin', and tryin' to, you know, just look like a regular person. [Employers] sayin' you probably look like a drug dealer to them; you know what I'm sayin'. They

look at you like, "He's *really* tryin' to apply here?" You wouldn't even get the call. So it's racially profile. I done walked up to plenty of restaurants: "Are you guys hiring?" They tell me no, then my [white] friend go ask. They tell him yes and then, you know what I'm sayin', I just be sittin' there lookin' like, "That's bogus!" You get the job but I can't. And, like, my mom used the term "Keisha doesn't get the call before Kimberly," you know. Like, the white girl gets the call before Keisha. You know. And that's how I been lookin' at it lately. Every time I try to go get a job or somethin', you know what I'm sayin', I do it on purpose. Like I said, I got white friends. So I go first, like I wanna see what they, you know, give it to me. I go up there like, "You guys hirin'?" Some jobs . . . they say "We hirin'," [and] give me an application and everything. . . . But my white friends, they be havin' jobs. Jobs call them back-to-back. I can't get one job. Like, it's harder. You know what I'm sayin'.

RM: Yeah, that's a messed-up situation. That's a real situation too. I've heard people having to change their name on applications . . . to use a white person's name—

LAMONT: [*Finishing my sentence*] —just for them to get the call. . . . And so after [learning] my name's Lamont, they don't know if I'm Black or white. They're like, "I wanna meet this guy." They finally meet me, you know what I'm sayin', they like, "Oh, he's Black. I'm not gonna call him back." It done happen like that before too.

RM: When you think about that . . . I can imagine it's frustrating. And . . . does it take up a lot of time for you to have to think about this on the regular?

LAMONT: Yes. I shouldn't even think about it. I should be, you know what I'm sayin', thinkin' about . . . I should be gettin' a job. It shouldn't be that hard, like, pretty sure there's a point in time where they [employers] didn't have no work history or anything like that, you know what I'm sayin'. And they goin' in and they got a job. Why can't I go in and get a job? Maybe I'll be a good fit for this job or somethin', you know. They won't give me a chance, it's crazy. It does take up more time thinkin' about it then, you know what I'm sayin'.

The time to find work for Lamont is protracted not only because of delays in callbacks, but due to the extra time spent over wrestling with the ontological question of why "Keisha doesn't get the call before Kimberly." Though this book resists the urge toward positivist sociology, I feel there is a useful opportunity to play with some of the criteria required to establish causality in experimental research. The three criteria include (1) correlation or association between the independent and dependent variables, (2) temporal order, and (3) nonspuriousness. Let us assess the extent to which Lamont's mother's claim that "Keisha doesn't get the call before Kimberly" meets such criteria. First, we can assume correlation in that Kimberly—a presumed white person—has an easier time finding a job than Keisha. Second, it seems that we can establish temporal order in that the cause (i.e., Kimberly's whiteness) comes before the effect (i.e., a job). Establishing that Kimberly finding a job before Keisha is nonspurious is a bit more challenging. Still, there is overwhelming evidence that white applicants are far more likely to find a job than their Black counterparts.[13] It is far too easy to play with sociological logic in this way. Perhaps there is way of thinking about temporal order more expansively when it comes to Keisha's and Kimberly's disparate experiences searching for work. What if "temporal order" referred not to the need to establish that a cause precedes the effect, but instead to a recognition of the overarching logic governing the distribution of time and opportunity? It is temporal order that ensures that Kimberly will always come before Keisha and thus remain on time and up to date.

"Processing time" consumes an inordinate amount of time that most Black youths already lack. Lamont knows that racism results in temporal costs for Keisha while giving Kimberly a temporal advantage. As illustrated in the previous sections, racialized bias in schooling and racial profiling in searches for employment are alike. Consider Lesko's description of adolescence as "a crucial point at which an individual (and a race) leaped to a developed, Western selfhood or remained arrested in a savage state."[14] Lesko helps substantiate this point through a critique of recapitulation theory:

> Within the framework of recapitulation theory, adolescence was deemed a crucial divide between rational, autonomous, moral, white, bourgeois men and emotional, conforming, sentimental, or mythical others, namely primitives, animals, women, lower classes, and children. Adolescence became a social space in which progress or degeneration was visualized, embodied, measured, and affirmed. In this way adolescence was a technology of "civilization" and progress and of white, male, bourgeois supremacy.[15]

When the life course is overrepresented as white, bourgeois, and male, it only makes sense that the social institutions designed to nurture both adolescence and adolescents would inevitably privilege some youths at the expense of others. Not only were Black youths rendered illegible within the concept of the Child, but they also failed to meet eligibility criteria established by recapitulation theory. Being denied not only coevalness but also access to the category of adolescence left many Black youths at Run-a-Way beginning from behind. Delayed starts, though, were the result of structural, not individual, failure.

Many Black youths know what it means to live, learn, and labor in setups—systems designed to fail. The schoolhouse, (s)low-wage work opportunities, and other racial enclosures are predicated on exploitation, extraction, symbolic and structural violence, and temporal harm. Being "held back" or "left back" in school. Being denied coevalness in their curriculum and their classrooms. Watching Kimberly get a job before Keisha. Being the last hired and first fired after finding employment. Working twice as hard to get half as far. These are all examples of temporal harm that leave Black youths suspended in time and consistently beginning from behind. So how can anyone expect them to abide by a time that does not abide by them? Why should they be in a hurry to be put on perpetual pause?

5

TABANCA TIME

In this chapter, I aim to funk the clock by funking with the temporal pace of this book. I do so by entering what I describe as an interminable interlude in *tabanca* time.[1] In Trinidad and Tobago, *tabanca* refers to a painful feeling of unrequited love, from loving someone, particularly a former lover or spouse, who does not love in return. A tabanca is not induced strictly by romantic relationships. In fact, it is no coincidence that tabanca rates seem to skyrocket toward the end of Trinidad carnival. The soca artiste Bunji Garlin details the symptoms of tabanca in his song "Carnival Tabanca," while bemoaning the thought of having to wait an entire year before carnival returns. Without festival, Garlin and other feters are more susceptible to a host of symptoms, including fever. These symptoms only intensified during COVID-19. Many hopeful revelers suffered from acute feelings of loss and longing in the absence of J'ouvert, fete, bacchanal, and any opportunity to "jump up," "wave up," "free up," "break way," "ramajay," "pelt waist," and/or "get on bad."

Like Garlin, I too have a tabanca. It is not a tabanca for *time*, but for *who and what* time has taken. What follows is more than a disclosure—it is, in truth, an exercise in time travel and part of a retroactive healing process. This exercise may do little to alter the course of time. Still, there is something generative within any refusal to allow linear progress narratives to proceed when so many poor and racialized subjects are attempting to reckon with racialized violence that allegedly resides in the past. So as white time urges so many to "get over it" and "put the past behind you" (despite the past seeming to lie ahead), I will take this opportunity to linger in tabanca time: a melancholic state located in what Michel-Rolph Trouillot calls "pastness"—which is not independent of the present.[2]

My biography informs my scholarship, but I do not treat my biography *as* scholarship. My hesitation to treat my biography as empirical evidence emanates not from concern over the pressures to remain "objective" or "neutral" or uphold similar racialized world-making logics. Rather, I am apprehensive about perpetuating the interpellation of Blackness through abjection and making my pain fungible and thus what Saidiya Hartman terms a "conduit for identification."[3] Here I am referring to the way in which empirical evidence is so often privileged over experience and embodied knowledge. As Renato Rosaldo writes, "By invoking personal experience as an analytical category one risks easy dismissal."[4] It is worth noting that incorporating aspects of one's biography is regarded by some as an acknowledgment of positionality and evidence of reflexivity. Like Rosaldo, I "make no claims for neutrality, detachment, and impartiality."[5] As Gloria Anzaldúa reminds us, "In trying to become 'objective,' Western culture made 'objects' of things and people when it distanced itself from them, thereby losing 'touch' with them. This dichotomy is the root of all violence."[6] My hope is to avoid such pitfalls and instead help expand a critique of time through an assessment of another source of time theft—namely, migration and deportation. I treat this chapter as an interminable interlude, a perpetual and ongoing "break." Deported time is one such break. Postremoval there is no resumption of family relations. There is no opportunity to "catch up." In fact, "catching up" is a misnomer because it presumes that the temporal coordinates of family relations can be charted linearly on a spatial plane that has not already been dissolved by deportation.

Deportation did not emerge as a theme in any part of my fieldwork. I do not seek to create a (false) equivalence between my father's story and the experiences of the youths at Run-a-Way. Instead I seek to funk with the pace and space of this book by resisting the teleological aims of writing and storytelling. I do not come from an academic lineage or socioeconomic privilege. Though my parents do not have any letters behind their names, they still taught me more than those that do. Despite the toxic culture of individualism permeating the university, I learned that "life is a mission [pronounced *mē-shän*], not no competition [pronounced *kōm-pē-tē-shän*]." Such sayings were uttered by my father and modeled by him and my mother. For most of our upbringing she held us down by working in local bookstores and what, back in the day, we called "health food stores." By contrast, my father dodged "legitimate" work before I was born. Before I came on the scene, my auntie Sandra helped sponsor my father's passage from Trinidad to Boston in the late 1970s. He made the journey with barely a secondary-school education (the equivalent of some high school in the United States).

Even though my dad had few "legitimate" jobs as an adult, he was quite a diligent child. On nonschool days, he and his brothers would work from six in the morning until six in the evening. They traveled over the Churchill-Roosevelt highway by way of donkey cart to harvest cabbage, *bhagi* (a kind of spinach), *baigan* (eggplant), *okroe* (ochra), *dasheen bush* (taro leaf), and bok choy, which they later sold in the croisee in San Juan. Farming on an island, though, was not the best job to list under "previous work experience," especially in the concrete jungle of Boston. Still, my dad managed to find work as a porter at a hotel in downtown Boston. My mom worked at a nearby bookstore in Copley Square, and they met on the subway, or the "T"—specifically the Orange Line.

At that time, my father was merely "service," not a "service worker." When white guests bemoaned the long wait for their bags, they rendered the carrier of the bags (i.e., my father) illegible and thus dysselected from the category of human. Sheraton management regularly conflated my father's ontological status with guests' *property*. As a natty dreadlocks who preached self-reliance, my father soon grew tired of, in his words, "making white people rich" (mind you, my mother is white). He knew that if he "applied himself" he could transgress time by making in a single day what many white bosses made in a week. Lacking both the prospects of advancement and personhood as a porter, my father decided to "fire de wuk" and began selling weed throughout the streets of Boston.[7]

My dad did dirt where he lived and moved through places like Dorchester, Roxbury, Mattapan, Hyde Park, and Mission Hill as if he were raised there and not in the economically depressed villages within San Juan. In the wake of increasing violence in the early 1990s, Boston's racialized enclosures acquired new names such as "Deathchester," "Glocksbury," and "Murderpan." As ominous as these labels sound, they were not hyperbole. Though my father only sold weed, he still posed a threat to competitors. The dangers of "pumping" any "product" in Boston in the early '80s proved dangerous to the dealer and those closest to them. Once my father's name started ringing bells, his rivals responded with stickups, making threats to my mother's life, and violating the code of the street.

Beyond the dangers of the fast life, Roxbury was literally on fire throughout the '80s and early '90s. In 1981, Roxbury's Highland Park neighborhood was deemed "the Arson Capital of the World."[8] The culprits? Gentrifying forces and predatory landlords. Property owners found a simple solution to reconcile increasing property values with the actual incomes of current residents: they could set their own properties ablaze and collect the liability insurance. In *Streets of Hope: The Rise and Fall of an Urban Neighborhood*, Peter Medoff and Holly Sklar document not only attempts to gentrify Roxbury, but also residents' organizing efforts in response to such destructive forces.[9] Explaining how arson became an opportunity for landlords to cash in on the suffering of poor people, Medoff and Sklar

128   **CHAPTER 5**

write, "A fire is of financial benefit to the developer . . . because: 1) it drives out low-income residents without the cost of waiting for attrition and without the potential political resistance to mass evictions, 2) it does the work of gutting the building for rehabilitation, 3) insurance provides tax-free, interest-free financing for the rehabilitation of the structure."[10]

Blocks in Roxbury were hot in more ways than one. Though my father maxed out (in height) at five feet five inches, his reputation in the streets kept growing and his hustling drew the ire of many enemies, including the police. He would eventually get "caught up" and was regularly arrested for attempting to survive in spaces where social life and social death coexist and sometimes compete. My mother told me a story about my father being arrested on Cambridge Common while my brother, Ja-Ja, and I were playing in a sandbox. According to my mom, someone asked my father for weed, but he ignored the request. My mother warned him not to sell the guy anything because he was a cop. The dude was persistent, though, so my father eventually made the transaction. Before they could return to their lunch on the Common, my parents found themselves surrounded by police. The entire incident must have lasted only a few minutes, as my brother and I were still doing our kid thing and were largely unaware of what had just gone down. Whenever the police arrested my father and identified him as just "Black," my mother expressed confusion and frustration that they did not acknowledge his Indian ancestry. When she brought the discrepancy to his attention, my father did not respond. The classification was only further confirmation of who he was/is.[11]

As we grew older, my brother and I learned that a "nine-to-five" was not the only way to stay alive. At the same time, my father's line of work was not appropriate for show-and-tell or bring-your-parent-to-school day. So we learned to lie. And we were nice at it. We were young, but we still knew the code of the street. So when my elementary school teachers would bring actual police into class in an attempt to desensitize all the poor Black and brown children to cops, I knew "Officer Friendly" was suspect. He would try to convince us to drop a dime but failed to recognize that we were ahead of our time and time itself. My father's fictitious jobs tended to rotate between plumber, construction worker, and artist. In fact, under "Father's Occupation," my birth certificate still reads "Artist." "Plumber" was almost true. Although my father did not finish secondary school in Trinidad, he did come close to completing a trade program in plumbing. My mother supplied plumbing textbooks to try to pull him away from the streets, but he had little patience for books that seemed to take time without offering anything in return. I am certain my father would have found a way to funk the clock as a plumber or an artist. Still, the opportunity to defy time and the state simultaneously was one he could not pass up.

My mother and father separated when I was two years old and Ja-Ja was one. We remained in Boston for a few more years, though, seeing my father whenever possible. My mom still came through for my dad whenever he was in a jam, but she would eventually reach her limit. Concerned that she would be unable to keep us safe from the streets and the state, my mom decided to move to Providence, Rhode Island. During our elementary school years, she would drive Ja-Ja and I to Dorchester to spend weekends with Dad. Once we hit middle school, my brother and I were able to make the trip on our own by bus. We would arrive at Back Bay Station and end up waiting for some sign of my father coming up Dartmouth Street in a car often different from the one he had driven during the previous visit.

"I Deh Ya!"

My father never wore a watch, but he always seemed to know what time it was. Knowing the time, though, did not mean he was on it. The traditional nine-to-five was not my father's gig. Instead he hustled from sunup to sunset, sometimes with us present. There was no time to *lime*.[12] Still, when people would call demanding to know where he was at, he usually responded by saying, "I deh ya" (I'm [t]here). Perhaps he truly believed that "any time is Trinidad time."[13] Once our impatience got the best of us, my brother and I would call or page Dad from a pay phone at Back Bay. When we eventually got ahold of him, he had the nerve to kick the same bullshit line to us, telling us he was "deh ya." In actuality, he was probably still in the hood and on the grind. Is it ironic that clockers funk the clock?[14]

Ja-Ja and I usually calibrated our spatial and temporal orientations according to our father's presence or absence. Sometimes it felt as if our father was cool with leaving us alone but had a harder time parting ways with the streets. Many mornings, we would wake to find ourselves by ourselves at my father's crib. At first we were both concerned, but eventually we learned to adapt to our pop's part-time presence. So, too, did my sister Amina and my brother Noah. Although we were not raised in the same homes, we all grew accustomed to the fact that my father was not always "deh ya," but like the Spinners sang, he was around.

The Transmutation of Space and Time

My father started living fast around the same time Randy Crawford started singing about the "street life" in her song of the same name.[15] Crawford sings that you can "run away from time," but that does not mean time won't catch up. Perhaps my father thought he could forever funk the clock and perhaps remain forever young. Time did not let my father get very far once he transgressed it. Instead, time held a grudge and sought revenge through space—specifically, containment in carceral space. Despite what some may think, selling herb in urbanized space is not easy. Living the fast life meant that my father was restive and rarely at (his) rest. Instead he was often held captive in the prison-industrial complex—a key site of temporal dispossession and domination. Communicating with my father through collect calls or a glass wall at South Bay Correctional Facility or Nashua Street Jail should have been intolerable but instead became banal.

I had a hard time reckoning with the metamorphosis of the space surrounding Nashua Street Jail, which changed from a place of excitement to a key site of incommensurable agony and impossible healing. You see, the jail was just under a half mile from the Museum of Science, Boston—a regular field trip site for kids in Providence and Boston public schools. Changes to the spatio-temporal location of schooling are something that many public school kids welcome, especially if they were learning in Providence public schools in the mid-'90s. There was a time when I felt warmed by the sight of the Charles River, the Charlestown High Bridge (now the Zakim Bridge), or the Museum of Science because I knew I was a little closer to my father. The enchantment did not last long, though. Maybe it was the fact that from the right vantage point, I could look across the Charles River, see Nashua Street Jail, be reminded of my father's time there, and know there were many other people like him still there for doing what they had to do to survive in Roxbury, Dorchester, Mattapan, Hyde Park, Jamaica Plain, Mission Hill, and other racial enclosures outside Boston.

The Museum of Science was not the only space that acquired a new and sobering meaning. In addition to weekend visits to the jailhouse, we also spent a lot of time at Dorchester District and Roxbury Municipal Courts. As a kid, I was unable to recognize the incongruity of a site of Black social death adjacent to a center of Black social life: namely, Dudley Square. Still, for many children, there is something intriguing about being in a majority-adult space that feels both serious and sobering. It was as if we had transgressed kid space to sneak a peek into the future. Unfortunately, the preview was not as promising as we would have hoped. I never really liked the inside of the courtroom. I was more interested in the murals on the walls outside, which sometimes served colorful camouflage used to conceal the structural violence within. Even at a young age, I knew that any courthouse filled with mostly Black and brown bodies made the legal system a primary site of racialized violence and captivity. Though my father did time, his time was never done. As much as he tried to funk the clock, the hands of time have a long reach, and they would eventually catch up with him.

Deported Time

Just as there are consequences for using time that does not belong to you, there are juridical protocols established to punish those for unauthorized use of space/land that does not belong to them. My father violated both temporal and spatial boundaries. As a result, the border followed my father's family as soon as they crossed it.[16] It followed them to Dorchester, Roxbury, and other poor urbanized spaces in Boston. The border maintained close lines of communication with Boston police and reminded officers to presume my father and uncles guilty until proven less guilty. In 1996, under the guise of "good border control," Immigration and Naturalization Services (INS) deported my father. The last time he was arrested in this country was around the start of 287(g) agreements that enabled the INS to cooperate with local police and round up "bad migrants." My father was the one that many immigrant-rights activists had in mind when chanting, "We are not criminals." In turn, "law abiding," "hardworking," and "desirable" migrants and their advocates esteemed themselves and their worth at my father's expense. As Lisa Cacho writes, "Because undocumented immigrants are marked as indelibly 'illegal' across various institutions, mobilizing support for undocumented immigrants' rights requires negotiating accusations of criminal intent. . . . By appealing to the needs of family members, immigrant rights advocates and their sympathizers attempt to lessen the perception of undocumented immigrants' criminal culpability by emphasizing their commendable commitments to their families."[17] I would eventually learn how the INS and its successor, Immigration and Customs Enforcement (ICE), came to be key regulators of time and temporal redistribution. In privileging the "good" migrants over the "bad" ones, INS and ICE increased the time of "lawful permanent residents" through the expedited removal of those deemed "unlawful."[18]

The last moment of coevalness I shared with my father in this country was when he was being escorted out of a courtroom in the John F. Kennedy Federal Building in Government Center. I was fourteen years old at the time. My mother and Ja-Ja were also present. None of us, including Amina and Noah, had a chance to say goodbye, show any type of affection, or say anything to my father that might preempt the perpetual pain inflicted by deportation and deported time. Instead we watched our father escorted out of the courtroom through double doors in an orange jumpsuit, chains around his ankles, waist, and wrists. Damn, I've been betrayed. Orange was supposed to be my favorite color. It was hard, though, to feel betrayed by a system that never cared for me and my father in the first place. Still, I could not help but wonder what kind of wretched system would deny a child the chance to hug, kiss, or even touch his parent before they are forever banned from the only place the child knew to be their home. Most

132 CHAPTER 5

survivors of the terror of *la migra* know that deportation is a process, not an event.[19] The aftermath of deportation belies a specific temporal location. It was then and there, here and now, and awaits so many of us in the not-yet-here.

Deportation requires time and space to collaborate in highly malicious ways to ensure that the deportee remains suspended in space and time. The absence of a loved one creates an unwanted space, specifically a void. This emptiness, though, is as temporal as it is spatial. For example, without him inside it, my father's crib on Humboldt Avenue Was hollow and devoid of coevalness. Postremoval train rides on the "T" required traversing not just space but time as well.[20] And despite being hemmed in by other riders, I remained unaccompanied in my spatio-temporal journey. Parks were not what they used to be. Rather than remaining a place of play, Malcolm X Park became the site of psychic violence. Any attempt to hoop would require me to go back in time and retrace my father's footsteps through the park's deepest recesses and most discreet paths to the secret spot where he would enter his "heavens" and "hold a meditation." Though I would not take my first sociology course for another six years, the "familiar" was quickly becoming "strange." But the familiar was made strange not by the sociological imagination, but by deportation.

Postremoval, families and children of the deportees are left wondering how to move forward when deportation puts life on pause. Is it possible to make up for time that is taken rather than lost? What strategies help to maintain relationship continuity with the incarcerated and deported?[21] Some may try to reassure those directly impacted by incarceration and deportation that time will heal all wounds. But how can time heal the same wounds it is complicit in inflicting? Is the rapper Nature right when he says, "The foulest thing about time, it still ticks when you're gone"?[22] Perhaps. It was quite clear that time had no problem ticking once my father was gone. Postremoval, I often felt that each tick (of the clock) brought another lick.[23] How could time proceed so mercilessly and act with such impunity, as if it were not complicit in the evisceration of such a central spatio-temporal organizing part of our lives?[24]

Despite my wanting to treat this chapter as an interlude, deported time exceeds containment within an interstice. Postremoval, there is no "picking up where we left off." There is only the obliteration of relations and the constant fumbling to pick up the pieces of what was. We would occasionally send my father and uncles barrels through local Caribbean shipping companies in Boston. Even though the barrels were filled to the brim with appliances, tools, clothes, and food not available in Trinidad, it was hard not to see them as only half full. Visits to T&T left a similar void and, in truth, only increased my anxiety and feelings of guilt. My father would always remind us to come and "check" him (or pay him a visit). He saw other deported fathers lose connection with their children in "foreign" and did not want us to forget about him.

When visiting my father, I was always extremely conscious of how to "use" time. As eager as I was to have a heartfelt conversation with my dad, it never felt that easy. Even as his child, I always had a hard time seeing him as approachable. When we asked him questions, he would pretend as if he did not hear us and simply remain silent. We were so intimidated that we refrained from asking the same question twice. This meant that most of the burning questions I wanted to ask were ironically placed on the back burner until the day before I left Trinidad or the half-hour car ride to the airport at five in the morning. I was young but empathetic. I knew that unloading all that was heavy on my mind, conscience, and heart would increase whatever burden my father was carrying. How could I disclose decades' worth of experiences within the span of a half-hour ride to an airport? Who would be there to help my father carry the hefty weight of emotions, ideas, and questions once he dropped me off and began the drive back to the ghetto? I have never heard my father describe himself as depressed. But he didn't have to tell it because it showed through his stoicism. I have seen my father cry only once. It was when I told him how I felt about his loyalty to the fast life. I told him that it felt like he put the streets and hustling before his family. I expressed frustration over knowing that he got to play the fun parent role, while my mother had to do the more challenging work of checking us on our misbehavior and making sure we were clothed, fed, and sheltered, all while holding on to the anxiety of whether she could keep us safe.

As I grew older, though, I became even more cautious about confronting my father. I tried to put myself in his position, without obliterating his suffering, and imagined what it must feel like to be so alone.[25] Deportation is a form of punishment that takes on a sort of autopoietic character as deportees are left to question their integrity and their personhood.[26] There is a sense of total powerlessness when the state forcibly removes a loved one through incarceration, deportation, and/or killing and then inflicts further pain through surveillance and retaliation against that person's family. Still, unloading my feelings on my father began to feel far too selfish. I knew he would not speak to anyone. He rarely, if ever, goes to the doctor, and therapy is nearly an anomaly in Trinidad. I had to hold the hefty weight of wondering how my father would react if I were to try and communicate the extraordinary pain and anguish I felt after his deportation. Would he dig himself into further isolation? I could vent to loved ones, but who would he talk to? Would he stop writing me letters? Would he stop calling? Would he lose an appreciation for life? Deportation left all these questions unanswered because I was too afraid to ask.

In the wake of my father's deportation, time inflicted greater pain through space (or the absence of it). Not being able to share space with my father meant that we could not share time. In fact, racialized violence took whatever time we allegedly had, through phone taps, tampered and stolen mail, the letter S on customs declaration forms (I assume the single or multiple Ses refer to some form of "selective screening," similar to the four Ses found on boarding passes, which stand for Secondary Security Screening Selection), sliced-up suitcases (presumably part of the Transportation Security Administration's "random" search process), being placed on "restricted" fly lists, and interrogations and detainment at the border. Racialized surveillance is another form of time theft. Due to my father's fear of being monitored, most phone calls to him remain largely unintelligible and end with an abrupt hang-up. One of the most torturous effects of deportation is subscribing to Michael Hardt and Antonio Negri's claim that "there is no outside."[27] I remain uncomfortable disclosing too much information in handwritten letters or when speaking to my father by phone. Such experiences are more evidence of the impossibility of revisiting the past. There is no "making up for lost time," precisely because time was never lost in the first place. It was stolen, along with my father.

With age came new ways of analyzing my father's removal. I wondered about the inadequacy of "cruel irony" to describe what it means to be deported for selling what is now "decriminalized" and legal in most US states, including Massachusetts. My father never referred to what he did as "crime." He called it "survival." Saidiya Hartman's engagement with Du Bois's notion of "open rebellion" illustrates the transmutation of survival strategies into "crime": "What was crime, but *the open rebellion of an individual against his social environment? There was a widespread feeling that something was wrong with a race that was responsible for so much crime and that strong remedies were called for.* Yet, how could they not rebel against the circumstances that made it impossible to live?"[28] If my father's hustling lifestyle was an act of rebellion against "circumstances that made it impossible to live," why was he removed? Why were there no retroactive clauses to pardon him and others whose survival strategies were transmuted into "criminal activity"? Like most Rastafari, he maintained that ganja was the "healing of the nation." So why did my father's past take precedence over his prescience?[29] The fact that I have yet to receive a "reasonable" answer to these questions is only greater evidence of the violent history of reason and the blanket immunity granted to progressive time as it marches onward, trampling over the multiply marginalized and dysselected.

The collusion between space and time sustains the prison-industrial complex and deportation regimes. So as I strive to think about ways to funk the clock, I must also think critically about the importance of transgressing space, including borders, jails, and prisons. When time comes to serve not only as a measurement device but also as a tool to protract pain, resistance to time becomes irresistible. As much as I have attempted to make space and let my biography inform my scholarship, there are so many stories left untold. It is easy to assume that returning someone to their country of origin marks the culmination of the removal process. But just as the border followed my father when he entered the United States, it passed the baton to immigration authorities in Trinidad, reminding us that deportation is a process and not an event. My father is still stopped, frisked, and shaken down by T&T police. During one of my previous visits, we were flagged three times in one trip at police roadblocks. After we were ordered out of Dad's Nissan Sunny, police searched the car and us, while other officers looked on, tightly gripping their machine guns strung over their chests. They were holding their weapons so tight you would have thought the guns were trying to escape.

One of the worst encounters with police took place during the one trip that all my father's children were on together for the very first time. We were on our way back from a river in St. Joseph when a jeep filled with police passed in the opposite direction. Each of the five officers maintained ice grills at each one of us as they passed. In Trinidad, it is fairly customary for drivers to greet one another, when passing on roads so tight that driver's-side mirrors must be pulled in to avoid being broken off. I do not recall my father offering such a greeting to the officers, though. The officers' scowls communicated everything my father needed to know about what was to come. Less than a minute after the police passed, they turned around and were right behind us. The cops sounded the siren and pulled us over as if we had just been in a high-speed chase, rather than driving ten miles per hour down a dirt road. They jumped out of the jeep with their guns drawn on all of us. By that time, most of us were accustomed to the shakedown. Most people who have been confronted by cops know that police are experts at asking the same condescending question in as many ways as possible. "Rastaman, yuh have any drugs in de vehicle?" "I smellin' weed, rastaman. Yuh sure yuh ain't have nothing in de car?" "Raise de trunk, nah. Wuh yuh have deh?" Despite my father maintaining that he had nothing on him, the police continued questioning all of us. My father explained that we were all his children, visiting from "foreign," which is why we did not have any "ID cards" to present. Eventually the police let us go. The car was not the only thing left in disarray after the incident. Being humiliated, disrespected, and violated in front of all his kids left my father's ego, pride, and dignity in shambles. We spent the ride back to San Juan processing the violence and listening to our father's advice on how to comport ourselves when encountering police. Such incidents reminded us that "making up for lost time" with our father was both impossible and inaccurate. Our time was taken, not lost. So we should not be surprised when Dad still urges us to "teef time."

136 **CHAPTER 5**

The state's antipathy to my family did not begin or end with my father. Two of my uncles were also deported. One died tragically in 2011, five years after returning to Trinidad. Back in the United States, the devolution of the state and the evisceration of social services and educational and employment opportunities required other family members to carry on tradition and hustle hard. So in the spirit of neoliberalism and the need to create an entrepreneurial self, other loved ones took up the charge of "personal responsibility" by dabbling in the fast life. They did so not because they wanted to follow in my father's footsteps, but because legitimate opportunity structures never let them step foot in the door. So rather than remaining on the path of the straight and narrow, they choreographed insurgent temporal movements, including dipping and dodging, swerving, and sidestepping. They were not in any rush to be the last hired and first fired. They were in no hurry to be exploited by (s)low-wage work intent on taking their time and garnishing their wages. They were not about to make haste by working twice as hard to get half as far. And despite fatalistic conceptions of racialized youth in poor urbanized space, they were *not* in a rush to die. Instead they hustled to live.

6

TRANSGRESSING TIME IN
THE FAST LIFE

Thirteen of the thirty youths I interviewed at Run-a-Way participated in the fast life. Like "CP Time," "the fast life" was an antiquated term to which only a few of the youths could relate. "Trapping," which involves making, selling, and/or distributing drugs, proved to have far greater relevance. "Trap" has multiple meanings. It is commonly associated with the space (i.e., the trap house) used to make and prepare drugs for sale. "Trap" may also refer to the ghetto, a space that exists in relation to its mutually constitutive counterpart: the suburbs. Among the various status symbols associated with trapping and the fast life are drugs, cars, designer clothes, jewelry, vernacular dexterity, money, and weapons. According to Elijah Anderson, the fast life involves "living on the edge."[1] Disturbing as it may appear to those with legitimate opportunities for success, the fast life holds a captivating appeal for both prescient and present-oriented youths.[2]

To view the fast life as merely a legal transgression is to ignore its commitment to violating time. In this chapter, I conceive of the fast life as an example of insurgent time—a brazen act of defiance among racialized and dysselected groups toward (s)low-wage labor. The fast life presents lucrative opportunities outside planned-obsolescent systems. Because time is money, the fast life holds immense value, especially to those financially and temporally bankrupt. Youths surviving in racial enclosures have little patience for typical nine-to-five jobs that short-change them both financially and temporally. The fast life, however, is transitory, and the notion that those who live it will likely end up dead or in jail is widely accepted in poor urbanized communities. Still, the prospects of the fast life may prove more appealing to those tired of hearing that "slow money is better than no money." Slow money may be better than no money, but is it really better than fast money? Some may say yes. Black youths at Run-a-Way seem to say it's debatable.

As a sort of icebreaker to introduce the topic of time, I presented the youths with several time-related expressions and asked whether there was any particular saying that most resonated with them. "Time is money" was by far the most identifiable phrase among the youths I interviewed. The equation of time and money is not strictly linked to the need to address exigent circumstances. Black youths saw time as money because job opportunities were habitually late. I asked eighteen-year-old Finesse about the easiest way someone his age could earn money in his community.

> FINESSE: Sellin' drugs. That's the easiest. Unless you can finesse . . . I mean, I was blessed with a *real good* mouthpiece. I can talk my way into anything, you know, so it's like . . . you got like three choices. You can finesse your way into getting a job that's gonna pay you decent enough money to live on. You can sell drugs. You can rob people. And that's like, growin' up that was the types of people that I seen in my hood, you know.
>
> RM: So you talked about the easiest way—what would you say is the fastest way?
>
> FINESSE: Sellin' drugs. Definitely. Sellin' drugs or, for females . . . I mean, I guess for males too, sellin' your body if you know some people that are into that sort of thing.

To Finesse and several other youths at Run-a-Way, selling drugs was both the easiest and fastest route to earn money. Finesse identified three "choices" to make money. "Finessing" one's way into getting a job reflects Elijah Anderson's notion of "code switching,"[3] where poor and marginalized Black youths comport themselves according to largely white, middle-class norms and etiquette in order to safely and effectively navigate situations, contexts, and social institutions. What makes code switching distinct from "performances" and "fronts" is that the codes that youths switch between are highly racialized.[4] Hence, the "presentation of self" is a product of racialized scripts, including the one that measures Black youths using what W. E. B. Du Bois called "the tape of a world that looks on in amused contempt and pity."[5] "Overdetermined from the outside," in the words of Frantz Fanon,[6] Black youths must finesse their way into legitimate work, revealing the continuity of slavery within emancipation. Not all racialized youths, however, can finesse their way into legitimate opportunity structures. Members of this further dysselected category, according to Finesse, may find their way to the fast life.

When communities are designed to fail, it makes sense that some youths would characterize them as "maybe environments." Asked about the fastest way to earn money in his community, Lamont responded, "I say trap. Fast money."

"Why is that?" I asked.

> LAMONT: Because it's hard to get jobs out here now, you know what I'm sayin'. Well, even though it's like seasonal jobs right now, it's just still hard to get a job. You know what I'm sayin', if you don't have a high school diploma or GED you're not really finna' to get a good job, you know what I'm sayin'.
>
> RM: Do you feel like it's harder for certain youth than others?
>
> LAMONT: I say it's harder for Black, you know what I'm sayin', colored youth . . . you know, from experience. . . . It's more white people than Black people with jobs. And . . . I don't have a work history because I never worked. . . . I'm not tryin' to be racist or nothin', but plenty of white people . . . they had a job and worked since they were like fifteen, fourteen. So they'd get hired quicker than . . . a person that never had a job before.

Anticipating obstructions in attempts to earn a high school diploma or find a job leads many youths to find expedited paths to making money. Though only sixteen, Lamont doesn't need to guess who is the last hired and first fired. This asymmetrical-temporal relation between Black and white applicants and workers confirms his belief that white people remain employed far longer than their Black and other racialized coworkers.[7] The cyclical problem of seeking work without prior employment experience and *within* a job racket is a futile pursuit. The absence of conventional life course transitions engenders an alternative relationship to time and opportunity structures. While Shanté also identified selling drugs as the easiest way to earn money in her community, when asked about the fastest way, she said, "A faster way. Drugs, that's easy, but fast way: it would be sellin' yourself."

Shanté was one of three girls and one gender-nonconforming youth who alluded to having been sexually exploited and trafficked during their life course. Being in "the life" as a Black girl, femme, and/or trans, however, troubles existing analyses of the gendered dimensions of the life course,[8] because misogynoir is irreducible to either sexism or racism. Involvement in "the life" requires girls to spend an inordinate amount of time processing multiple forms of violence that exceed containment within the conceptual limitations of a transition or trajectory.[9] Life course scholars and criminologists conveniently avoid the role of state terror in shaping life course transitions and trajectories. Instead, arrest

140   CHAPTER 6

and incarceration become volitional life course transitions. When state terror punishes not just dissent but defense, survival strategies become liable to arrest and incarceration. Historically, police and sociologists have collaborated to create the exact crime they fight and study, *not* respectively.[10] Saidiya Hartman makes this point exceptionally clear by detailing how Black girls and women defied the linear life course through "wayward" acts:

> What the law designated as crime were forms of life created by young black women in the city. The modes of intimacy and affiliation being fashioned in the ghetto, the refusal to labor, the forms of gathering and assembly, the practices of subsistence and getting over were under surveillance by the police as well as sociologists and the reformers who gathered the information and made the case against them, forging their lives into tragic biographies of poverty, crime, and pathology. The activity required to reproduce and sustain life is, as Marx noted, a definite form of expressing life, it is an art of survival, social poesis. Subsistence—scraping by, getting over, making ends meet—entailed an ongoing struggle to produce a way to live in a context in which poverty was taken for granted and domestic work or general housework defined the only opportunity available to black girls and women.[11]

Hartman exposes the "open rebellion and beautiful experiments produced by young women in the emergent ghetto—a form of racial enclosure that succeeded the plantation."[12] How might selling drugs signify an "open rebellion" or "beautiful experiment" in refusing so-called equal opportunity, freedoms, rights, and liberties that serve more as a pretext for punishment than as pathways toward upward social mobility? Finesse, Lamont, Shanté, and several other youths maintained a clear vision of the particular way their life courses unfold and believed that selling drugs or selling themselves was the fastest and easiest way to earn money in their communities.

Given that transgressing time may involve expedited and potentially illegal survival strategies, what if, rather than viewing selling drugs as "going down the wrong path in life" or a "commitment to a life (course) of crime," there was greater acknowledgment of the level of resourcefulness among Black and other racialized youths forced to do more with less (time)? When forced to work twice as hard to get half as far, you "work smarter, not harder."[13] Constructions of Black and other racialized youths involved in the underground economy as impetuous ignores the unyielding pressures of time associated with beginning one's life course from behind. I argue that youths' involvement in the underground economy is not only a legal transgression but a temporal one as well. Because of the dilatory payoff associated with (s)low-wage labor, the insurgent time of the fast life is a competitive substitute for the typical nine-to-five job. Prepared to begin a long and hard road filled with roadblocks, Black youths in urbanized space learn various shortcuts and detours along the life course. Some are efficient. Some are transgressive. Some exemplify both.

The Hard Road to a Fast Life (Course)

Educational enclosures and (s)low-wage work have little purchase for youths who read more as temporally consumable than as temporal consumers. The fast life helps bypass conventional sites of time theft by functioning as an "accelerated life course" with which the standard life course paradigm cannot keep pace.[14] Devon described the fast life this way. "The fast life? Well, where I grew up, the fast life was the person that sold the drugs, you know, had all the fancy cars and basically had a chance of dying at any moment because of what he did. That was the fast life. Because if you were in that type of business . . . your life was gonna end pretty quickly."

Devon associates the fast life with truncated life expectancies. To live the fast life is to abide by an insurgent time, one that rejects patience in favor of nowness. Mandated to work twice as hard to get half as far, Black youths participating in this underground economy prefer to work smarter, not harder. If Black youths must work twice as hard to get half as far, they have less time than their white counterparts. Working smarter and not harder gives them the opportunity to recoup their lost and stolen time. But the fast life is not a long-term solution for addressing the enduring forms of racialized violence over the life course.

The fast life is *fast*, hence its name. It is fast in the sense that it may not last. Fast-life pursuits therefore require special orientations to time. Acting according to perceived temporal positions is what Robert Merton calls "socially expected durations."[15] Merton contends that people make decisions based on the perceived length of experiences and their personal life expectancy. Socially expected durations serve a specific purpose for seniors and the terminally ill, who tend to calibrate their decisions based on perceptions of their own mortality. The possibility that Black youths in poor urbanized space hold similar socially expected durations as those approaching the end of life warrants concern and critique. What I wish to make clear is that participation in the fast life is both a survival strategy and a chance to defy social death—even if selling drugs accelerates actual mortality.

According to Richard Settersten, the pressure to meet certain developmental deadlines is more salient among marginalized youths whose life chances seem already "foreclosed."[16] Settersten finds that, in addition to other marginalized

142 **CHAPTER 6**

teens, Black and Latinx youths enter adult roles at earlier ages than their white counterparts.[17] What prompts earlier deadlines among nonwhite youths, however, remains absent from Settersten's analysis. Perhaps Black and other racialized youths are attempting to get a head start on "beating the odds" and defying the then and there of anti-Blackness and other forms of racialized violence. The fast life represents the most convenient and sometimes the sole detour along a hard road riddled with roadblocks. When I asked eighteen-year-old Finesse about who usually participates in the fast life, he paused and then said, "People that really got no other choice. I never heard nobody gettin' into [the] trap that wanted to be in the trap. You know? Nobody wakes up and is like, 'Hey, I'm gonna go sell some crack.'"

According to Finesse, structural violence inures people into the fast life. Questions surrounding youths' "motivations" for entering the fast life ignore their limited chances at life. In centering the experiences of racialized youths with state repression, Lisa Cacho adopts Orlando Patterson's concept of "social death" to describe a "desperate space, overwrought with and overdetermined by the ideological contradictions of ineligible personhood."[18] Cacho questions the utility of rights-based discourse for the "racialized" and "rightless"—those "ineligible to personhood," unprotected within the realm of deservingness and innocence and denied a right to life. In turn, "total powerlessness, natal alienation, and generalized dishonor," as Patterson puts it,[19] become life course constants for the "racialized" and "rightless."

Constructing the fast life, or trapping, as a crime ignores the importance it holds for those who rely on it as a survival strategy when conventional opportunities come slowly or not at all. Sean was more familiar with the notion of trapping. When I asked him to describe trapping, he broke it down this way: "Trapping is like you're from the trap. You're out there doin' what you have to do to make money and to live, what you've gotta do. That's like gangbanging, all type of stuff. It could even be sex trafficking. None of that is me." Though Sean himself does not trap, he recognizes that those who do are doing what they "have to do to make money and to live."

Trapping as a form of survival is no overstatement. In fact, when I attempted to have a heartfelt conversation with my father about his time in the fast life, I began by saying, "I know you sold weed to support us . . ." He immediately cut me off with a vexed response: "Ah ain't do dat to support you! Da'is wuh ah do to survive. Yuh ovahs [overstand]?"[20] My father's words left me feeling both hurt and intrigued. He did not mean to put me down or make me feel unimportant. Perhaps he was trying to prevent me from feeling as if I and my siblings were responsible for him selling weed. He did not want us to feel guilty or carry any burdens because of his deportation. Rather, he was trying to make clear that if he could not survive, neither could we. To diminish my father's claim that selling weed was survival is to deny the existence of those marked for social death. The "survival" my father referred to was different from trying to "make a living." He was referring to surviving the hunt, the hunter, and the threat of captivity.

The equation of crime and survival is not an exaggeration. As Steve Martinot notes,

> To continually remove a sizable number of people from a community in this way constitutes a massive disruption of its social coherence. . . . As a community gets the reputation for criminality, businesses close and leave, decreasing the possibilities for a communal economic life. A general financial obstruction of community asset accumulation ensues, leading to further impoverishment and misery. The "collateral damage" of this process is that crime itself actually becomes a major (if not the only) means of survival for those growing up under such forms of induced economic famine.[21]

My father was not about to die of "economic famine." He needed to eat and to ensure that his kids were also fed. He knew hustling guaranteed food on the table, while the American dream would surely leave him and us hungry. You can't eat dreams. Previous ethnographic research on the experiences of Black youth in urbanized space suggests that the American dream remains exclusive, elusive, and illusive.[22] In studying the experiences of Black teens in urbanized space, Linda Burton, Dawn Obeidallah, and Kevin Allison make the case that exigent needs and obstructed opportunities impair youths' vision of what is possible over their life course. In response, the authors argue that Black youths pursue a "revised American Dream" oriented toward the fast life.[23]

This revised American Dream features prominently in the chorus of "Fast Life" by Kool G. Rap and Nas.[24] In the song, the rappers signal an acute awareness of the American Dream and the need to still plot and scheme to achieve it. Kool G. Rap and Nas reveal that the fast life and the American Dream are not so much contradictory as complementary. Both concepts endorse neoliberal notions of the entrepreneurial self and prize investments in property. A key difference between the two is that the state reveres one and reproves the other. What makes the fast life transgressive is not just a connection to illegal activity but its threat to existing temporal and temporal-capital protocols for "success." Seeking faster routes to escape racialized enclosures and opportunities designed without you in mind requires a transgressive relationship to time.

When I asked Tanisha how long it takes kids her age to find a job, she recounted her brother's struggles to find legitimate work:

CHAPTER 6

> TANISHA: It depends on if you're experienced with the job or if it's your
> first time or if you've been fired a lot. But probably it'd take a month
> or at least two or three weeks.
>
> RM: Does that seem like a long time?
>
> TANISHA: Um, kinda. 'Cuz my brother . . . he was tryin' to . . . like, my
> sister was tryin' to help him find a better way and she got him a job
> with her at a Burger King and he decided to do it to stay out the
> streets but . . . they started him off with two hours a week. . . . And
> then they kept givin' him those hours and he was like, "I'd rather just
> keep doin' the same stuff I was doin' then just to come to a place for
> two hours and get paid like eight dollars or seven dollars an hour." So
> he stopped. And then he ended up in jail.

For Tanisha's brother, the fast life represented an appealing alternative to precarious labor, and when labor is precarious, time is precious. Tanisha's brother saw little incentive in working a job offering a negligible return on his temporal investment. To what extent did he perceive work in the streets as a greater temporal investment than time in the formal economy? Rather than seeing the fast life as a waste of time, perhaps youths like Tanisha's brother treat time as a highly coveted resource and optimize it by forgoing slow money in favor of more efficient and insurgent paths.

After reminiscing over their own fast-life ventures, "ol' heads" are quick to insist that "slow money is better than no money." But the dilatory procedural tactics of employers leave Black youths wondering, "How slow can they go?" Opportunities for slow money are either habitually late or nonexistent for Black youths in urbanized space. Given the legacy of slavery and its afterlife, equating "slow money" with "slave money" is not hyperbole. According to Paul Gilroy, "In the critical tradition of blacks in the West, social self-creation through labour is not the core of emancipatory hopes. For the descendants of slaves, work signifies only servitude, misery and subordination."[25]

Participation in the fast life serves as an opportunity for Black youths to revise their life course trajectories in accordance with demands to work twice as hard only to get half as far. The fast life, however, is not strictly a response to structural inequalities. Such dialectical interpretations of youth resistance obscure the role of desire and the pursuit of leisure in youths' decision to participate in the fast life. As Robin D. G. Kelley contends, "The pursuit of leisure, pleasure, and creative expression is *labor*, and . . . some African-American urban youth have tried to turn that labor into cold hard cash."[26] Kelley helps invert mainstream conceptions of labor and what is labeled "productive activity" for youth. The appeal of working less and achieving similar or greater levels of financial success as workers in the conventional labor market is an irresistible incentive, especially for youths with limited work experience.

Child development scholars treat a desire for immediate reward as "maladaptive" behavior and antithetical to "delayed gratification."[27] Others attribute demands for instant payoff to children's lack of "environmental reliability."[28] Both theories deny that delayed gratification is a racialized concept privileging white middle-class life.[29] In turn, scholars wield delayed gratification as a tool to scold "impatient" nonwhite youths for wanting, while ignoring the white youths who tease and taunt them with what they have so often been refused (e.g., symbols of wealth and privilege). Perhaps instant gratification signals poor youths' awareness of what is (not) to come.

I would be remiss not to acknowledge that participation in the fast life is not a defining life course transition for all Black youths in urbanized space. Still, the opportunity to make in one week what many people make in a month is a compelling proposition to those required to work twice as hard to get half as far. The mutually constitutive relationship between urbanized space and suburbanized space prompts consideration of how the fast life and conventional work opportunities are to a large degree codependent.[30] The fast life is predicated on the proliferation of jobs and youths' exclusion from them. Put differently, the slow, leisurely life course integral to the development of a white, suburbanized habitus depends on the evisceration of opportunity for many racialized subjects in poor urbanized space.

7

WHY IS THE TIME ALWAYS RIGHT FOR WHITE AND WRONG FOR US?

In *The Possessive Investment in Whiteness*, George Lipsitz alludes to a double meaning of "possessive." White people are not only possessive of whiteness but, according to Lipsitz, also predisposed to possession. That is, they are susceptible to being *possessed* by whiteness. "Possession," though, is just a few letters short of "dispossession." To what extent does a possessive investment in whiteness require a possessive investment in time and space? Without examining the extent to which possession requires dispossession, we place ourselves at risk of possession (i.e., being spellbound) by antirelational thought. In this chapter, I explore how Black youths at Run-a-Way interpret time in relation to whiteness and their assessments of white youth. To what extent do Black youths see their relationship to time as distinct from that of their white counterparts? Like race, whiteness is relational; hence, understanding how Black youths reckon with time also requires examining whether they perceive white youths doing the same. The effects of whiteness as a "condition," as Lipsitz puts it,[1] do not negate its potential to *condition* or harm nonwhite people.

The Temporality of Whiteness

In *Black Reconstruction in America*, W. E. B. Du Bois observed that white laborers, by dint of phenotype (and the social value ascribed to such a phenotype) benefited from a "public and psychological wage."[2] Du Bois's prescient formulation of whiteness paved the way for critical race theorists, critical whiteness theory, and countless sociologists to explore the way in which whiteness works as a set of power relations between poor white workers and their Black counterparts. By taking Du Bois's notion of a "wage" literally, David Roediger shows how poor white laborers capitalized on their whiteness while forfeiting the opportunity to forge alliances with their poor Black counterparts in favor of solidifying a higher position within a constructed racial hierarchy.[3] In offering allegiance to their capitalist bosses, poor white laborers failed to recognize that their class interests were more reflective of those they worked *with* (Black people) than those they worked *for* (white elites).[4] In short, poor whites were "tricked" by their own whiteness and the future orientation of white time.[5]

Cheryl Harris describes whiteness as a "consolation prize" that white people redeem in case of (nonwhite) emergency (i.e., ontological threats to the episteme).[6] Regardless of how challenging the stressors of life may be, white people will always be winners, precisely because whiteness is everywhere they want to be. Harris expands on the covetous relationship between whites and whiteness by suggesting that whiteness evolved "from color to race to status to property."[7] This is in part why Saidiya Hartman describes whiteness as an "incorporeal hereditament or illusory inheritance from chattel slavery."[8] It is what Hartman calls "the property of enjoyment." Referencing *Black's Law Dictionary*, she notes that to "enjoy" entails "the exercise of a right, the promise and function of a right, privilege or incorporeal hereditament. Comfort, consolation, contentment, ease, happiness, pleasure and satisfaction."[9] Whiteness provokes an orientation toward the future while ignoring the presence of the past, including the interminable "inheritance from chattel slavery." White people attempting to distance themselves from this inheritance are actively seeking to evade accountability for what Dionne Brand describes as the "cumulative hurt of others":

> Only the brazen can say, "I was not here, I did not do this and feel that." One hears that all the time in Canada; about what people feel they are and are not responsible for. People use these arguments as reasons for not doing what is right or just. It never occurs to them that they live on the cumulative hurt of others. They want to start the clock of social justice only when they arrived. But one is born into history, one isn't born into a void.[10]

It is clear that the clock of social justice is not synchronized to the time of slavery. The equation between time and money requires an acknowledgment of the temporal benefits that accrue concomitantly with the "wages of whiteness." As a public and psychological wage, whiteness provides both unconditional reassurance and insurance to whites, guaranteeing that even when times get tough, whiteness will be there. As Harris maintains, whiteness undergirds the "settled

148 CHAPTER 7

expectations of whites," which are legally affirmed through an anti-Black juridical system.[11] The unlimited protection of whiteness, according to Eduardo Bonilla-Silva, is subsidized by a "white habitus"—"a racialized, uninterrupted socialization process that *conditions* and *creates* whites' racial taste, perceptions, feelings and emotions and their views on racial matters." As a racial critique of "structuring structures," white habitus opens a window to whiteness.[12]

Similarly, "the white spatial imaginary" represents a cognitive frame entertained by sponsors of whiteness who describe affirmative action as "reverse racism," interpret personal success as a product of a strong, individualistic work ethic, and are generally more concerned with fairness, once the terms and conditions of existence for certain groups make fairness impossible. Within this solipsistic space, there is little room for self-interrogation of the structured advantages woven in whiteness. Personal successes and gains are then deemed "natural," ahistorical, and part of a "self-actualized achievement" as opposed to products of the institutionalization of whiteness in education, employment, housing, the criminal legal system, and public policy.[13] Despite its ubiquity, whiteness and its consequences remain hidden in plain sight.[14] This is partly why Charles Mills sees whiteness as a "political commitment to white supremacy. . . . Whiteness is not really a color at all, but a set of power relations."[15]

Though implied in critical whiteness scholarship, the temporal orientation of whiteness is not typically centered as a primary site of analysis. It is not enough to ask, "What is whiteness?" Like Michelle M. Wright's proposal for examining the physics of Blackness, perhaps there is a need to ask "when" and "where" whiteness is. In answering the "when" part of this question, countless scholars have established that whiteness signifies that which is future oriented and modern.[16] The "where" part of the question is more obvious given the white-supremacist context in which asymmetrical ontologies form. Sara Ahmed takes a phenomenological approach to studying the "what," "when," and "where" of whiteness and views it as the "what" that is "around."[17]

The phenomenologist Helen Ngo invokes Shannon Sullivan's conceptualization of "ontological expansiveness" to highlight the spatial and, by extension, temporal dimension of whiteness: "Similar to Sara Ahmed's thinking on a 'phenomenology of whiteness,' Sullivan looks at how white people tend to act and think as if all spaces—whether geographical, psychical, linguistic, economic, spiritual, bodily, or otherwise—are or should be available for them to move in and out of as they wish."[18] To fully apprehend the implications of ontological expansiveness, we must consider those consistently under threat of ontological reduction/dissolution. As shown in chapter 2, many Black youths must account for the fears and anxieties of white people. Not doing so makes them vulnerable to white violence. Not only do white people take up space, but their ontological expansiveness takes time from Black and other racialized people. In becoming more possessive of and possessed by whiteness, white people are simultaneously *dispossessing* nonwhite people of the chance to claim any spacetime for themselves.

Where many critical phenomenologists are concerned with "how whiteness is 'real,' material and lived," as Ngo puts it,[19] my intervention comes through an examination of how whiteness infringes on the time perspectives of Black youth relegated to a spatio-temporal abyss. The association between whiteness and future orientations explains the equation of Black youth in poor urbanized space with present orientations. As I demonstrate in chapter 8, however, rather than being a paralyzing force suspending youth in time, present orientations mark a site of nowness, in light of a prescient vision of what is to come. Remaining ahead of ~~their~~ time, the youths I worked with found ways to invert the temporal terms of whiteness and their own racialized-temporalized positions by depicting their white counterparts as cultural appropriators and behind what was most up to date. In the end, Black youths at Run-a-Way ensured that their temporalities were most culturally relevant, while casting whiteness into a "played-out" past.

This chapter not only intervenes in existing literature on the sociology of time and whiteness but also presents new directions in youth resistance scholarship. Resistance to white time, like many forms of dissent, runs the risk of deeper embeddedness in the systems and structures that remain the target of criticism.[20] As the youths I spoke with repurposed time to their benefit, many reinscribed linear conceptions of temporality rooted in whiteness and androcentric thought. "Counter-frames" to the future orientations of whiteness, to use Joe Feagin's term, were still couched in what Wright describes as progress narratives embedded in linear time.[21] Wright critiques progress narratives for endorsing a return to an "origin" or singular point in history where Blackness begins, rendering Black (queer) women illegible.[22] Despite the rhetorical limitations of linear progress narratives,[23] Black youths at Run-a-Way invoke these counter-frames in a spirit of resistance by remembering a past under continuous threat of evisceration by the future orientations of whiteness.[24] While their resistance may be situational, the content of these counter-frames illustrates not only how temporal power of whiteness works but how it is contested. In the following section, youths explain why they believe white youths' lives are calibrated to vastly different temporalities than their own.

"They Got All the Time in the World"

How did Black youths at Run-a-Way assess their life chances given that opportunity structures remain calibrated to white time? They were poised to speak

150   CHAPTER 7

about what they perceived as disparate temporalities between themselves and their white counterparts. I am not seeking to validate youths' perceptions according to empirical standards. In fact, US Supreme Court cases like *McCleskey v. Kemp* make clear that attempts to litigate racism and racialized violence are futile when racial bias remains anomalous, in the absence of clear "evidence of conscious, discriminatory action."[25] In a similar analysis of the case, Joy James writes, "Where one cannot prove intent, racist violence is merely a theoretical possibility or improbability on the part of the state. Such improbability was insufficient ground for the court to issue a stay of execution."[26] Still, Black youths do not need the courts or judges to prove that anti-Blackness exists. Consider the tautological error of attempting to make the case that anti-Blackness exists within an anti-Black structure like the legal system or the law itself.[27] Why is the experiential evidence of Black people never surmounting? Are the "hieroglyphics of the flesh," as Hortense J. Spillers puts it,[28] too difficult to decipher? How can the courts and the legal system not read their own writing? The indelible mark of state terror left on Black bodies, Black flesh, and Black psyches is a reminder that "who feels it knows it."[29]

Not only did these Black youths know and feel anti-Blackness, but they also saw clearly how anti-Blackness remained a central organizing principle in the social identity of whiteness. As they show, understanding whiteness or white culture does not entail formal study. The oppressive ubiquity of whiteness makes it the most common educational default, one that Black and other racialized subjects have no choice but to learn. In this crash course, some nonwhite people choose to appease whiteness. Some inhabit it. Others challenge or resist it. In my research, I observed Black youths interacting with whiteness in some of these ways while also redefining the terms of this relationship. To operationalize Black youths' relation to whiteness, I asked them to describe how their life chances differed from those of their white counterparts and how such perceptions shaped their relationship to time. Below is part of my conversation with seventeen-year-old Tanisha. Before I could finish my sentence and ask whether she had more or less time than white youths, Tanisha interjected with this:

> TANISHA: Oh, they can sit on they rich behinds.
> RM: OK. So what are some of the things that you think take up your time but don't take up their time?
> TANISHA: Workin'. They don't have to worry about that because their parents do it.... Like, just in case they did wanna get a job, they probably won't be turned around for a job at an interview. They probably get it on the spot.

While the extent of Tanisha's contact with "rich" white youths is unknown, she speaks with confidence and in detail about what their lifeworlds look like. With opportunity structures already established in their favor, white youths, according to Tanisha, hold significant levels of privilege. Enhanced life chances were linked not solely to institutional opportunity structures (e.g., employment, education) but also to social/familial ones. The intergenerational transmission of wealth led many Black youths at Run-a-Way to believe that white youths benefited from the luxury of time, while they and others like them remained in a race against it.

When I asked sixteen-year-old Dominique about differences in time use between white and Black youths, they presented a picture of disparate schedules for both groups:

> Dominique: Mm, I feel with white youth, stuff is more, like, either planned . . . planned and busy. Like, they . . . they have the resources to stay busy. Like . . . we're going hiking. But for Black youth, I feel like those occasions are rare and special and stuff like that. However, there are some routines like Saturday morning cartoons or whatever . . . oh, especially like in my house, we didn't eat dinner until ten at night. While here [at Run-a-Way] it's six . . .
>
> RM: Why would you say you had dinner later when you were at home?
>
> Dominique: I don't know, because I guess we got to bed earlier. But with my mom I didn't have a bedtime, so there's a lot more, like, awareness of time with white people. . . . They're more set to the system. I shouldn't say aware, because . . . time is a man-made system. [*Smacks lips*] Bam!

Dominique unveils a budding sociological imagination by exposing the social constructedness of time. They also answer an orienting question of this book: Whose time is it? According to Dominique, time is "man-made." In their opinion, time is not only man-made but also white-man-made.[30] White people, according to Dominique, seem to have a better relationship to time and, in their words, are more "set to the system." In further exploring the racialization of time, I asked Dominique about other differences in time perspectives.

> RM: Do you ever think that maybe certain people function on a separate . . . like white people have their own time?
>
> Dominique: Yes. Yes, definitely. 'Cuz no person of color would dare start school at frickin' eight in the morning! We do not get up that early! Yes. Okaaaaay.
>
> RM: Do you feel like time itself is a white-people thing?

DOMINIQUE: Yes, definitely! Because, you know, like . . . we don't have enough time to live. . . . I wish everything could be twenty-four hours because that way the party doesn't end. You can be nocturnal if you wanted to.

Notice how Dominique immediately links time, when marked as white, to education. This reflects not only Dominique's earlier point that time is man-made but also the idea that education is controlled by white people. White space is inextricably linked to white time, and both present a threat to Dominique's Black and trans identity. The temporal constraints of whiteness force Dominique and other Black youths into more than a race against time—they are also racing to survive. In imagining the possibility of a "nocturnal" existence, Dominique invokes important connections between time and marginality.

J. Jack Halberstam emphasizes the importance of queering time through "nonnormative logics and organizations of community, sexual identity, embodiment, and activity."[31] Queer time reflects the heterogeneity of time and serves as a response to what Halberstam conceives of as "family time": "the normative scheduling of daily life (early to bed, early to rise) that accompanies the practice of child rearing."[32] Insofar as Dominique desires to live in a spacetime when and where "the party doesn't end," they are effectively queering linear time and reproductive family time in favor of nocturnality. Queering time may be both a cause and effect of what Kara Keeling calls "queer temporality," which "names a dimension of time that produces risk . . . that dimension of the unpredictable and the unknowable in time that governs errant, eccentric, promiscuous, and unexpected organization of social life."[33]

Multiplicative forms of marginalization make adherence to such "normative scheduling" an anomalous virtue and virtually anomalous to queer and trans people of color. Coping with anti-Blackness, homophobia, and transphobia demands an inordinate amount of time from Black queer and trans people. Like racialization and racism, anti-Blackness and transphobia, including transmisogynoir, steal time by forcing Black queer and trans subjects to process multiplicative forms of violence. The threat of being clocked as Black and trans,[34] for example, takes time. "Clocking" is, interestingly enough, a reminder of the violence of time and the clock itself. Healing from cumulative forms of racialized and sexualized violence sometimes requires new spaces of sociality where, in Dominique's words, "the party doesn't end." This may take the form of actual parties or social gatherings that occur when most people are asleep.

Surviving while Black, queer, and/or trans sometimes necessitates laboring outside the logic of capital accumulation and bourgeois time. In a critique of David Harvey's description of the gender politics of time/space, Halberstam explains why queer and trans survival strategies remain at odds with "chrononormative" logics of what counts as "labor":

> All kinds of people, especially in postmodernity, will and do opt to live outside of reproductive family time as well as on the edges of labor and production. By doing so, they also often live outside the logic of capital accumulation: here we could consider ravers, club kids, HIV-positive barebackers, rent boys, sex workers, homeless people, drug dealers, and the unemployed. Perhaps such people could be productively called "queer subjects" in terms of the ways they live (deliberately, accidentally, or of necessity) during the hours when others sleep and in the spaces (physical, metaphysical, and economic) that others have abandoned, and in terms of the ways they might work in the domains that other people assign to privacy and family.[35]

In marking time as white, Dominique provides a racial critique of time that is missing from Halberstam's work. Living outside "reproductive family time" and what Elizabeth Freeman calls "domestic time" does not offer refuge from white time—a persistent threat to the life of Black queer and trans youth.[36] Each additional murder of a Black trans woman gives Dominique legitimate reason to feel as though time is robbing them of life. Perhaps Dominique does not feel like they have enough time to live because white time is predicated on the extraction of Black life.

Black youths at Run-a-Way were acutely aware of the benefits conferred by whiteness, including accrued time. I asked sixteen-year-old Shanté whether she has more or less time than her white counterparts.

> SHANTÉ: Less time. They got all the time in the world.
>
> RM: And why do you say that?
>
> SHANTÉ: People wait on them like it's nothin', like they Jesus or somethin'. . . . It's just 'cuz they white. They automatically get more respect just 'cuz of the color of their skin. They even got a higher credit score than us already. . . . We gotta hustle, we gotta struggle, we gotta work hard to really get what we want. And they don't have to work hard at all. They can get it just like that.

Shanté's response helps answer Erykah Badu's question when she sings, "Time to save the world / Where in the world is all the time?"[37] Like Tanisha and Dominique, Shanté views white youths as endowed with proprietary claims to time. Shanté identifies several structured advantages characteristic of a "possessive investment in whiteness" while extending Lipsitz's conceptualization by showing

154   CHAPTER 7

how an investment in whiteness subsidizes temporal capital. Because time is money, "temporal capital" reads as a redundancy. I use the term not simply to signal the commodification of time, but rather to illustrate whiteness's worth and exchange value. In other words, temporal capital grants white people access not only to modernity but, as Shanté notes, to higher credit scores. Hence, a possessive investment in whiteness reflects a possessive investment in time. Among the many privileges conferred by whiteness, time may be conceived of as material and immaterial capital maintaining whites' "settled expectations," in Harris's formulation. Shanté reveals how these settled expectations mutually reinforce the unsettled experiences of Black youth. In other words, white youths "got all the time in the world" because white people have *taken* all the time in the world by amassing tremendous amounts of wealth through global capitalism, enslavement, conquest, genocide, displacement, dispossession, and ecological destruction. With all the time in the world, a higher credit score is just one of many bonuses for white people. Black youths, however, don't "got it like that" and instead must receive a temporal and temporary loan before actually using time.

Less Time to Work Twice as Hard to Get Half as Far

The protracted estimates the youths at Run-a-Way gave for completing school and finding a job, as illustrated in the previous chapters, suggest that they were aware that the paths toward such life course transitions were filled with roadblocks and detours that limited their life chances. If Black youths must work twice as hard as their white counterparts to get half as far, does this mean they have half the time to accomplish the same goal? In the following narrative, sixteen-year-old Lamont explains why he feels he must do more with less (time):

> RM: So how much harder do you feel you have to work compared to white kids your age to achieve the same goal?
> LAMONT: One hundred percent. You really gotta work just to get to where they at because their moms and dads, they got companies so they just pass down. . . . You know what I'm sayin'? And it's gonna be super hard for me to . . . come from the bottom to the top. . . .
> RM: So that's like . . . twice as hard?
> LAMONT: Yeah, twice. Yeah.
> RM: If you have to work twice as hard, does that mean you have less time to do it?

LAMONT: Well, yeah. You could say that. I have less time to do more. 'Cuz, like, they're always ahead. It's always gonna be a point in time they're gonna be ahead of you so, you know what I'm sayin'. Just to catch up . . . it's one times harder [harder the first time] and then the second time is like twice as harder. You should be . . . right there with them. Not above but with them, you know what I'm sayin'?

Lamont feels forced to work 100 percent harder to achieve some sort of parity with white youths. Working 100 percent harder may not always mean that you are working twice as hard. In some cases, youths like Lamont may already be working significantly harder than his white counterparts. Hence, when he works 100 percent harder, he may be working *at least* twice as hard as his white counterparts to achieve similar goals. The need to "catch up" to white youths "always ahead" in time signals Lamont's awareness that race is temporalized. Lamont has "less time to do more," due to the cumulative advantages associated with whiteness, as well as the cumulative struggles for Black youths. Lamont describes an intergenerational transmission of wealth and privilege, best exemplified in what Robert Merton calls "the Matthew Effect" (or the "cumulative dis/advantage hypothesis"),[38] which posits that advantages or disadvantages of individuals and groups cumulate over the life course, explaining why "the rich get richer, and the poor get poorer."[39] In *Black Wealth/White Wealth*, Melvin Oliver and Thomas Shapiro illustrate the relationality of wealth and economic and temporal dispossession:

Whites in general, but well-off whites in particular, were able to amass assets and use their secure economic status to pass their wealth from generation to generation. What is often not acknowledged is that the accumulation of wealth for some whites is intimately tied to the poverty of wealth for most blacks. Just as blacks have had "cumulative disadvantages," whites have had "cumulative advantages." Practically, every circumstance of bias and discrimination against blacks has produced a circumstance and opportunity of positive gain for whites. When black workers were paid less than white workers, white workers gained a benefit; when black businesses were confined to the segregated black market, white businesses received the benefit of diminished competition; when FHA policies denied loans to blacks, whites were the beneficiaries of the spectacular growth of good housing and housing equity in the suburbs. The cumulative effect of such a process has been to sediment blacks at the bottom of the social hierarchy and to artificially raise the relative position of some whites in society.[40]

CHAPTER 7

Oliver and Shapiro reveal not just the intergenerational transmission of wealth but also the way in which such transfers require the systematic withdrawal and theft of opportunities and resources. It was clear to many youths at Run-a-Way that the opportunities that racialized youths lacked, white youths possessed in abundance. I asked Miguel, a seventeen-year-old Latino youth, whether he had more or less time than white kids:

> MIGUEL: Less time. . . . Because I'm usually working to help my mom.
> RM: So what are some things that you think take up your time every day, but may not take up time for white kids?
> MIGUEL: School. . . . It's just I have to work harder than them 'cuz I usually [have] thirty minutes before school ends to go to work, so I always be asking for all the notes [from] teachers and doing the homework on the bus, focusing on schoolwork on the bus until I get to the bus stop to work, then go home, change real fast, leave the backpack, and go directly to work. . . . They [white kids] usually don't 'cuz their parents either pick them up or give them a bike to go home.

In addition to school, Miguel is one of many students who hold down part-time jobs while still earning a high school diploma. Contrary to depictions of racialized youth in urbanized space as incapable of planning or thinking long-term, Miguel has a well-structured routine built around his school/work life. Miguel also identifies employment as a key source of time use. While his peers may be doing homework at home, he must do his homework on his way to work. When forced to do homework on the bus on the way to work, is Miguel using time or being used by it? When school and work are synchronized to white time, racialized youths will inevitably be late. Miguel cannot possibly keep up in school when white time requires many migrant youths to work after-school jobs to make ends meet.[41] As Miguel shows, white time demands deference to temporal standards to ensure that white wealth increases at the expense, extraction, and exploitation of nonwhite life.

"White People—Do You Believe in Black Privilege?"

To youths at Run-a-Way, whiteness, white identity, and white culture were synonymous. In some cases, they found ways to resist whiteness, white identity, white culture, and white time simultaneously. Take, for example, an exchange during a shift change meeting in the emergency shelter program. Around three thirty in the afternoon every day, staff and youths gather in the program's living room to recount the day's events and run down the evening agenda. Staff usually begin the discussion with the "question of the day," such as "What is your favorite color?" or "If you had a superpower, what would it be?" As the youths begrudgingly answer, most staff members awkwardly wait for the ordeal to end. At the conclusion of one shift change meeting, Remy eagerly asked, "Can we talk about race?" The three staff members present looked sheepishly at each other, as if engaged in a telepathic deliberation over how best to respond to the question. Eventually one halfheartedly said, "Yeah, let's do it." Remy proceeded by asking, "White people—do you believe in Black privilege?" The looks on the faces of the white staff members conveyed regret for their invitation. Their best defense was to ask, "What do you mean by 'Black privilege'?" Remy then explained the problem of whites' claims of "reverse racism" in the wake of accomplishments by an "exceptional" group of Black people. Remy then went on to disabuse believers in "Black privilege" of the absurdity of such claims by reminding them that systemic racism keeps Black people locked into the criminal legal system and locked out of educational and employment opportunities.

While not explicitly naming it, Remy conceptualized whiteness as a normalizing orientation of the world and its way of functioning. If whiteness is, as Lipsitz asserts, "a condition," then Remy was questioning what they believe is a symptom of that condition: the notion of "Black privilege." The question was intended not simply as a corrective but also as a screening tool to assess whether any of the white staff members actually subscribed to such beliefs. What seems most instructive about Remy's conceptualizations of whiteness is that they were interrogating its egocentric character, as it allows many whites to use white culture and white identity as a reference category for all social life. Remy also made an important rhetorical move by questioning the links between whiteness and time. If whiteness is synonymous with modernity, then it makes no sense for white people to entertain a backward concept like "Black privilege." By screening the white people in the room, Remy sought to make sure that "Black privilege" became antiquated before it became relevant.

The Wackness of Whiteness

What strategies do Black youths use to keep up with the times when the time is always right for white and wrong for them? With whiteness being associated with those who are future oriented, where are Black and other racialized youths positioned and where do they position themselves on the temporal spectrum? Black youths at Run-a-Way refused to entertain the notion that they somehow lagged behind their white counterparts. Instead it was their tastes, worldviews, trends, and culture that remained both culturally and temporally relevant. When I asked fifteen-year-old Tasha if she had ever felt targeted based on her race, she described how she responded to an anti-Black question from a white peer in school: "I used to when I was little . . . yeah. 'Cuz I'd be the only . . . 'cuz I went to a mostly all-white school and I had poofy hair with my glasses on. And they used to just look at me like, 'Why is your hair like that?' I'm just like . . . like why *isn't* your hair like this?"

Tasha's clapback is both dignified and self-affirming. She checks her white peers while simultaneously making whiteness wack and reminding herself that she is *stunningly* fabulous and fabulously *stunning*. The apparent consternation of Tasha's white peer is a product of whiteness's discomfort with contradiction and ambiguity. Tasha's hair represents an ontological threat to Eurocentric standards of beauty, which causes her white peer to go haywire while also short-circuiting whiteness. At sixteen, Tasha seems acutely aware that racialized violence is a life course constant—one that does not come and go but resides in the afterlife of slavery. By flipping the script, Tasha places her white peers outside a spacetime familiar to her and other Black youths. As Tasha relocates her white peer to an alternative spacetime, she also limits the increase of what Shannon Sullivan describes as "ontological expansiveness."[42] Tasha's response is but one example of ways in which Black youths resist temporal protocols in order to make white time "late."

Inverting white logic through ridicule is a long-established tradition among Black scholars. In search of explanations for the hubris and inflated worth associated with whiteness, W. E. B. Du Bois asks, "But what on earth is whiteness that one should desire it? Then always, somehow, some way, silently but clearly, I am given to understand that whiteness is the ownership of the earth forever and ever, Amen!"[43] Du Bois poses such a simple yet generative question—one that mocks whiteness in several ways. First, he questions why anyone would want to be possessive of whiteness. Second, he critiques whiteness itself for being so possessive that it must claim ownership of the entire world. Finally, what appears to be a rhetorical question is Du Bois pointing out the "psychological wage" of whiteness,[44] particularly its potential to possess white people. To be possessed by whiteness is to risk becoming possessed by time.

In *African Religions and Philosophy*, John Mbiti devotes an entire chapter to the "concept of time" and offers the following critique of foreigners socialized and synchronized to white time: "When foreigners, especially from Europe and America, come to Africa and see people sitting down somewhere without, evidently, doing anything, they often remark, 'These Africans waste their time by just sitting down idle!' Another common cry is, 'Oh, Africans are always late!' . . . Those who are seen sitting down, are actually not wasting time, but either waiting for time or in the process of 'producing' time."[45] Mbiti highlights whiteness's intolerance for ambiguity. Whiteness and white people require coherence and answers. Not knowing what Africans could possibly be doing sitting down drives white people to consternation. What white people perceive as stillness, tarrying, skylarking, and loitering might be a form of temporal manipulation, production, and/or destruction.[46] Each maneuver is made in the spirit of funking the clock and funking with whiteness. Michelle M. Wright describes the way that prominent Black scholars depict whiteness as backward and Blackness as most modern. She references James Baldwin's *Notes of a Native Son*, revealing the novelist's "rhetorical trick," where he "frames modernity as closer to Blackness than whiteness."[47] Other scholars have effectively flipped the script on whiteness by refusing to absolve it of the "problems" it creates. "The Negro problem," for example, does not reside in Black America, but within enslavement, Jim Crow, residential segregation, police terror, racialized violence, whiteness, and white America.[48]

By turning the fundamental principles of whiteness on their head, Black scholars have also defied the mandates of modernity by locating whiteness and white people within anachronistic space. I am interested in exploring how Black youths at Run-a-Way carry on this tradition of repurposing time to ensure that their styles, tastes, and worldviews are most culturally relevant and up to date, while leaving behind whiteness in a played-out past. As youths reconfigure the terms and conditions of whiteness and time, they become producers of new temporalities and reposition themselves on the temporal spectrum. In this section I highlight some of the strategies Black youths use to not only keep up with the times but also ensure that no matter what they do, they are always on time or up to date and that their sociality is never late.[49]

Despite the coevalness of whiteness and modernity and future orientations,[50] Black youths at Run-a-Way found a way to invert whose culture was up to date. They viewed their white counterparts, as well as white culture, as behind time, lame, or just plain wack (uncool). Fashion trends, musical tastes, and social media content (e.g., Facebook posts, tweets, memes, Vines) all represented (temporal) status symbols. As the youths centered nonwhite sociality, they transgressed time while demanding others keep pace. The following fieldnotes help illustrate the wackness of whiteness.

> We are all in the case management office. Melissa, 16-year-old black girl, stops by and asks Steve, a white male in his late forties, "When are you going to stop wearing those sandals?" Steve is wearing a pair of black Birkenstock sandals with white socks. "I wear these from April 'til October," he replied. "Uugghhhh!" Melissa replies with exasperation.
> —Fieldnote from July 16, 2015

160   **CHAPTER 7**

> After dinner, we returned to the floor. Steve informs the youth that they can participate in one of two activities: (1) mini-golf (2) trip to the park to play ultimate Frisbee. When the youth asked Steve if he was coming, they mentioned that he can't leave wearing his Birkenstock sandals.
>
> —Fieldnote from July 24, 2015

Attending to the minutiae of youth sociality helped me interpret what they deemed most relevant and up to date. Black youths tend to know the latest fashion trends and, according to their footwear index, Steve's Birkenstocks were *not* up to date. Birkenstocks are not typically marketed or sold in poor communities of color. Despite their hefty price tag, the sandals hold little weight among Black youth. Similar to the way nonwhite people are relegated to anterior time when in predominantly white institutions, Steve and his footwear are rendered illegible within the spacetime of youths at Run-a-Way.

Whiteness was tantamount to wackness in other leisure and labor spaces at Run-a-Way, including the "dance floor" of the basement conference room:

> We gather in the basement conference room for the evening activity. Staff expect youth to play Nintendo Wii Fit as their physical activity for the day. Among the many games to choose from, the most popular seemed to be "Dance, Dance Revolution." Before beginning the game, Lisa, a middle-aged white staff person, tells youth she was warned not to participate. When someone asks why, Gerard [sixteen-year-old] interjects, saying, "Unacceptable! White people can't dance."
>
> —Fieldnote from July 28, 2015

One of Gerard's favorite words was "unacceptable," and he used it effortlessly to mock many white staff members. The stereotype that "white people can't dance" is reminiscent of the 1992 film *White Men Can't Jump*. It is an allusion to stereotypical representations of white people as having less physical prowess than nonwhites generally and Black people in particular. Gerard was not just mocking white people and whiteness but reorienting the when and where of whiteness. He located white time outside the realm of what is most relevant and up to date. In mocking white people's inability to keep pace with the latest dance trends, Melissa and Gerard also funked the clock by temporalizing whiteness behind the spacetime of Black youth. Both of them created an interesting racial-temporal inversion by locating whiteness, white people, and white time in the anterior and "premodern" space typically reserved for Black and other racialized persons.

The coherence between whiteness and modernity loses strength as Black youths link an incapacity to keep up with the latest and timeliest trends to white ineptitude. Inverting the relationship between whiteness and modernity, fourteen-year-old Shanice suggests that what is most inept is white people emulating those they view as "worthless."

> RM: How important is the past to you?
> SHANICE: It's important because it's talkin' about our generation, it's talkin' about our color, the things that happened back in the day. For one, we really need to learn about that . . . because we still got white people constantly talkin' about us, constantly tryin' to be better than us but also tryin' to be like us! You know. It doesn't make sense to me. You're talkin' about us but tryin' to be like us, you know. We make up stuff, they wanna take that and make it as their own! You know. But at the same time I still don't get it because they say Black people are stupid, you know, worthless, but also you're tryin' to take what we have made into your own.

Shanice loves her Blackness and the Blackness of others. A love for Blackness, Black life, and Black people warrants defense. Shanice feels obligated to protect Blackness from the consistent threat of whiteness and what Joe Feagin calls the "white racial frame." Protecting Blackness from whiteness comes in multiple forms, including "counter-framing."[51] According to Feagin, counter-frames originally formed as survival strategies but later developed into tools for analyzing and resisting racialized violence. Shanice's counter-frame calls out the irony of whiteness co-opting the exact culture it deems backward.

Cultural appropriation was a recurring theme among the Black youths at Run-a-Way. Many endorsed the idea that white people view Black culture as what Andrea Smith terms "inherently violable" and hence theirs for the taking.[52] Consider the following remarks from Remy when they were asked how they perceive white youth in relation to time:

> I dunno. Sometimes I feel like they should just stop with whatever they're doing. I don't really think about what white people wear or how they do things or the things that they're up to date really. I don't really care. But I guess I just don't think about it too much. And if I am thinking about what white people are doing modernly, I am looking to make sure that what they're doing isn't appropriating someone else's culture. 'Cuz to white people, someone else's culture from years back, they think that they can just make it their own and all of a sudden it's some new thing. . . . They act like it's a new thing when really it's been someone's culture since day one and they're taking it from people who actually own that culture and it's their life, they do it every day and they're taking credit for it.

Remy cares less about whether white people are up to date than about whether they are stealing from Black culture. Frank Wilderson asserts that, "as a general rule, it is difficult for Black people to make anything and to hold onto it for more than thirty seconds before the world takes it for its own purposes."[53] Cultural appropriation is one thing, but cultural *misappropriation* makes the wounds of such theft even rawer. George Lipsitz describes the "misappropriation of memory" familiar to 1950s sitcoms like *Mama*.[54] Such television programs sponsor a romanticized past that never was.[55] Both Shanice and Remy express concern about white exploitation of Black culture, but to witness their culture displayed in contradictory ways evokes even greater disdain for such theft.

Black youths at Run-a-Way were acutely aware that Black culture's appeal to whites (and other non-Black people) meant that Blackness itself had significant value, despite broader attempts to lessen its worth. There is an unspoken understanding among many nonwhite people: when white folks start doing something, that is a cue to stop doing that thing. Similarly, Black youths at Run-a-Way knew that when white people begin to adopt their style, they must stop it because it is officially played out. Johannes Fabian argues that the commodification of Black culture for a white audience requires a temporal shift from the "primitive" state of "the other" to the "civilized" state of the self:

> Resources have been transported from the past of their "backward" locations to the present of an industrial, capitalist economy. A temporal conception of movement has always served to legitimize the colonial enterprise on all levels. Temporalizations expressed as a passage from savagery to civilization, from peasant to industrial society, have long served an ideology whose ultimate purpose has been to justify the procurement of commodities for our markets. African copper becomes a commodity only when it is taken possession of by removing it from its geological context, placing it into the history of Western commerce and industrial production. Something analogous happens with "primitive art."[56]

While the concept of "temporalization" was not a part of everyday parlance at Run-a-Way, youths like Remy saw how cultural traditions go from worthless to worthy over time. As time elapses, that which is "primitive" is refined and redefined as "modern." Temporalization requires spatialization. Hence, African goods and resources, as Fabian notes, must first be spatially placed on the "dark continent" before being relegated to a past retrievable only through Western civilization's benevolence.

Exemplifying that which is modern and future oriented, whiteness plays a significant role in temporalization. Whiteness usurps the "primitive" or "backward" under the guise of "development" or "progress." Aware that what is "new" is not always true, Remy demands that white people be held accountable for cultural appropriation and their attempts to temporalize Blackness. Despite the trick of temporalization to make intimate cultural traditions appear new and innovative, many Black youths have immense pride in their cultural past and take back what was stolen. Quincy, for example, uses contemporary fashion trends as a link to and site of enslavement and Black resistance:

> It's just stuff that, you know, seems to make the culture of white people mad. Like, the shoes I'm wearin' right now . . . the Timberlands. The tree that they put on it symbolizes when they used to burn Black people. And if they didn't realize—the white people that make the shoes—that Black people are the person [sic] who put your shoes out here [made them popular]. Like, the only reason your shoes are runnin' for two hundred and three hundred dollars is because Black people are wearing them. Like, I can see a couple white people wear Timberlands but I can go into my school that's seventy-five percent Black people and . . . every one of them has a pair of Tims. Like, they don't see that. If we weren't here they wouldn't be able to do what they are doing now. Like, if . . . one hundred years ago if they didn't have us, where would you be right now? So I'm just sayin', like, that's what white people need to realize that if we weren't here, where would you be right now? Like, if I wasn't wearin' your style of shoes, where would you be right now? You would be nowhere, 'cuz . . . the shoes didn't even become a brand name until 1973 and these shoes wasn't really even all that [in style] 'til the 2000s 'til the Black people started wearing them . . . and even when we wear them, we have respect. We . . . we cover up the tree. Like . . . there's a tree on the boot heel. We can't cover that [one] up, but I have a big face one and I cover that up when I wear them. 'Cuz . . . even though I'm gonna buy your shoes, I'm gonna respect my kind, my people. So yeah. That's what they need to realize. Where would you be if we weren't here right now? Where? Yeah.[57]

As I have argued in various parts of this book, white life and white time are subsidized by Black life, Black debt, and Black death. Quincy makes clear that the accumulation of white life, white time, and white wealth also requires racial capitalism. Thus, he reminds white people of the "unpayable debt" owed to Black people.[58] Capital accumulation within the fashion industry, as Quincy notes, is predicated on Black extraction and dispossession. The Black community's patronage of white-owned corporations, however, is not reciprocal.

Coincidentally, in the 1993 *New York Times* article that sparked the controversy over Timberlands, Carl McCaskill, the president of Cheryl Johnson McCaskill Communications, a public relations firm in New York,

> was repeatedly surprised by the lack of cooperation from outdoor apparel companies when he approached them with ideas for recycling some of those dollars back into programs intended for black and Hispanic youths.
>
> "When I think about it, I get disgusted," Mr. McCaskill said. "I think it's so stupid for the kids to continue to wear it."[59]

Ironically, the incessant quest toward conspicuous consumption and the attainment of material markers of temporal status gives way to the construction of those residing in poor urbanized space as guided by a set of distorted values and priorities. Quincy and many of his peers, however, see things differently. Rather than completely withdraw their financial support from white-owned companies like Timberland, Black youths like Quincy linger in the contradictions of capitalism by supporting corporations that do not necessarily support them in what Robin D. G. Kelley calls their "pursuit of leisure, pleasure, and creativity."[60] Though seldom credited for their production of surplus value, Black youths in urbanized space consistently resist whiteness by making and remaking various forms of culture while also defining the temporal terms of what is most up to date. By asking, "Where would you be if we weren't here right now?" Quincy is given license to temporalize whites as backward for exploiting Black culture with impunity.

The importance of counter-framing should not lead us to overestimate the transformative potential of mocking whiteness and white culture within such a localized context as Run-a-Way. Rejecting whiteness and white culture often backfires in "white space."[61] As Black youths transition to adulthood, they remain in a race against time not simply because they reject mainstream opportunity structures, but because opportunity rejects them. Black youths at Run-a-Way discerned notable differences between the temporal squeeze they felt when seeking opportunity and the leisurely timetables of their white peers. In the race against time, these Black youths saw themselves as beginning from delayed starting points compared to white youths. Perceiving their starts as delayed left many of them feeling that time was compressed. They saw their white peers as joint owners of a time that they could only borrow.

White time has strict eligibility criteria that excludes Black youths as prospective investors. With time being money, the intergenerational transmission of wealth signifies an intergenerational transmission of (available or free) time. Coming from mostly poor and working-class backgrounds, Black youths at Run-a-Way were temporally bankrupt. Not only did they lack time, but they also began from temporal deficits. They regularly stewed over multiplicative forms of oppression that left them behind in the race against time. Compared to the abundance of time they believed white youths possess, they saw their timetables for achieving conventional benchmarks (such as school) as compressed.

Using whiteness and white life as reference categories, time-use studies ignore the time taken and accumulated by racialized violence. Time diaries may be useful for enumerating the daily time use of white youths, but how do these diaries account for the time *used by* racism and racialization?[62] It remains unclear whether time diaries can capture the experiences that do not fit neatly into the margins of printed time intervals. How does a time diary calculate the time Lamont spends working (at least) twice as hard to get half as far? How do time diaries quantify the time Black youths lose when learning, living, and laboring within the many social institutions designed without them in mind? How do time diaries accurately detail Miguel's time use when his travel time by bus is also his study time? Can a time diary capture the time Remy spends disabusing white staff of "Black privilege"?

Systemic racism and the labor required to reckon with racialized violence are not measurable within seconds, minutes, days, or years. Not only do time diaries fail to enumerate Black youths' time use, but there remain serious holes in white youths' schedules as well. How do we account for the time white youths save in schools by learning from a curriculum that constructs them as *individuals* without culture yet also the default racial category?[63] How much time do white youths save by not having to learn about the lived experiences of their racialized counterparts? If there are more white youths who, proportionally, occupy positions of class privilege than Black youths, should we be that surprised that white youths have more time?

Though processing acts of racialized violence, including whiteness, offers little financial return for racialized laborers, this work is highly generative for racialized social systems. Racialized violence yields significant material and immaterial profit. Profits derive from any of the following: enslavement, stolen land, convict leasing, the prison-industrial complex, the overrepresentation of racialized youth in congregate-care settings (e.g., foster care, group homes, residential programs), the mutually constitutive relationship between poor urbanized space and wealthy suburbanized space, and white people relying on Black people to set trends while denying them compensation as trendsetters. In the end, white people depend on the physical, emotional, and psychic labor of nonwhite people to maintain a modern and future-oriented temporal position in the race against time. White people have the "luxury of time" precisely because they steal time from an exploitable class of youth.

When in a race against white time that offers less time to get half as far as the winners, finding a way to "run your own race" is a challenge. Black youths at Run-a-Way preferred to redefine the race by transgressing time and creating what J. Brendan Shaw describes as "radical ruptures in contemporary scripts of progress."[64] In this race, Black youths had already declared themselves the winners because whiteness was wack and incapable of keeping pace with Black sociality. While constructing whiteness as wack may present a negligible threat to white time, "resistance is revelatory" (to paraphrase Robin D. G. Kelley),[65] and the existence of these counter-frames shows that Black youths recognized that being most up to date was more a matter of being off white time than on it.

8

PRESCIENCE WITHIN PRESENT ORIENTATIONS

A salient theme in the 2016 presidential election was undoubtedly time. Whether it was Bernie Sanders proclaiming "a future to believe in," Hillary Clinton's iconic campaign logo of a red arrow signaling progress forward, or Donald Trump's intention to "make America great again," time was a not-so-hidden cast member in this particular act of political theater. The 2020 election cycle offered more of the same future-oriented logic and speculative investment in the not-yet-here. Campaign slogans promoting a future "not built by somebody better than you, not built for you, but built with you," as Deval Patrick put it,[1] led voters to believe that, as Joe Biden declared, "Our best days still lie ahead."[2] Yet as most politicians calibrate their prospective presidencies according to future-oriented time horizons, it is worth asking again, "Whose time?" and "Whose future?"

Unlike politicians on either side of the aisle committed to the prospect of a better tomorrow, the youths at Run-a-Way were more circumspect about what was to come. In 2015, seventeen-year-old Tanisha had her own predictions about the future: "To be honest, something bad's gonna happen. Like, 'cuz Obama's not gonna be president no more and there's a man that's running and a woman that's running. And the man that's running seems very racist. And I think that he'll try to get . . . I think that he'll try to turn us into slaves again. Black people." My purpose here is not to assess the accuracy of Tanisha's premonition, but to offer a counter-frame to the "ethnographic present" and urban sociology's preoccupation with "present orientations."[3] Tanisha's ominous outlook reflected not only her insight into the future but also a deep and abiding connection to the past. She foresaw problems for Black people based on past and present violence. Will

167

168   CHAPTER 8

scholars dismiss Tanisha's perspicacity as mere superstition or acknowledge her prescience? All too often, scholars construct youths like Tanisha as being hyper-focused on the now and devoid of future orientations. Ironically, it was Tanisha's connection to the past that made her way ahead of her time. Witnessing increasing anti-Black violence, many youths saw the past and present as indistinguishable.

In this final chapter, I make the case that Black youth, particularly Black youth in poor urbanized space, are less present oriented and more prescient. Having seen the multiplicative forms of oppression they will inevitably face over their life course, Black youth from poor urbanized space retain a unique ability to foretell their futures. This chapter reveals the ways in which Black youth are not only ahead of their time but ahead of time itself. What to the untrained sociological eye seem like present orientations rooted in "deviant temporal perspectives," as Lewis A. Coser and Rose L. Coser put it,[4] are in fact earnest considerations regarding what the future holds. Perhaps we can reframe "deviant temporal perspectives" as what Victor Rios calls a "critical consciousness" among racialized youth.[5] Referencing *The Gang as an American Enterprise* (1992), by Felix Padilla, Rios secondarily cites the following passage from Henry Giroux:

> In some cases . . . youngsters may not be fully aware of the political grounds of the position toward the conventional society, except for a general awareness of its dominating nature and the need to somehow escape from it without relegating themselves to a future they do not want. Even this vague understanding and its attendant behavior portend a politically progressive logic.[6]

Rejecting foreclosed futures predicated on "equal opportunity" in favor of now-ness does not make youth present oriented. Rather, it makes them prepared to confront structural violence that appears to lack any foreseeable end.

Suspended in the Ethnographic Present

As urban ethnographers seek to make the mundane matter and to make sense of the lived experiences of "disadvantaged populations" in real time, they run the risk of freezing racialized subjects within what Johannes Fabian calls the "ethnographic present."[7] Seeking not only to make the familiar strange but the strange familiar, urban ethnographers bear tremendous responsibility for placing the lived realities of poor and racialized people on perpetual pause.[8] The lives of poor and racialized people are then crystallized and suspended in time to create a coherent and intelligible story. To be suspended in time is to be in limbo. Time is at a standstill, and so are individual aspirations. The ethnographic present, though, is predicated on a set of unequal power relations between the observer and observed. Not only does the ethnographic present freeze an observed subject in time, but it also freezes temporal orientations. Future orientations are sacrificed in order to live in the moment. What to the observer (and consumer) is the ethnographic present is, for the observed, past tense. In other words, although urban sociologists spatially-temporally assign poor and racialized people to the ethnographic present, those people do not stay there.

"Urban jungle" serves as a metonym for poor urbanized space and as an indicator of nonnormative temporalities.[9] "Random violence" and the need to "watch your back" invoke fear of the unknown. Black and brown youths racing bikes in between heavy traffic as if they have "nothing to lose" and without fear of what may come signals a desire to "live for the moment." Youths navigating the streets past curfew lead outside observers to wonder how they manage to survive. Urban sociologists endorse the idea that youth have difficulty extending personal motivations beyond the present. Present orientations are products of "social disorganization," violence, and economic insecurity. Consequently, the long-term implications of individual actions are bridges that youth will cross upon arrival and no sooner.[10]

Urban sociologists rely on the ethnographic present as a heuristic to make sense of deviant temporalities among youth lacking long-term goals for the life course. The ethnographic present, though, relies on two-dimensional models of sociality that risk suspending youth in time. The logic of the ethnographic present requires those residing in poor urbanized space to move from the inner city to the inert city. Once they reach their destination, they remain stuck in "stillville." Yet images of the ethnographic present are but snapshots of space-time and ultimately fail to see the broader picture.

This chapter extends my engagement with the notion of transgression by revealing how youth's prescience exceeds the temporal parameters of the ethnographic present. How does shifting representations of Black youth from present oriented to prescient stretch the sociological imagination by making the familiar (i.e., the ethnographic present) strange and making the mundane matter? This question remains largely unexamined within urban sociology. Instead, static representations of Black life continue to conceal vibrant and dynamic forms of sociality. A walk down the block easily turns into encounters with friends and foes, neighbors and strangers, all of whom contribute to a limitless tempo of rich social life. Instead of isolating people in poor urbanized space to the ethnographic present, urban sociologists and ethnographers may benefit from considering their own limited capacity to remain on beat to unfamiliar temporal rhythms. Scenes of poor people waiting in a local welfare office, for example, may lead a researcher to assume that time in this context is suspended. Is waiting, though,

170   **CHAPTER 8**

the only discernible activity in such situations? Is there room to acknowledge how submitting applications for work or welfare benefits is a future-oriented activity? What activities does physical idleness conceal? How does this activity bely someone's location in the ethnographic present? Perhaps they are in transit, moving between the past, present, and future, as they adhere to nonlinear forms of time free from linear progress narratives.

Rather than extend urban sociology's legacy of reifying poor urbanized space as dangerous, chaotic, and inert, this chapter contributes to an ongoing process to de-arrest Black youth from the ethnographic present.[11] Within urban sociology and urban ethnography, "thinking for the moment" signifies a present orientation to time and a product of an unpredictable life course marked by "social disorganization" and violence. Depictions of poor urbanized space as immutably anachronistic obscures Black youth's ability to see the not-yet-here. In this chapter, Black youths at Run-a-Way demonstrate that their prescience exceeds the conceptual capacity of the ethnographic present.

Despite being introduced in the mid-1980's, the concept of the ethnographic present prevailed throughout the 1990s and well into the current moment. During this period, life course scholars, urban sociologists, and criminologists utilized the ethnographic present to assess the values, worldviews, and aspirations of poor families living in urbanized space. With the family being widely accepted as a key site of socialization, Black parents, particularly Black mothers, were deemed responsible for their children's in-the-moment thinking and abbreviated aspirations. Despite being widely taken to task by a range of social scientists and Black feminists,[12] the Moynihan Report is still revived and recited almost verbatim for many seeking to make sense of race, space, and family dynamics.[13] For instance, Alex Kotlowitz casts aspersions on Black mothers for failing to think about both their own and their children's futures: "She [Lajoe] rarely felt she could sail through a day and enjoy such simple moments as the coming of spring, Pharoah's smile or Lafeyette's playful teasing. There was no time to reflect on the past or plan for the future. If it wasn't the shooting outside, it was her daughter's drug habit or Lafeyette's troubles at school or Pharoah's stammer."[14]

Kotlowitz's book's title—*There Are No Children Here*—says it all. If in fact there are no children here, there are also no parents (read: adults capable of effectively bearing and rearing children). When the Child is prefigured as white, however, it is no surprise that Kotlowitz cannot find "children" (or "qualified" parents) in poor urbanized space. The unpredictability of such space, according to urban sociologists, explains why Black youth are present oriented and why they judge the future as futile. Present orientations are thus the product of limited knowledge of the middle class or a passive acceptance of the future.

Consider the work of sociologists striving to distinguish between "risk" and "resilience" in poor communities. In *Managing to Make It: Urban Families and Adolescent Success*, Frank Furstenberg and colleagues examine adolescent development within poor urbanized space using the "risk and resiliency framework." While the authors note some limitations of the framework, their conceptualization of "development" remains confined to an "iterative and ongoing process between children and the settings in which they grow up."[15] Lacking any analysis of the racialization of time or the temporalization of race, Furstenberg and colleagues attribute present orientations to an intergenerational transmission of dysfunction: "Most parents in our study devoted their attention to the here and now, believing that the future would take care of itself if their children managed to remain in school and stay out of trouble.... [P]arents were applying expectations appropriate for a past rather than a future economy.... [M]any parents simply didn't have adequate knowledge of the middle-class world to guide their children in how to succeed."[16]

Focus on the "here and now," according to Furstenberg and colleagues, is a consequence of limited exposure to middle-class norms and values and what they describe as "functional communities."[17] Rather than acknowledging struggles to reckon with routinized structural violence, the authors believe low-income families suffer from a poverty of middle-class norms and values. They accuse families of passively letting the future "take care of itself" as opposed to actively shaping it. Consequently, sociologists treat present orientations as symptoms of unemployment, unstructured schedules, and a general disregard for time.[18]

Critiquing the ethnographic present's past should not distract from its contemporary manifestations in urban ethnography. Carrying on the tradition of using culture as a proxy for anti-Blackness and racialized and spatialized violence, David Harding calls for greater attention to "cultural heterogeneity" and "neighborhood effects" to explain the social organization of violence in Black and Latinx communities in Boston:[19] "Instead of worrying about violence, victimization, and involvement in crime, Lower Mills parents have the time and energy to worry about other challenges that most adolescent boys will undoubtedly face, like staying focused on school, avoiding becoming a father at a young age, and avoiding sexually transmitted infections."[20]

In constructing families from Roxbury Crossing and Franklin as constantly "worrying about violence, victimization, and involvement in crime," Harding isolates them within an ethnographic present devoid of future orientations. To escape this temporal suspension, he recommends that social scientists adopt a "culturally informed theory of neighborhood effects on adolescents."[21] The term "neighborhood effects," though, is specious, given its use among urban sociologists as a proxy for making sense of what Robert J. Sampson and his coauthors describe as "delinquency, violence, depression, [and] high-risk behavior," particularly among Black youth.[22] Countless urban sociologists and ethnographers have skillfully evaded accusations of reproducing culture-of-poverty discourse by deploying terms like "structure," "neighborhood effects," and "social isolation" in order to draw trite conclusions about the intimate connections between culture and structure.[23] I take issue with Harding not because of any alleged disregard of youth agency but because of the way he reifies the equation of Black youths' agency with risk, deviance, and criminality. For Harding and many other urban ethnographers, Black youth and Blackness become "pure function."[24] As Chad Benito Infante writes, "The most pernicious violence against Black and Indigenous life is their transformation into literary metaphor and device."[25] "Living the drama" and "inner-city boys" become metonymic devices for understanding violence and Blackness. The consequence, as Calvin L. Warren suggests, is that "utility eclipses the thing itself."[26]

The acclaim given to Alice Goffman's *On the Run: Fugitive Life in an American City* is symptomatic of persistent racialized myopia, abjection fetish, and the fungibility of Blackness within urban ethnography. Preserving constructions of Black social life as inherently errant, chaotic, and antithetical to normative conceptions of time and future planning, Goffman writes,

> Young men looking over their shoulder for the police find that a public and stable daily routine becomes a path to confinement. A stable routine makes it easier for the police to locate a man directly, and makes it easier for his friends and family to call the police on him. Keeping a secret and unpredictable schedule—sleeping in different beds, working irregular hours, deceiving others about one's whereabouts, and refusing to commit to advance plans—serves as a generalized technique of evasion, helping young men avoid getting taken into custody.[27]

The challenge of creating a stable routine is, according to Goffman, a product of the "War on Drugs," surveillance, policing, and the criminalization of communities of color. Through dramatic tales of crime, gang violence, and betrayal, Goffman undermines her own critique of the structural forces conditioning Black life. Crime is not the only conduit for interpellating Black and other racialized youth in urban ethnographic studies. Time serves a similar function. "Refusing to commit to advance plans" appears to be Goffman's way of explaining deviant temporal orientations among young Black men, including a failure to remain future oriented. Consequently, her interlocutors remain suspended in time and inured to living in the moment.

Urbanized space is conducive to the production not only of present orientations but of pathology as well. What appears to be an attempt to engage the

PRESCIENCE WITHIN PRESENT ORIENTATIONS   173

question of positionality becomes another instance of an urban ethnographer pathologizing poor urbanized space by treating crime as infectious. In the book's methodological appendix, Goffman describes her return to Princeton as a "culture shock":

> The first day, I caught myself casing the classrooms in the Sociology Department, making a mental note of the TVs and computers I could steal if I ever needed cash in a hurry. I got pulled over for making a U-turn, and then got another ticket for parking a few inches outside the same designated dotted line on the street that I hadn't even noticed.... The students and the even wealthier townies spoke strangely; their bodies moved in ways that I didn't recognize.... The Princeton students discussed indie rock bands—white-people music, to me—and drank wine and imported beers I'd never heard of.... Who were these white men in tight pants who spoke about their anxieties and feelings? They seemed so feminine, yet they dated women.[28]

Goffman's "shock" pales in comparison to the astonishment of readers critical of white social scientists seeking to live vicariously through racialized others. The above passage rehearses the consequences of "going native"—a (settler) colonial expression used to describe the risks of a researcher adopting the characteristics and customs of a local group or culture they study. "Going native," however, distracts the reader from an even greater perniciousness in Goffman's reflection—treating Blackness as both fungible and pathological.[29] Goffman's return to Princeton is marked by a self-awareness of a newly acquired predisposition to crime, perpetuating the notion that "Black crime" is redundant, while "white crime" is virtually an anomaly.[30] At the same time that Goffman empties and occupies Black bodies, she also attempts to psychically disown whiteness.[31] The impossibility of doing so reveals Goffman's scholastic solecism. What does it mean for a white person to suggest that "indie rock" sounds like "white-people music"? It means a white person can treat a nonwhite life as fungible and interchangeable with their own while entertaining the fanciful prospect of renouncing whiteness.

On the Run exemplifies urban ethnography's capacity to study Black social life from the position of abstraction. "Who feels it, knows it" is a popular aphorism in Jamaica and many other majority-Black Caribbean nations that signifies the subjective side to oppression that only the oppressed can understand. Goffman, however, uses the fungibility of Blackness as an opportunity for those who don't feel it to claim to know it. From an abstracted position, the ethnographic present becomes a temporalizing tool used to suspend poor racialized people in time while holding constant racialization, anti-Blackness, and routinized state terror.

174   CHAPTER 8

I am not alone in critiquing urban sociology and urban ethnography for their depictions of poor and racialized persons. I find myself in the company of other sociologists and Black studies scholars. For example, Roderick Ferguson, in *Aberrations in Black: Toward a Queer of Color Critique*, takes canonical sociology to task for its reading of "American modernity through the category of social disorganization" and for using African American culture as "evidence of modernity's course and society's disorganization."[32] Others like Robin D. G. Kelley critique the "culture wars" as a pretext for neoliberal and neoconservative debates over who can best diagnosis the condition(s) of the inner city. In *Yo' Mama's Disfunktional!* Kelley indicts social scientists for constructing Black communities as "dysfunctional," "lazy," "irresponsible," and "sociopathic."[33] The book's title is an allusion to "the dozens"—a competition familiar to many Black youth involving mental maneuverability, vernacular dexterity, and, most important, potent punchlines. The title serves as a comeback to the racializing logics of social science that depict the ghetto as dysfunctional—"Nah. Yo' mama's dysfunctional!" Freeden Blume Oeur also seeks to challenge pathological constructions of youth in poor urbanized space through a study of all-male public schools. Blume Oeur argues that in their attempts to push students toward academic excellence, both schools and communities reproduce troubling dichotomies between "deviant" Black boys destined to remain "stuck in place" and those who are actively preparing to take control of their futures.[34]

My critique draws additional insights and inspiration from Saidiya Hartman's *Wayward Lives, Beautiful Experiments*. Disabusing social scientists of the notion that "crime" and "pathology" remain the central modes of interpellating in urbanized space, Hartman centers the experiences of Black girls as catalysts for a cultural movement that radically renarrated sociological scripts for the urban poor. Hartman recovers the stories of Black girls openly rebelling against "circumstances that made it impossible to live" in New York and Philadelphia at the beginning of the twentieth century.[35] As she notes, "The reformers and sociologists come in search of the truly disadvantaged failing to see her and her friends as thinkers or planners, or notice the beautiful experiments crafted by poor black girls."[36] Even the most prominent sociologists succumbed to the cult of perfunctory social science. Hartman draws on Du Bois's *The Philadelphia Negro* to illustrate the tensions that emerge when the "scholar denied" becomes the scholar admitted to predominantly white space predicated on the extraction and exploitation of Black sociality:[37]

> Their eyes looked straight into his, as if imploring Du Bois for a solution. Was there some answer or remedy that might have escaped them? The sociologist was silent. . . . The conversations humbled him. His

gentlemanly comportment and reserved New England manner—even his friends called him dear Du Bois—was off-putting, and it exaggerated the gulf between him and ordinary black folks. The distance was a requirement of the research and a studied performance.[38]

Sociologists, too, have critiqued urban ethnographers for stigmatizing Black sociality. Alford Young, for example, seeks to "de-pathologize the image of poor black men" through a new cultural analysis:[39] "Cultural models, paradigms, and interpretations must be built from analyses of the experience of low-income African Americans that are not restricted to social problem solving or to illustrating the everyday realities of their lives."[40] Young goes on to propose "elevating the African American urban poor to the analytical landscape that other groups share so that rather than these people being viewed as a special social problem case, they acquire full recognition as informers of the human experience and condition."[41] Young's apparent commitment to liberal humanism presupposes a belief that "elevating" Black people will result in "full recognition." Such an argument, though, rehearses what Denise Ferreira da Silva calls a "sociological analytics of exclusion" and ignores the violence associated with racially affectable others seeking to approximate the "post-Enlightenment European" subject.[42] Young fails to consider the terms and conditions under which Black people gain "full recognition" and how the recognition of some is predicated on the misrecognition and illegibility of others. For example, the false opposition of "street" and "decent" Black folk is indicative of the way in which some racialized persons are esteemed at the expense of members of the same racial category.[43]

The centrality of time marks my departure from previous critiques of urban sociology and urban ethnography. There exist countless studies replete with rich descriptions of Black youth reckoning with racialized social systems. The story of how Black youth reckon with time, however, remains untold. No longer will time be ignored as a tool of racial power and subordination. Rather than allow urban sociologists to continue to serve as the masters of the ethnographic clock, I center the voices of Black youth to remind social scientists what and whose time it is. Through their stories, we come to appreciate that being present is a form of prescience, and that, for many Black youth, history does more than repeat itself—it also hurts.

Presenting a racial critique of time serves as a necessary rejoinder to the ethnographic present in urban sociology. If time, as I argue, is a racialized construct, then any discussions of youths' time use and temporal orientations must acknowledge the role of power and how some gain greater temporal value over others by dint of their racialized status. Without attending to the racialization of time and the temporalization of race, urban sociologists legitimate and

176 **CHAPTER 8**

naturalize the ethnographic present while locating Black and other racialized youth squarely inside it.

When "What Is to Come" Has Already Gone

While youth are believed to maintain a present orientation to time, such assessments fail to appreciate the possibility that many of them have already thought deeply about their futures and concluded that there is not a whole lot to look forward to. The stigma surrounding present orientations is one that Elliot Liebow takes to task in *Tally's Corner: A Study of Negro Streetcorner Men*:

> From the inside looking out, what appears as a "present time" orientation to the outside observer is, to the man experiencing it, as much a future orientation as that of his middle-class counterpart. . . . Thus when Richard squanders a week's pay in two days it is not because, like an animal or a child, he is "present-time oriented," unaware of or unconcerned with his future. He does so precisely because he is aware of the future and the hopelessness of it all.[44]

Age and experience certainly help "streetcorner men" recognize "the hopelessness of it all"; however, even youths can gather enough experiential evidence to figure out that pursuing liberal futures is futile. How much space and time do Black youths have to think about a future conditioned by anti-Blackness in the present? According to Kara Keeling, insofar as visions of the future are filtered through an anti-Black world, the future cannot be entertained as something radically different from the present: "From within the logics of existing possible worlds and the range of possible trajectories into the future that they currently make perceptible, a Black future looks like no future at all."[45]

Having had a preview of structural inequalities associated with "possible trajectories into the future," Black youths must adjust their time horizons accordingly. Because the Black youths at Run-a-Way had a strong sense of what was to come, they refused to entertain false promises. For example, Kendra, age fifteen, shared why she felt Black youths may think in the moment:

> KENDRA: . . . because I guess they might think the moment is what we're living in now. Why think about the future if it might not really come? Some people might not think that there is a future 'cuz the future isn't promised. So they might just think, "Well, I'm gonna think about now, right now at this moment so I can live in this moment and not in some fairy tale that might not even happen."

RM: Why do you think the future is so uncertain?

KENDRA: Because it's never been confirmed that we're gonna have another day. We might make plans in the future, but there's no telling if it will really happen. This world could end right now, we wouldn't even . . . we wouldn't have anything to say about it.

In suggesting that "it's never been confirmed that we're gonna live another day," Kendra does not limit the threat of a premature death to environmental risk factors but widens the definition of risk to include the threat of state-sanctioned violence. I asked whether she felt that the notion that tomorrow is not promised is a "realer" feeling for Black people and Black youth:

> Yeah. Definitely. Because . . . Black kids don't really . . . they don't really look up to anything. . . . I mean, we see Black people get killed for absolutely no reason at all. Police officer is not gonna spare my life because I'm a kid. They're not gonna spare my life because I'm a girl. I'm still Black! The color of my skin is still the same as Trayvon Martin or Eric Brown [sic]. So . . . sometimes I feel like I might not even have a future . . . or my brothers might not have a future. I mean, we can say . . . we wanna go to college and stuff. But how many youth have said they wanted to go to college and ended up on the street? I mean, all youth say they wanna go to college.

At the time of this interview, the Black Lives Matter movement was in full effect, and to youths like Kendra, so were anti-Blackness and misogynoir. With an athletic physique, long braids, and a dark complexion, Kendra "fit the description" sketched by many police officers. When the "description" is always already Black, Kendra must emphasize, "I'm still Black." In other words, Kendra is still the description. What does it mean to fit what one is? To Kendra, it means that describing the future is a challenge because she has already been described as the description. The possibility that the future, in Kendra's words, "might not really come" signals its fugitivity. Or perhaps Kendra's future remains held within what John Mbiti calls "no time"—"what has not taken place or what has no likelihood of an immediate occurrence."[46] As Mbiti writes, "The future is virtually absent because events which lie in it have not taken place, they have not been realized and cannot, therefore constitute time. . . . Since what is in the future has not been experienced, it does not make sense, it cannot, therefore constitute part of time, and people do not know how to think about it—unless, of course, it is something which falls within the rhythm of natural phenomena."[47]

Could it be that youths like Kendra find it futile to always try to capture that which is already held captive within the realm of "no time"? Not only does

Kendra see her future under threat of expropriation by police terror, but she also questions liberal futurities, including the popular "college for all" trope. Is Kendra rejecting the possibility of improving her life chances over time? Or is she rejecting a future she does not want? Perhaps she is rejecting what Dylan Rodríguez calls a liberal futurity predicated on false promises of "equal opportunity," civil liberties, and neoliberal "freedoms" that backfire as soon as she attempts to become an entrepreneurial subject.[48] Because liberalism requires universality, mutuality, and commensurability, liberal futurities stand in as the aspirational goals for all. In rejecting liberal futurities, youths at Run-a-Way also rejected key frames to colorblind racism, including "abstract liberalisms" predicated on the false equivalences of "choice," "individualism," and "equal opportunity." As Kendra says, "I mean, we can say . . . we wanna go to college and stuff. But how many youth have said they wanted to go to college and ended up on the street? I mean, all youth say they wanna go to college." Kendra's reluctance to embrace such universalisms brings greater nuance to previous research examining the sources of unrealistically high educational expectations among Black students. Blume Oeur links such expectations to the myth of meritocracy and its adverse impact on Black students:

> A majority of students still saw college in their future; fifteen of twenty-five students I interviewed (60 percent) mentioned college as part of their future plans. Educational researchers have found that poor youth hold unrealistically high academic expectations for themselves: many believe that they will earn a bachelor's degree when in fact the odds against that are very high. High educational expectations are driven, in part, by an enduring meritocracy discourse in the United States, which maintains that success is primarily driven by individual work ethic. This narrative—what many call a myth—has taken on new life in a neoliberal era that further reduces achievement to a matter of individual choice. This has an especially devastating impact on poor Blacks.[49]

Despite being repeatedly told that "education is the key," many Black youths at Run-a-Way saw through the veneer of progress narratives and "education-for-all" discourse. Present-day structural violence had already foretold their futures. Kendra's prescience belies notions that she and other Black youths are present oriented. She has received a preview of that which has yet to come and opts out of a future undergirded by empty promises. Kendra and other Black youths at Run-a-Way echo José Esteban Muñoz's critique of Lee Edelman for prefiguring the Child as white. As Muñoz writes, "The future is only the stuff of some kids. Racialized kids, queer kids, are not the sovereign princes of futurity."[50]

According to Pierre Bourdieu, "Today is tomorrow, because yesterday tomorrow was today."[51] What Bourdieu illustrates is the fluidity and iterativeness of time. Bourdieu's astute observation is shared by sixteen-year-old Marlon, who, when asked about the future, stated, "I think of now, not really the future. . . . 'Cuz it's happening now. I dunno, just when the future comes it comes. I'm thinkin' about now. It's more important." What Marlon and Bourdieu both acknowledge is that time does not stop. Hence, isolating a "point in time" is counterproductive. "The future," Carmen Sirianni writes, "appears only as an abstract and linear continuation of the present."[52] The abstractness of the future does not concern Marlon. What is most clear and apprehensible is the now. Marlon knows the future will come, but until then he stays in the now.

If the present is any predictor of the future, then current voids will likely persist later in life. Black youths at Run-a-Way were perceptive enough to recognize that the protracted nature of structural inequalities made the current moment and the future largely indistinguishable. Rarely did they reject the future without offering some rationale for thinking and being "in the now." Complicating conventional understandings of time as contained in isolated intervals of the past, present, and future, sixteen-year-old Remy views life as one continuous struggle in which the only endpoint or deadline is death itself. Responding to my question about how they think about the future, Remy said,

> I don't think about the future. . . . I'm in the moment. To me, the moment right now is the future. What you're doin' in this moment is going to affect what's going on in the future. I see this very stressful road because my life has been hard since day one. I don't really think about the future 'cuz people keep telling me it's going to get better. But it's like, if I have to go through all this shit in order for it to get better, I dunno if I wanna see it at all 'cuz I don't wanna . . . I wanna stop. I don't wanna do it no more. 'Cuz the more I keep going the more shit keeps happening. I don't like that. So I just don't really think about the future like that.

For Remy, contemplating the future is futile, precisely because tomorrow's struggles are so evident today. In turn, Remy rejects what La Marr Jurelle Bruce calls "Western Standard Time" (WST) predicated on a hegemonic teleology directed "toward normative futures, toward narrow horizons of happily ever after tailored to white, heteronormative, middle-class, rationalist subjects."[53] What would it look like for Remy to embrace what Bruce describes as "depressive time"?

> Depressive time also centers sorrow. . . . Antiblack regimes of slavery, terror, brutality, degradation, and death have systematically induced

180   CHAPTER 8

sadness in black people. Then, to add insult to atrocity, agents of anti-blackness and WST consistently devalue that sadness, insisting that black people just get over it and move on. Depressive time invites aggrieved subjects to mobilize their sadness, ironically by tarrying within it.[54]

As a Black, nonbinary youth, Remy sees the struggle in the future because to them, "right now is the future." Why should Remy "get over it and move on," when "more shit keeps happening?" Though only sixteen, Remy has had a pre-view of their life course and knows what to expect. The foresight with which Remy assesses time is a product of multiple ways of knowing and being. By being in the moment or in the now, Remy is also in the know. In the final sentences of his essay on William Faulkner and desegregation, James Baldwin writes, "There is never time in the future, in which we will work out our salvation. The challenge is in the moment; the time is always now."[55]

Perhaps Remy is calibrating their time perspective to what Michelle M. Wright calls "epiphenomenal time":

> Epiphenomenal time understands one spacetime: the moment of the now, through which we imagine the past and also move into the future possibilities (walking, thinking, talking). . . . [O]nce located in the now on that linear timeline, the moment is freed for exploring a broad vari-ety of intersecting spacetimes for Blackness, some of which contradict interpellations that make sense in other moments. Linear progress nar-ratives are, as it were, "allergic" to contradictory interpellations, almost forcefully expelling them from discourse, especially when they fail to cohere to the cause-and-effect dynamic that drives their spacetime. Because they cannot interpellate dimensions of Blackness that offer nonlinear or nonprogressive interpretations . . . forcing nonprogressive narratives into linear narrative frameworks will cause a qualitative col-lapse of Blackness.[56]

By asking not only what Blackness is but where and when is Blackness, Wright expands the possibility of interpellating Blackness outside progress narratives that inevitably require negation within an already negated category. Remy's Blackness and queerness exceed containment within linear spacetime privileg-ing future orientations. They refuse to entertain teleological assessments of race and racism.[57] Epiphenomenal time's embrace of "nonprogressive" narratives and interpretations expands Remy's ability to be in the moment of now.

Remy's perceptiveness of what is to come illustrates the breadth and timeless-ness of Du Bois's "double consciousness." If we take seriously that Black youth are "born with a veil," Remy may be simply narrating their biography according to the "tape of a world that looks on in amused contempt and pity."[58] Describing how their "life has been hard since day one," Remy implies that their double consciousness and multiple consciousness began at birth. Remy must travel a "very stressful road" over their life course in the "other world" (i.e., the white world). In its current form, urban sociology as a subfield lacks the theoretical, conceptual, and methodological capacity to fully comprehend Remy's journey.

Within existing paradigms, Remy's comments about being "in the moment" serve as evidence of their cognitive confinement to the ethnographic present. If thinking for the moment is the problem, future orientations become the sociological solution to get Black youth unstuck from the present. As I listen again to Remy's words, I cannot help but consider their unwillingness to "keep going" alongside the (temporal) expectations of "Black excellence." I think about how Remy and other Black youth are rarely granted enough grace to simply be "a'ight" rather than excellent. Does "Black excellence" preclude the possibility of "Black a'ightness" when being a'ight is conflated with personal failure and thus subject to discipline?[59] Can we create space to celebrate both Black excellence and a'ightness? Or does "excellence" require the castigation of a'ightness? When Black excellence represents an exemplary reference point, a'ightness seems unacceptable. Any sense of sadness, sorrow, or resignation over the struggles of living within the context of slavery's afterlife becomes anomalous. Black excellence is cause for celebration, while Black a'ightness is cause for refutation/renunciation/rejection. Perhaps there is a need to let Remy and other Black youths know that it's OK to be a'ight and it's a'ight to be OK. Black youths like Remy should not be punished by the ableist undertones of an "excellence" that denies them access to feel weary, exhausted, sad, and depressed after recurring bouts with anti-Blackness and transmisogynoir. I am not suggesting that Black excellence should not be acknowledged or celebrated, but rather emphasizing the need to consider how constructions of excellence require the production of those deemed "subpar," "mediocre," and/or "inferior" while dismissing the many "radiant moments of ordinariness," as Dionne Brand puts it,[60] that are integral to Black life.

Recognizing the importance of Black a'ightness is also a sign of respect for what Kevin Quashie describes as the "sovereignty of quiet."[61] Black a'ightness is not merely an example of being in one's feelings, but an appreciation of Black interiority. As Quashie writes, "The interior is the inner reservoir of thoughts, feelings, desires, fears, ambitions that shape a human self; it is both a space of wild selffullness, a kind of self-indulgence, and 'the locus at which self interrogation takes place' (Spillers, *Black, White, and in Color*, 383)."[62] Quashie's broader intervention lies in unsettling the consistent interpellation of Black culture through public displays of resistance, including violence and "risk behaviors." When sociological narratives such as "living the drama" conscript Black youth sociality into

182   CHAPTER 8

the spectacular, the spectacle of the spectacular comes to subsume the richness of and heterogeneity within Black interiority.[63] As if directly speaking to urban sociology, Quashie states, "The determination to see blackness only through a social public lens, as if there were no inner life, is racist."[64] Depictions of Black life as overdetermined by an exterior render invisible Black interiority, including a'ightness and quiet. While Black excellence relishes the opportunity to take center stage in publicness, Black a'ightness holds a meditation in the "sovereignty of quiet."

When examining Black excellence and a'ightness in relation to time, we come to see the two maintain contradictory orientations. Black excellence exemplifies the active, forward motion of progressive time, while a'ightness is comfortable lingering in the past and/or the current moment. While linear, progressive time is quantifiable in seconds, minutes, and hours, Black a'ightness, like interiority, represents a place, according to Quashie, "where time is without measure and where change and stillness cohabitate."[65] In the hood, "maintaining," "doing the best I can," and "surviving" are common responses to the question, "How are you doing?" The present orientation of "maintaining," "getting by," and "surviving," though, remains at odds with the vigor, drive, and future orientation of Black excellence. This is not an attempt to interpellate Black life through abjection, but rather a refusal to use the "master's tools," including time. If Black excellence requires an endorsement of neoliberal multicultural logics that selectively incorporate minoritized difference while esteeming some at the expense of others, then funking the clock may also require a funking of "excellence."

Despite my emphasis on the antagonism between Black excellence and a'ightness, I see both as intimately connected to double consciousness. One possible, though not exclusive, impetus behind the pursuit of Black excellence might be an acute awareness of the representational and symbolic violence used to depict Black life. Similarly, tarrying in a'ightness may also emanate from the weight of racial capitalism, racialized impoverishment, and other anti-Black logics and operations used to extract Black energy, life, and time. Du Bois describes double consciousness as a "second sight," one that serves not only as a window into the world of whiteness but also as a portal to witnessing what a white-made world might do to Black youth.[66] Between the "unreconciled strivings" of being both "American and Negro" exists a temporal orientation—one that remains undertheorized within urban sociology.[67] In taking seriously the psychic dimension of double consciousness, this chapter fills many of the theoretical voids within urban sociology while revealing clairvoyance within youths' present orientations.

In privileging future orientations as an indicator of youths' direction in life, urban sociologists have ignored Remy's assertion that "now is the future." Echoing the work of queer-of-color theorists, Remy recognizes that "the future is in the present."[68] As Muñoz writes, "Rather than invest in a deferred future, the queer citizen-subject labors to live in a present that is calibrated through the protocols of state power, to sacrifice our liveness for what Laruen Berlant has called the 'dead citizenship' of heterosexuality."[69] Remy is laboring to live in the present while within the "'dead citizenship' of heterosexuality" and anti-Blackness. It is no surprise, then, that Remy envisions the future as so stressful. According to them, to be oriented to the future is to also be oriented to the present, and vice versa. By asserting that "right now is the future," Remy complicates enduring representations of the time perspectives of racialized youth living in poor urbanized space. Much of this scholarship treats urbanized space as a self-generated pathogen that breeds violence and spreads uncertainty.

There are several urban sociologists and ethnographers who intentionally speak back to constructions of poor urbanized space as anachronistic zones of disorder. For example, Loïc Wacquant describes present orientations as products of economic and political marginalization. In studying "hustling as structure and strategy," Wacquant states, "Much like the people who live from it, money from hustling 'ain't goin' nowhere' and is consumed by and in the moment: better play today when you have no assurance of having a tomorrow."[70] Missing from Wacquant's analysis, however, is a racial critique of time itself. Poor and Black youth in urbanized space see what stands ahead and reject not only what Wacquant describes as "advanced marginality,"[71] but also white time oriented to future opportunities that remain fugitive. It is unclear whether Wacquant considers the possibility that youths privilege nowness over the future because they can foretell the future based on present forms of structural and racialized violence. When time is compressed and the future is both fugitive and flee(t)ing, it is no surprise that youths prioritize the urgent and insurgent power of now.

In spite of perceived uncertainty about what is to come, there remain fairly reliable aspects of poor urbanized space.[72] In the ghetto, there exists the certainty of joblessness, that law enforcement will neither protect nor serve, that Black youth are presumed guilty until proven less guilty, and that the legal system will remain in contempt of justice. There also exists the certainty that the depleting budgets of social services cannot contend with the proliferating profits of carceral systems and their capacity to expropriate time and eviscerate the future, particularly for poor Black youth.[73]

Despite attempts to resist reproducing representations of urbanized space as pathological, unpredictable, and, in the words of Elijah Anderson, "bereft of hope," a substantial portion of urban ethnography still constructs poor and racialized communities as preoccupied with the present and relegated to a state of abjection.[74] The problem lies not just in sociologists (re)presenting Black people and Black life as devoid of agency but in the terms and conditions under which Black people become

184   **CHAPTER 8**

agentic within urban sociology.[75] Just as Saidiya Hartman opens *Scenes of Subjection* by asking, "Why is pain always the conduit for identification?," why is abjection so often the primary mode of interpellation for Black people and Blackness within urban ethnography?[76] In other words, why are Black people and Blackness most legible within the study of "crime," "urban poverty," and "pathology"? Within urban sociology, this set of "ghetto-specific" conditions function as self-regenerating phenomena, inherent to and products of the ghetto. What is then of interest to the urban ethnographer is not how "crime," "poverty," and "pathology" came to be central tenets of urban sociological knowledge production, or even the genealogy of such constructs within the discipline, but the way in which racialized subjects "make sense of" and "cope with" these constructs as inextricable elements of Black social life.

It is far too convenient to explain the suffering and survival of racialized people in urbanized space through "adaptations," "concentration effects," and "cultural repertoires." If sociology were truly committed to revealing what is hidden in plain sight, the discipline would be more cognizant of how it remains complicit in the hiding. Sociological discourse serves as a prime hiding place for racist theories on the "urban poor." For Hartman, "the normative character of terror insures its invisibility; it defies detection behind rational categories like *crime, poverty,* and *pathology*" (emphasis in the original).[77] Terror cloaks itself in many other sociological concepts. "Social capital," for example, functions as a proxy for culture-of-poverty tropes that discipline those poor and nonwhite for a failure to conform to racialized and classist measures of sociality. Similarly, cultural racism conceals itself within "race relations" while obscuring the violence of "self-obliteration."[78] These sociological concepts serve to regulate, rather than accurately represent, racialized youth in poor urbanized space.[79] Consequently, "cultural repertoires" and "ghetto-specific behavior," "social disorganization," and futureless youth become key indices of urban sociological knowledge production.[80] For the youths at Run-a-Way, remaining present-oriented was not as temporally debilitating as urban sociology would lead us to believe. Instead of being a paralyzing force that keeps youth suspended in time, present orientations and the production of nowness help buffer the impact of colliding with a future that always already designates Black youth as temporally expendable.

"You Can Plan a Picnic, but You Can't Predict the Weather"

Rather than assume that Black youth in the inner city place a moratorium on their own future orientations because of the "disorder" of their social contexts, this chapter reveals a prescience within present orientations. Certain predictions among the youths at Run-a-Way were eerily noteworthy and illustrative of the way that racialized people, especially Black youth, remain (in) a race against time. Tanisha, featured in the opening of this chapter, believed that then candidate Donald Trump would turn Black people into slaves "again." To what extent is Tanisha's expectation also preparation? What does it mean to have to defend yourself from what you are said to be emblematic of (i.e., the future)? What would it look like to frame Black youths' present orientations within the psychic dimensions of double consciousness? Some youths I spoke with saw the future as unpredictable, but not necessarily because of the wildness of poor urbanized space.

Tariq, who at the time of our interview was sixteen years old and prepared to enter the eleventh grade, was a resident of the independent living program at Run-a-Way. Tariq was known for making efficient use of time while also realizing that the time he used was not his own. Here, he describes how his future ends up in the hands of others:

> I think of the future as unpredictable. 'Cuz really anything can happen in the future. If you plan something, it doesn't always have to happen. It's not guaranteed to happen. It's guaranteed that you can try, but the future is unpredictable. . . . Because everyone around the world makes decisions and my decisions can be affected by someone else's decisions. So therefore, you can't predict someone else's decisions. So if your decisions are affected by another person's decisions, you can't really see that coming until it happens. . . . [T]here's this saying, "You can plan a picnic, but you can't predict the weather."

To urban sociologists and life course scholars, Tariq's uncertainty is a product of "environmental risk factors." Violence within poor urbanized space, according to both urban sociologists and life course scholars, makes it impossible for Black youths like Tariq to effectively plan for what is to come. Yet Tariq's skepticism regarding the future is a product not strictly of his "environment" but of an acute awareness of what an anti-Black climate has to offer Black youth.

In *In the Wake: On Blackness and Being*, Christina Sharpe uses "the weather" to illustrate how "antiblackness is as pervasive as climate." According to Sharpe, the weather of being "in the wake" is part of "the atmosphere: slave law transformed into lynch law, into Jim and Jane Crow, and other administrative logics that remember the brutal conditions of enslavement after the event of slavery has supposedly come to an end."[81] What role does structural violence play in shaping weather patterns? When it rains, do Black youth experience a downpour of systemic forms of oppression? Though meteorological weather may be unpredictable, Sharpe's conceptualization suggests that the forecast of anti-Blackness is quite predictable and extends well beyond five- or even ten-day projections.

186   **CHAPTER 8**

When part of one's predictions involves tragedy, however, prescience may feel more like a burden. Toward the end of my interview with Tariq, I asked him how long he expected to live.

> Honestly, I expect myself to die almost every day. It sounds a bit odd to say that I expect to die almost every day, but literally anything that can happen that can cause me to die every day. About two hours ago I could have died. I didn't, but I expect myself to die every ... almost every day. Any day I go outside, I expect to die in some way. That's just because of the whole unpredictable world we live in.

It is not Tariq's environment or community that prevents him from planning a picnic. It is state terror—a condition far more inclement than the threat of rain or snow. Approximately eighteen months after I left Run-a-Way, police from a suburb approximately twenty minutes from the program shot eighteen rounds at Tariq while he was brandishing an airsoft gun in an empty park. Tariq was hit twice—once in his brain and once in his spinal cord. Though he survived the shooting, his allotted time at life was significantly truncated by racialized terror. "Policing" is yet another example of the limitations of sociological discourse. Talk of "policing" makes the "distinction" between "good policing" and "bad policing" theoretically possible while ignoring the question of whether "police violence" is a redundancy.[82] It was not the chaos of the "urban jungle" that precipitated the shooting. Rather, it was Tariq's presence in a community that is over three-quarters white.

Tariq's mental health was the subject of much scrutiny by the police and the press. A report by the Minnesota Bureau of Criminal Apprehension noted his history of depression and paranoid schizophrenia. Applying what Jina B. Kim calls a "crip-of-color critique," though, allows for an analysis of Tariq's encounter with police through the lens of disability, race, and the role of the state in the production of racialized disablement. As Kim notes, there is an urgent need to shift the concept of disability "from noun—a minority identity to be claimed—to verb: the state-sanctioned disablement of racialized and impoverished communities via resource deprivation."[83] In short, disablement is a process—one that requires the systematic abuse and neglect of Black youth by the state through educational enclosures, police terror, and racialized dispossession that results in unmet demands for mental health services in poor urbanized space.[84] In response to the shooting, nearly one hundred of Tariq's family and friends took to the streets in protest, condemning the police for treating mental illness as a death sentence.[85] Instead of acknowledging Tariq's mental health needs and a wailing psyche yearning to be heard, police treated the coexistence of Blackness and disability as a threat.

PRESCIENCE WITHIN PRESENT ORIENTATIONS 187

Tariq's orientation to time during this incident is unclear. Locating him in the ethnographic present, however, elides clairvoyance. Within the context of what La Marr Jurelle Bruce calls "madtime," Tariq's actions signal a rejection of normative time and liberal futurities:

> Madtime refers to any mode of doing time or feeling time that coincides with renegade rhythms of madness. Its variations are endless, including, for instance, manic time, depressive time, schizophrenic time, and melancholic time. . . . Madtime is multidirectional and polymorphous, errant and erratic, dazed and dreamy, unruly and askew. It tears calendars, smashes clocks, dances to the lilt of the voices in its heads, builds makeshift time machines from scraps, and ignores calls for timeliness. Furthermore, it tends to stagger, lunge, twirl, moonwalk, or sit still, rather than march teleologically forward. In the process, madtime defies the Eurocentric, heteronormative, capitalist, rationalist clock-bound time that prevails in the modern West. Let's call that normative temporality Western Standard Time (WST).[86]

What does it mean to be young, Black, and prescient within Western Standard Time? It means that Tariq can hold aspirations of finishing high school, going to college, and pursuing a career, while apprehending the many structural barriers to achieving such goals. In other words, he can plan his picnic, but when it comes to the weather within an anti-Black climate, there ain't no tellin' what could happen. Tariq may have been taking a stand against WST by living in the now as a way of protecting himself from liberal futurities and progress narratives that, according to Bruce, treat "madness as a liability." Within "schizophrenic time," the time is always now. "Schizophrenic time," Bruce notes, "collapses everything into an exigent now, thus frustrating fantasies of triumphal teleology and thwarting the seductions of nostalgia."[87] The "exigent now," however, differs from the "ethnographic present" in that it acknowledges the future but also rejects it in favor of the moment. Where the ethnographic present "freezes" racialized persons through observation, nowness belies such temporal suspension. Nowness is not static but fluid.

We should not think that youths like Tariq, Remy, and Marlon are not present oriented because of the chaos of their communities. Instead, structural violence necessitates that Black youth be simultaneously oriented to the past, present, and future. Many youths at Run-a-Way maintained a prescient vision of what was to come based on intimate ties to the past and its presence today. In communion with Toni Morrison, Christina Sharpe writes, "We, Black people, exist in the residence time of the wake, a time in which 'everything is now. It is all now' (Morrison 1987: 198)."[88] What is the power of nowness? Maybe the power we seek lies

188   CHAPTER 8

in the "ungovernable, anarchic here and now" that, according to Kara Keeling, "harbors Black futures."[89] Tomorrow may not be guaranteed, and the future may indeed be fugitive, but to many Black youths, the past was always inching closer and closer to the present.

Repeating or Remixing History?

A popular trend among dancehall reggae and hip hop DJs alike is playing the first few lines or bars of a song and then restarting the track. The process begins when a dancehall DJ screams (in Jamaican patois), "Come again," "Wheel up," or "Puuuuuull up." With this cue, the crowd is prepped to hear the song once more. Similarly, hip hop DJs and emcees at live shows will often ask to "run it back." DJs pull up or run back a hit record to give all partygoers an opportunity to reexperience a moment in time. There exist intimate connections between race, space, time, and sound. As George Lipsitz notes, "The rhythmic complexity of Afro-American music encourages listeners to think of time as a flexible human creation rather than as an immutable outside force."[90] To pull up or run a track back is, I argue, a form of time travel.

Just as Afrofuturism creates new temporal-spatial imaginaries for Black sociality to flourish, music serves as a catalyst to produce epistemic spacetimes that defy what is.[91] While Black sci-fi focuses on future possibilities, I assess the importance of the past to Black youth. Nearly every one of the youths I interviewed at Run-a-Way considered their past to be very important. They forged substantive connections between legacies of slavery, conquest, genocide, and contemporary struggles for a more just world, and the significance of their racial histories shaped their present realities. For sixteen-year-old Shanté, who identifies as Black and Native, "slavery is real important."

> . . . 'Cuz those is my people. They went through literally hell and back for us. And look where we are today, we still gettin' treated disrespectful. We still gettin' beat for no reason. Look at how many Black kids have gotten shot by cops. We still gettin' killed for nothin', literally! I mean, it [racial justice movements] was worth it. We're way better off today than how we was a hundred fifty years ago, but it still ain't no different. It's just a different way of disrespect. They're disrespecting us legally now. . . . Like . . . especially the way they talk to us it's like you act like slavery never happened. Like, y'all just did this to our same people. Like, the way cops is gettin' away with killin' kids, the same way white people is

gettin' away with hangin' us back in the day. Y'all still gettin' away with the same petty crimes. Well, not petty but ridiculous crimes.

In Shanté's opinion, little has changed over the last 150 years, a perspective that alludes to her intimate connection to the past and the presence of the afterlife of slavery. A decade before introducing "slavery's afterlife" as a description of the material and epistemic forces confronting Black life, Hartman offered this theoretical scaffolding: "The enduring legacy of slavery was readily discernible in the travestied liberation, castigated agency, and blameworthiness of the free individual."[92] "Castigated agency" is why Shanté asserts, "We still gettin' killed for nothin', literally!" To Shanté, the difference between the legal lynchings of the past and those of today is negligible. While those synchronized to white time have the capacity to construct the past as a blank page in history, Shanté's biography and those of many Black people are densely narrated.

In an analysis of the social structure of time, Eviatar Zerubavel claims that marked time has a higher "mnemonic density" than "unmarked time."[93] That is, particular periods in time occupy greater mnemonic space depending on their biographical significance for the individual. Racialized violence is not only mnemonically dense but temporally taxing. In other words, the mnemonic density of oppression requires a substantial amount of processing time. But what does it mean to process something that is in continuous process? Can racialized violence ever be fully processed? Echoing some of Shanté's sentiments, sixteen-year-old Tasha described racialized violence as a recurring trend. I asked her about the importance of Black history to her present reality:

> Important. Because I do feel history do repeat itself. Like history is repeating itself right now with the racist thing. Like white cops killing Black people. Like back then they used to do it and now it's startin' again. And you heard about the white man who went in the church and killed Black people? Isn't he out or they're bailin' him out?[94]

The youths at Run-a-Way did not see the present-day violence against Black people as anything new and instead described it as "history repeating itself." Many, including Tasha, likened the police killings of Black people to slavery and the continued criminalization of Blackness. Tasha's connection to the past makes her acutely aware that "white cops killing Black people" is not a new trend but one that is simply "startin' again." Social scientists indict the past for hampering racialized persons' "progress," but for youths like Tasha, the past is prologue, and the iterative process of being backward- and forward-looking creates landscapes of meaning for Black youths to navigate.

190   **CHAPTER 8**

As the saying goes, "You don't know where you're going until you know where you're coming from." What happens, though, when where you are going looks a lot like where you have already been? While the clockwise direction of minute and second hands symbolizes progression in time, racialized temporalities are recursive. That is, racialized violence cannot be isolated to a single point in time. Instead, oppressions travel—swaying back and forth, around and around, from past to present. For some "mnemonic communities,"[95] the heavy rotation of racialized violence makes the past present.[96] As Hartman reminds us, "This pain [chattel slavery] might best be described as the history that hurts—the still-unfolding narrative of captivity, dispossession, and domination that engenders the black subject in the Americas."[97]

Those responsible for making history so painful often seek to ensure that the past is always past and to a large degree nonexistent. In an ethnographic examination of identity formation, Pamela Perry finds that white students see only "ethnic" people as having a connection to the past, while their own white identity is rendered "cultureless."[98] Without any connection to the past, white people evade accountability for what Hartman calls their "incorporeal hereditament,"[99] which is, according to Ferreira da Silva, both a "wage" and an "unpayable debt."[100] Perry asserts, "Naturalized whiteness is securely grounded in and validated by the normal way of things in the present and therefore does not seek meaning in cultural or past orientation."[101] Thus, future orientations validate whiteness while invalidating the historical continuity of conquest and enslavement in the present. Black youth lack the luxury of time to ignore the past when it haunts them today. For youths like Remy, the past is far from gone. It is here and now:

> You know how your history teacher will say, "If you don't learn history you'll be forced to repeat it." Then she'll laugh it off or whatever. I just feel like, shit, my history teacher was right 'cuz I didn't learn about nothing. I don't wanna hear not a damn thing. But now it's like the stuff she was trying to tell us, it's happening right in front of our eyes. It's been happening! We're watching it happen. . . . I literally just feel like we're going back in time. . . . These days people are so openly racist it's just blowing my mind. 'Cuz they don't necessarily have any consequence unless we can prove that it's keeping us from getting to things that they can get to.

Remy raises an important theme echoed by other youths at Run-a-Way. In suggesting that time moves backward, Remy is alluding to the lack of progress made toward a more just world for racialized people generally, and Black people in particular. In *The Fire Next Time*, James Baldwin writes, "To accept one's past—one's history—is not the same thing as drowning in it; it is learning how to use it."[102] Rather than drowning in their history, Remy is figuring out how to navigate the current and maybe even catch a wave. They are also challenging whiteness as a cultureless identity, suggesting that their teacher's advice also applies to white people. In other words, "If you don't learn white history (i.e., conquest, enslavement), you'll be forced to repeat it."

Mark Twain is thought to have said, "History doesn't repeat itself, but it rhymes." Eviatar Zerubavel observes, "Such rhyming implies that, while clearly distinct, the past and the present are nonetheless fundamentally similar to the point of evoking a déjà-vu sense of 'there we go again.'"[103] The continued onslaught of state power against Black people and other racialized people living in the United States suggests that history has been "rhyming" for quite some time. The phrase-turning charm of the quote attributed to Twain is one of many diluted references to time. For example, the saying "time heals all wounds" warrants critique and intense skepticism among those whose wounds run deep in a past that continues to inform the present and a seemingly recurring history. In other words, history does not need to repeat itself or rhyme when the soundtrack of racialized violence is like clockwork and has not skipped a beat. The notion that time heals all wounds is a comfort only to those who inflict the wounds and benefit from harming others. Cumulative disadvantage theory reminds us that the passage of time is more likely to worsen wounds than to heal them. Hence, when urban sociologists construct racialized youth in urbanized space as lingering in a perpetual state of delay, it is worth asking: Are Black, Indigenous, and racialized youth "killing time," or is time is killing them?

How else might we rethink representations of youth killing time? Why must "killing time" have such a negative connotation? Perhaps youths' attempts to kill time are also an attempt to kill capitalism—to kill the rigid and racialized strictures of time that demand their mental, physical, emotional, and psychic labor. Killing time may be a form of self-defense, a way of trying to kill that which is trying to kill you every day. Perhaps Black youth are keeping in communion with Lucille Clifton and her famous invitation to "come celebrate / with me that everyday / something has tried to kill me / and has failed."[104]

How does remaining present oriented serve as a defense mechanism against structural violence in the future? Put another way, what potential does living in the moment hold for survival in the future? In thinking with scholars like Michelle M. Wright and Kara Keeling, how might Blackness and Black sociality engender new forms of temporality that lie beyond linear time and outside the ethnographic present? If history is repeating itself, is racialized violence on repeat? While "fast forward" and "skip" are common features on most stereos, Black people cannot neglect the rewind button, especially when particular soundtracks of oppression never seem to pause but only stay stuck on play/repeat. The creative control of

192   CHAPTER 8

sound, however, makes time travel an integral feature of Black music. I asked the youths to utilize their time-traveling talents and imagine what they would be doing in five years. Dominique, age sixteen, had this to say:

> DOMINIQUE: Um, I think I will be twenty-one. I hope to be doing really good in college and I hope to have an apartment and be working and just trying to free myself from depression and free myself from time. Like, I hope I have a soulmate by then.
> RM: How will you work towards those goals?
> DOMINIQUE: Just [*pause*] . . . forget about time. I feel like that's so essential. Even though, like, [we're] basically oppressed by this time infinitely, you know. Just try to fight back and enjoy things instead of regretting that they're gone. . . . You understand what I'm saying? . . . 'Cuz when you think of things like that, you're thinking of a stopwatch for your life. . . . I don't think you should think like that. I think you should enjoy the moments and, you know, let them go and then like, surround yourself with things that remind you of moments such as that. Like pictures and videos and food that remind you of those people and moments. You know?

Within Dominique's response exists both liberal and liberatory futurities. Dominque endorses liberal ideals of attending college but also emphasizes the importance of temporal liberation, or liberation from time. Perhaps they are calling for a commitment to what Damien Sojoyner describes as "black radical time," which "places human concerns over the material demands of a Western racial capitalist infrastructure."[105] Dominque also confirms Muñoz's theorizations on queerness. As he writes, "Queerness is essentially about the rejection of a here and now and an insistence on potentiality or concrete possibility for another world."[106]

Refusing a "stopwatch for [their] life," Dominique yearns for the freedom to enjoy the moment and escape depression. Refusing to "blithely romanticize madness," Bruce admits that there are risks associated with depressive time and other modes of "madtime": "I want to briefly acknowledge the risks that haunt these temporalities: manic time might rush recklessly into danger; depressive time might become so wedged in its woe that it cannot ever get free; schizophrenic time might be crushed between history's hurt and future's threat; melancholic time might break beneath its heaping load of lost objects."[107] "Wedged in [the] "woe" of the present, Dominique remains committed to transgressing what is in favor of otherwise futurities. Despite time's infinite oppression, they are prescient enough to see the possibility of achieving freedom from depression and possibly "depressive time." Perhaps Dominique seeks to live in a world where time (and thus money) is no object. Their remarks are a reminder of the "mighty agency" that Bruce says is linked to a "colored people's praxis of black time." As Bruce writes, "The abyss may have no bottom, but blackness has no top, no limit."[108]

By definition, abolishing time is an anticapitalist act. It is unclear whether Dominique identifies as an anticapitalist, but they do appear to be anti-time. What would a telos of time look like? For many adults whose identities are inextricably linked to their labor or industry, the thought of a world without time is unfathomable. For Black youths like Dominique, who are emblematic of the future yet assigned to the ethnographic present, transgressing time is essential to creating another world. Transgressive temporalities and insurgent forms of time are already in full effect and often found in sound.

Sonic Spacetime

Throughout this book, I have used music as a tool to put the "tempo" in "temporality." Since my father's removal, music has come to serve as a sort of temporal index to help me reckon with the present past of deportation. I have a sort of sobering interest in thinking about songs that were released before and after my father's removal. It is no coincidence that listening to specific songs warms my spirit in indescribable ways. It was not so much which song was playing, but the where and when of the song. For example, I maintain vivid memories of driving with my brother down Warren Street past the Roxbury YMCA while listening to Groove Theory's "Tell Me" on Jam'N 94.5. My mind has constructed a sort of pre- and postremoval playlist. Without knowing the exact year a song was released, I can likely guess whether the record dropped before or after my father's removal. This may be in part why I have such an antagonistic relationship with time and why I insist on funking the clock.

Just as the DJ and emcee control time through calls to "pull up" or "run it back," the turntablist also possesses a unique capacity to dictate a hip hop audience's orientation to time. "Scratching" is a technique the turntablist uses to create music within music by moving a vinyl record back and forth to produce percussive or rhythmic sounds. Scratching creates "a break" in the record at play. At parties, the turntablist/DJ may scratch a popular verse in a song for purposes of emphasis. The skilled turntablist/DJ knows what verse is likely to "get the crowd hype." The turntablist/DJ will run a track back several times to allow the crowd to collectively experience the lyrical effect of a particular verse. Scratching, I argue, functions as a transgressive temporality that the turntablist/DJ uses to violate white time. Unlike white time, however, scratching a record does not

194   **CHAPTER 8**

efface history. It remakes and remixes it. As racialized people turn the tables of time and DJs spin the turntables, they place the direction of time under their discretion. Both the audience and the DJ cooperate by manipulating the tempo and temporality of a song. In turn, Blackness becomes a moderator of time. In other words, time goes when Black people say so. As the Black youths I spoke with both funked and queered the clock, they placed the direction of time under their discretion and within the context of nowness.

The Power of Nowness

On the rare occasion that my father ventured out of San Juan, car rides were always a trip. My father decided to go to the country because one of my uncles was visiting from Boston. We all packed into my father's Nissan Sunny and began our two-hour-plus one-way journey. My father likes to drive as if he has X-ray vision and can see behind each curve of the very high mountains we climb to travel to and from the country. It is as if he tells himself that if the tires are not screeching when taking sharp turns, you are not driving right. During this trip, we had just come off one such turn and were on a much straighter path when my uncle, who was sitting in the passenger seat, emphasized the need for my father to think about the future. My father cut him off, saying, "Deh ain't no future, mi bredda. De future ain't is. Yuh ovahs?"

What did my father mean? This passage from Earl Lovelace's *The Dragon Can't Dance* may offer some insights: "All we thinking about is to play dragon. All we thinking about is to show this city, this island, this world, that we is people, not because we own anything, not because we have things, but because we is. We are because we is. You know what I mean?"[109] In this particular scene, the novel's protagonist, Aldrick, is arguing with a landlord, Guy, and one of his partners, Philo, over the circumstances in their village. During the exchange, Aldrick conveys the importance of playing mas (masquerade) for Trinbagonians, but also the significance of "is" to Afro-Trinidadians. According to Aldrick, material possessions do not make him and other Afro-Trinidadians people. In other words, Black people are more than beings. They are being because they is. For Aldrick, "is" becomes a pronouncement of (Black) presence and being within presumed absence.

Perhaps my father was thinking of the future, and thus of time, as less of a noun and more of a verb. I like to think he was thinking along similar wavelengths as Katherine McKittrick when she conceives of the "human as a verb" and "being human as a praxis."[110] Perhaps he was signaling a refusal to treat the future as a static endpoint and instead regarding it as something constantly in motion, in process, and thus alterable. So when Black youths at Run-a-Way

PRESCIENCE WITHIN PRESENT ORIENTATIONS   195

express skepticism over the prospect of the future, they may be rejecting notions of the future that are already fixed and predestined. If the future, according to my father "ain't is," what is "is"? I would argue that the "is" is a site of life-giving energy that stands in contradistinction to the dead time of the future.[111] "Is" is an action word. It signals the dynamism and transformative possibilities within nowness. "Is" is what it means to conceive of "being human as a praxis." Finally, "is" is a threat to the clock and the linear progress of time. "Is" is what tugs on time when it attempts to proceed into the future without tarrying in the now (what is) and the past (what still is, not was). "Is" is what reins time in before it can declare the past to be past, while pleading with those beaten by the hands of time to "forgive and forget."

"Is" is then a response to the construction of those who is/are not. Still, Calvin Warren curbs my urge to bring this chapter to a close without acknowledging what he calls the "tension of the copula"—namely, the "'is-ness' of a [non]being."[112] For Warren, "is" cannot bridge the subject ("black") and subject complement ("being") because "being is not universal or applicable to blacks."[113] Warren asserts that "black thinking is given a tremendous task: to approach the ontological abyss and the metaphysical violence sustaining the world."[114] It is a journey that few are willing to take, out of what Warren describes as a fear of nothingness. Still, I wonder whether entering the abyss and bidding farewell to the human might also reveal how integral "is" is to what Warren calls the aim "to shift emphasis from the human toward the spirit."[115] I also wonder whether there is room to appreciate that many Black people have already bid adieu to the human and don't feel the urge to be or become human simply because they is.

In the final lines of *Habeus Viscus*, Alexander Weheliye speaks to the notion of "being human as a praxis":

> A habeus viscus unearths the freedom that exists within the hieroglyphics of the flesh. For the oppressed the future will have been now, since Man tucks away this group's present in brackets. Consequently, the future anterior transmutes the simple (parenthetical) present of the dysselected into the nowtime of humanity during which the fleshly hieroglyphics of the oppressed will have actualized the honeyed prophecy of another kind of freedom (which can be imagined but not [yet] described) in the revolutionary apocatastasis of human genres.[116]

According to Weheliye, a habeus viscus engenders the possibility of new human genres and thus new forms of personhood beyond Man. Within this "nowtime" exists freedom beyond ontological impossibilities and neoliberal multicultural logics that treat (racial) difference as a mode of capital accumulation. Weheliye's nowtime also contains prescience—a "honeyed prophecy" for a new and/or revolutionary restoration of human genres. Hence, it is important to distinguish this nowtime from the present-orientedness found within urban sociology.

What are the consequences of constructing those emblematic of the future as present oriented? In urban sociology, a preference for the present works to legitimate temporal, discursive, and material violence. Consider the double standard that exists when it comes to the question of who is permitted to live in the moment and remain oriented to the present or what is. When white, middle-class, working professionals heed the advice of Thích Nhất Hạnh, Eckhart Tolle, and/or John Kabat-Zinn on "mindfulness,"[117] they are lauded for "surrendering to the present." When poor, Black youths in urbanized space live in the present, they are not mindful but "mindless," "reckless," and devoid of future orientations. To "be in the moment" becomes a therapeutic kind of cultural capital for some and, for racialized others, particularly Black youth, a marker of "ghetto-specific behavior."[118] Despite many benchmarks for young adults being synchronized to the "stopwatch," Dominique strives to forget about time and enjoy the moment. So what power can come from "living in the moment"? More importantly, whose moment are we talking about?[119]

Rather than endorsing "the power of now," the Black youths at Run-a-Way emphasized the possibilities within nowness. Urban ethnography's limited engagement with critical ethnic studies generally, and Black studies in particular, renders it ineffectual in representing the temporal orientations of Black youth. James Baldwin, Toni Morrison, Christina Sharpe, Alexander Weheliye, Michelle M. Wright, and many other Black scholars have emphasized the importance of nowness for Black people. They do not endorse an ethnographic present that suspends Black people in time and the moment. Rather, nowness privileges nonlinearity and the potential to create liberatory futurities on spatio-temporal planes. Black youths at Run-a-Way center the now, despite being assailed by liberal futurities that promise a lot and guarantee little. This is what makes them more prescient than present oriented.

In this chapter, I have made the case that Black youths in poor urbanized space retain a psychic ability to see into a future that exceeds the conceptual capacity of existing paradigms within urban ethnography and sociology. Black youths at Run-a-Way invoked the part of the Black radical tradition that Fred Moten describes as illuminating a "forecast of a future in the present and in the past here and there, old-new, the revolutionary noise left and brought and met, not in-between."[120] Urban sociologists and ethnographers are complicit in relegating Black youth to the ethnographic and not only suspending them in time but also denying them coevalness. Youths' asynchronous relationship to white time is not, however, indicative of their preoccupation with the present. Instead, present orientations are grounded in a prescience familiar to many Black youths at Run-a-Way. As they looked through "the veil," they saw themselves through "the revelation" of a white world that renders them outside modernity and outside white time. I frame double consciousness as a temporal orientation bestowing youth with a second sight to bear witness to a not-yet-here and comport themselves accordingly. This chapter has revealed why Black youth are wary of investing in liberal futurities undergirding white youth's temporal orientations. Not only were futures foreclosed due to limited educational opportunities and pathways to stable jobs, but racialized violence constantly infringed on youths' time horizons. Racialized violence, including police terror, created an inhospitable climate, making it difficult for youths like Tariq to plan a picnic.

Still, youths like Tanisha were clairvoyant enough to know what was to come. How did they know? The past told them so. Any discussions of what is require some understanding of what was. What happened and what is still happening. For many youths, the killings of unarmed Black people marked both the repetition and the mutation of history. History repeated itself each time police killed another Black person. State-sanctioned violence and legal lynchings also contributed to history's mutation. As Shanté reminds us, "The way cops is gettin' away with killin' kids, the same way white people is gettin' away with hangin' us back in the day." Most of the youths acknowledged the gains of the civil rights movement and the freedoms and liberties won through struggle. They also recognized that "human rights" meant little to those declared "racialized" and "rightless" by the state.[121]

This chapter contributes to an undoing of discrete temporal boundaries between the past, present, and future. For youths at Run-a-Way, the past was always present, and struggles in the present foreshadowed foreclosed futures. An always already present past made Black youths acutely aware of what was to come. With past oppressions residing in the present, these youths anticipated that which is not yet here. They rejected the future because they see and know what a racist-carceral, colonial state has in store for them today. Their preparedness was a product of their perspicacity and overall awareness that racial struggles are extending, not ending. Blurred temporal boundaries induced experimentation with new and often nonlinear spacetimes, such as nowness. Many of the youths tarried within the moment, knowing that the future is now. For them, it was now or never. At the same time, Dominique sought liberation by forgetting about time altogether. While it may be difficult to imagine a world without time, this chapter has revealed how these worlds may already be in the making. The architects, though, are not chronologically gifted—adults with greater age and experience—but rather those of a younger generation who remain ahead of their time.

Black youth living in urbanized space retain a unique ability to foretell their futures based on the multiplicative forms of oppression they will inevitably face over their life course. So it is not as though Black and other racialized youth have not thought about the not-yet-here. It is precisely because they have cogitated so deeply over their futures that they reject many of the oppressions that have yet to come. That Black youth, including Black queer and trans youth, choose not to entertain "deferred" or foreclosed futures directed toward "freedoms" and liberties associated with a postraciality does not make them present oriented. It makes them prepared.

CONCLUSION

On April 24, 2021, a couple of local organizing collectives in Washington, DC, organized an event demanding the release of Mumia Abu-Jamal and all political prisoners. The rally was held on Mumia's sixty-seventh birthday. Before attending it, I was with a few comrades offering support to people being released from DC jails. After the rally, I headed back to the mutual aid site to check in with fellow organizers. As many were celebrating Mumia's life, many others were commemorating the death of Prince Rogers Nelson. It was the fifth anniversary of the Artist's passing on April 21, 2016. During my drive back to the site, the "4 p.m. Faceoff" on WHUR was in full effect, and this week's battle was between Prince and Rick James. As I was nearing my destination, the DJ began playing Prince's "Adore." In the song, Prince professes an undying love for another and makes clear that the only expiration date for his affection is the end of time itself. In short, it's a forever thang.

For whatever reason, on this particular day, "Adore" hit me in a special way. I began wondering whether there was any room to turn what was once a love ballad into a goodbye song by thinking about the literal end of time. It is unclear whether Prince believed that anything, including his love for another, would remain after the end of time. Most people use "till the end of time" to describe an impossibility, foreclosing the likelihood that something like love will never end because time itself is so seemingly eternal.

Still, if we can imagine the actual end of time, what else might need to be brought to a conclusion? If time is money, will the end of time mark the end of capitalism? If "time" is a metonym for incarceration, will end of time mark the end of the prison-industrial complex? If time and space are mutually constitutive, will the elimination of time help undo colonial relations to space? The end of time need be equated not with the end of life or the apocalypse but with the end of what Frank Wilderson describes as the anti-Black project of world making.[1] Perhaps we can think of the end of time in the way Ruth Wilson Gilmore thinks of abolition: as a "presence."[2]

To some, *until* the end of time feels far too reactive.[3] What about those who have no interest in waiting for the abstract end of time? For some Black youth, waiting until the end of time is not an option, but funking the clock is. When Dominique expresses a desire to free themself from time, they seem less interested in waiting until the end of time than in ending time itself. How many other Black youth are committed to a similar mission? The uprisings of 2020 suggest that Black people, and Black youth in particular, are not interested in waiting on time because it is clear that white time takes its/their time. Instead the goal is to funk the clock now. Many of the Black youths at Run-a-Way refused white time, punctuality, the temporal orientations of "maybe environments," the time discipline of schooling and jobs, and liberal futurities predicated on freedoms, liberties, and rights. Perhaps they see the end of time as the end of the world *as they know it.* Is that not what abolition demands? As Gilmore reminds us, "Abolition requires that we change one thing: everything."[4] To this end, we might ask: What would the abolition of time look like?

Unlearning is integral to abolition. Schools have a duty to help students unlearn, as much as, if not more than, they learn. In doing so, students unlearn that school resource officers, police, jails, cages, and prisons keep them safe. They unlearn the idea that we can heal through harm (security and surveillance, arrest, incarceration). Healing through (temporal) harm is not sustainable, but healing through the abolition of time is. In accordance with Joy James, though, I am not referring to some aspirational abolition.[5] I am referring to the strategies and tactics that Black and other racialized youth employ in the here and now to render systems of racialized violence and oppression obsolete. I am shouting out the countless students across the Twin Cities still leading workshops on how to get cops out of schools. I am showing love to all the organizers and activists throughout the Twin Cities modeling mutual aid, transformative justice, and healing justice to make carceral logics and systems obsolete. I am centering the many liberation lovers still going head up with law enforcement because they know that "police violence" is a redundancy and that brutality is standard operating procedure for all cops. Finally, I am amplifying the calls of comrades behind and beyond the wall committed to abolishing not just prisons but a society that allow prisons to exist.[6]

COVID-19, Disorientation, Rebellion, and the Wounds Time Cannot Heal

Many described COVID-19 as a "disorienting" experience—one that left people disconnected from familiar spatio-temporal coordinates. Losing track of time or the day of the week was further evidence of disorientation and the unmooring of time and space. Some went as far as to conflate "sheltering in place" or the lockdown with incarceration. Soon enough, I learned that disorientation was largely limited to the level of the individual. What became even clearer was that most people in the United States were not disoriented toward systems and institutions complicit in a form of world making that naturalizes Black dispossession, captivity, debt, and death. The pandemic sparked fears that "the world will never be the same." But what about those who worried that things would not be all that different?

Even fewer people seem to have been disoriented to time itself. Some may express concern over the provocation to funk the clock: "Without time, how will we educate students?" "Will we simply get rid of deadlines?" "Are we promoting laziness, procrastination, waywardness, and an overall devolution of societal norms?" "If we don't teach punctuality now, youth will never gain the skills necessary to join the workforce." I tend to respond to such inquiries by encouraging the asker to question the question. How might flexibility with deadlines be a commitment to disability justice and to helping Black and other racialized youths reclaim the time taken from structures of racialized violence? Moreover, why are we so quick to individualize disorder and ignore systemic forms of temporal violence? What if before punishing Black youths for lateness, we first sought to transform the onto-epistemological conditions that make lateness possible in the first place? How can teachers mark Black youths tardy when systems and structures are consistently late in delivering "equal" educational opportunities "with all deliberate speed"?[7] What would it take to eliminate logics that equate Black youths' time use with time theft? What would it look like for adults, including teachers, youthworkers, and others in positions of authority, to encourage Black youths to take/reappropriate their time, rather than chastising them for doing so? What must be done to transform the social conditions that make "maybe environments" so very real? How can we upend the logics that equate survival with "crime"? Before condemning Black youths for 'living for the moment," why not question why they are denied access to liberal futurities when whiteness is equated with modernity and future orientations?

Black youths seek not only an exit from the here and now of anti-Blackness and racialized violence but an escape from white time necessitating an anti-Black future. Black youths at Run-a-Way were not interested in going "back to the future," precisely because they knew that the future was foreclosed by white time. Rather, they found ways to create Black futures in the present. While reckoning with time, they also wrecked it in order to design new possibilities for being. Drawing inspiration from Robin D. G. Kelley's conceptualization of the "black radical imagination," Kara Keeling states, "Black existence is a condition of possibility for moving beyond the what is. At the same time, it presently anchors a set of possibilities for 'something else to be.'"[8]

As Black youth transgress the "what is" of white time and liberal futurities, they bring new meaning to the notion of time travel. Just as Dionne Brand taught readers the importance of traveling "without a map" and "without a way," Black youth find a way in disorientation and "misdirection."[9] Perhaps we might think of disorientation as direction, in the sense that losing our coordinates from the current spacetime is integral to charting new paths and constructing otherwise ways of being. As Édouard Glissant writes, "There is no place that does not have its elsewhere. No place where this is not an essential dilemma."[10]

Abiding by CP Time, inverting the temporal terms of whiteness, "teefing" time, and rejecting liberal futurities are evidence of Black youths' desire to free themselves from time and create what Tiffany Lethabo King, Jenell Navarro, and Andrea Smith describe as "otherwise worlds": "*Otherwise: something or anything else; something to the contrary*" (emphasis in the original).[11] Funking the clock is key to the creation of liberatory futurities and otherwise worlds. Youths, however, are not "the ones we've been waiting for," because, in truth, nobody is waiting. The uprisings of 2020 are a reminder that an otherwise world is possible, but not without struggle. Black youths know the stakes are high. As King, Navarro, and Smith, write, "*Otherwise: if not, or else.*"[12]

In addition to being about time, this book has made the case that it is also *about time* that sociology catch up to the racialized temporalities of Black youth in urbanized space. Sociology's reliance on measures of linear time, the linear life course, and an overall linear logic will keep it suspended in white time. Perhaps sociology is not meant to keep up with the temporalities of Black youth in urbanized space. Black youth consistently resist the disciplinary urge of sociology to suspend them in time and space by upholding several key tasks of Black studies: namely, to rewrite knowledge and unwrite racial taxonomies,[13] challenge the truth of the current episteme, and redefine the human as a verb. By running *a way*, rather than away, Black youth reveal their prescience and their connection to past and present realities, as well as otherwise futurities.

"Fugitivity," as conceptualized by Black studies scholars, does not require a person to run *a* way. Rather, the act of running is itself generative. To flee, escape, and abscond represent modes of acting with purpose. Fugitivity is also an opportunity to repurpose. Yet "runaway youth" have little chance of escaping the grips of what La Marr Jurelle Bruce calls the "symbiotic interrelation between material and discursive violence."[14] The stigma of being a "runaway" speaks for those presumed guilty until proven less guilty—namely, Black youth. The stigma linked to "runaways" renders motivations for running invisible, even if running a way is the only option. It does not matter what youth are running from or where they are running to. Running itself is transgressive, as it defies the designated space and time.

To inquire about youths' motivations for running is to risk learning that Black youth have become superfluous to the concept of the Child and thus warrant no protection. As Black youth begin to share their reasons for running, we see they are breaking fast from a compost of violence largely produced by adult-led systems. So they boogie from detention and the schoolhouse. They bounce from (s)low-wage work and other planned-obsolescent space. Perhaps many Black youths at Run-a-Way were seeking the haven that many of their ancestors sought and that Saidiya Hartman describes:

> And the dreams of what might be possible were enshrined in the names of these towns and villages founded by fugitives, *safe at last, we have come together, here where no one can reach us anymore, the village of free people, here we speak of peace, a place of abundance, haven.* Haven like communities of maroons and fugitives and outliers elsewhere, their identity was defined as much by what they were running from as by what they were running toward. (emphasis in the original)[15]

We need not privilege physicality, however, to understand the concept of "running." Many youths are running a way without moving at all. As fugitives fleeing racism, settler colonialism, and anti-Blackness, they run away, both physically and psychically, from racialized violence and toward another spacetime. As fugitives of white time, Black youths are not only "on the run"; they are wanted for attempting to use time that does not belong to them. Hence, their time use is read as time theft and is deemed criminal behavior. They are charged with "walking up to no good" while walking *down* the street in their own neighborhood. It is not that they are in the wrong place at the wrong time. Rather, they are in the wrong space according to white time, which remains the product of Black debt and dispossession. In short, Black youth are accused of stealing that which was already stolen (from them).

Black youths' temporalities are not only transgressive but transformative. To transform time requires exercising what Robin D. G. Kelley describes as the "black radical imagination": "We must remember that the conditions and the very existence of social movements enable participants to imagine something different, to realize that things need not always be this way. It is *that* imagination, that effort to see the future in the present, that I shall call 'poetry' or 'poetic knowledge.'"[16] Youths not only see foreclosed futures in the present but also imagine a "then and there" of Black sociality free from white time and racialized violence. As long as some persons remain exploited by white time, there will exist an exigent need to resist and, in the words of Toni Cade Bambara, "make revolution irresistible."[17] For adherents of Western Standard Time navigating the world through the future, the prospects of a revolution against time remain to be seen. The residence of slavery's afterlife in the present, though, leads many Black youths to imagine the not-yet-here. As Kara Keeling notes, "The past appears with every present, harboring dimensions of itself that might challenge what has been perceived about it."[18]

After the murder of George Floyd, Black youth took to the streets, not necessarily to run a way but to show the way through disorientation. They refused to be oriented to the notion that cops, cuffs, and cages keep people safe. They felt the same about school resource officers. More importantly, they were disoriented to the notion of "police reform." The risk of dying from COVID-19 was real, but the threat of police terror was even more imminent. At the time, there was no end in sight for the pandemic. But Black youth recognized that the enduring lifespan of police terror was sure to outlive any global health crisis. If their demands were not met today, tomorrow would lose importance. In turn, they showed that direct action is itself a mode of transgressing time and funking the clock.

Engaging in direct action signals one's refusal to have a seat, take a number, hold for the next representative, and/or wait their turn. Instead the goal was to bring the ruckus right to the front door of systems and institutions that only claim to "stand with Black lives" when their property, particularly whiteness and capital, is at risk. Thus, rather than continuing to be teased by capitalism and what is so often denied, many racialized youth from across the Twin Cities came to collect and did so through another form of direct action: shoplifting, or, as some activists called it, "reappropriation." Other youths did not believe in charges of "destruction of property," particularly when the "property" (e.g., the Third Precinct in South Minneapolis) was destructive. Perhaps the proper charge would then be "destruction of destructive property." Each of these tactics are examples of insurgent time that have no interest in entertaining the status quo and/or "business as usual."

Black and other racialized youth were prescient enough to know that you cannot treat a disease (i.e., police terror) with a symptom of that disease (e.g., databases to track "police misconduct"; national standards for accrediting police departments; body cameras; liability insurance; de-escalation training; diversity, equity, and inclusion (DEI) initiatives; implicit bias or antiracism trainings).

CONCLUSION   205

They knew that hiring more Black and brown officers would not only not end police terror but inaugurate and legitimate new forms of racialized violence. Black youth refuse to entertain postraciality simply because the cop brutalizing a Black person is no longer white. DEI disciples fail to recognize that "inclusion," by definition, requires exclusion. As Dylan Rodríguez notes, campaigns like "Join LAPD" function as "counterinsurgency" strategies used to incorporate minoritized difference while simultaneously legitimating state terror against members of the same racialized groups who join the ranks.[19] Hence, the inclusion of more Black and brown cops will always come at the expense of marginalized Black and brown communities. It makes sense that policing and DEI and/or antiracist education are so compatible. Both are temporally oriented toward a future of postraciality. Police and other institutions of racial terror use DEI and liberal antiracisms as fronts to mete out more palatable and seemingly race-neutral forms of violence.

Today's remedies for racism come specially packaged in individualized, future-oriented how-to guides that do more to expand racial capitalism and the state than dismantle them. Black youth, however, are not buying. They will not be fooled by (neo)liberal antiracisms that encourage them to be the best antiracist they can be because "only you can prevent racism." At the same time, Black youth refuse to let a largely white "reading class" reinforce Enlightenment logic by reading their way "out of trouble," just so they can become harbingers of a postracial world.[20] Entertaining such a postracial future is a pretext for legitimating violence in the present. Antiracists emphasize the difference between not being racist and being antiracist; however, when being antiracist necessitates reforms to unparalleled catastrophe and the afterlife of slavery, then such a distinction is meaningless. Just as you cannot reform slavery, you cannot reform time. Any attempt to do so would be fascist.[21] A radical praxis urges us to get at the root of temporal violence, while reforms push us to refashion time so that the watch bears a striking resemblance to the whip.

Throughout the pandemic, many Black youth knew what lay ahead and had no interest in things "returning to normal," precisely because the "normal" so many longed to return to was fatal as fuck. So it is no surprise that Black and many other racialized youth, acting in solidarity, were largely responsible for setting things off in the Twin Cities. They demanded the abolition of police and prisons, and some were even motivated by a desire to abolish civil society.[22] They checked anyone who tried to critique them for being impetuous and yearning for "instant gratification," because the(ir) time was/is now.

Black youths at Run-a-Way knew what's up and still know what time it is. They know their ABCs and 1-2-3s, but it is still fuck alphabet boys and fuck 12, respectively, but with the utmost disrespect. Even though they know how to count, they know they cannot count on cops. So fuck Five-O. Fuck slave patrol. Fuck watchmen. Matter fact fuck the watch. Fuck Jake. Fuck "the man." Matter fact fuck Man. Fuck "one time." Matter fact fuck time. All day every day. They say time heals all wounds. But can time heal the same wounds it inflicts for nine minutes twenty-nine seconds? George Floyd. Can time heal the wounds of delaying lifesaving treatment to a Black woman physician imperiled by racialized medicine and COVID-19? *Doctor* Susan Moore. Some might say it's only a matter of time before Black time matters, but on the matter of time, Black youth have already rendered a decision—Ayo, fuck the clock!

Methodological Appendix: Interview Schedule

Opportunity Structures

Orienting remarks: This first section asks about some of the different opportunities available to youth in communities like your own. Some experiences may be more familiar than others. Please answer the questions the best you can.

Methodological utility: By placing this section first, I hope to get youth thinking about the connection between time and opportunity structures.

1. Are you familiar with the notion of the "fast life"? Prompt: Provide explanation if youth are unfamiliar with the term.
   a. If so, how do you define it? Examples of the fast life may include selling drugs, selling illegal products (e.g., bootlegging), or earning money in an illegitimate way.
   b. If not, are you familiar with the term "trapping"? What does it mean to you?
   c. Are there particular hours people live the fast life?
2. What type of kids your age usually live the "fast life"?
3. For girls/femmes: Do you ever hear people talk about girls who are "in the life"? Prompt: Provide explanation if they are unfamiliar with the term.
   a. What does this mean?
4. What types of kids your age tend to get caught up in "the life"?
5. What is the easiest way someone your age can earn money in your community?
6. What is the fastest way someone your age can earn money in your community?
7. How do you differentiate between "easy" money and "fast" money?
8. Have you ever lived the "fast life"?
   a. If yes, are you still living the "fast life"?
   b. If yes, while living the fast life, do your thoughts about time change at all? If so, how?
   c. If no, how do people living the "fast life" think about time?
9. Have you ever been "in the life"?

208 **METHODOLOGICAL APPENDIX**

    a. Are you still "in the life"? While being "in the life," do your thoughts about time change at all? If so, how?

    b. If no, how do people who are "in the life" think about time?

There's also ways people earn legitimate money. This next section asks about people's experiences trying to follow a legit route to success.

10. On average, how long do you think it takes someone your age to find a job in your community? Does this seem like a long time?

11. How long do you think it takes to complete college?

Perceptions of Time

Orienting remarks: So we've talked a little bit about what it means to "live fast." This section focuses more on the pace of your own life. Most of the questions are related to your perceptions of time. I ask specific questions about the way you organize your time based on daily responsibilities. Please focus more on your experiences outside of the program.

    Methodological utility: Explore the extent to which youth construct their own temporalities in relation to institutionalized notions of time. I expect some responses to reflect some efforts to subvert conventional notions of time that do not reflect the lived experiences of youth of color in urbanized space.

1. People describe time in a variety of ways. For example "time on my hands," "killing time," "buy time," "time is money," "the luxury of time," "take your time," "time flies when you're having fun," "time waits for no one," "the race against time," and/or "time is of the essence." Which of these expressions are most familiar to you? Do you identify with any one in particular? Why? Do you not identify with any of these expressions of time?

2. Can you describe how you think about the future? For example, are you someone that tends to think only for the moment or the now, rather than consider what is yet to come?

3. What do you see in your future? Struggle? Easy street?

Certain groups have their own cultural notions of time. For example, Black people/African Americans living in this country jokingly refer to their own notions of time as "CP Time" or "CPT."

4. Are you familiar with the concept of "CP Time" or "CPT" or "Black People's Time"?

INTERVIEW SCHEDULE 209

   a. If so, how do you understand it? Prompt: Provide explanation, if they are unfamiliar with the term.
   b. What purpose does CP Time serve? Why do you think it exists?
   c. Are you familiar with similar notions of time within your own racial/ethnic group(s)?

5. Describe your relationship to time. Positive? Negative? Why?
6. Does time only move forward?
7. Do you follow CP Time?
8. Do you consider yourself to be someone that has a personal schedule? On average (when not in the program), what does your daily schedule consist of/look like?

Sometimes certain circumstances make it hard to get things done on time. This next series of questions explore different ways you cope with the pressures of time.

9. How do you use time? Do you ever consider yourself to be used by time? If so, how?
   a. Prompt: Wasting time or wisely using time?
10. Consider your experiences in your community, at school, at Run-a-Way. Who or what usually controls your time? When do you feel you are in control of your time?
11. How do people show respect for your time? How do people show a lack of respect for your time?
12. In what situations do you feel you are racing against time?
13. In what situations or contexts does time matter most to you? When do you make the most of your time?
14. How do you define lateness?
15. How important is it for you to be on time?
16. In your opinion, what causes people to be late?
17. In general, how often do you get to places on time? If you don't get to places on time, what prevents you from doing so?
18. How do you usually go about completing daily tasks? Weekly tasks? What sorts of things prevent you from completing your tasks on time?
19. When you think about what you have to accomplish every day, do you feel you have more or less time than your white peers?
20. What are some things that you feel consume your time, but not that of white youth?
   a. For girls of color in relation to boys of color.
   b. For girls of color in relation to white girls.
   c. For Black girls in relation to non-Black girls.

210   METHODOLOGICAL APPENDIX

21. How much harder do you feel you have to work compared to your white counterparts to achieve similar goals?
    a. How is your time constrained based on how much harder you have to work? Do you feel you have half the time to accomplish what more privileged youth do?
22. Does time move quicker for white youth or youth of color? Why?

Race, Racialization, and Racism

Orienting remarks: So we talked a little bit about the way certain racial/ethnic groups develop their own conceptions of time. This next set of questions focuses on particular experiences familiar to people of color that interfere with their personal schedules.

Methodological utility: This section is meant to explore the extent to which racism and racialization are in and of themselves time-consuming processes. It is also an opportunity to explore how one's awareness of racism and other forms of structural inequality condition youth temporality in relation to life chances.

1. Do you feel targeted by others based on your race?
2. How does being a target of racism impact your day-to-day functioning?
    a. Prompt: How are you fazed by this?
3. How do you interact with white people in positions of authority?
4. In your opinion, how important are events of the past? Cultural past?
5. Do you think about racism? If so, how often?
6. How often do you do something about racism?
7. How do you expect to be treated by employees of:
    a. convenience stores?
    b. major department stores?
    c. social service agencies (e.g., the Run-a-Way, [names of similar youth programs inserted here], etc.)
    d. state agencies (Child Protection Services, juvenile court, food assistance, etc.)
8. Who usually gets placed in the "slow" (remedial) classes in your school?
9. Have you ever been arrested? If so, why were you arrested? What were the charges?
10. Have you ever been locked up (in jail or prison)? If so, why were you locked up?
11. How do you cope with the possibility that you may be unfairly targeted by police?

12. How do you cope with the possibility that you may be harmed or killed by police?
13. When people talk about your community, how do they usually describe it? Up to date/new or old/backwards/behind time/slow/run down?
14. How do you think white people view you in relation to time (e.g., backwards, slow, quick thinker)?
15. How do you view the relationship between white people and time? "Up to the times, up on the latest fashions" or "slow and played out"?

Developmental Deadlines

Orienting remarks: Having to think about your own mortality or death may make people think more seriously about what they would like to accomplish before they die. This next set of questions asks about particular life experiences and the age at which you think people should achieve them.

Methodological utility: The purpose of this section is to establish a better understanding of how future orientations are temporally structured.

1. Around what age do you think people should have children?
2. Around what age do you think people should get married?
3. If you had a choice, what would be the minimum age at which you would allow children to start working?

Life Expectancy

Orienting remarks: This final section contains questions about your own life expectancy.

Methodological utility: The purpose of this section is to explore the accuracy of claims that youth of color living in urbanized space are present-oriented and incapable of thinking about the future and long-term implications of their actions.

1. What would you like to be doing 5 years from now?
   a. How will you work towards this goal?
2. How long do you expect to live?
   If age is under 30, why do you expect to die at this age?
      a. How does the thought of dying at this age shape your understanding of time?

3. What type of things would you like to accomplish as you grow into adulthood? Do you feel you have time to do these things? Why or why not?
4. What gives you hope?

Date _____
Interview # _____

Demographics

I'd like to ask you a few questions about your background. This information will help me better understand your perspectives on time. This brief questionnaire is also voluntary, and you can skip any questions you don't feel comfortable answering. If you have any questions while answering, please feel free to ask the researcher. When you are finished, please give this sheet to the researcher.

1. Age in years _____
2. Gender _____   Pronouns _____
3. Sexual orientation _____
4. What racial/ethnic group or groups do you and your family identify with being a member of? (Please list as many as you feel are important to who you are.)

   _____
   _____

5. Enrolled in school? Please circle one of the following responses: Yes or No
   a. If you answered no, you have completed this questionnaire.
6. What is your grade in school? _____
7. Do you receive free or reduced lunch? Please circle one: Yes or No
8. What school do you go to?
9. What is your zip code?

Notes

INTRODUCTION

1. Denise Ferreira da Silva uses this term to describe the production of the racial within post-Enlightenment theories of the racial "other" and their placement within the category of the human. Denise Ferreira da Silva, *Toward a Global Idea of Race* (Minneapolis: University of Minnesota Press, 2007), xviii.

2. I use "urbanized" rather than "urban" to attend to the ongoing construction of space. There exists a mutually constitutive relationship between urbanized space and suburbanized space. In other words, the suburbs cannot exist without the many ghettos across the globe. It is worth noting that "urban space" is just a few letters short of "suburban space." "Urban areas" ignores the ongoing and processual character of urbanization. The reification of "urban communities" as such obscures the systematic construction of the ghetto and suburbs through white suburbanization, blockbusting, block bombings, restrictive covenants, redlining, zoning laws, and "urban renewal," or what James Baldwin calls "Negro removal." In short, a compost of institutional artifice, private actions, and racialized policy catering to a white public yields arable terrain for the co-construction of white habitus within white habitats and suffering in majority-nonwhite space. James Baldwin, interviewed by Kenneth Clark, "Urban Renewal . . . Means Negro Removal—James Baldwin (1963)," posted June 3, 2015, YouTube, https://www.youtube.com/watch?v=T8Abhj17kYU.

3. Elizabeth Freeman, *Time Binds: Queer Temporalities, Queer Histories* (Durham, NC: Duke University Press, 2010), 3.

4. L. H. Stallings, *Funk the Erotic: Transaesthetics and Black Sexual Cultures* (Chicago: University of Illinois Press, 2015), xvi.

5. Stallings, *Funk the Erotic*, xvi.

6. Stefano Harney and Fred Moten, *The Undercommons: Fugitive Planning and Black Study* (New York: Minor Compositions, 2013), 132.

7. It is possible that Dominique intended to self-identify as "gender fluid," a more commonly accepted identity along the gender spectrum. This should not, however, diminish the applicability of "gender fluent." While less conventional among gender scholars, "gender fluent" conveys a sense that one is fluent in gender discourse, especially when it comes to articulating their own gender identity.

8. Barry Glassner, "An Essay on Iterative Social Time," *American Sociological Review* 30, no. 4 (1982): 668–81, and Elliott Jaques, *The Form of Time* (London: Heinemann, 1982), are two examples of social scientists engaging with time's iterative and nonlinear character.

9. M. Jacqui Alexander, *Pedagogies of Crossing: Meditations on Feminism, Sexual Politics, Memory, and the Sacred* (Durham, NC: Duke University Press, 2005), 309.

10. Alexander, *Pedagogies of Crossing*, 309.

11. Sylvia Wynter, "No Humans Involved: An Open Letter to My Colleagues," *Forum N.H.I. Knowledge for the 21st Century* 1, no. 1 (1994): 68.

12. Sylvia Wynter, "Unsettling the Coloniality of Being/Power/Being/Truth/Freedom: Towards the Human, after Man, Its Overrepresentation—an Argument," *CR: The New Centennial Review* 3, no. 3 (2003): 318.

214   **NOTES TO PAGES 4–6**

13. Stallings, *Funk the Erotic*, 6.

14. Alexander G. Weheliye, *Habeus Viscus: Racializing Assemblages, Biopolitics, and Black Feminist Theories of the Human* (Durham, NC: Duke University Press, 2014), 20.

15. I would be remiss not to note my reservations regarding "criminalized." I believe "criminalized," "criminalization," etc., remain complicit in the reproduction of solecism. Each of these concepts requires the existence and production of an always already racialized "criminal." Who then is the criminal? To what extent does the presence of a "criminal" legitimate the existence of and need for the criminal legal system and the prison-industrial complex? What are the limitations of a discourse of "criminalization" within the context of abolition? While language may be limited, developing more precise terminology and liberatory discourse is key to measuring what we intend to measure, and perhaps abolishing what we intend to abolish.

16. To the extent that Black youth are interpellated within the temporal context of school, they are, according to Ann Arnett Ferguson, "tagged with futures: 'He's on the fast track to San Quentin Prison,' and 'That one has a jail-cell with his name on it.'" Ann Arnett Ferguson, *Bad Boys: Public Schools in the Making of Black Masculinity* (Ann Arbor: University of Michigan Press, 2000), 95–96. Zero-tolerance policies and racialized discipline ensure that Black students will be not only consistently held back, left back, and expelled from school, but *suspended* in time.

17. In their study exploring whether Black youths are afforded similar protections of the category of "childhood" as their non-Black counterparts, Goff et al. find that Black youths are consistently seen as older, less innocent than their peers, and thus less worthy of the protections that accompany the ontological status of "child." According to the authors, "The perceived innocence of Black children aged 10–13 was equivalent to that of non-Black children aged 14–17, and the perceived innocence of Black children aged 14–17 was equivalent to that of non-Black adults aged 18–21." Philip A. Goff et al., "The Essence of Innocence: Consequences of Dehumanizing Black Children," *Journal of Personality and Social Psychology* 106, no. 4 (2014): 529.

18. Lee Edelman, *No Future: Queer Theory and the Death Drive* (Durham, NC: Duke University Press, 2004), 3.

19. Edelman, *No Future*, 2.

20. Edelman, *No Future*, 28.

21. I would be remiss to not push back against Edelman's pessimistic claim by acknowledging the many ways in which queer and trans people form families outside the heteronormative logics of reproductive futurisms. Heteronormative logics, Edelman argues, render queer and trans people incapable of being active participants in reproductive futurisms; still, this should not ignore the many ways in which queer and trans people form families, through kinship, care, choice, and childbearing, without reproducing hegemonic heteronormativity.

22. Frank Wilderson describes Black youth as an ontological impossibility because "*Black* and *Child* cannot be reconciled" (emphasis in the original). Frank B. Wilderson III, *Red, White & Black: Cinema and the Structure of U.S. Antagonisms* (Durham, NC: Duke University Press, 2010), 331.

23. Wynter, "Unsettling the Coloniality."

24. Outside sociology, anthropologists have explored how time is objectified in the lives of youth in several countries, including the Philippines, Brazil, Romania, Uganda, Nepal, Denmark, Georgia, Cameroon, and the United States. There is still little attention paid to the temporal perspectives of racialized youth in poor, urbanized space in the US. In their edited volume based on transnational comparisons of youth temporality, Dalsgård et al. seek to understand "what an anthropology of youth has to offer to wider anthropological theorizing on time." Anne Line Dalsgård et al., *Ethnographies of*

Youth and Temporality: Time Objectified (Philadelphia: Temple University Press, 2014), 4. In the only comparative case in the anthology to include the US, Jennifer Johnson-Hanks explores how college-educated American women "make a living and meaningful life" under uncertain prospects for the future. Jennifer Johnson-Hanks, "Waiting for the Start: Flexibility and the Question of Convergence," in Dalsgård et al., *Ethnographies of Youth and Temporality*, 25.

25. Johannes Fabian, *Time and the Other: How Anthropology Makes Its Object* (New York: Columbia University Press, 1983), 74.

26. My decision to use strikethrough here is not simply a writing style but also a site of critical thinking. In several chapters of this book, I describe what it means for Black youth to use time that doesn't belong to them. Hence, I use strikethrough to make clear that even though we'd like to believe that Black youth have ownership over their time, they are more likely to owe rather than own time. This is similar to Calvin Warren's use of "black ~~being~~." Warren leverages an Afro-pessimist critique to argue that "being is not universal or applicable to blacks." The literary effectiveness comes through a recognition among readers that while "black being" may be a familiar-enough phrase, it remains, according to Warren, oxymoronic. The use of the strikethrough becomes another tool to uphold a key task of Black studies—namely, to rewrite knowledge. Calvin Warren, *Ontological Terror: Blackness, Nihilism, and Emancipation* (Durham, NC: Duke University Press, 2018), 5.

27. José Esteban Muñoz, *Cruising Utopia: The Then and There of Queer Futurity* (New York: New York University Press, 2009).

28. Cedric Robinson, preface to *Futures of Black Radicalism*, ed. Gaye Theresa Johnson and Alex Lubin (New York: Verso, 2017), 3.

29. In *Act Your Age!: A Cultural Construction of Adolescence* (New York: Routledge-Falmer, 2001), Nancy Lesko writes, "On the future of white boys the civilized nations would rise or fall" (45).

30. Among this group of girls and boys, there are two youths who identify as trans—one boy and one girl.

31. According to a report created by Wilder Research, "Out of all homeless youth age 24 and younger, 23% identified as LGBTQ." Virginia Pendleton, Walker Bosch, Margaret Vohs, Stephanie Nelson-Dusek, and Michelle Decker Gerrard, "Characteristics of People Who Identify as LGBTQ Experiencing Homelessness: Findings from the 2018 Minnesota Homeless Study," Amherst H. Wilder Foundation, September 2020, https://www.wilder.org/sites/default/files/imports/2018_HomelessnessInMinnesota_LGBTQ_9-20.pdf, 2.

32. Kiese Laymon, *Long Division* (Chicago: Bolden Books, 2013), 1.

33. Michelle M. Wright describes qualitative collapse as "meaningful, layered, rich and nuanced interpellations that occur when seeking to interpellate the diversity of Blackness through the patterns of linear spacetime." Michelle M. Wright, *Physics of Blackness: Beyond the Middle Passage Epistemology* (Minneapolis: University of Minnesota Press, 2015), 142.

34. I am riffing on a virtual lecture delivered by Hortense J. Spillers in conversation with Lewis R. Gordon. Soka University of America, "Afropessimism and Its Others: A Discussion between Hortense J. Spillers and Lewis R. Gordon," YouTube video, 1:23:31, May 24, 2021, https://www.youtube.com/watch?v=Z-s-Ltu06NI.

35. Javier Auyero and Débora Alejandra Swistun, *Flammable: Environmental Suffering in an Argentine Shantytown* (Oxford: Oxford University Press, 2009), 16.

36. Katherine McKittrick, *Dear Science and Other Stories* (Durham, NC: Duke University Press, 2021), 44. McKittrick draws extensively on Édouard Glissant's *Poetics of Relation*. As Glissant writes, "Description is no proof; it simply adds something to Relation insofar as the latter is a synthesis-genesis that never is complete." Édouard Glissant, *Poetics of Relation* (Ann Arbor: University of Michigan Press, 1997), 174. Sylvia Wynter also

216   NOTES TO PAGES 10–15

critiques the ontological violence of biocentric "descriptive statements" of the human, man, and Man's overrepresentation. Sylvia Wynter, "Unsettling the Coloniality," 268.

37. I sometimes wonder whether sociology PhDs forget that they are doctors of philosophy as opposed to medical doctors. Sociology's emphasis on prescribing solutions to social problems seems laudable; however, so often what sociologists prescribe are solutions conceived of through the individualization of social disorder. For example, criminologists' emphasis on delinquency and deviance results in pathologizing prescriptions to improve human, social, and cultural capital, as opposed to condemning the systems and institutions responsible for constructing "delinquency" and "deviance" in the first place.

38. Fabian writes, "In simple terms, the ethnographic present is the practice of giving accounts of other cultures and societies in the present tense. . . . [T]he present tense 'freezes' a society at the time of observation; at worst, it contains assumptions about the repetitiveness, predictability, and conservatism of primitives." Fabian, *Time and the Other*, 80–81.

39. "Flicka Da Wrist," MP3 audio, track 7 on Chedda Da Connect, *Chedda World: The Album*, eOne Entertainment, 2015.

40. "New York (Ya Out There)," MP3 audio, track 10 on Rakim, *The 18th Letter/The Book of Life*, Universal Records, 1997.

41. Renato Rosaldo, *Culture and Truth: The Remaking of Social Analysis* (Boston: Beacon, 1989), 207.

42. I would be remiss not to acknowledge the privileges of being "racially ambiguous." If violence against Black people, as Wilderson suggests, is not contingent but gratuitous, I recognize that while I may be subject to police terror, I still exist within a particular position of thought/field of psychic and ontological relation that diminishes a cop's instinct to kill. Frank B. Wilderson III, "The Black Liberation Army and the Paradox of Political Engagement," in *Postcoloniality-Decoloniality-Black Critique: Joints and Fissures*, ed. Sabine Broeck and Carsten Junker (Chicago: University of Chicago Press, 2014), 7.

43. Steve Mann, "Veilance and Reciprocal Transparency: Surveillance versus Sousveillance, AR Glass, Lifelogging, and Wearable Computing," in *2013 IEEE International Symposium on Technology and Society (ISTAS): Social Implications of Wearable Computing and Augmediated Reality in Everyday Life* (Toronto: Institute of Electrical and Electronics Engineers, 2013), 3.

44. Simone Browne, *Dark Matters: On the Surveillance of Blackness* (Durham, NC: Duke University Press, 2015), 21.

45. Richard Majors and Janet Billson describe how some young Black men rely on the "cool pose" as a physical and psychological deportment to counter the effects of racialized and structural violence. As the authors note, a "cool pose can be used to keep social service workers, mental health professionals, and therapists off guard. Some African-American males suspect that white counselors do not give them honest feedback, so they tell counselors what they want to hear; they resort to playing games and faking it by adopting a cool pose." Richard Majors and Janet Billson, *Cool Pose: The Dilemmas of Black Manhood in America* (New York: Lexington Books, 1992), 40.

46. Yarimar Bonilla, *Non-sovereign Futures: French Caribbean Politics in the Wake of Disenchantment* (Chicago: University of Chicago Press, 2015), xvii.

47. Trans youths' room preferences did not always affirm their gender identity. I observed some tensions among male-identified youths over the staff's decision to assign a transmasculine youth to a boy's room, which matched that youth's gender identity. Ostracized by families, friends, and community, many queer and trans youths remained in constant search of gender-affirming programs and programming. There were no specific rooms reserved for nonbinary youths. I observed at least one nonbinary youth placed in a gendered bedroom.

48. Sara Ahmed, *Queer Phenomenology: Orientations, Objects, Others* (Durham, NC: Duke University Press, 2006), 121.

49. I expand on the mutual construction of poor urbanized space and wealthy urbanized space in chapter 3.

50. During my time at Run-a-Way, "gas" was one of the most current slang terms to refer to marijuana.

51. George Lipsitz, *The Possessive Investment in Whiteness: How White People Profit from Identity Politics* (Philadelphia: Temple University Press, 2006).

52. Eduardo Bonilla-Silva, *Racism without Racists: Color-Blind Racism and the Persistence of Racial Inequality in the United States* (Lanham, MD: Rowman & Littlefield, 2010), 104.

53. The average length of stay for many youths in the emergency shelter program was seven to ten days, and most who left went home with family. I maintained the longest relationships with youths from of the independent living program, some of whom had transitioned from the emergency shelter program.

54. In some cases, however, parents, guardians, social workers, and/or staff members assigned youths' racial and ethnic identities.

55. Grace Kyungwon Hong, "Intersectionality and Incommensurability: Third World Feminism and Asian Decolonization," in *Asian American Feminisms and Women of Color Politics*, ed. Lynn Fujiwara and Shireen Roshanravan (Seattle: University of Washington Press, 2018), 36.

56. Dylan Rodríguez, *White Reconstruction: Domestic Warfare and the Logics of Genocide* (New York: Fordham University Press, 2021), 7.

57. I would be remiss not to acknowledge the limitations of "hauntings"—a term that evokes the presence of something or someone from the past. Throughout this book, however, I make clear that the past is always present for racialized, particularly Black and Native, youth.

58. Steve Martinot, *The Machinery of Whiteness: Studies in the Structure of Racialization* (Philadelphia: Temple University Press, 2010), 172.

59. Martinot, *Machinery of Whiteness*, 172.

60. Martinot, *Machinery of Whiteness*, 10–11.

61. Frantz Fanon, *Black Skins, White Masks*, trans. Richard Philcox (New York: Grove Press, 2008), xv.

62. Fanon, *Black Skins, White Masks*, 95.

63. I feel "penal-legal system" captures the perfunctory, technocratic, cold, and impersonal nature of a system that remains not just devoid of "justice" but antithetical to it. Because the penal-legal system functions to decriminalize white supremacy, racialized violence, and the perpetrators of both, it can never be a site of justice. When "justice" itself "produces and requires Black exclusion and death as normative," as James Joy and João Costa Vargas put it, it will always elude its own point of reference (i.e., Black people). James Joy and João Costa Vargas, "Refusing Blackness-as-Victimization: Trayvon Martin and the Black Cyborgs," in *Pursuing Trayvon: Historical Contexts and Contemporary Manifestations of Racial Dynamics*, ed. George Yancy and Janine Jones (Lanham, MD: Lexington Books, 2012), 193.

64. Here I am thinking of Richard Iton's theorization of Blackness as engendering "possibilities in excess of and beyond modernity" as well as the "modern nation-state." Richard Iton, *In Search of the Black Fantastic: Politics and Popular Culture in the Post-Civil Rights Era* (Oxford: Oxford University Press, 2008), 15.

65. Martinot, *Machinery of Whiteness*, 173.

66. Nandita Sharma, "Strategic Anti-essentialism: Decolonizing Decolonization," in *Sylvia Wynter: On Being Human as Praxis*, ed. Katherine McKittrick (Durham, NC: Duke University Press, 2015), 175.

218   NOTES TO PAGES 21–22

67. Michael Omi and Howard Winant, *Racial Formation in the United States: From the 1960s to the 1990s*, 2nd ed. (New York: Routledge, 1994), 82.

68. Omi and Winant, *Racial Formation*, 111.

69. I agree with Martinot, who writes, "For whites to think that they too were a race only valorized the concept of race as whites had invented it and allowed them to pretend that it had a foundation in something natural. It also places the relation of races on a horizontal plane, while the process of racialization that whites impose on others is by that token hierarchical, a vertical system of domination. Many whites have hidden their awareness of their hierarchical status from themselves by trying to think of themselves as simply human." Martinot, *Machinery of Whiteness*, 86.

70. Helen Ngo, *The Habits of Racism: A Phenomenology of Racism and Racialized Embodiment* (Lanham: Lexington Books, 2017), xiii. As Martinot states, "By defining itself as the primary difference, whiteness defines itself as the power to define." Martinot, *Machinery of Whiteness*, 100.

71. See Ashley W. Doane Jr., "Dominant Group Ethnic Identity in the United States: The Role of 'Hidden' Ethnicity in Intergroup Relations," *Sociological Quarterly* 38, no. 3 (1997): 375–97; Amanda E. Lewis, "'What Group?' Studying Whites and Whiteness in the Era of 'Color-Blindness,'" *Sociological Theory* 22, no. 4 (December 2004): 623–46; Pamela Perry, "White Means Never Having to Say You're Ethnic: White Youth and the Construction of 'Cultureless' Identities," *Journal of Contemporary Ethnography* 30, no. 1 (2001): 56–91.

72. Rosaldo, *Culture and Truth*, 202.

73. Nell Irvin Painter, *The History of White People* (New York: W. W. Norton, 2010).

74. Mike King conceptualizes "aggrieved whiteness" as a "white identity politics aimed at maintaining white sociopolitical hegemony through challenging efforts to combat actual material racial inequality, while supporting heavily racialized investments in policing, prisons, and the military, and positing a narrative of antiwhite racial oppression loosely rooted in an assortment of racialized threats." Mike King, "Aggrieved Whiteness: White Identity Politics and Modern American Racial Formation," *Abolition Journal*, May 4, 2017, https://abolitionjournal.org/aggrieved-whiteness-white-identity-politics-and-modern-american-racial-formation.

75. See Ferreira da Silva, *Global Idea of Race*, 30–31.

76. Several critical ethnic studies scholars have embraced a similar engagement with such ideas. See, for example, Tiffany Willoughby-Herard, "'The Whatever That Survived': Thinking Racialized Immigration through Blackness and the Afterlife of Slavery," in *Relational Formations of Race: Theory, Method and Practice*, edited by Natalia Molina, Daniel Martinez Hosang, and Ramóna A. Gutiérrez (Berkeley: University of California Press, 2019), 145–61. Consider scholarship in critical whiteness studies that acknowledge, in their respective essays' subtitles, "The Role of 'Hidden' Ethnicity in Intergroup Relations" (Doane) and "The Construction of 'Cultureless' Identities" (Perry). For more on the formation of white identity from a position of race neutrality, see Toni Morrison, *Playing in the Dark: Whiteness and the Literary Imagination* (New York: Vintage, 1992); Lewis, "'What Group?'"; Martinot, *Machinery of Whiteness*; David R. Roediger, *The Wages of Whiteness: Race and the Making of the American Working Class* (Brooklyn, NY: Verso, 1991); France Winddance Twine, "Brown Skinned White Girls: Class, Culture and the Construction of White Identity in Suburban Communities," *Gender, Place & Culture: A Journal of Feminist Geography* 3, no. 2 (1996): 205–24; Sara Ahmed, "A Phenomenology of Whiteness," *Feminist Theory* 8, no. 2 (2007): 149–68. Not only does whiteness signify the absence of race, but it also poses the threat of erasing racial identity for those who attempt to "act white." For more on this, see Signithia Fordham and John Ogbu, "'Black Students' School

Success: Coping with the 'Burden of Acting White,'" *Urban Review* 18 (1986): 176–206. It is then no surprise that many racialized and Indigenous peoples equate assimilation with death. In short, whiteness is as much of a sociohistorical construct as other racial formations, but in reality it operates as a hidden ethnicity. We might think of this as an *a priori* and autopoietic character of whiteness.

77. Alia Al-Saji's work on racialization and time also suggests that racialized subjects are not only stuck but delayed. Al-Saji writes, "The racialized subject is temporally decentred and delayed in regard to this virtual (absent but real) subject, incapable of catching up." Alia Al-Saji, "Too Late: Racialized Time and the Closure of the Past," *Insights* 6, no. 5 (2013): 8.

78. Michelle M. Wright critiques such provincializing logics and representations as a "qualitative collapse": "The collapse of meaningful, layered, rich and nuanced interpellations that occurs when seeking to interpellate the diversity of Blackness through the patterns of linear spacetime." Michelle M. Wright, *Physics of Blackness: Beyond the Middle Passage Epistemology* (Minneapolis: University of Minnesota Press, 2015), 142.

79. Saidiya Hartman, *Lose Your Mother: A Journey along the Atlantic Slave Route* (New York: Farrar, Straus & Giroux, 2007), 7.

80. For more on the role of CP Time as a tool of resistance, see Ronald Walcott, "Ellison, Gordone, and Tolson: Some Notes on the Blues, Style and Space," *Black World* 22, no. 2 (1972): 4–29.

81. Eduardo Bonilla-Silva, "Rethinking Racism: Toward a Structural Interpretation," *American Sociological Review* 63, no. 3 (1997): 469.

82. To "teef" is to steal. The word's genealogy can be traced to Jamaica. The significance of Jamaican patois and "chat" to the sociolinguistic styles of neighboring islands in the Caribbean and countries around the world cannot be overstated.

83. Derek Thompson, "The Miracle of Minneapolis," *The Atlantic*, March 2015, https://www.theatlantic.com/magazine/archive/2015/03/the-miracle-of-minneapolis/384975/; Jessica Nickrand, "Minneapolis's White Lie," *The Atlantic*, February 21, 2015, https://www.theatlantic.com/business/archive/2015/02/minneapoliss-white-lie/385702/.

84. Mark Rifkin, *Beyond Settler Time: Temporal Sovereignty and Indigenous Self-Determination* (Durham, NC: Duke University Press, 2017).

85. Despite being used colloquially among youths at Run-a-Way, "lame" is also problematic from a critical disability studies and disability justice perspective.

86. Lesko, *Act Your Age!*, 137.

87. Homi K. Bhabha, "'Race,' Time and the Revision of Modernity," in *Theories of Race and Racism: A Reader*, 2nd ed., ed. Les Back and John Solomos (New York: Routledge, 2009), 427.

1. WHOSE TIME IS IT?

1. Time is a racialized, gendered, and capitalist construct that precludes the coevalness of Black and Indigenous people, among many other racialized subjects. White time is synchronized to white life and asynchronized to nonwhite life. Hence, white people, according to George Lipsitz, maintain a "possessive investment in whiteness" (see his book of the same name) and time, while nonwhite people can only owe rather than own time. White time supports the construction of white people, mostly male/masculine identified, and whiteness as modern, civilized, and future oriented, while marking racialized subjects as backward, premodern, and other. Charles Mills describes "white time" as a product of the exploitation and extraction of nonwhite life. Charles Mills, "White Time: The Chronic Injustice of Ideal Theory," *Du Bois Review* 11, no. 1 (2014): 28.

220   **NOTES TO PAGES 29–30**

2. Barbara J. Fields, "Whiteness, Racism, and Identity." *International Labor and Working-Class History* 60 (2001): 53.

3. The transition from the category of dysselected to selected comes with a variety of risks. Here I am thinking with scholars like Denise Ferreira da Silva and Saidiya Hartman, who both attend to the violence of representation. In *Toward a Global Idea of Race* (Minneapolis: University of Minnesota Press, 2007, Ferreira da Silva distinguishes the "transparent I" that exists within the "scene of representation" from the "affectable other" subjugated to the "scene of regulation" (38). Any attempt by the affectable other to move from the scene or regulation to the scene of representation requires what Ferreira da Silva describes as "self-obliteration" (162). Similarly, in *Scenes of Subjection: Terror, Slavery, and Self-Making in Nineteenth-Century America* (New York: Oxford University Press, 1997), Saidiya V. Hartman asks, "Why is pain the conduit for identification?" (20). Why are pain, subjugation, and abjection the primary mode for interpellating Black life? It is worth asking, then, how representation itself comes to legitimate violence against those who remain the targets of asymmetrical violence.

4. Adrienne Rich, "'Disloyal to Civilization': Feminism, Racism, and Gynephobia," in *On Lies, Secrets, and Silence: Selected Prose* (New York: W. W. Norton, 1995), 299. Rich describes white solipsism as the ability to "think, imagine, and speak as if whiteness described the world." Consequently, white people fail to, or refuse to, acknowledge the significance of nonwhite experience and/or existence.

5. John Hassard, ed., *The Sociology of Time* (New York: St. Martin's, 1990), 1.

6. Johannes Fabian expresses a preference for "reflexion" over reflection. Fabian, *Time and the Other: How Anthropology Makes Its Object* (New York: Columbia University Press, 1983), 91. Reflexion is a product of reflexivity, which itself derives from memory and an appreciation of how subjectivity and social location inform our research. In contrast, reflection tends to reproduce observations as objective fact rather than understanding the role of the self in constructing the other.

7. The notion that social time is a product of social structure is well established by several scholars of the sociology of time. For further discussions of social time, see Pitirim Sorokin and Robert Merton, "Social-Time: A Methodological and Functional Analysis," in Hassard, *Sociology of Time*, 56–66; Lewis Coser and Rose Coser, "Time Perspective and Social Structure," in Hassard, *Sociology of Time*, 191–202; Barry Schwartz, *Waiting and Queuing: Studies in the Social Organization of Access and Delay* (Chicago: University of Chicago Press, 1975); David J. Lewis and Andrew J. Weigart. "The Structures and Meanings of Social-Time," in Hassard, *Sociology of Time*, 77–101; Barry Glassner, "An Essay on Iterative Social Time," *American Sociological Review* 30, no. 4 (1982): 668–81; Blanka Filipcová and Jindřich Filipec, "Society and Concepts of Time," *International Social Science Journal* 107 (1986): 19–32; Norbert Elias, *Time: An Essay* (Cambridge: Blackwell, 1992); Mustafa Emirbayer and Ann Mische, "What Is Agency?," *American Journal of Sociology* 103, no. 4 (1998): 962–1023.

8. Émile Durkheim, *The Elementary Forms of Religious Life*, trans. Carol Cosman (Oxford: Oxford University Press, 2001), 12.

9. As Frieda Johles Forman notes, "In ancient Greek myth, Cronus, son of mother earth and father heaven, who devours his own children, is identified with Chronos, the personification of time: thus our chronology." Frieda Johles Forman, "Feminizing Time: An Introduction," in *Taking Our Time: Feminist Perspectives on Temporality*, edited by Frieda Johles Forman and Caroran Sowton (Oxford: Pergamon, 1989), 4.

10. Hassard, *Sociology of Time*, x.

11. Antonio Negri, *Time for Revolution*, trans. Matteo Mandarini (New York: Bloomsbury, 2003), 77. Negri writes, "It then becomes possible to grasp the relation between

external time (as the time of composition) and *internal time* (as the human time of the subjects that compose it)."

12. Vanessa Ogle, "Whose Time Is It? The Pluralization of Time and the Global Condition, 1870s–1940s," *American Historical Review* 118, no. 5 (2013): 1377.

13. Hassard, *Sociology of Time*, 3.

14. See Michael G. Flaherty, *A Watched Pot: How We Experience Time* (New York: New York University Press, 1999) and *Textures of Time: Agency and Temporal Experience* (Philadelphia: Temple University Press, 2011). Flaherty suggests that "time work" and "temporal agency" are key to bringing about a particular kind of "temporal experience." See *Textures of Time*, 3.

15. Sorokin and Merton, "Social-Time," 61.

16. Sorokin and Merton, "Social-Time," 61.

17. On sociogenesis and sociogeny, see Frantz Fanon, *Black Skin, White Masks*, trans. Richard Philcox (New York: Grove, 2008); and Sylvia Wynter, "Unsettling the Coloniality of Being/Power/Being/Truth/Freedom: Towards the Human, after Man, Its Overrepresentation—an Argument," *CR: The New Centennial Review* 3, no. 3 (2003): 257–337.

18. Eviatar Zerubavel, "The Standardization of Time: A Sociohistorical Perspective," *American Journal of Sociology* 88, no. 1 (1982): 4.

19. Zerubavel, "Standardization of Time," 5.

20. Frank B. Wilderson III, *Red, White, & Black: Cinema and the Structure of U.S. Antagonisms* (Durham, NC: Duke University Press, 2010), 283–84.

21. A central concern of most quantitative research methods in sociology is causality or causal validity. These methods emphasize the importance of "temporal order"—a cause must come before an effect.

22. Rather than critique "Western civilization" and its reliance on temporal domination to maintain a coevalness with modernity, Zerubavel naturalizes time and legitimates modernity as defining characteristics of progress narratives. "Given that temporal coordination serves to solidify 'organic' ties among people (Zerubavel 1979, pp. 60–83; Zerubavel 1981, pp. 67–69), this system also seems to be a perfect manifestation of the modern prevalence in the West of interdependence and complementary differentiation over 'mechanical' ties of similitude and uniformity and is thus one of the key characteristics of modern Western civilization." Zerubavel, "Standardization of Time," 21.

23. Elizabeth Freeman, *Time Binds: Queer Temporalities, Queer Histories* (Durham, NC: Duke University Press, 2010), 80.

24. Coser and Coser, "Time Perspective and Social Structure," 196.

25. Coser and Coser, "Time Perspective and Social Structure," 202.

26. Coser and Coser, "Time Perspective and Social Structure," 193.

27. Coser and Coser, "Time Perspective and Social Structure," 196.

28. John S. Mbiti, *African Religions and Philosophy* (New York: Praeger, 1969), 27–28.

29. Coser and Coser, "Time Perspective and Social Structure," 201. In chapter 7, I demonstrate how Black youths in urbanized space remain ahead of time, as a result of their prescience within present orientations.

30. Saidiya Hartman describes "slavery's afterlife" as a still-unfolding process in the wake of "emancipation." The afterlife of slavery subjects Black people to "skewed life chances, limited access to health and education, premature death, incarceration, and impoverishment." Saidiya V. Hartman, *Lose Your Mother: A Journey along the Atlantic Slave Route* (New York: Farrar, Straus & Giroux, 2007), 6.

31. Dylan Rodríguez, "Inhabiting the Impasse: Racial/Racial-Colonial Power, Genocide Poetics, and the Logic of Evisceration," *Social Text* 33, no. 3 (2015): 19–44.

32. Walter Mignolo, *The Idea of Latin America* (Oxford: Blackwell, 2005), 153.

33. Paul Gilroy, *The Black Atlantic: Modernity and Double-Consciousness* (Cambridge, MA: Harvard University Press, 1993), 163.

34. Clarissa Rile Hayward, *How Americans Make Race: Stories, Institutions, Spaces* (Cambridge: Cambridge University Press, 2013), 30.

35. Eviatar Zerubavel, *Time Maps: Collective Memory and the Social Shape of the Past* (Chicago: University of Chicago Press, 2003), 92.

36. Renato Rosaldo, *Culture and Truth: The Remaking of Social Analysis* (Boston: Beacon, 1989), 87.

37. Ferreira da Silva, *Global Idea of Race*, 94.

38. Zerubavel, *Time Maps*, 4.

39. Zerubavel, *Time Maps*, 10.

40. Crystal Fleming, *Resurrecting Slavery: Racial Legacies and White Supremacy in France* (Philadelphia: Temple University Press, 2017), 16. Prior to the publication of *Resurrecting Slavery*, Helen Ngo introduced the concepts of "racialized temporality" and "racialized time" in *The Habits of Racism: A Phenomenology of Racism and Racialized Embodiment* (Lanham, MD: Lexington, 2017).

41. Michael Hanchard, "Afro-modernity: Temporality, Politics, and the African Diaspora," *Public Culture* 11, no. 1 (1999): 247.

42. Here I am thinking with Black studies scholars who acknowledge "slavery's afterlife." For more on this topic, see Saidiya V. Hartman, "The Time of Slavery," *South Atlantic Quarterly* 101, no. 4 (2002): 757–77; Christina Sharpe's concept of "the wake" in Sharpe, *In the Wake: On Blackness and Being* (Durham, NC: Duke University Press, 2016), 3; Jamaica Kincaid's focus on the presence of the past in Kincaid, *A Small Place* (New York: Farrar, Straus & Giroux, 1988), 54; and Michel-Rolph Trouillot's concept of slavery as a "living presence" in Trouillot, *Silencing the Past: Power and the Production of History* (Boston: Beacon 1995), 147.

43. Eduardo Bonilla-Silva, *Racism without Racists: Color-Blind Racism and the Persistence of Racial Inequality in the United States* (Lanham, MD: Rowman & Littlefield, 2010), 104. Bonilla-Silva defines "white habitus" as "a racialized, uninterrupted socialization process that *conditions* and *creates* whites' racial taste, perceptions, feelings and emotions and their views on racial matters."

44. James C. Scott, *Domination and the Arts of Resistance: Hidden Transcripts* (New Haven, CT: Yale University Press, 1990), 220.

45. Kamala Harris, "Smart on Crime: Elevating the Discussion in Our City, State, and Nation," speech to the Commonwealth Club, January 14, 2010, quoted in Dan MacGuill, "Did Kamala Harris Once Boast about Prosecuting a Homeless Mother?," Snopes, February 1, 2019, https://www.snopes.com/fact-check/kamala-harris-homeless-mother/.

46. I use "fugitive" here in a similar tradition to other critical theorists and Black studies scholars to describe futures that for many Black youth are continuously on the run. See Hartman, *Lose Your Mother*; Stefano Harney and Fred Moten, *The Undercommons: Fugitive Planning and Black Study* (New York: Minor Compositions, 2013); Frank B. Wilderson III, "Social Death and Narrative Aporia in *12 Years a Slave*," *Black Camera* 7, no. 1 (2015): 134–49; and Alexis Pauline Gumbs, *Spill: Scenes of Black Feminist Fugitivity* (Durham, NC: Duke University Press, 2016).

47. Hanchard, "Afro-modernity," 263.

48. Ronald Aminzade, "Historical Sociology and Time," *Sociological Methods Research* 20, no. 4 (1992): 458.

49. Hanchard, "Afro-modernity," 247.

50. Hanchard, "Afro-modernity," 247.

51. Hanchard, "Afro-modernity," 253.

52. Denise Ferreira da Silva defines affectability as "the condition of being subjected to both natural (in the scientific and lay sense) conditions and to others' power." Denise Ferreira da Silva, *Toward a Global Idea of Race*, xv.

53. Frank Wilderson writes, "For the slave, historical 'time' is not possible." Wilderson, "Social Death and Narrative Aporia," 136. Elsewhere he states, "The idea of 'going back' imbues Black suffering with a temporality that it doesn't have; emplots the slave in the arc of equilibrium, disequilibrium, equilibrium restored; when, in point of fact, Blackness and Slaveness are coterminous." Frank B. Wilderson III, "The Black Liberation Army and the Paradox of Political Engagement," in *Postcoloniality-Decoloniality-Black Critique: Joints and Fissures*, ed. Sabine Broeck and Carsten Junker (Chicago: University of Chicago Press, 2014), 29. My aim is not to introduce CP Time as an example of how Black people reclaim ownership over time. Instead, I see CP Time as a way in which Black people and other racialized persons transform white time into an internally functional metric to cope with the timelessness of racialized violence.

54. Joe R. Feagin, *The White Racial Frame: Centuries of Racial Framing and Counterframing* (New York: Routledge, 2013).

55. CP Time is a general referent to the temporal patterns of Black people living in the United States. Similar expressions, however, exist among other racialized groups. "West Indian time," "Dominican time," "Indian standard time," "Laos time," and "Cape Verdean time" ("CV time") share similar connotations to CP Time in that lateness is to be expected, not rejected. I argue that these different conceptions of time reveal not only the discordant relationship between racialized subjectivity and time but also resistance to white time. I would be remiss to ignore what I have heard described as "Spirit time" among Native and Indigenous peoples. Spirit time emphasizes the communion between Native peoples, the Creator, land, and space. Daniel R. Wildcat writes, "To the Western mind, human beings look backward and forward in time to get a sense of their place in history, whereas American Indians literally looked around the natural world to get a sense of their place in history." Daniel R. Wildcat, "Indigenizing the Future: Why We Must Think Spatially in the Twenty-First Century," *American Studies* 46 (2005): 432. "Crip time" is an expression familiar to people with disabilities, signaling the unique and often antagonistic relationship between disability and clock time. The "persistence of past forms of power under seemingly new conditions" is what Eric Tang calls "refugee temporality." As Tang writes, "Refugee temporality is not another way of stating that the refugee is haunted by the past—through trauma or survivor guilt. Instead, it is the distinct way in which refugees know that the power of their past captivities remains in the present—in the supposed land of salvation that promised safety and freedom." Eric Tang, *Unsettled: Cambodian Refugees in the New York City Hyperghetto* (Philadelphia: Temple University Press, 2015), 173. Tang describes how for many Cambodian refugees attempting to survive in spaces not meant for living, the present is "unbroken" from the past given the nexus between "colonial warfare" and "warfare in the hyperghetto" (21).

56. Ronald Walcott, "Ellison, Gordone, and Tolson: Some Notes on the Blues, Style and Space," *Black World* 22, no. 2 (1972): 8–9.

57. Fred Moten, *Black and Blur: Consent Not to Be a Single Being* (Durham, NC: Duke University Press, 2017), 76.

58. Bonnie J. Barthold, *Black Time: Fiction of Africa, the Caribbean, and the United States* (New Haven, CT: Yale University Press, 1981), 23.

59. Mark M. Smith, *Mastered by the Clock: Time, Slavery, and Freedom in the American South* (Chapel Hill: University of North Carolina Press, 1997), 5.

60. Smith, *Mastered by the Clock*, 137.

61. Quoted in Smith, *Mastered by the Clock*, 136.

224   NOTES TO PAGES 39–47

62. Smith, *Mastered by the Clock*, 130.

63. Rosaldo, *Culture and Truth*, 110.

64. For more research on Black workers' resistance to time discipline, see Philip S. Foner and David R. Roediger, *Our Own Time: A History of American Labor and the Working Day* (New York: Verso, 1989), 272.

65. Robin D. G. Kelley, *Race Rebels: Culture, Politics, and the Black Working Class* (New York: Free Press, 1994), 20.

66. Kelley, *Race Rebels*, 50.

67. Rodríguez says, "'Disparity' is a bullshit concept, when we already know that the inception of criminal justice is the de-criminalization of white people, particularly propertied white citizens and those willing to bear arms to defend the white world. 'Mass Incarceration' is worse than meaningless, when it's not the 'masses' who are being criminalized and locked up. So there is some furtive and fatal white entitlement involved in this discursive political structure." Casey Goonan, "Policing and the Violence of White Being: An Interview with Dylan Rodríguez," *Black Scholar* 12 (2016): 13. Rodríguez makes clear that the arrest and incarceration of racialized groups require the "de-criminalization of white people."

68. Consider how approximately ten thousand people participated in the attempted coup at the US Capitol on January 6, 2022, while less than one thousand have been arrested at the time of this writing. Nik Popli and Julia Zorthian, "What Happened to the Jan. 6 Rioters Arrested since the Capitol Attack," *Time*, last updated May 26, 2023, https://time.com/6133336/jan-6-capitol-riot-arrests-sentences/. The trial of Kyle Rittenhouse is yet another example of how "those willing to bear arms to defend the white world" (to quote Dylan Rodríguez; see previous note) will always be decriminalized in relation to those constructed as threats to the white world.

69. Dylan Rodríguez, *White Reconstruction: Domestic Warfare and the Logics of Genocide* (New York: Fordham University Press, 2021), 195.

70. Jared Sexton, "The Social Life of Social Death: On Afro-pessimism and Black Optimism," in *Time, Temporality and Violence in International Relations: (De)fatalizing the Present, Forging Radical Alternatives*, ed. Ann M. Agathangelou and Kyle D. Killian (New York: Routledge, 2016), 62.

71. Though memory fades with the passage of time, some may recall when it was in bad taste to make haste. For example, Pierre Bourdieu observed, "Haste is seen as a lack of decorum combined with diabolical ambition." Pierre Bourdieu, "Time Perspectives of the Kabyle," in Hassard, *Sociology of Time*, 221.

72. Gayatri Chakravorty Spivak, "'Can the Subaltern Speak?,'" in *Marxism and the Interpretation of Culture*, ed. Cary Nelson and Lawrence Grossberg (Urbana: University of Illinois Press, 1988), 271–313.

73. Pierre Bourdieu, *Pascalian Meditations* (Stanford, CA: Stanford University Press, 1997), 223.

74. Bourdieu, *Pascalian Meditations*, 228.

75. Bourdieu, *Pascalian Meditations*, 228.

76. Bourdieu, *Pascalian Meditations*, 228.

77. Quoted in Rosaldo, *Culture and Truth*, 111–12.

78. Rosaldo, *Culture and Truth*, 112–13.

79. See Hartman, *Lose Your Mother*, 5.

80. Walcott, "Ellison, Gordone, and Tolson," 8.

81. With over 125 sites nationwide, Job Corps is a free education and vocational training program administered by the US Department of Labor. The program aims to help youths between the ages of sixteen and twenty-four strengthen their preparedness for careers and/or help them meet educational benchmarks such as earning a high school

diploma or GED. Job Corps has also come under intense criticism, mainly from the political Right, for failing to keep its students safe. According to a June 2017 report from the Office of the Inspector General, Job Corps staff reported 49,836 safety incidents, most of which involved serious illnesses or injuries, assaults, and drugs, between January 1, 2007, and June 30, 2016. US Government Accountability Office, *Job Corps: Preliminary Observations on Student Safety and Security Data*, June 22, 2017, https://www.gao.gov/assets/gao-17-596t.pdf.

82. Michelle M. Wright, *Physics of Blackness: Beyond Middle Passage Epistemology* (Minneapolis: University of Minnesota Press, 2015), 146.

83. Wright, *Physics of Blackness*, 20, italics in the original.

84. Wright shared this analysis during a meeting with the critical race and ethnic studies (CRES) graduate writing group at the University of Minnesota on March 25, 2016.

85. Wright, *Physics of Blackness*, 145.

86. W. E. B. Du Bois, *Darkwater: Voices from within the Veil* (New York: Verso, 2016), 23. Within critical race theory (CRT), racism should be treated not as an anomaly or a contradiction, but rather as a central organizing principle of liberalism and democracy.

87. Wright, *Physics of Blackness*, 82.

88. Alexander Weheliye writes, "As W.E.B. Du Bois asked in 1944, if the Universal Declaration of Human Rights did not offer provisions for ending world colonialism and legal segregation in the United States, 'Why then call it the Declaration of Human Rights?'" Alexander Weheliye, *Habeus Viscus: Racializing Assemblages, Biopolitics, and Black Feminist Theories of the Human* (Durham, NC: Duke University Press, 2014), 76.

89. Bourdieu, *Pascalian Meditations*, 206.

90. Bourdieu, *Pascalian Meditations*, 206.

91. It is worth noting that many social institutions were designed precisely with racialized youth in mind. They are the ones that schools reject and employers refuse.

92. Damien M. Sojoyner, *First Strike: Educational Enclosures in Black Los Angeles* (Minneapolis: University of Minnesota Press, 2016).

93. The Movement for Family Power used the term "family regulation system" in a tweet as a more accurate name for the "child welfare system." Movement for Family Power (@movfamilypower), "AND INSTEAD OF PREVENTING HARM, THE FAMILY REGULATION SYSTEM THRUSTS AND CREATES VIOLENCE!!!," Twitter, June 11, 2020, 9:54 p.m., https://twitter.com/movfamilypower/status/1271259572938985472.

94. Shanté may have also been moved by what Max Weber calls "the 'spirit' of capitalism." Weber references a "sermon" delivered by Benjamin Franklin in which he declared that "time is money" and "credit is money." Max Weber, *The Protestant Ethic and the "Spirit" of Capitalism and Other Writings* (New York: Penguin Books, 2002), 11–13.

95. Deborah K. King, "Multiple Jeopardy, Multiple Consciousness: The Context of Black Feminist Ideology," *Signs* 14, no. 1 (1988): 42–72.

96. In chapter 6, I further explore youths' participation in the "fast life" as a means of transgressing time.

97. Benjamin Franklin, quoted in Weber, *Protestant Ethic*, 10.

98. Kemi Adeyemi, "The Practice of Slowness: Black Queer Women and the Right to the City," *Gay and Lesbian Quarterly* 25, no. 4 (2019): 561.

99. J. Jack Halberstam, *In a Queer Time and Place: Transgender Bodies, Subcultural Lives* (New York: New York University Press, 2005), 2.

100. Kara Keeling, *Queer Times, Black Futures* (New York: New York University Press, 2019), 17.

101. Halberstam, *Queer Time and Place*, 7.

102. Lisa M. Cacho, *Social Death: Racialized Rightlessness and the Criminalization of the Unprotected* (New York: New York University Press, 2012), 166–67.

NOTES TO PAGES 55–62

103. "Pass-ons" are individual reports for each youth, containing a short summary of occurrences and significant events from previous shift(s).

104. Erving Goffman, *The Presentation of Self in Everyday Life* (New York: Doubleday, 1959), 2.

105. See James C. Scott, *Weapons of the Weak: Everyday Forms of Peasant Resistance* (New Haven, CT: Yale University Press, 1987); and James C. Scott, *Domination and the Arts of Resistance* (New Haven, CT: Yale University Press, 1990).

106. For Sylvia Wynter, "the overrepresentation of Man as Human" and the use of race as a "genetic status-organizing principle" signify central concepts structuring the current episteme. Wynter argues that "'descriptive statements' or governing master codes" established strict eligibility criteria turned "objective set of facts" for being human. See Wynter, "Unsettling the Coloniality," 271.

2. *TEEFING* TIME

1. According to Jared Sexton, "Whereas blackness precedes and precipitates anti-blackness, anti-blackness presumes and presupposes blackness. Call them blackness1 and blackness2, with the key qualification that the strange temporality of retroaction disallows the possibility of any strict chronology. In this *perverse* sense, then, black social death is black social life. The object of black studies is the aim of black studies. The most radical negation of the anti-black world is the most radical affirmation of a blackened world. Afro-pessimism is 'not but nothing other than' black optimism.'" Jared Sexton, "The Social Life of Social Death: On Afro-pessimism and Black Optimism." In *Time, Temporality and Violence in International Relations: (De)fatalizing the Present, Forging Radical Alternatives*, ed. Ann M. Agathangelou and Kyle D. Killian (New York: Routledge, 2016), 73.

2. Johannes Fabian, *Time and the Other: How Anthropology Makes Its Object* (New York: Columbia University Press, 1983), 31.

3. I am referring to white people who function as extensions of the state by criminalizing nonwhite people through surveillance (i.e., the white gaze) and/or seizure.

4. David Harvey, *The New Imperialism* (Oxford: Oxford University Press, 2005), 142.

5. Pierre Bourdieu, *Pascalian Meditations* (Stanford, CA: Stanford University Press, 1997), 223.

6. Michael Hanchard, "Afro-modernity: Temporality, Politics, and the African Diaspora," *Public Culture* 11, no. 1 (1999): 253.

7. Charles W. Mills, "White Time: The Chronic Injustice of Ideal Theory," *Du Bois Review* 11, no. 1 (2014): 36.

8. Mills, "White Time," 29.

9. Claiming that racialized violence remains inconsequential is not hyperbole, especially when litigating racism remains a site of continuous debate. For example, US Supreme Court cases like *McCleskey v. Kemp* not only make racism largely unintelligible but institutionalize and legalize its unintelligibility. *McCleskey* ruled that racial bias in sentencing cannot be challenged under the Fourteenth Amendment in the absence of clear "evidence of conscious, discriminatory action." In other words, the legislative, judiciary, and executive branches of government all play a role in legitimating the exclusion of racism as a decisive part of racialized persons' everyday lives. How, then, does one calculate or quantify something like racism, which according to the most powerful systems of government does not exist legally or socially? Perhaps this is the wrong question.

10. See Raygiene C. DiAquoi, "Critical Race Life Course Perspective Theory: A Framework for Understanding Racism over the Life Course," *International Journal of Qualitative Studies in Education* 3, no. 1 (2018): 36–54; Celia B. Fisher, Seyatta A. Wallace,

and Rose E. Fenton, "Discrimination Distress during Adolescence," *Journal of Youth and Adolescence* 6 (2000): 679–95; and Andrea J. Romero and Robert E. Roberts, "Perceptions of Discrimination and Ethnocultural Variables in a Diverse Group of Adolescents," *Journal of Adolescence* 21 (1998): 641–56.

11. In "The Souls of White Folk," Du Bois continues to invert questions related to the "Negro Problem." Other scholars, including Gunnar Myrdal (*An American Dilemma: The Negro Problem and Modern Democracy*) and James Baldwin ("The Negro Problem: A Conversation with James Baldwin"), soon followed suit.

12. W. E. B. Du Bois, *The Souls of Black Folk* (New York: Barnes & Noble Classics, 2003), 143.

13. August Wilson, introduction to *May All Your Fences Have Gates*, ed. Alan Nadel (Iowa City: Iowa University Press, 1988), 8. Although white people's survival does not depend on knowing Blacks and other nonwhites, this has not stopped them from claiming to know "the other." Sociology generally, and white urban ethnographers in particular, remain in a relentless quest not just to make the familiar strange, but also to make the strange familiar (to whiteness).

14. Helen Ngo, *The Habits of Racism: A Phenomenology of Racism and Racialized Embodiment* (Lanham, MD: Lexington Books, 2017), 70–71.

15. Sara Ahmed, "A Phenomenology of Whiteness," *Feminist Theory* 8, no. 2 (2007): 159.

16. Mills, "White Time," 28.

17. See Du Bois's description of the relationship between Black and white workers in the early twentieth century in W. E. B. Du Bois, *Black Reconstruction in America, 1860–1880* (New York: Atheneum, 1998), 6. David Roediger extends many of Du Bois's ideas by revealing the psychic and material "wages" gained from whiteness in David Roediger, *The Wages of Whiteness: Race and the Making of the American Working Class* (Brooklyn: Verso, 1991). In *Black Wealth/White Wealth: A New Perspective on Racial Inequality* (New York: Routledge, 1995), Melvin Oliver and Thomas Shapiro show how the cumulative advantage is a product of cumulative disadvantage and dispossession. The authors make clear that white wealth is a product of unjust enrichment and the exploitation of Black labor. Dalton Conley builds on these ideas in *Being Black, Living in the Red: Race, Wealth, and Social Policy in America* (Berkeley: University of California Press, 1999). Finally, Manning Marable, in *How Capitalism Underdeveloped Black America: Problems in Race, Political Economy, and Society* (Cambridge: South End, 1999), makes clear that capitalism continues to ravage poor Black communities.

18. Javier Auyero explores poor people's experiences waiting for social and administrative services, as well as the tactics of those who make them wait. Auyero describes waiting as a "strategy of domination" used to dispossess the poor in Argentina of time, information, and a sense of certainty. Javier Auyero, *Patients of the State: The Politics of Waiting in Argentina* (Durham, NC: Duke University Press, 2012), 15.

19. Denise Ferreira da Silva, "Unpayable Debt: Reading Scenes of Value against the Arrow of Time," in *The documenta 14 Reader*, ed. Quinn Latimer and Adam Szymczyk (Munich: Prestel, 2017), 81. Ferreira da Silva invokes the main character of Octavia Butler's *Kindred*, Dana, to conceptualize unpayable debt as "a debt someone owes but is not hers to pay." As Ferreira da Silva observes elsewhere, however, "The debt is hers because her blackness signals both slavery and lack of equity." Denise Ferreira da Silva, *Unpayable Debt* (London: Sternberg), 14.

20. Harvey, *New Imperialism*, 142.

21. For a critique of teleological assessments of race and racism, see Louise Seamster and Victor Ray, "Against Teleology in the Study of Race: Toward the Abolition of the Progress Paradigm," *Sociological Theory* 36, no. 4 (2018): 315–42.

228 NOTES TO PAGES 68–72

22. Du Bois describes how white people remain the beneficiaries of a "public and psychological wage" Du Bois, *Black Reconstruction in America*, 700–701. In *Wages of Whiteness*, Roediger takes Du Bois's ideas literally to describe how poor white workers failed to forge alliances across racial lines because they believed they had more in common with the people they *worked for* (i.e., their white elite bosses) than with the people they *worked with* (i.e., their poor Black counterparts). Cheryl Harris extends many of Du Bois's ideas by describing whiteness as a "consolation prize" ensuring that, regardless of the competition, white people win. Cheryl Harris, "Whiteness as Property," *Harvard Law Review* 106, no. 8 (1993): 1758.

23. Observing that the limitations in Marx and Engels's ideas about the prospects of a "[European] bourgeois society would rationalize social relations and demystify social consciousness," Cedric Robinson set out to develop a more complete analysis of capitalism through greater attention to its racial dimensions. He states, "The tendency of European civilization through capitalism was thus not to homogenize but to differentiate—to exaggerate regional, subcultural and dialectical differences into 'racial' ones." Cedric Robinson, *Black Marxism: The Making of the Black Radical Tradition* (Chapel Hill: University of North Carolina Press, 1983), 26.

24. Bonilla-Silva conceptualizes racialized social systems as "societies in which economic, political, social and ideological levels" are structured according to the hierarchical organization of racial categories or races. Eduardo Bonilla-Silva, "Rethinking Racism: Toward a Structural Interpretation," *American Sociological Review* 63, no. 3 (1997): 469.

25. Frantz Fanon, *Black Skin, White Masks*, trans. Richard Philcox (New York: Grove, 2008), xv.

26. Fanon, *Black Skin, White Masks*, 95. Fanon's words are as dense as they are poetically terse. To be "overdetermined from the outside" calls attention to the multitude of forces that (over)determine Blackness. The "outside" for Fanon is the social, which privileges white being as the reference category for determining each person's fitness within the category of the human.

27. Denise Ferreira da Silva, *Toward a Global Idea of Race* (Minneapolis: University of Minnesota Press, 2007), 28.

28. Simone Browne, *Dark Matters: On the Surveillance of Blackness* (Durham, NC: Duke University Press, 2015), 16.

29. Browne, *Dark Matters*, 7.

30. Fanon, *Black Skin, White Masks*, 92.

31. Additional critiques of straight time, family time, and heteronormative time can be found in Lee Edelman, *No Future: Queer Theory and the Death Drive* (Durham, NC: Duke University Press, 2004); J. Jack Halberstam, *In a Queer Time and Place: Transgender Bodies, Subcultural Lives* (New York: New York University Press, 2005); José Esteban Muñoz, *Cruising Utopia: The Then and There of Queer Futurity* (New York: New York University Press, 2009); and Elizabeth Freeman, *Time Binds: Queer Temporalities, Queer Histories* (Durham, NC: Duke University Press, 2010).

32. Tavia Nyong'o, "Non-binary Blackness: After the End of the World with Samuel R. Delany," Art Practical, November 21, 2019, http://www.artpractical.com/feature/non-binary-blackness-after-the-end-of-the-world-with-samuel-r.-delany/, cited in Joshua Aiken, Jessica Marion Modi, and Olivia R. Polk, "Issued by Way of 'The Issue of Blackness,'" *Transgender Studies Quarterly* 1.7, no. 3 (2020): 429.

33. Elizabeth Freeman describes "chrononormativity" as "a mode of implantation, a technique by which institutional forces come to seem like somatic facts." Freeman, *Time Binds*, 3.

34. Katherine McKittrick, *Demonic Grounds: Black Women and the Cartographies of Struggle* (Minneapolis: University of Minnesota Press, 2006), 93.

NOTES TO PAGES 72–78

35. Muñoz describes straight time as "a naturalized temporality that is calibrated to make queer potentiality not only unrealized but also unthinkable." Muñoz, *Cruising Utopia*, 165.

36. Quoted in Walter D. Mignolo, "Sylvia Wynter: What Does It Mean to Be Human," in *Sylvia Wynter: On Being Human as Praxis* (Durham, NC: Duke University Press, 2015), 116.

37. Steve Martinot, *The Machinery of Whiteness: Studies in the Structure of Racialization* (Philadelphia: Temple University Press, 2010), 43.

38. "The World's Most Valuable Resource Is No Longer Oil, but Data," *The Economist*, May 6, 2017, https://www.economist.com/leaders/2017/05/06/the-worlds-most-valuable-resource-is-no-longer-oil-but-data.

39. Ruha Benjamin, *Race after Technology: Abolitionist Tools for the New Jim Code* (Cambridge: Polity, 2019), 80.

40. See Frieda Johles Forman and Caroran Sowton, eds., *Taking Our Time: Feminist Perspectives on Temporality* (Oxford: Pergamon, 1989); Neferti X. M. Tadiar, "Life-Times in Fate Playing," *South Atlantic Quarterly* 111, no. 4 (2012): 783–802; and Barbara Adam, "The Gendered Time Politics of Globalization: Of Shadowlands and Elusive Justice," *Feminist Review* 70 (2002): 3–29.

41. Here I am particularly reflecting on the contributions of Anne McClintock in *Imperial Leather: Race, Gender, and Sexuality in the Colonial Contest* (New York: Routledge, 1995).

42. La Marr Jurelle Bruce, *How to Go Mad without Losing Your Mind: Madness and Black Radical Creativity* (Durham, NC: Duke University Press, 2021), 4.

43. Elizabeth Deeds Ermath, "The Solitude of Women and Social Time," in *Taking Our Time: Feminist Perspectives on Temporality*, ed. Frieda Johles Forman and Caroran Sowton (Oxford: Pergamon, 1989), 37.

44. Ermath, "Solitude of Women," 37.

45. Patricia Hill Collins, *Black Feminist Thought: Knowledge, Consciousness, and the Politics of Empowerment* (New York: Routledge, 2000), 57.

46. See McClintock, *Imperial Leather*.

47. Captive Maternals, according to James, "may be either biological females or those feminized into caretaking and consumption." Membership within the category of the Captive Maternal requires sacrifice, resistance, and complicity against/with the predations of the state. Joy James, "The Womb of Western Theory: Trauma, Time Theft and the Captive Maternal," *Carceral Notebooks* 12, no. 1 (2016): 255.

48. Bonnie J. Barthold, *Black Time: Fiction of Africa, the Caribbean, and the United States* (New Haven, CT: Yale University Press, 1981), 101.

49. Hortense J. Spillers, "Mama's Baby, Papa's Maybe: An American Grammar Book," *Diacritics* 17, no. 2 (Summer 1987): 67.

50. Spillers, "Mama's Baby, Papa's Maybe," 80.

51. Deborah K. King, "Multiple Jeopardy, Multiple Consciousness: The Context of Black Feminist Ideology," *Signs* 14, no. 1 (1988): 46–47.

52. King, "Multiple Jeopardy, Multiple Consciousness," 45.

53. Spillers, "Mama's Baby, Papa's Maybe," 68.

54. Spillers, "Mama's Baby, Papa's Maybe," 67. As Spillers writes, "Before the 'body' there is the 'flesh,' that zero degree of social conceptualization that does not escape concealment under the brush of discourse, or the reflexes of iconography."

55. Ferreira da Silva, *Global Idea of Race*, 60. David Couzens Hoy describes Kant as having a more ambivalent assessment of the origins of time. In response to whether Kant saw the source of time as being either of the world or of the mind, Hoy writes, "On the one hand, insofar as time is a *form* of intuition, it comes from the mind. On the other hand,

230 **NOTES TO PAGES 80–86**

however, insofar as it is a form of *intuition*, and intuition receives data from the real world, time is empirically real." David Couzens Hoy, *The Time of Our Lives: A Critical History of Temporality* (Cambridge, MA: MIT Press, 2012), 5–6.

56. Marx, *Early Writings* (New York: Penguin, 1992), 351.

57. See Harris, "Whiteness as Property"; and George Lipsitz, *The Possessive Investment in Whiteness: How White People Profit from Identity Politics* (Philadelphia: Temple University Press, 2006).

58. Tadiar, "Life-Times in Fate Playing," 794.

59. Tadiar, "Life-Times in Fate Playing," 791.

60. See the National Youth Rights Association, "Top Five Reasons to Abolish Curfews," accessed June 5, 2023, https://www.youthrights.org/issues/curfew/reasons-to-abolish/.

61. Jodi Rios, *Black Lives and Spatial Matters: Policing Blackness and Practicing Freedom in Suburban St. Louis* (Ithaca, NY: Cornell University Press, 2020), 84.

62. Rios, *Black Lives and Spatial Matters*, 91.

63. In *Invisible No More: Police Violence against Black Women and Women of Color* (Boston: Beacon, 2017), Andrea J. Ritchie exposes incommensurable levels of violence against Black women, Native women, and women of color by local, state, and federal authorities. The simultaneity and multiplicative connections between race, gender, sexuality, citizenship status, and class place racialized women at higher risks of being targeted as threats to the state and to heteropatriarchal constructions of womanhood and femininity.

64. Frank B. Wilderson III, "The Black Liberation Army and the Paradox of Political Engagement," in *Postcoloniality-Decoloniality-Black Critique: Joints and Fissures*, ed. Sabine Broeck and Carsten Junker (Chicago: University of Chicago Press, 2014), 7.

65. It is worth noting that some of my peers called me "croissant" in middle and high school. Their jokes were not a critique of my racial identity, but rather a way of making fun of the sound of my name. "Croissant" and "Rahsaan" may not sound phonetically similar, but to kids from the hood, it was a convenient way of calling me out my name.

66. Du Bois, *Souls of Black Folk*, 9.

67. Calvin Warren, "Black Time: Slavery, Metaphysics, and the Logic of Wellness," in *The Psychic Hold of Slavery: Legacies in American Expressive Culture*, ed. Soyica Diggs Colbert, Robert J. Patterson, and Aida Levy-Hussen (New Brunswick, NJ: Rutgers University Press, 2016), 63.

68. Saidiya V. Hartman, *Wayward Lives, Beautiful Experiments: Intimate Histories of Social Upheaval* (New York: W. W. Norton, 2019), 242.

69. Saidiya V. Hartman writes, "It is a tricky matter to detail the civil existence of a subject who is socially dead and legally recognized as human only to the degree that he is criminally culpable." Saidiya V. Hartman, *Scenes of Subjection: Terror, Slavery, and Self-Making in Nineteenth-Century America* (New York: Oxford University Press, 1997), 24.

70. See Stephanie H. Donald and Cristoph Lindner, *Inert Cities: Globalization, Mobility and Suspension in Visual Culture* (New York: I. B. Taurus, 2014).

71. Michelle M. Wright reveals how Thomas Jefferson temporalizes race, privileging whiteness as dynamic and Blackness as static. As Wright observes, "Jefferson suggests that 'Blackness' can be altered when mixed with white blood. His rhetoric already assumes Black inertia and white activity." Michelle M. Wright, *Becoming Black: Creating Identity in the African Diaspora* (Durham, NC: Duke University Press, 2004), 58.

72. City of Sanford, Florida, "Transcript of George Zimmerman's Call to the Police," Internet Archive, March 20, 2012, https://archive.org/details/326700-full-transcript-zimmerman.

73. Hartman, *Scenes of Subjection*, 6.

3. THE MAKINGS OF A "MAYBE ENVIRONMENT"

1. Sara Ahmed, *Queer Phenomenology: Orientations, Objects, Others* (Durham, NC: Duke University Press, 2006), 121.

2. Terrion L. Williamson, ed., *Black in the Middle: An Anthology of the Black Midwest* (Cleveland: Belt, 2020).

3. Mark Rifkin, *Beyond Settler Time: Temporal Sovereignty and Indigenous Self-Determination* (Durham, NC: Duke University Press, 2017). The "white spatial imaginary" is what George Lipsitz, in *The Possessive Investment in Whiteness: How White People Profit from Identity Politics* (Philadelphia: Temple University Press, 2006), describes as a product of segregation and a broader "possessive investment" in the myth of meritocracy. Mills draws on Lipsitz's concept to describe a "white temporal imaginary." Charles W. Mills, "White Time: The Chronic Injustice of Ideal Theory," *Du Bois Review* 11, no. 1 (2014): 29.

4. "Hot Cheetos and Takis" is a song created by Da Rich Kidzz—a hip hop group consisting of eight members between the ages of ten and thirteen from Minneapolis's Northside.

5. Andrea Smith, "Sovereignty as Deferred Genocide," in *Otherwise Worlds: Against Settler-Colonialism and Anti-Blackness*, ed. Tiffany Lethabo King, Jenell Navarro, and Andrea Smith (Durham, NC: Duke University Press, 2020), 120.

6. Such representations seem to fall into the category of what Teresa Gowan describes as "ethnonoir." Gowan distinguishes between "ethnonoir" research that "makes a virtue of deliberately gritty, sometimes overblown realism" and neoromantic ethnography and ethnographers who "inflate and romanticize those aspects of the poor that illustrate how *similar* they are to other Americans—their mainstream aspirations, their law-abiding behavior, their conventional morality." Teresa Gowan, *Hobos, Hustlers, and Backsliders: Homeless in San Francisco* (Minneapolis: University of Minnesota Press, 2010), 174.

7. "The Black Midwest Initiative is a progressive collective of scholars, students, artists, organizers, and community-involved people who are committed to advocating for the lives of people of African descent as they are situated throughout the Midwest and Rust Belt regions of the United States." "Mission—Vision—Values," Black Midwest Initiative, accessed June 5, 2023, https://www.theblackmidwest.com/mission-vision-values.

8. Terrion L. Williamson, "This Place We Know: An Introduction," in Williamson, *Black in the Middle*, 15.

9. Saidiya V. Hartman, *Scenes of Subjection: Terror, Slavery, and Self-Making in Nineteenth-Century America* (New York: Oxford University Press, 1997), 42.

10. Derek Thompson, "The Miracle of Minneapolis," *The Atlantic*, March 2015, https://www.theatlantic.com/magazine/archive/2015/03/the-miracle-of-minneapolis/384975/.

11. Jessica Nickrand, "Minneapolis's White Lie," *The Atlantic*, February 21, 2015, https://www.theatlantic.com/business/archive/2015/02/minneapoliss-white-lie/385702/.

12. "Note: The Highest Poverty Rate Gap category describes the poverty rate of a certain ethnicity in relation to that of whites. For reference, 100% would mean twice the poverty rate of whites." Adam McCann, "2023's States with the Biggest and Smallest Wealth Gaps by Race/Ethnicity," WalletHub, January 25, 2023, https://wallethub.com/edu/states-with-the-highest-and-lowest-financial-gaps-by-race/9842/. Even the *Washington Post* took aim at Thompson's article. Jeff Guo, "If Minneapolis Is So Great, Why Is It So Bad for African Americans?," *Washington Post*, February 17, 2015, https://www.washingtonpost.com/blogs/govbeat/wp/2015/02/17/if-minneapolis-is-so-great-why-is-it-so-bad-for-black-people/.

13. Nickrand, "Minneapolis's White Lie."

14. Samuel Stebbins and Evan Comen, "These Are the 15 Worst Cities for Black Americans," *USA Today*, November 16, 2018, https://www.usatoday.com/story/money/2018/11/16/racial-disparity-cities-worst-metro-areas-black-americans/38460961/.

15. "By surprise," McKittrick writes, "I mean the outcome of wonder: an unexpected or astonishing event, circumstance, person, or thing; the emotion caused by this; astonishment, shock, or amazement; a gift or a present; a person or thing that achieves unexpected success; an attack or an approach made upon an unsuspecting victim; an act contrary to the expectations of a person; just as one might expect—no surprise at all." Katherine McKittrick, *Demonic Grounds: Black Women and the Cartographies of Struggle* (Minneapolis: University of Minnesota Press, 2006), 91.

16. Richard Iton, *In Search of the Black Fantastic: Politics and Popular Culture in the Post–Civil Rights Era* (Oxford: Oxford University Press, 2008), 22.

17. Fred Moten writes, "The history of blackness is testament to the fact that objects can and do resist. Blackness—the extended movement of a specific upheaval, an ongoing irruption that anarranges every line—is a strain that pressures the assumption of the equivalence of personhood and subjectivity." Fred Moten, *In the Break: The Aesthetics of the Black Radical Tradition* (Minneapolis: University of Minnesota Press, 2003), 1; Michelle M. Wright, *Physics of Blackness: Beyond the Middle Passage Epistemology* (Minneapolis: University of Minnesota Press, 2015).

18. McKittrick reminds readers that when studying Black geographies, there is a need to appreciate the "rupture" that is the Middle Passage. Katherine McKittrick, *Dear Science and Other Stories* (Durham, NC: Duke University Press, 2021), 32.

19. Council on Black Minnesotans, report, January 15, 2013, https://mn.gov/cmah/assets/2013%20Annual%20Report_tcm32-356559.pdf.

20. US Census Bureau, 2017 American Community Survey Five-Year Estimates (2013–17), unemployment and below-poverty rates, accessed September 14, 2023, https://data.census.gov/table?q=unemployment+in+minnesota+2015&tid=ACSST1Y2015.S2301; racial demographics, accessed September 14, 2023, https://data.census.gov/table/ACSDP5Y2017.DP05?g=040XX00US27.

21. See Eve Tuck and K. Wayne Yang, "Decolonization Is Not a Metaphor," *Decolonization: Indigeneity, Education and Society* 1, no. 1 (2012): 1–40.

22. Tiffany Lethabo King, Jenell Navarro, and Andrea Smith, "Beyond Incommensurability: Toward an Otherwise Stance on Black and Indigenous Relationality," in King, Navarro, and Smith, *Otherwise Worlds*, 1.

23. Jared Sexton, "The *Vel* of Slavery: Tracking the Figure of the Unsovereign," *Critical Sociology* 42, no. 4–5 (2014): 9.

24. Smith, "Sovereignty as Deferred Genocide," 125.

25. Sexton, "*Vel* of Slavery," 9.

26. Smith, "Sovereignty as Deferred Genocide," 126.

27. Frank Wilderson critiques Leslie Marmon Silko's *Almanac of the Dead* for structurally adjusting Blackness to conform to the esteemed qualities of Native peoples. As Wilderson writes, "She makes the Black safe for sovereignty and rescues sovereignty from the Black." Frank B. Wilderson III, *Red, White, & Black: Cinema and the Structure of U.S. Antagonisms* (Durham, NC: Duke University Press), 244.

28. Helen Ngo, "'Get Over It'? Racialised Temporalities and Bodily Orientations in Time," *Journal of Intercultural Studies* 40, no. 2 (2019): 246.

29. Waziyatawin, *What Does Justice Look Like? The Struggle for Liberation in Dakota Homeland* (St. Paul: Living Justice, 2008), 32.

30. Waziyatawin, *What Does Justice Look Like?*, 32.

31. Wilder Research, *Characteristics and Trends among Minnesota's Homeless Population*, 2018 Minnesota Homeless Study, May 2019, https://www.wilder.org/sites/default/files/imports/2018_HomelessStudy_CharacteristicsFactSheet_5-19.pdf, 4.

32. Andrea Smith, "Heteropatriarchy and the Three Pillars of White Supremacy: Rethinking Women of Color Organizing," in *Color of Violence: The Incite! Anthology*, ed. Incite! Women of Color against Violence (Cambridge, MA: South End, 2006), 68.

33. Smith, "Sovereignty as Deferred Genocide," 125.

34. Smith, "Sovereignty as Deferred Genocide," 126.

35. Tiya Miles, "Uncle Tom Was an Indian: Tracing the Red in Black Slavery," in *Relational Formations of Race: Theory, Method, and Practice*, ed. Natalia Molina, Daniel Martinez Hosang, and Ramóna A. Gutiérrez (Berkeley: University of California Press, 2019), 136.

36. Molina, Hosang, and Gutiérrez emphasize the need to analyze racialized (non-white) groups in relation to one another and not just in relation to whiteness, while demonstrating how colonialism and white supremacy have always been relational projects. Molina, Hosang, and Gutiérrez, introduction to *Relational Formations of Race*, 1.

37. See Kenyon S. Chan and Shirley Hune, "Racialization and Panethnicity: From Asians in America to Asian Americans," in *Toward a Common Destiny: Improving Race and Ethnic Relations in America*, ed. Willis D. Hawley and Anthony W. Jackson (San Francisco: Jossey-Bass, 1995), 205–23; Lisa Lowe, "Heterogeneity, Hybridity, Multiplicity: Marking Asian American Differences," *Diaspora* 1, no. 1 (1991): 24–44; Claire Jean Kim, "The Racial Triangulation of Asian Americans," *Politics and Society* 27 (1999): 105–38; Henry Yu. *Thinking Orientals: Migration, Contact, Exoticism in Modern America* (New York: Oxford University Press), 2001; Sunaina Marr Maira, *Missing: Youth, Citizenship, and Empire after 9/11* (Durham, NC: Duke University Press, 2009); Sun Ah Laybourn, "Adopting the Model Minority Myth: Korean Adoption as a Racial Project," *Social Problems* 68 (2021): 118–35. Eric Tang helps fill this void by exploring how Cambodian refugees comport to tenuous timelines structured by the state, particularly the executive branch of government. Tang offers "refugee temporality" as an epistemological tool to theorize and name the refugee's knowledge of the way in which previous forms of power are reinscribed with each resettlement, displacement, and dislocation. Eric Tang, *Unsettled: Cambodian Refugees in the New York City Hyperghetto*. (Philadelphia: Temple University Press, 2015), 21.

38. Nandita Sharma, "Strategic Anti-essentialism: Decolonizing Decolonization," in *Sylvia Wynter: On Being Human as Praxis*, ed. Katherine McKittrick (Durham, NC: Duke University Press, 2015), 171.

39. As Saskia Sassen writes, "International migrations are produced, they are patterned and they are embedded in specific historical phases." Saskia Sassen, *Guests and Aliens* (New York: New Press, 1999), 155.

40. For more on the processes of relational racial formation, see Kim, "Racial Triangulation"; and Molina, Hosang, and Gutiérrez, *Relational Formations of Race*. See also Omi and Winant's conceptualization of "racial formation" in *Racial Formation in the United States: From the 1960s to the 1990s* (New York: Routledge, 1994).

41. Wilder Research, *Homelessness in Minnesota: Youth on Their Own; Findings from the 2015 Minnesota Homeless Study*, April 2017, https://www.wilder.org/sites/default/files/imports/2015_HomelessYouth_4-17.pdf, 8.

42. Charles W. Mills, "The Chronopolitics of Racial Time," *Time and Society* 29, no. 2 (2020): 301.

43. See Vanessa Ogle, "Whose Time Is It?: The Pluralization of Time and the Global Condition, 1870s–1940s," *American Historical Review* 118, no. 5 (2013): 1376–402.

44. Richard Wright, *Native Son* (New York: New American Library, 1950), 68.

45. Bonnie J. Barthold, *Black Time: Fiction of Africa, the Caribbean and the United States* (New Haven, CT: Yale University Press, 1981), 35.

46. Johannes Fabian, *Time and the Other: How Anthropology Makes Its Object* (New York: Columbia University Press, 1983), 25.

47. William Julius Wilson, *The Truly Disadvantaged: The Inner City, the Underclass, and Public Policy* (Chicago: University of Chicago Press, 1987), 60–61.

48. See C. Wright Mills, *The Sociological Imagination* (Oxford: Oxford University Press, 1959). As Bourdieu asserts, "The function of sociology, as of every science, is to reveal that which is hidden." Pierre Bourdieu, *On Television* (New York: New Press, 1996), 17.

234 NOTES TO PAGES 101–105

49. Simone Browne defines "racializing surveillance" as "a technology of social control where surveillance practices, policies, and performances concern the production of norms pertaining to race and exercise a 'power to define what is out of place.'" Simone Browne, *Dark Matters: On the Surveillance of Blackness* (Durham, NC: Duke University Press, 2015), 16.

50. William Fielding Ogburn uses the notion of "cultural lag" to describe any nonnormative adjustments to technological development. William Fielding Ogburn, *Social Change with Respect to Culture and Original Nature* (New York: B. W. Huebsch, 1922), 200. William Julius Wilson adapts Ogburn's idea to describe how Black people in poor urbanized space remain in a suspended state of delay due to "ghetto-related" behaviors. William Julius Wilson, *When Work Disappears: The World of the New Urban Poor* (New York: Vintage, 1996), 52. Comparing poor urbanized space to the wild, Ulf Hannerz writes, "There are slums which are more like villages and others which are more like jungles. At times one would look down Winston Street, see only the neighborliness and tranquility, and place this neighborhood close to the village end of the spectrum. But the people who live there know that it also has some attributes of the urban jungle. Some people and places mean trouble, and there is danger in the dark and the unknown." Ulf Hannerz, *Soulside: Inquiries into Ghetto Culture and Community* (New York: Columbia University Press, 1969), 20.

51. "U, Black Maybe," compact disc, track 8 on Common, *Finding Forever*, Good Music and Geffen Records, 2007.

52. Geof D. Wood rehearses the idea that "the determining condition for poor people is uncertainty." Geof D. Wood, "Staying Secure, Staying Poor: The Faustian Bargain," *World Development* 31 (2003): 468. See also Geof D. Wood, "Desperately Seeking Security," *Journal of International Development* 13 (2001): 523–34. Scholarship on intimate partnerships also traffics in the concept of uncertainty. See, for example, Linda M. Burton and M. Belinda Tucker, "Romantic Unions in an Era of Uncertainty: A Post-Moynihan Perspective on African American Women and Marriage," *Annals of the American Academy of Political and Social Science*. 621 (2009): 132–48; and Kathryn Edin and Maria Kefalas, *Promises I Can Keep: Why Poor Women Put Motherhood before Marriage* (Berkeley: University of California Press, 2005).

53. Evelyn Nakano Glenn, "From Servitude to Service Work: Historical Continuities in the Racial Division of Paid Reproductive Labor," *Signs: Journal of Women in Culture and Society* 18, no. 1 (1992): 18.

54. E. P. Thompson, "Time, Work-Discipline, and Capitalism," *Past and Present* 38 (1967): 61. For more on the relationship between time and money, see Nigel Thrift, "The Making of a Capitalist Consciousness," in *The Sociology of Time*, ed. John Hassard (New York: St. Martin's, 1990), 105–29.

55. Anne McClintock, *Imperial Leather: Race, Gender, and Sexuality in the Colonial Contest* (New York: Routledge, 1995), 121.

56. Baldwin made the remarks during a 1963 interview with Kenneth Clarke. See "A Conversation with James Baldwin," in *Conversations with James Baldwin*, ed. Fred R. Standley and Louis H. Pratt (Jackson: University of Mississippi Press, 1989), 42.

57. Allen Costantini, "Rondo Neighborhood Gets Apologies for I-91," KARE, July 17, 2015, https://www.kare11.com/article/news/local/rondo-neighborhood-gets-apologies-for-i-94/89-105454642.

58. See Rondo Ave., Inc. (website), accessed September 14, 2023, https://rondoavenueinc.org/.

59. "Near North Neighborhood Data," Minnesota Compass, 2013–17 data, https://www.mncompass.org/profiles/neighborhoods/minneapolis/near-north.

60. Edward G. Goetz, Brittany Lewis, Anthony Damiano, and Molly Calhoun, *The Diversity of Gentrification: Multiple Forms of Gentrification in Minneapolis and St. Paul,*

Center for Urban and Regional Affairs, University of Minnesota, January 25, 2019, https://gentrification.umn.edu/sites/gentrification.umn.edu/files/files/media/diversity-of-gentrification-012519.pdf, 34.

61. Douglas S. Massey and Nancy A. Denton, *American Apartheid: Segregation and the Making of the Urban Underclass* (Cambridge, MA: Harvard University Press, 1993).

62. Massey and Denton, *American Apartheid*, 118.

63. Paula Chakravartty and Denise Ferreira da Silva, "Accumulation, Dispossession, and Debt: The Racial Logic of Global Capitalism; An Introduction," *American Quarterly* 64, no. 3 (2012): 361–85.

64. Massey and Denton, *American Apartheid*, 229. The authors recommend that the Department of Housing and Urban Development (HUD) adhere to existing federal legislation such as the Fair Housing Act and the 1974 Equal Credit Opportunity Act.

65. "Across 110th Street," MP3 audio, track 1 on Bobby Womack and Peace, *Across 110th Street*, United Artists, 1973.

66. George Lipsitz, *How Racism Takes Place* (Philadelphia: Temple University Press, 2011), 28.

67. Mills, "White Time," 29.

68. I would be remiss not to acknowledge Jodi Rios's important analysis of the spatialization of identity and how "space can easily change, or be recodified, from urban to suburban and back again, depending on who lives there and what they are doing." Jodi Rios, *Black Lives and Spatial Matters: Policing Blackness and Practicing Freedom in Suburban St. Louis* (Ithaca, NY: Cornell University Press, 2020), 125. Rios describes how Blackness, when constructed as "risk," threatens the authenticity of white, suburbanized space and white spatial imaginaries. Phrases like "suburban ghetto," Rios argues, become part of the many "discursive regimes" used to regulate Black sociality and Blackness in North St. Louis (119).

69. For more details on the documentary series, see *Jim Crow of the North*, Twin Cities PBS, https://www.tpt.org/jim-crow-north/.

70. Saidiya V. Hartman, *Lose Your Mother: A Journey along the Atlantic Slave Route* (New York: Farrar, Straus & Giroux, 2007), 87–88.

4. "KEISHA DOESN'T GET THE CALL BEFORE KIMBERLY"

1. Studies on the transition to adulthood have a long lineage within the social sciences. There is an extensive amount of research using education and employment as indicators of the transition to adulthood. For more on this topic, see John Modell, Frank F. Furstenberg Jr., and Theodore Hershberg, "Social Change and Transitions to Adulthood in Historical Perspective," *Journal of Family History* 1 (1976): 7–32; Margaret M. Marini, "The Transition to Adulthood: Sex Differences in Educational Attainment and Age at Marriage," *American Sociological Review* 43 (1978): 483–507; Michael J. Shanahan. "Pathways to Adulthood in Changing Societies: Variability and Mechanisms in the Life Course Perspective," *Annual Review of Sociology* 26 (2000): 667–92; Monica Kirkpatrick Johnson, "Social Origins, Adolescent Experiences, and Work Value Trajectories during the Transition to Adulthood," *Social Forces* 80, no. 4 (2002): 1307–40; Janel E. Benson and Frank F. Furstenberg Jr., "Entry into Adulthood: Are Adult Role Transitions Meaningful Markers of Adult Identity?," *Advances in the Life Course Research* 11 (2007): 199–224; Jennifer M. Silva, "Constructing Adulthood in an Age of Uncertainty," *American Sociological Review* 77, no. 4 (2012): 505–22; Karl Alexander, Doris Entwisle, and Linda Olson, *The Long Shadow: Family Background, Disadvantaged Urban Youth, and the Transition to Adulthood* (New York: Russell Sage Foundation, 2014).

2. Consider Michel Foucault's analysis of the disciplinary function of the bell within schools. Michel Foucault, *Discipline and Punish: The Birth of the Prison* (New York: Vintage Books, 1995), 150.

NOTES TO PAGES 115–127

3. Saidiya V. Hartman, *Lose Your Mother: A Journey along the Atlantic Slave Route* (New York: Farrar, Straus & Giroux, 2007), 6.

4. Assata Shakur, *Assata: An Autobiography* (Chicago: Zed Books, 1978), 181.

5. Paul Willis, *Learning to Labor: How Working Class Kids Get Working Class Jobs* (New York: Columbia University Press, 1977), 28–29.

6. Damien M. Sojoyner, *First Strike: Educational Enclosures in Black Los Angeles* (Minneapolis: University of Minnesota Press, 2016), xiii. Also see Clyde Woods, *Development Arrested: The Blues and Plantation Power in the Mississippi Delta* (New York: Verso, 2017), 127.

7. William H. Watkins, *The White Architects of Black Education* (New York: Teachers Education Press, 2000).

8. Gloria Ladson-Billings, "From the Achievement Gap to the Education Debt: Understanding Achievement in U.S. Schools," *Educational Researcher* 35, no. 7 (2006): 5.

9. Cheryl Harris, "Whiteness as Property," *Harvard Law Review* 106, no. 8 (1993): 1754. Despite the Supreme Court's decision in *Brown v. Board of Education*, white people still managed to "control, manage, postpone, and, if necessary, thwart change."

10. Nancy Lesko, *Act Your Age! A Cultural Construction of Adolescence* (New York: RoutledgeFalmer, 2001), 183.

11. Anne Arnett Ferguson, *Bad Boys: Public Schools in the Making of Black Masculinity* (Ann Arbor: University of Michigan Press, 2000), 230.

12. Michael Hardt and Antonio Negri, *Empire* (Cambridge, MA: Harvard University Press, 2000), 153.

13. Richard Q. Shin, Lance C. Smith, Jamie C. Welch, and Ijeoma Ezeofor, "Is Allison More Likely Than Lakisha to Receive a Callback from Counseling Professionals? A Racism Audit Study," *Counseling Psychologist* 44, no. 8 (2016): 1187–211. See also Devah Pager and Hana Shepherd, "The Sociology of Discrimination: Racial Discrimination in Employment, Housing, Credit, and Consumer Markets," *Annual Review of Sociology* 34, (2008): 181–209.

14. Lesko, *Act Your Age!*, 34.

15. Lesko, *Act Your Age!*, 35.

5. TABANCA TIME

1. This phrasing is a riff on La Marr Jurelle Bruce, "Interludes in Madtime: Black Music, Madness, and Metaphysical Syncopation," *Social Text* 35, no. 4 (2017): 1–31. My riff off Bruce should not be confused with ripping off Bruce. I find the concept of "interlude" both provocative and generative. Like Bruce, I am drawing on the musicality of "interlude," but I am also thinking more about the impossibility of interlude within the context of deportation and deported time.

2. Michel-Rolph Trouillot, *Silencing the Past: Power and the Production of History* (Boston: Beacon, 1995), 15.

3. Saidiya V. Hartman, *Scenes of Subjection: Terror, Slavery, and Self-Making in Nineteenth-Century America* (New York: Oxford University Press, 1997), 20.

4. Renato Rosaldo, *Culture and Truth: The Remaking of Social Analysis* (Boston: Beacon, 1989), 11.

5. Rosaldo, *Culture and Truth*, 221.

6. Gloria Anzaldúa, *Borderlands/La Frontera: The New Mestiza*, 4th ed. (San Francisco: Aunt Lute Books, 2007), 59.

7. To "fire de wuk" is to quit a job. The phrase reflects the vernacular dexterity and overall creativity among many Trinis and Caribbean neighbors who consistently subvert

power relations through language. In this case the employee fires their job, not the other way around.

8. Peter Medoff and Holly Sklar, *Streets of Hope: The Rise and Fall of an Urban Neighborhood* (Boston: South End, 1994), 31.

9. Aware that the police were not going to protect the community from fires or other forms of harm, many Roxbury residents, including my mother, formed their own community defense groups.

10. Medoff and Sklar, *Streets of Hope*, 31.

11. Contact with the prison-industrial complex signifies a site of racial formation. Contrary to criminological theories on the "race of a criminal record" (see Aliya Saperstein and Andrew M. Penner, "The Race of a Criminal Record: How Incarceration Colors Racial Perceptions," *Social Problems* 57, no. 1 [2010]: 92–113), my father did not become Black when the police arrested him. The classification only matched his racial identity.

12. "Lime" is a colloquialism in Trinidad used to describe an intentional effort to relax in the company of others. Those perceived to be working too hard are often encouraged to "take a lime, nah." As Kevin Birth writes, "Liming is an essential social activity. The term . . . could be misconstrued as simply doing nothing, but there are two significant differences between truly doing nothing and liming: (1) one cannot lime by oneself; and (2) one can do an infinite number of things (other than 'work') while liming with others." Kevin Birth, *Any Time Is Trinidad Time: Social Meanings and Temporal Consciousness* (Gainesville: University Press of Florida, 1999), 4.

13. "Anytime is Trinidad time" is a popular expression among Trinbagonians to highlight both the spontaneity and the organization of temporal rhythms. On the 1971 album *Curfew Time*, Lord Kitchener popularized the phrase in the song "Trinidad Time." "Trinidad Time," vinyl, track A2 on Lord Kitchener, *Sock It to Me Kitch*, International Recording Co., 1970. For more on this concept, see Birth, *Any Time is Trinidad Time*. My father's refusal to conform to Western standard time reflected his refusal to comport to Western space: namely, the United States. Believing that anytime is Trinidad time is also a belief that any space is Trinidad (space). To this day, my father lauds himself for swiftly moving through Boston with the kind of swag he carried while navigating the streets of San Juan or any other part of Trinidad. Perhaps he was prescient enough not to get too comfortable in the US. Did he know his stay would be temporary, regardless of whether his kids were born in the US? Though he established roots in the country, my father was intent on not assimilating to American culture. He had no desire to speak proper English. Instead he accentuated his accent while mocking our slang. I see this as one way the subaltern speak back to Western imperialism. In believing that "anytime is Trinidad time" and believing that "any space is Trinidad," my father contributed to the provincialization of the West while centering the lived experiences of those subjugated by empire and imperialism.

14. "Clocker" is a slang term used to describe someone who sells drugs.

15. "Street Life," 7-inch vinyl, track 1 on The Crusaders, *Street Life*, MCA, 1979.

16. Linda Bosniak argues that constructions of citizenship as "hard on the outside and soft on the inside" are inaccurate and that such a separation is in fact "elusive." As Bosniak writes, "Noncitizen immigrants have entered the spatial domain of universal citizenship, but they remain outsiders in a significant sense: the border effectively follows them inside." Linda Bosniak, *The Citizen and the Alien: Dilemmas of Contemporary Membership* (Princeton, NJ: Princeton University Press, 2006), 4.

17. Lisa M. Cacho, *Social Death: Racialized Rightlessness and the Criminalization of the Unprotected* (New York: New York University Press, 2012), 117. For more on the limitations of esteeming "desirable" migrants at the expense of those deemed "undesirable," see Harsha Walia, *Undoing Border Imperialism* (Oakland: AK Press, 2013).

238 **NOTES TO PAGES 131–134**

18. Harsha Walia describes how migrant justice collectives like No One Is Illegal (NOII) resisted such false oppositions: "NOII movements . . . challenge Darwinian constructions of good/desirable/real migrant (read: English-speaking, employed and/or conforming to heteropatriarchal norms) versus bad/undesirable/bogus migrant (read: unemployed, without formal education and/or with a criminal record). Such dichotomies reinforce state controls on self-determination, strengthen the capitalist exploitation of labor, and maintain social hierarchies based on race, class, gender, sexuality and ability" Harsha Walia, *Undoing Border Imperialism*, 77–78.

19. A significant amount of the perpetual emotional, psychic, and physical agony of deportation remains enshrined in legislation. For example, the 1996 Anti-terrorism and Effective Death Penalty Act (AEDPA) and Illegal Immigration Reform and Immigrant Responsibility Act (IIRAIRA) resulted in four devastating changes to immigration policy: (1) an increased number of categories warranting deportation and expanded categories of "aggravated felonies," (2) reduced judicial power to grant relief from deportation, (3) an expedited process of deportation, and (4) limited avenues for appeal.

20. Despite differing opinions among immigration attorneys, state prosecutors, and ICE, I argue that there is no such thing as "postdeportation," only "postremoval."

21. The fledgling stages of my writing career are easily traceable to the many letters I sent to my father and uncles pre- and postremoval. I imagined what it was like for my father to be alone and so far removed from his loved ones. Thus, I took this undertaking very seriously. I injected more love and aspects of my being into countless handwritten letters. My aim was to maintain a sense of temporal continuity with loved ones behind the wall. I hoped my words would help them "stay up" within a system designed to keep them locked down.

22. "Time," featuring AZ and Nas, MP3 audio, track 13 on Nature, *Queen's Classics*, DCM, 2016.

23. "Licks" is a common phrase in the Caribbean used to refer to the use of physical discipline.

24. Anyone that has lost someone knows the brutality of time. To go on living when a family member, spouse, friend, or other loved one is gone is an extraordinary undertaking. Crying out, "I can't go on" is an acknowledgment of the interminable pain of loss. Still, although time continues to violently press forward, those subjected to time's foulness find a way to push on/back. My hope is that readers find some signs of resistance to time in the pages of this text.

25. Saidiya Hartman offers a compelling appraisal of empathy, writing, "Empathy is double-edged, for in making the other's suffering one's own, this suffering is occluded by the other's obliteration." Hartman, *Scenes of Subjection*, 19.

26. See Humberto R. Maturana and Francisco J. Varela, *Autopoiesis and Cognition: The Realization of Living* (Holland: D. Reidel, 1980).

27. Michael Hardt and Antonio Negri, *Empire* (Cambridge, MA: Harvard University Press, 2000), 194.

28. Saidiya V. Hartman, *Wayward Lives, Beautiful Experiments: Intimate Histories of Social Upheaval* (New York: W.W. Norton, 2019), 107. Words in italics are direct quotes to Du Bois's *The Philadelphia Negro*.

29. See Amanda Chicago Lewis, "How Black People Are Being Shut Out of America's Weed Boom: Whitewashing the Green Rush," BuzzFeed News, March 16, 2016, https://www.buzzfeednews.com/article/amandachicagolewis/americas-white-only-weed-boom. I sometimes wonder whether my father predicted that white people would be the only ones going gangbusters once the weed bonanza hit. With so many Black people still incarcerated for minor drug offenses, this is yet another example of white people capitalizing on Black dispossession, debt, and incarceration. I am reminded of Dylan Rodríguez's words previously cited in chapter 1: "'Disparity' is a bullshit concept, when we already

NOTES TO PAGES 137–139

know that the inception of criminal justice is the de-criminalization of white people, particularly propertied white citizens and those willing to bear arms to defend the white world. 'Mass Incarceration' is worse than meaningless, when it's not the 'masses' who are being criminalized and locked up. So there is some furtive and fatal white entitlement involved in this discursive political structure."

6. TRANSGRESSING TIME IN THE FAST LIFE

1. Elijah Anderson, *Code of the Street: Decency, Violence, and the Moral Life of the Inner City* (New York: W. W. Norton, 1999), 117.

2. Social scientists have a long track record of constructing Black youths in poor urbanized space as "present oriented." See Oscar Lewis, *The Children of Sánchez: Autobiography of a Mexican Family* (New York: Random House, 1961); William Julius Wilson, *The Truly Disadvantaged: The Inner City, the Underclass, and Public Policy* (Chicago: University of Chicago Press, 1987); Martin Sánchez-Jankowski, *Islands in the Streets: Gangs and American Urban Society* (Berkeley: University of California Press, 1991); Anderson, *Code of the Street*; Frank Furstenberg Jr. et al., *Managing to Make It: Urban Families and Adolescent Success* (Chicago: University of Chicago Press, 1999); Jay MacLeod, *Ain't No Makin' It: Aspirations and Attainment in a Low-Income Neighborhood*, 3rd ed. (Boulder, CO: Westview, 2009).

3. Anderson, *Code of the Street*, 36. "Code switching" as a concept, however, seems to fit into Denise Ferreira da Silva's critique of overemphasis on the logic of racialized exclusion, while ignoring how any attempts to be included by effectively alternating codes places the racialized other at risk of self-obliteration through assimilation. See Denise Ferreira da Silva, *Toward a Global Idea of Race* (Minneapolis: University of Minnesota Press, 2007), 162. Perhaps it is time to do more code sticking and less code switching.

4. Erving Goffman, *The Presentation of Self in Everyday Life* (New York: Doubleday, 1959), 22.

5. W. E. B. Du Bois, *The Souls of Black Folk* (New York: Barnes & Noble Classics, 2003), 9.

6. Frantz Fanon, *Black Skin, White Masks*, trans. Richard Philcox (New York: Grove, 2008), 95.

7. See Devah Pager and Lincoln Quillan, "Walking the Talk: What Employers Say versus What They Do," *American Sociological Review* 70 (2005): 355–80; and Devah Pager, Bruce Western, and Bart Bonikowski, "Discrimination in a Low-Wage Labor Market: A Field Experiment," *American Sociological Review* 74 (2009): 777–99.

8. See Phyllis Moen, "The Gendered Life Course," in *Handbook of Aging and the Social Sciences*, ed. Robert H. Binstock and Linda K. George (New York: Academic Press, 1996), 175–96; and Phyllis Moen and Robert M. Orrange, "Careers and Lives: Socialization, Structural Lag, and Gendered Ambivalence," *Advances in Life Course Research* 7 (2002): 231–60. The gendered division of labor ensures that men work a single shift outside the home, while women have double and triple duty. Reproductive labor, affective labor, care-work, and the labor-time required to reckon with acts of sexual violence, however, remain incommensurable within the logics of capital. Women and femmes, particularly women and femmes of color, may borrow time, but they take severe risks when attempting to spend it. Time is not simply lost due to the unequal value ascribed to women's labor. Rather, it is stolen by gender-based violence.

9. Jody Miller brings greater attention to gender-based violence against African American girls. Miller's specific aim is to "investigate how the structural inequalities that create extreme—and racialized—urban poverty facilitate both cultural adaptations and social contexts that heighten and shape the tremendous gender-based violence faced by African American girls." Jody Miller, *Getting Played: African American Girls, Urban*

240   NOTES TO PAGES 140–143

Inequality, and Gendered Violence (New York: New York University Press, 2008), 3. But Miller struggles to avoid interpellating both Black girlhood and Black boyhood through the lens of abjection, pathology, and heteronormativity. Moreover, her analysis is based on an indivisible concept of gender violence devoid of processes of racialization. Consequently, she ends up reproducing a variety of culture-of-poverty tropes and appears to fall into the second-wave feminist trap of equating womanhood with whiteness.

10. "Not respectively" because, as I have argued elsewhere, sociology departments do more than produce knowledge—they also produce police. See Rahsaan Mahadeo, "As Campuses Cut Ties to Police, Sociology Departments Must Do the Same," Truthout, July 21, 2020, https://truthout.org/articles/as-campuses-cut-ties-to-police-sociology-departments-must-do-the-same/.

11. Saidiya V. Hartman, "The Anarchy of Colored Girls Assembled in a Riotous Manner," *South Atlantic Quarterly* 117, no. 3 (2018): 469.

12. Hartman, "Anarchy of Colored Girls," 470.

13. It would be a mistake, however, to assume that work within the underground economy is at all easy. The risks of arrest, incarceration, and police terror, along with unconventional work hours and meager earnings, remain undesirable to most with access to legitimate opportunities for work.

14. Linda M. Burton, Dawn A. Obeidallah, and Kevin Allison, "Ethnographic Insights on Social Context and Adolescent Development among Inner-City African-American Teens," in *Ethnology and Human Development: Context and Meaning in Social Inquiry*, ed. Richard Jessor, Anne Colby, and Richard A. Shweder (Chicago: University of Chicago Press, 1996), 409.

15. Robert K. Merton, "Socially Expected Durations: A Case Study of Concept Formation in Sociology," in *Conflict and Consensus: A Festschrift in Honor of Lewis A. Coser*, ed. Walter W. Powell and Richard Robbins (New York: Free Press, 1984), 264.

16. Richard A. Settersten Jr., "Age Structuring and the Rhythm of the Life Course," in *Handbook of the Life Course*, ed. Jeylan T. Mortimer and Michael J. Shanahan (New York: Springer Science and Business Media, 2004), 91.

17. Settersten writes, "Non-whites, non-professionals, and those with lower educational levels cited age deadlines more often than their counterparts." Settersten, "Age Structuring," 91.

18. Lisa M. Cacho, *Social Death: Racialized Rightlessness and the Criminalization of the Unprotected* (New York: New York University Press, 2012), 145.

19. Orlando Patterson, *Slavery and Social Death: A Comparative Study* (Cambridge, MA: Harvard University Press, 2018), 10.

20. "Overstand" is a common phrase within Rastafari culture, which seeks to eliminate hierarchy in practice and discourse. For many Rastafari, "understand" constructs some as subordinate to the person who is presenting specific information or asking a question. By contrast, an "overstanding" is an effort to remain steps ahead of conventional knowledge.

21. Steve Martinot, *The Machinery of Whiteness: Studies in the Structure of Racialization* (Philadelphia: Temple University Press, 2010), 74.

22. See Anderson, *Code of the Street*; MacLeod, *Ain't No Makin' It*; Richard Majors and Janet Billson, *Cool Pose: The Dilemmas of Black Manhood in America* (New York: Lexington Books, 1992); Katherine S. Newman, *No Shame in My Game: The Working Poor in the Inner City* (New York: Alfred A. Knopf, 1999); Philippe Bourgois, *In Search of Respect: Selling Crack in El Barrio* (Cambridge: Cambridge University Press, 2003); David J. Harding, *Living the Drama: Community, Conflict, and Culture among Inner-City Boys* (Chicago: University of Chicago Press, 2009).

23. Burton, Obeidallah, and Allison, "Ethnographic Insights," 400.

NOTES TO PAGES 143–147 241

24. "Fast Life," featuring Nas, MP3 audio, track 8 on Kool G. Rap, *4, 5, 6*, Cold Chillin' and Epic Street, 1995.

25. Paul Gilroy, "The Dialectics of Diaspora Identification," in *Theories of Race and Racism: A Reader*, 2nd ed., ed. Les Back and John Solomos (New York: Routledge, 2009), 571.

26. Robin D. G. Kelley, *Yo' Mama's Disfunktional! Fighting the Culture Wars in Urban America* (Boston: Beacon, 1997), 45.

27. Walter Mischel, Yuichi Shoda, and Philip K. Peake, "The Nature of Adolescent Competencies Predicted by Preschool Delay of Gratification," *Journal of Personality and Social Psychology* 54 (1988): 687–96.

28. As Celeste Kidd, Holly Palmeri, and Richard N. Aslin note, "Consider the mindset of a 4-year-old living in a crowded shelter, surrounded by older children with little adult supervision. For a child accustomed to stolen possessions and broken promises, the only guaranteed treats are the ones you have already swallowed. At the other extreme, consider the mindset of an only-child in a stable home whose parents reliably promise and deliver small motivational treats for good behavior." Celeste Kidd, Holly Palmeri, and Richard N. Aslin, "Rational Snacking: Young Children's Decision-Making on the Marshmallow Task Is Moderated by Beliefs about Environmental Reliability," *Cognition* 126 (2013): 111.

29. Joseph Scott, "Black Science and Nation Building," in *The Death of White Sociology: Essays on Race and Culture*, ed. Joyce A. Ladner (Baltimore: Black Classic Press, 1973), 293. Tracing the origins of white manhood through histories of anti-Black violence, Gail Bederman writes, "Middle-class parents taught their sons to build a strong, manly 'character' as they would build muscle, through repetitive exercises of control over impulse.... By gaining the manly strength to control himself, a man gained the authority, as well as the duty, to protect and direct those less manly than himself, whether his wife, his children, his employees, or his racial 'inferiors.'" Gail Bederman, *Manliness and Civilization: A Cultural History of Gender and Race in the United States, 1880–1917* (Chicago: University of Chicago Press, 1995), 48.

30. Jodi Rios reveals the intimate connections between urbanized space and suburbanized space. By studying the racial and spatial politics in North St. Louis County, Missouri, Rios reveals how discursive regimes perpetuate logics of cultural inferiority while legitimating policing and anti-Black violence in suburbanized space. Rios argues that racializing and spatializing logics work to attach "risk" to Black bodies based on cultural norms associated within a "white spatial imaginary of suburban citizenship." For example, municipal leaders justified the use of "extreme policing practices" under the guise that Black people moving from the projects to the suburbs "don't know how to act." Jodi Rios, *Black Lives and Spatial Matters: Policing Blackness and Practicing Freedom in Suburban St. Louis* (Ithaca, NY: Cornell University Press, 2020, 25.

7. WHY IS THE TIME ALWAYS RIGHT FOR WHITE AND WRONG FOR US?

1. George Lipsitz, *How Racism Takes Place* (Philadelphia: Temple University Press, 2011), 37.

2. W. E. B. Du Bois, *Black Reconstruction in America, 1860-–1880* (New York: Atheneum, 1998), 700–701.

3. David Roediger, *The Wages of Whiteness: Race and the Making of the American Working Class* (Brooklyn, NY: Verso, 1991), 13.

4. Steve Martinot describes how fear, anxiety, and paranoia became key elements for structuring white solidarity and cohesion. Steve Martinot, *The Machinery of Whiteness: Studies in the Structure of Racialization* (Philadelphia: Temple University Press, 2010), 49.

242 NOTES TO PAGES 147–149

5. Tim Wise, *Speaking Treason Fluently: Anti-racist Reflections from an Angry White Male* (Berkeley: Soft Skull, 2008).

6. Cheryl Harris, "Whiteness as Property," *Harvard Law Review* 106, no. 8 (1993): 1758.

7. Harris, "Whiteness as Property," 1714.

8. Saidiya V. Hartman, *Scenes of Subjection: Terror, Slavery, and Self-Making in Nineteenth-Century America* (New York: Oxford University Press, 1997), 24.

9. Hartman, *Scenes of Subjection*, 24.

10. Dionne Brand, *A Map to the Door of No Return: Notes to Belonging* (Toronto: Random House, 2001), 81–82.

11. Harris, "Whiteness as Property," 1777.

12. Eduardo Bonilla-Silva, *Racism without Racists: Color-Blind Racism and the Persistence of Racial Inequality in the United States* (Lanham, MD: Rowman & Littlefield, 2010), 104; Pierre Bourdieu, *Outline of a Theory of a Practice* (Cambridge: Cambridge University Press, 1977), 72.

13. Owen J. Dwyer and John Paul Jones III, "White Socio-Spatial Epistemology," *Social & Cultural Geography* 1, no. 2 (2000): 212.

14. As noted in the introduction, whiteness is as much of a sociohistorical construct as other racial formations. In quotidian life, however, whiteness proceeds as if it were race neutral and ahistorical.

15. Charles W. Mills, *The Racial Contract* (Ithaca, NY: Cornell University Press, 1997), 126–27.

16. For more on this topic, see Édouard Glissant, *Poetics of Relation* (Ann Arbor: University of Michigan Press, 1997); David Theo Goldberg, *Racist Culture: Philosophy and the Politics of Meaning* (Malden: Blackwell, 1993); Pamela Perry, "White Means Never Having to Say You're Ethnic: White Youth and the Construction of 'Cultureless' Identities," *Journal of Contemporary Ethnography* 30, no. 1 (2001): 56–91; Sara Ahmed, "A Phenomenology of Whiteness," *Feminist Theory* 8, no. 2 (2007): 149–68; Eduardo Bonilla-Silva, "'This Is a White Country!' The Racial Ideology of the Western Nations of the World Systems," *Sociological Inquiry* 70, no. 2 (2000): 188–214; and Renisa Mawani, "Law as Temporality: Colonial Politics in Indian Settlers," *University of California Irvine Law Review* 4, no. 65 (2014): 65–96. I would be remiss not to acknowledge the "good stories" (see chapter 1) that white people tell to convince themselves of the need to return to the "good old days." For example, many white nationalists, white nativists, and other white supremacists long to return to a time when white being was not troubled by the presence of racialized others.

17. Ahmed, "Phenomenology of Whiteness," 151.

18. Helen Ngo, *The Habits of Racism: A Phenomenology of Racism and Racialized Embodiment* (Lanham, MD: Lexington Books, 2017), 81.

19. Ngo, *Habits of Racism*, 150.

20. Paul Willis, *Learning to Labor: How Working Class Kids Get Working Class Jobs* (New York: Columbia University Press, 1977); Alford A. Young, *The Minds of Marginalized Black Men: Making Sense of Mobility, Opportunity, and Future Life Chances* (Princeton, NJ: Princeton University Press, 2004); Jay MacLeod, *Ain't No Makin' It: Aspirations and Attainment in a Low-Income Neighborhood* (Boulder, CO: Westview, 2009).

21. Joe R. Feagin, *The White Racial Frame: Centuries of Racial Framing and Counterframing* (New York: Routledge, 2013); Michelle M. Wright, *Physics of Blackness: Beyond the Middle Passage Epistemology* (Minneapolis: University of Minnesota Press, 2015), 46.

22. Wright, *Physics of Blackness*, 60.

23. See Victor E. Ray et al., "Critical Race Theory, Afro-pessimism, and Racial Progress Narratives," *Sociology of Race and Ethnicity* 3, no. 2 (2017): 147–58; Louise Seamster and Victor Erik Ray, "Against Teleology in the Study of Race: Toward the Abolition of the Progress Paradigm," *Sociological Theory* 36, no. 4 (2018): 315–42.

NOTES TO PAGES 149–153   243

24. See Ray et al., "Critical Race Theory"; Seamster and Ray, "Against Teleology." It is no surprise that whiteness remains future oriented. Whiteness looks to the future because it seeks to ignore a present past (i.e., slavery, settler colonialism, imperialism, etc.). Consider the Nick Estes critique of "settler narratives" that "use a linear conception of time to distance themselves from the horrific crimes committed against Indigenous peoples and the land. This includes celebrating bogus origin stories like Thanksgiving. But Indigenous notions of time consider the present to be structured entirely by our past and by our ancestors. There is no separation between past and present, meaning that an alternative future is also determined by our understanding of our past. Our history is our future." Nick Estes, *Our History Is the Future: Standing Rock versus the Dakota Access Pipeline, and the Long Tradition of Indigenous Resistance* (New York: Verso Books, 2019), 14–15.

25. McCleskey v. Kemp, 481 U.S. 279 (1987) ruled that racial bias in sentencing cannot be challenged under the Fourteenth Amendment in the absence of clear evidence of conscious discriminatory intent.

26. Joy James, *Resisting State Violence: Radicalism, Gender, and Race in U.S. Culture* (Minneapolis: University of Minnesota Press, 1996), 36.

27. The courts and legal system often deny structural racism and anti-Blackness while reproducing both in the same breath. Consider how Derek Chauvin's defense attorneys attempted to blame George Floyd for his own death, rather than acknowledge the systemic nature of anti-Blackness in policing.

28. Hortense J. Spillers, "Mama's Baby, Papa's Maybe: An American Grammar Book," *Diacritics* 17, no. 2 (Summer 1987): 67.

29. "Who feels it knows it" is a popular aphorism in Jamaica, and many other majority-Black Caribbean nations invoke signifying the subjective side to oppression that only the oppressed can understand. It is worth asking what happens when those who don't feel it claim to know it. I am specifically considering Hartman's theorizing of fungibility and the possibility of interchanging people with cultural capital. Hartman (*Scenes of Subjection*, 21) describes fungibility as "the joy made possible by virtue of the replaceability and interchangeability endemic to the commodity—and by the extensive capacities of property—that is, the augmentation of the master subject through his embodiment in external objects and persons." What concerns me, then, is the possibility that the fungibility of Blackness provides an opportunity for those who don't feel it to claim to know it.

30. As a "gender-fluent" and trans person, Dominique's critique signals an attempt to speak back to chrononormativity and the heteronormative logics surrounding "family" and "domestic time." Both queer and queer-of-color theorists, including J. Jack Halberstam, *In a Queer Time and Place: Transgender Bodies, Subcultural Lives* (New York: New York University Press, 2005); José Esteban Muñoz, *Cruising Utopia: The Then and There of Queer Futurity* (New York: New York University Press, 2009); and Kara Keeling, *Queer Times, Black Futures* (New York: New York University Press, 2019), critique time as privileging a social time in which queer and trans lives literally and figuratively don't count. Like each of these theorists, Dominique answers the question "Whose time is it?" For Dominique and other queer and trans youth of color at Run-a-Way, time was concentrated in the hands of those privileged along the lines of race, gender, class, and sexuality.

31. Halberstam, *Queer Time and Place*, 5.

32. Halberstam, *Queer Time and Place*, 5.

33. Keeling, *Queer Times, Black Futures*, 19.

34. To be "clocked" is to be "read" or identified as trans by a cisgender person.

35. Halberstam, *Queer Time and Place*, 10.

36. Elizabeth Freeman describes "domestic time" as "a gendered form of and contributor to class habitus." Elizabeth Freeman, *Time Binds: Queer Temporalities, Queer Histories* (Durham, NC: Duke University Press, 2010), 44.

37. "Didn't Cha Know," MP3 audio, track 1 on Erykah Badu, *Mama's Gun*, Motown, 2000.

38. Robert K. Merton, "The Matthew Effect in Science: The Reward and Communication Systems of Science Are Considered," *Science* 159, no. 3810 (1968): 56–63.

39. Andrew Pallas, "Educational Transitions, Trajectories, and the Pathways," in *Handbook of the Life Course,* ed. Jeylan T. Mortimer and Michael J. Shanahan (New York: Springer Science and Business Media, 2004), 174.

40. Melvin L. Oliver and Thomas Shapiro, *Black Wealth/White Wealth: A New Perspective on Racial Inequality* (New York: Routledge, 1995), 51.

41. Migration is itself a product of white time's synchronization to global capitalism, free trade, US interventionism, and "low-intensity conflicts" that destroy local economies in dispossessed nations, lower wages, and reduce social spending on social services, all in the name of "progress."

42. Shannon Sullivan, *Revealing Whiteness: The Unconscious Habits of Racial Privilege* (Bloomington: Indiana University Press, 2006), 10. Helen Ngo writes, "Sullivan looks at how white people tend to act and think as if all spaces—whether geographical, psychical, linguistic, economic, spiritual, bodily, or otherwise—are or should be available for them to move in and out of as they wish." Ngo, *Habits of Racism*, 81.

43. W. E. B. Du Bois, "The Black Man Brings His Gifts," in *W.E.B. Du Bois: A Reader*, ed. David Levering Lewis (New York: Henry Holt, 1995), 454.

44. Du Bois, *Black Reconstruction in America*, 700–701.

45. John Mbiti, *African Religions and Philosophy* (New York: Praeger, 1969), 19.

46. La Marr Jurelle Bruce writes, "Whereas fugitivity, wandering, waywardness, and derangement are modes of motion defying modern mandates for 'proper' movement, loitering is slowness or stillness that violates said mandates. The fugitive goes when told to stay, while the loiterer stays when told to go." La Marr Jurelle Bruce, "Shore, Unsure: Loitering as a Way of Life," *GLQ: A Journal of Lesbian and Gay Studies* 25, no. 2 (2019): 353.

47. Michelle M. Wright, *Physics of Blackness: Beyond the Middle Passage Epistemology* (Minneapolis: University of Minnesota Press, 2015), 133.

48. See W. E. B. Du Bois, *The Souls of Black Folk* (New York: Barnes & Noble Classics, 2003); Ralph Ellison, *Invisible Man* (New York: Vintage, 1947); Richard Wright, *Native Son* (New York: New American Library, 1950).

49. While "late" is typically used as a reference to chronological delay, it is also an expression, particularly among youth, to signal a delay in picking up on recent trends.

50. On whiteness and modernity, see Frantz Fanon, *The Wretched of the Earth*, trans. Richard Philcox (New York: Grove, 2004); Edward W. Said, *Orientalism* (New York: Vintage Books, 1979); Anne McClintock, *Imperial Leather: Race, Gender, and Sexuality in the Colonial Contest* (New York: Routledge, 1995); Roderick A. Ferguson, *Aberrations in Black: Toward a Queer of Color Critique* (Minneapolis: University of Minnesota Press, 2004); M. Jacqui Alexander, *Pedagogies of Crossing: Meditations on Feminism, Sexual Politics, Memory, and the Sacred* (Durham, NC: Duke University Press, 2005); Halberstam, *Queer Time and Place*; Homi K. Bhabha, "'Race,' Time and the Revision of Modernity," in *Theories of Race and Racism: A Reader*, 2nd ed., ed. Les Back and John Solomos (New York: Routledge, 2009), 422–36; Steph Lawler, "White Like Them: Whiteness and Anachronistic Space in Representations of the English Working Class," *Ethnicities* 12, no. 4 (2012): 409–26; Mawani, "Law as Temporality"; Wanda Nanibush, "Outside of Time: Salvage Ethnography, Self-Representation and Performing Culture," in *Time, Temporality and Violence in International Relations: (De)fatalizing the Present, Forging Radical Alternatives*, ed. Ann M. Agathangelou and Kyle D. Killian (New York: Routledge, 2016), 104–18.

On future orientations, see Mbiti, *African Religions and Philosophy*; George De Vos, "Ethnic Pluralism: Conflict and Accommodation," in *Ethnic Identity: Cultural Continuities*

NOTES TO PAGES 161–165   245

and Change, ed. George De Vos and Lola Romanucci-Ross (Chicago: University of Chicago Press, 1975); Perry, "White Means Never Having to Say You're Ethnic"; Daniel R. Wildcat, "Indigenizing the Future: Why We Must Think Spatially in the Twenty-First Century," *American Studies* 46 (2005): 417–40.

51. Feagin, *White Racial Frame*, 21.

52. Andrea Smith, *Conquest: Sexual Violence and American Indian Genocide* (Cambridge, MA: South End, 2005), 12.

53. Frank B. Wilderson III and Tiffany Lethabo King, "Staying Ready for Black Study," in *Otherwise Worlds: Against Settler-Colonialism and Anti-Blackness*, ed. Tiffany Lethabo King, Jenell Navarro, and Andrea Smith (Durham, NC: Duke University Press, 2020), 56.

54. George Lipsitz, *Time Passages: Collective Memory and American Popular Culture* (Minneapolis: University of Minnesota Press, 1990), 80.

55. Stephanie Coontz, *The Way We Never Were: American Families and the Nostalgia Trap* (New York: Basic Books, 1992).

56. Johannes Fabian, *Time and the Other: How Anthropology Makes Its Object* (New York: Columbia University Press, 1983), 95.

57. Most of Quincy's response is based on a November 7, 1993, *New York Times* article in which Timberland's former executive vice president, Jeffrey Swartz, described his intended consumer base as "honest working people." Swartz went on to say that he was not going to "build his business on smoke," referring to what he perceived as the fickle and unreliable fashion sense among racialized youth in the inner city. "We are cutting back the number of doors we do business in. So if you want to buy us and you are not our target customer, we don't have a point of distribution that speaks to your life style. We are making hip-hop come to our distribution." Michel Marriott, "Out of the Woods," *New York Times*, November 7, 1993, https://www.nytimes.com/1993/11/07/style/out-of-the-woods.html. Though Swartz refuted claims that he and the Timberland Corporation would dissociate themselves from a "hip-hop" consumer base, critics see this as further evidence of the way in which corporations (intentionally) underestimate the economic power of poor communities of color in order to advance a broader agenda of economic exploitation. Black youths at Run-a-Way relied on localized knowledge of status symbols (such as Timberlands) to screen peers and staff on their ability to keep pace with the most culturally relevant trends.

58. Denise Ferreira da Silva, "Unpayable Debt: Reading Scenes of Value against the Arrow of Time," in *The documenta 14 Reader*, ed. Quinn Latimer and Adam Szymczyk (Munich: Prestel, 2017), 81–112.

59. Marriott, "Out of the Woods."

60. Robin D. G. Kelley, *Yo' Mama's Disfunktional! Fighting the Culture Wars in Urban America* (Boston: Beacon, 1997), 45.

61. For more on this point, see Signithia Fordham and John Ogbu, "Black Students' School Success: Coping with the 'Burden of Acting White,'" *Urban Review* 18 (1986): 176–206; Wendy Leo Moore, *Reproducing Racism: White Space, Elite Law Schools, and Racial Inequality* (Lanham, MD: Rowman & Littlefield, 2008); Elijah Anderson, *Code of the Street: Decency, Violence, and the Moral Life of the Inner City* (New York: W. W. Norton, 1999); and Elijah Anderson, "The White Space," *Sociology of Race and Ethnicity* 1, no. 1 (2015): 10–21.

62. Time diaries are widely celebrated among life course and youth development scholars alike. See Anne Gauthier and Frank Furstenberg Jr., "Historical Trends in Patterns of Time Use among Young Adults in Developed Countries," in *On the Frontier of Adulthood: Theory, Research and Public Policy*, ed. Richard Settersten Jr., Frank Furstenberg Jr., and Rubén G. Rumbaut (Chicago: University of Chicago Press, 2005), 150–76; Cathleen D. Zick, "The Shifting Balance of Adolescent Time Use," *Youth & Society* 41, no. 4 (2010):

246 **NOTES TO PAGES 165–170**

569–96; Joseph L. Mahoney and Andrea E. Vest, "The Over-scheduling Hypothesis Revisited: Intensity of Organized Activity and Participation during Adolescence and Young Adult Outcomes," *Journal of Research on Adolescence* 22, no. 3 (2012): 409–18; Vanessa R. Wright et al., "The Time Use of Teenagers." *Social Science Research* 38 (2009): 792–809.

63. Perry, "White Means Never Having to Say You're Ethnic"; Ashley W. Doane Jr., "Dominant Group Ethnic Identity in the United States: The Role of 'Hidden' Ethnicity in Intergroup Relations," *Sociological Quarterly* 38, no. 3 (1997): 375–97.

64. J. Brendan Shaw, "'I Don't Wanna Time Travel No Mo': Race, Gender, and the Politics of Replacement in Erykah Badu's 'Window Seat,'" *Feminist Formations* 27, no. 2 (2015): 63.

65. Robin D. G. Kelley, "Resistance as Revelatory," in *Youth Resistance Research and Theories of Change*, ed. Eve Tuck and K. Wayne Yang (New York: Routledge, 2014), 82–96.

8. PRESCIENCE WITHIN PRESENT ORIENTATIONS

1. Deval for All, "Deval Patrick Announcement Video," YouTube video, 2:35, November 14, 2019, https://www.youtube.com/watch?v=IJCY7qN48hU.

2. Jill Lepore, "Don't Let Nationalists Speak for the Nation," *New York Times*, May 25, 2019, https://www.nytimes.com/2019/05/25/opinion/sunday/nationalism-liberalism-2020.html.

3. Johannes Fabian, *Time and the Other: How Anthropology Makes Its Object* (New York: Columbia University Press, 1983), 80.

4. Lewis A. Coser and Rose L. Coser, "Time Perspective and Social Structure," in *The Sociology of Time*, ed. John Hassard (New York: St. Martin's Press, 1990), 196.

5. Victor Rios, *Punished: Policing the Lives of Black and Latino Boys* (New York: New York University Press, 2011), 103.

6. Quoted in Rios, *Punished*, 103.

7. Fabian, *Time and the Other*, 80. These populations, as George Lipsitz writes, are "not so much disadvantaged as taken advantage of." Lipsitz, *The Possessive Investment in Whiteness: How White People Profit from Identity Politics* (Philadelphia: Temple University Press, 2006), 107.

8. Renato Rosaldo states, "The ethnographic perspective develops an interplay between making the familiar strange and the strange familiar." Renato Rosaldo, *Culture and Truth: The Remaking of Social Analysis* (Boston: Beacon, 1989), 39.

9. Ulf Hannerz, *Soulside: Inquiries into Ghetto Culture and Community* (New York: Columbia University Press, 1969), 20.

10. See Kathleen M. Harris, Greg J. Duncan, and Johanne Boisjoly, "Evaluating the Role of 'Nothing to Lose' Attitudes on Risky Behavior in Adolescence," *Social Forces* 80, no. 3 (2002): 1005–39.

11. It is worth noting that urban sociology adopted the ethnographic present from anthropologists to construct the "other." Fabian's major intervention, then, lies in taking his own field to task for reproducing discourses of power and domination. One potential target of Fabian's critique could have been Oscar Lewis, who writes, "On the level of the individual, major characteristics are a strong feeling of marginality, of helplessness, of dependency and of inferiority . . . weak ego structure, confusion of sexual identification, lack of impulse control . . . little ability to defer gratification and to plan for the future . . . resignation and fatalism and belief in male superiority . . . tolerance for psychological pathology . . . provincial and locally oriented . . . very little sense of history." Oscar Lewis, *The Children of Sánchez: Autobiography of a Mexican Family* (New York: Random House, 1961), xlvii–xlviii, quoted in Charles Valentine, *Culture and Poverty: Critique and Counterproposals* (Chicago: University of Chicago Press, 1968), 133.

NOTES TO PAGES 170–173

12. See Hortense J. Spillers, "Mama's Baby, Papa's Maybe: An American Grammar Book," *Diacritics* 17, no. 2 (Summer 1987): 65–81.

13. See Spillers, "Mama's Baby, Papa's Maybe"; Ron Haskins, "Moynihan Was Right. Now What?," *Annals of the American Academy of Political and Social Science* 621 (2009): 281–314; Sara McLanahan and Christopher Jencks, "Was Moynihan Right? What Happens to Children of Unmarried Mothers," *Education Next* 15, no. 2 (2015): 14–20.

14. Alex Kotlowitz, *There Are No Children Here: The Story of Two Boys Growing Up in the Other America* (New York: Doubleday, 1991), 80. Though not a sociologist by training, Kotlowitz is widely read, cited, and taught within sociological subfields, including the life course perspective, sociology of families, urban sociology, and criminology. Even more disconcerting is that *No Children Here* is categorized as "Sociology/Black Culture."

15. Frank Furstenberg Jr. et al., *Managing to Make It: Urban Families and Adolescent Success* (Chicago: University of Chicago Press, 1999), 10.

16. Furstenberg et al., *Managing to Make It*, 226.

17. Furstenberg et al., *Managing to Make It*, 230.

18. See Alford A. Young, *The Minds of Marginalized Black Men: Making Sense of Mobility, Opportunity, and Future Life Chances* (Princeton, NJ: Princeton University Press, 2004), 42; and William Julius Wilson, *The Truly Disadvantaged: The Inner City, the Underclass, and Public Policy* (Chicago: University of Chicago Press, 1987), 60–61.

19. David Harding, *Living the Drama: Community, Conflict and Culture among Inner-City Boys* (Chicago: University of Chicago Press, 2010), 134.

20. Harding, *Living the Drama*, 65.

21. Harding, *Living the Drama*, 244.

22. Robert J. Sampson, Jeffrey D. Morenoff, and Thomas Gannon-Rowley, "Assessing Neighborhood Effects: Social Processes and New Directions in Research," *Annual Review of Sociology* 28 (2002): 443.

23. William Julius Wilson, *The Truly Disadvantaged: The Inner City, the Underclass, and Public Policy* (Chicago: University of Chicago Press, 1987), 60–61.

24. Calvin L. Warren, *Ontological Terror: Blackness, Nihilism, and Emancipation* (Durham, NC: Duke University Press, 2018), 32.

25. Chad Benito Infante, "Murder and Metaphysics," in *Otherwise Worlds: Against Settler-Colonialism and Anti-Blackness*, ed. Tiffany Lethabo King, Jenell Navarro, and Andrea Smith (Durham, NC: Duke University Press, 2020), 136.

26. Warren, *Ontological Terror*, 45.

27. Alice Goffman, *On the Run: Fugitive Life in an American City* (Chicago: University of Chicago Press, 2014), 39.

28. Goffman, *On the Run*, 247.

29. Saidiya Hartman asserts, "The fungibility of the commodity makes the captive body an abstract and empty vessel vulnerable to the projection of others' feelings, ideas, desires, and values; and as property, the dispossessed body of the enslaved is the surrogate for the master's body since it guarantees his disembodied universality and acts as the sign of his power." Saidiya V. Hartman, *Scenes of Subjection: Terror, Slavery, and Self-Making in Nineteenth-Century America* (New York: Oxford University Press, 1997), 21. What concerns me, then, is Goffman's attempt to treat Black people as empty vessels for the projection of her own feelings, desires, and knowledge production while interchanging Black social life with criminality.

30. Michelle Alexander writes, "In the era of mass incarceration, what it means to be a criminal in our collective consciousness has become conflated with what it means to be black, so the term *white criminal* is confounding, while the term *black criminal* is nearly redundant. . . . Whiteness mitigates crime, whereas blackness defines the criminal." Michelle Alexander, *The New Jim Crow: Mass Incarceration in the Age of Colorblindness*

NOTES TO PAGES 173–177

(New York: New Press, 2010), 193. Goffman treats "Black" and "crime" as synonymous, making the study of one a study of the other.

31. Here I am thinking with Dionne Brand, who describes how the Door of No Return transformed Black people into "bodies emptied of being, bodies emptied of self-interpretation into which new interpretations could be placed." Dionne Brand, *A Map to the Door of No Return: Notes on Belonging* (Toronto: Random House, 2001), 93. Brand illustrates the violence of fungibility, where social scientists like Goffman can empty Black bodies of being in order to occupy them and inscribe new interpretations and meanings for their enjoyment.

32. Roderick A. Ferguson, *Aberrations in Black: Toward a Queer of Color Critique* (Minneapolis: University of Minnesota Press, 2004), 32.

33. Robin D. G. Kelley, *Yo' Mama's Disfunktional! Fighting the Culture Wars in Urban America* (Boston: Beacon, 1997), 2.

34. As Blume Oeur writes, "While Northside students had a sense of control over their participation in the long race to college, the school community members often described deviant young men as stuck in place. They were taking 'passive, receptive stances towards an approaching future over which [they had] little control.' While hope has forward momentum, despair lacks it or has downward momentum." Freeden Blume Oeur, *Black Boys Apart: Racial Uplift and Respectability in All-Male Public Schools* (Minneapolis: University of Minnesota Press, 2018), 92.

35. Saidiya V. Hartman, *Wayward Lives, Beautiful Experiments: Intimate Histories of Social Upheaval* (New York: W. W. Norton, 2019), 107.

36. Hartman, *Wayward Lives, Beautiful Experiments*, 4.

37. See Aldon D. Morris, *The Scholar Denied: W. E. B. Du Bois and the Birth of Modern Sociology* (Oakland: University of California Press, 2015).

38. Hartman, *Wayward Lives, Beautiful Experiments*, 104.

39. Young, *Minds of Marginalized Black Men*, 13.

40. Alford A. Young, "White Ethnographers on the Experiences of African America Men: Then and Now," in *White Logic, White Methods: Racism and Methodology*, ed. Tukufu Zuberi and Eduardo Bonilla-Silva (Lanham, MD: Rowman & Littlefield, 2008), 197.

41. Young, "White Ethnographers," 197.

42. Ferreira da Silva argues that a "sociological analytics of exclusion . . . does no more than to recount the many ways in which states fail to fulfill their task of promoting social equality (causing social harm, social exclusion, poverty, environmental damage . . .)." Denise Ferreira da Silva, "Reading the Dead: A Black Feminist Poethical Reading of Global Capital," in *Otherwise Worlds: Against Settler-Colonialism and Anti-Blackness*, ed. Tiffany Lethabo King, Jenell Navarro, and Andrea Smith (Durham, NC: Duke University Press, 2020), 40.

43. Elijah Anderson, *Code of the Street: Decency, Violence, and the Moral Life of the Inner City* (New York: W. W. Norton, 1999), 35. Though Anderson acknowledges the thin and blurry line between "street" and "decent," there exists a line, nonetheless. Here I am paraphrasing Jodi Melamed, who writes, "Esteeming some people of color of the same race, according to conventional categories, makes it easier to accept that others of that same race may be systematically treated unequally." Jodi Melamed, *Represent and Destroy: Rationalizing Violence in the New Racial Capitalism* (Minneapolis: University of Minnesota Press, 2011), 153.

44. Elliot Liebow, *Tally's Corner: A Study of Negro Streetcorner Men* (Lanham, MD: Rowman & Littlefield, 1967), 42.

45. Kara Keeling, *Queer Times, Black Futures* (New York: New York University Press, 2019), 67.

46. John S. Mbiti, *African Religions and Philosophy* (New York: Praeger, 1969), 17.

47. Mbiti, *African Religions and Philosophy*, 17.

48. Rodríguez uses "futurity" as a way of disrupting teleological assumptions related to civil rights regimes. See Dylan Rodríguez, "Inhabiting the Impasse: Racial/Racial-Colonial Power, Genocide Poetics, and the Logic of Evisceration," *Social Text* 33, no. 3 (2015): 34.

49. Blume Oeur, *Black Boys Apart*, 102.

50. José Esteban Muñoz, *Cruising Utopia: The Then and There of Queer Futurity* (New York: New York University Press, 2009), 95.

51. Pierre Bourdieu, *Outline of a Theory of a Practice* (Cambridge: Cambridge University Press, 1977), 9.

52. Carmen Sirianni, "Economies of Time in Social Theory: Three Approaches Compared," *Current Perspectives in Social Theory* 8 (1987): 165.

53. La Marr Jurelle Bruce, "Interludes in Madtime: Black Music, Madness, and Metaphysical Syncopation," *Social Text* 35, no. 4 (2017): 4.

54. Bruce, "Interludes in Madtime," 11.

55. James Baldwin, *The Price of the Ticket: Collected Nonfiction, 1948–1985* (London: St. Martin's, 1985), 148.

56. Michelle M. Wright, *Physics of Blackness: Beyond the Middle Passage Epistemology* (Minneapolis: University of Minnesota Press, 2015), 145–46.

57. See Louise Seamster and Victor Ray, "Against Teleology in the Study of Race: Toward the Abolition of the Progress Paradigm," *Sociological Theory* 36, no. 4 (2018): 315–42.

58. W. E. B. Du Bois, *The Souls of Black Folk* (New York: Barnes & Noble Classics, 2003), 9.

59. I think it is worth thinking about Black a'ightness alongside Savannah Shange's notion of "black girl ordinary." As Shange writes, "Black girl ordinary is that which signifies on (but does not conform to) normative notions of gender through a performative blackness shaped by hip hop, social media, and conspicuous consumption: it is a mode of queer(ed) disidentification (Muñoz 1999)." Savannah Shange, "Black Girl Ordinary: Flesh, Carcerality and the Refusal of Ethnography," *Transforming Anthropology* 27, no. 1 (2019): 6.

60. Brand, *Map to the Door*, 19.

61. Kevin Quashie, *The Sovereignty of Quiet: Beyond Resistance in Black Culture* (New Brunswick, NJ: Rutgers University Press, 2012).

62. Quashie, *Sovereignty of Quiet*, 21.

63. See Harding, *Living the Drama*.

64. Quashie, *Sovereignty of Quiet*, 4.

65. Quashie, *Sovereignty of Quiet*, 18.

66. Du Bois, *Souls of Black Folk*, 9.

67. Du Bois, *Souls of Black Folk*, 9.

68. Muñoz adapts "the future is in the present" from C. L. R. James's first volume of collected writings, *The Future in the Present* (1977). Muñoz, *Cruising Utopia*, 55.

69. Muñoz, *Cruising Utopia*, 49.

70. Loïc Wacquant, "Inside 'the Zone': The Social Art of the Hustler in the American Ghetto," in *The Weight of the World: Social Suffering in Contemporary Society*, ed. Pierre Bourdieu et al. (Stanford, CA: Stanford University Press, 1993), 155.

71. Loïc Wacquant, *Urban Outcasts: A Comparative Sociology of Advanced Marginality* (Cambridge: Polity, 2008), 2.

72. Javier Auyero demonstrates how waiting functions as a tool of political subordination used to exploit the time and labor of poor people. The political production of "subjective uncertainty" among poor people, according to Auyero, "finds its roots in objective unpredictability." Javier Auyero, *Patients of the State: The Politics of Waiting in Argentina* (Durham, NC: Duke University Press, 2012), 82.

250 NOTES TO PAGES 183–186

73. Waverly Duck describes such certainties as part of local "interaction orders." Within poor urbanized space, an interaction order functions as "a rational adaptation to otherwise impossible circumstances." Waverly Duck, *No Way Out: Precarious Living in the Shadow of Poverty and Drug Dealing* (Chicago: University of Chicago Press, 2015), 3.

74. Anderson, *Code of the Street*, 135.

75. See Loïc Wacquant, "Scrutinizing the Street: Poverty, Mobility, and the Pitfalls of Urban Ethnography," *American Journal of Sociology* 107, no. 6 (2002): 1468–532. Wacquant critiques Mitchell Duneier, *Slim's Table: Race, Respectability, and Masculinity* (Chicago: University of Chicago Press, 1992); Katherine S. Newman, *No Shame in My Game: The Working Poor in the Inner City* (New York: Alfred A. Knopf, 1999); and Anderson, *Code of the Street*. Wacquant accuses the authors of flattening difference within heterogenous subgroups and rendering agency invisible while creating "*unitary* tales of *difference*" (emphasis in the original). Wacquant, "Scrutinizing the Street," 1521.

76. Hartman, *Scenes of Subjection*, 20.

77. Saidiya V. Hartman, "The Time of Slavery," *The South Atlantic Quarterly*. 101, no. 4 (2002): 772.

78. Denise Ferreira da Silva critiques postcolonial studies and critical race and ethnic studies (CRES) for an overemphasis on the exclusion of the racial other from modernity and post-Enlightenment knowledge projects. Critiques of the racial subaltern's exclusion prompts scholars to imagine possibilities for inclusion. But it is precisely such a curiosity that Ferreira da Silva criticizes for producing Europe's affectable racial "other" in relation to the (white) "transparent I." As she writes, "Race relations has produced racial subjection as an effect of the fundamental impossibility of certain strangers' becoming . . . modern. Not only does this produce blackness as an impossible basis for formulating any project of emancipation; it suggests that, because it is always already the exclusive attribute of a transparent I, the racial subaltern's desire for emancipation, for inclusion in the dominant (white Anglo-Saxon society), is fundamentally a desire for self-obliteration." Denise Ferreira da Silva, *Toward a Global Idea of Race* (Minneapolis: University of Minnesota Press, 2007), 162.

79. See the distinction Ferreira da Silva makes between "scene of regulation" and "scene of representation" in *Global Idea of Race*, 38.

80. Hannerz, *Soulside*, 185–86. Hannerz classifies "cultural repertoires" and "ghetto-specific behavior" as learned behavior within poor urbanized space. William Julius Wilson argues that high levels of joblessness undermine social organization, leading to increasing crime, gang violence, drug dealing, and family breakups. Wilson, *When Work Disappears: The World of the New Urban Poor* (New York: Vintage, 1996), 21.

81. Christina Sharpe, *In the Wake: On Blackness and Being* (Durham, NC: Duke University Press, 2016), 106.

82. Here I am thinking of the use of "police violence" as a tool to reaffirm the logic of policing itself. Steve Martinot and Jared Sexton write, "There are two possibilities: first, police violence is a deviation from the rules governing police procedures in general. Second, these various forms (e.g., racial profiling, street murders, terrorism) are the rule itself as standard operating procedure." Steve Martinot and Jared Sexton, "The Avant-Garde of White Supremacy," *Social Identities: Journal for the Study of Race, Nation and Culture* 9, no. 2 (2003): 170.

83. Jina B. Kim, "Toward a Crip-of-Color Critique: Thinking with Minich's 'Enabling Whom?,'" *Lateral* 6, no. 1 (2017), https://csalateral.org/issue/6-1/forum-alt-humanities-critical-disability-studies-crip-of-color-critique-kim/.

84. Damien M. Sojoyner, *First Strike: Educational Enclosures in Black Los Angeles* (Minneapolis: University of Minnesota Press, 2016).

NOTES TO PAGES 186–190   251

85. Ableism cannot be divorced from anti-Blackness and other forms of racialized violence. For example, Jason Whitesel suggests that the simultaneity, intersection, and interaction between racism, fat hatred, ageism, ableism, and classism cooperated to justify the police killings of Eleanor Bumpurs and Eric Garner. Jason Whitesel, "Intersections of Multiple Oppressions: Racism, Sizeism, Ableism, and the 'Illimitable Etceteras' in Encounters with Law Enforcement," *Sociological Forum* 32, no. 2 (2017): 426–33.

86. Bruce, "Interludes in Madtime," 3–4.

87. Bruce, "Interludes in Madtime," 15.

88. Sharpe, *In the Wake*, 41.

89. Keeling, *Queer Times, Black Futures*, 32.

90. George Lipsitz, *Time Passages: Collective Memory and American Popular Culture* (Minneapolis: University of Minnesota Press, 1990), 112.

91. Ytasha Womack credits Mark Dery with coining the term "Afrofuturism" in his 1994 essay, "Black to the Future." Womack describes Afrofuturism as a tool taken up by "sci-fi-loving black college students and artists" seeking to affect transformative social change through science and technology in the 1980s and '90s. Ytasha Womack, *Afrofuturism: The World of Black Sci-Fi and Fantasy Culture* (Chicago: Chicago Review Press, 2013), 16. Octavia Butler is another one of Afrofuturism's earliest innovators, and since her passing she has been widely celebrated for her own literary prescience. See *Parable of the Sower* and *Parable of the Talents*—two-thirds of a trilogy that was never finished. See also *Survivor* (1978) and *Wild Seed* (1980) for evidence of Butler's rich imagination and capacity to construct alternative worlds and universes that defy normative conceptions of time and space, all while centering Black life.

92. Hartman, *Scenes of Subjection*, 6.

93. Zerubavel makes this distinction between "marked" and "unmarked time": "As a strictly mathematical entity, time is homogenous, with every minute essentially identical to every other minute, as demonstrated by the way they are conventionally measured by the clock." Eviatar Zerubavel, *Time Maps: Collective Memory and the Social Shape of the Past* (Chicago: University of Chicago Press, 2003), 23. This form of time, for Zerubavel, is "unmarked" because of its banality and synchronization to calendar days, weeks, months, etc. "Marked" time, by contrast, reflects those "extraordinary chunks of social reality" that help distinguish between "eventful" and "uneventful" historical periods (26).

94. Tasha is referring to Dylann Roof, a white man convicted of killing nine Black worshipers at the Emanuel AME church in Charleston, South Carolina, on June 17, 2015. He was sentenced to nine consecutive life sentences without parole after pleading guilty to nine state counts of murder, and he was sentenced to the death penalty on federal charges after being found guilty at trial.

95. Zerubavel, *Time Maps*, 4.

96. DJs use the term "heavy rotation" to describe the high frequency of plays of a particular record.

97. Hartman, *Scenes of Subjection*, 51.

98. Pamela Perry, "White Means Never Having to Say You're Ethnic: White Youth and the Construction of 'Cultureless' Identities," *Journal of Contemporary Ethnography* 30, no. 1 (2001): 58.

99. Hartman describes whiteness as an "incorporeal hereditament or illusory inheritance from chattel slavery." Hartman, *Scenes of Subjection*, 24.

100. Denise Ferreira da Silva, "Unpayable Debt: Reading Scenes of Value against the Arrow of Time," in *The documenta 14 Reader*, ed. Quinn Latimer and Adam Szymczyk (Munich: Prestel, 2017), 81–112.

101. Perry, "White Means Never Having to Say You're Ethnic," 73.

252   NOTES TO PAGES 191–200

102. James Baldwin, *The Fire Next Time* (New York: Vintage International, 1962), 81.

103. Zerubavel, *Time Maps*, 25.

104. Lucille Clifton, "won't you celebrate with me," in *Book of Light* (Port Townsend, WA: Copper Canyon, 1993), 25.

105. Damien M. Sojoyner, "Dissonance in Time: (Un)making and (Re)mapping of Blackness," in *Futures of Black Radicalism*, ed. Gaye Theresa Johnson and Alex Lubin (New York: Verso, 2017), 67.

106. Muñoz, *Cruising Utopia*, 1.

107. Bruce, "Interludes in Madtime," 23.

108. Bruce, "Interludes in Madtime," 5.

109. Earl Lovelace, *The Dragon Can't Dance* (New York: Persea Books, 1979), 111.

110. Katherine McKittrick, "Yours in the Intellectual Struggle: Sylvia Wynter and the Realization of Living," in *Sylvia Wynter: On Being Human as Praxis*, ed. Katherine McKittrick (Durham, NC: Duke University Press, 2015), 7–8.

111. Lauren Berlant, "Live Sex Acts (Parental Advisory: Explicit Material)," *Feminist Studies* 21, no. 2 (1995): 379–404.

112. Warren, *Ontological Terror*, 37.

113. Warren, *Ontological Terror*, 12.

114. Warren, *Ontological Terror*, 7.

115. Warren, *Ontological Terror*, 171.

116. Alexander G. Weheliye, *Habeus Viscus: Racializing Assemblages, Biopolitics, and Black Feminist Theories of the Human* (Durham, NC: Duke University Press, 2014), 138.

117. For more on mindfulness, see *The Miracle of Mindfulness* (1975), by Thích Nhất Hạnh; and *The Power of Now: A Guide to Spiritual Enlightenment* (1999) and/or *Mindfulness for Beginners: Reclaiming the Present Moment—and Your Life* (2006), by John Kabat-Zinn.

118. Wilson, *Truly Disadvantaged*, 14.

119. In a critique of Hegel's construction of the transcendental subject as the "culmination of a temporal trajectory," Ferreira da Silva asks, "How could the recognition of transcendentality be limited to particular human beings located in a rather small corner of the globe?" Ferreira da Silva, *Global Idea of Race*, 86.

120. Fred Moten, *Black and Blur: Consent Not to Be a Single Being* (Durham, NC: Duke University Press, 2017), 13.

121. Lisa M. Cacho, *Social Death: Racialized Rightlessness and the Criminalization of the Unprotected* (New York: New York University Press, 2012).

CONCLUSION

1. Frank B. Wilderson III and Tiffany Lethabo King, "Staying Ready for Black Study," in *Otherwise Worlds: Against Settler-Colonialism and Anti-Blackness*, ed. Tiffany Lethabo King, Jenell Navarro, and Andrea Smith (Durham, NC: Duke University Press, 2020), 68.

2. Rachel Kushner, "Is Prison Necessary? Ruth Wilson Gilmore Might Change Your Mind," *New York Times*, April 17, 2019, https://www.nytimes.com/2019/04/17/magazine/prison-abolition-ruth-wilson-gilmore.html.

3. Here I am thinking about Jodi Byrd's critique of an "affective investment in multicultural liberal democracy." Byrd writes, "The Hopi (who became the site of a national affective investment in multicultural liberal democracy as the 2008 U.S. presidential campaign circulated the faux-Hopi prophecy 'We are the ones we've been waiting for') are transformed into the logocentric imperial order that cannot tolerate any systemic line of flight." Jodi Byrd, *Transit of Empire: Indigenous Critiques of Colonialism* (Minneapolis: University of Minnesota Press, 2011), 15. What about those who are not waiting but actively creating the not-yet-here?

4. Gilmore, *Change Everything*. Gilmore's book is forthcoming; her quotation appears in the book description on the publisher's website, accessed September 17, 2023, https://www.haymarketbooks.org/books/1597-change-everything.

5. In a panel discussion titled "The Architects of Abolitionism," Joy James suggests that "abolition democracy" is a "promissory note" rooted in ideals and aspirations, without a sufficient critique of the state and adequate mobilization against the organized terror of fascism and genocidal systems. James offers a broader critique of the way the state has systematically deradicalized prison struggles. Brown University, "Joy James: The Architects of Abolitionism," YouTube video, 1:45:57, May 6, 2019, https://www.youtube.com/watch?v=z9rvRsWKDx0.

6. I am thinking with Fred Moten and Stefano Harney, who make this important clarification about abolition: "Not so much the abolition of prisons but the abolition of a society that could have prisons, that could have slavery, that could have the wage, and therefore not abolition as the elimination of anything but abolition as the founding of a new society." Fred Moten and Stefano Harney, "The University and the Undercommons: Seven Theses," *Social Text* 22, no. 2 (2004): 114.

7. I am referring to the 1954 US Supreme Court decision *Brown v. Board of Education*.

8. Kara Keeling, *Queer Times, Black Futures* (New York: New York University Press, 2019), 34.

9. As Brand writes, 'To travel without a map, to travel without a way. They did long ago. That misdirection became the way. After the Door of No Return, a map was only a set of impossibilities, a set of changing locations." Dionne Brand, *A Map to the Door of No Return: Notes to Belonging* (Toronto: Random House, 2001), 224.

10. Édouard Glissant, *Poetics of Relation* (Ann Arbor: University of Michigan Press, 1997), 153.

11. King, Navarro, and Smith, *Otherwise Worlds*, 8.

12. King, Navarro, and Smith, *Otherwise Worlds*, 13.

13. Katherine McKittrick, *Dear Science and Other Stories* (Durham, NC: Duke University Press, 2021), 33.

14. La Marr Jurelle Bruce, *How to Go Mad without Losing Your Mind: Madness and Black Radical Creativity* (Durham, NC: Duke University Press, 2021), 75.

15. Saidiya V. Hartman, *Scenes of Subjection: Terror, Slavery, and Self-Making in Nineteenth-Century America* (New York: Oxford University Press, 1997), 226.

16. Robin D. G. Kelley, *Freedom Dreams: The Black Radical Imagination* (Boston: Beacon, 2002), 9.

17. Kay Bonetti, "An Interview with Toni Cade Bambara," in *Conversations with Toni Cade Bambara*, ed. Thabiti Lewis (Jackson: University Press of Mississippi, 2012), 3.

18. Keeling, *Queer Times, Black Futures*, 126.

19. Dylan Rodríguez, *White Reconstruction: Domestic Warfare and the Logics of Genocide* (New York: Fordham University Press, 2021), 107.

20. Melissa Phruksachart, "The Literature of White Liberalism," *Boston Review*, August 21, 2020, https://bostonreview.net/articles/melissa-phruksachart-literature-white-liberalism/.

21. George Jackson writes, "We will never have a complete definition of fascism, because it is in constant motion, showing a new face to fit any particular set of problems that arise to threaten the predominance of the traditionalist, capitalist ruling class. But if one were forced for the sake of clarity to define it in a word simple enough for all to understand, that word would be 'reform.'" George L. Jackson, *Blood in My Eye* (Baltimore: Black Classic Press, 1990), 118. Jackson speaks to the hegemonic character of reform that requires coercion and consent before being naturalized as common sense.

22. As Haunani Kay Trask states, "For Indigenous people, civil society is . . . a creation of settler colonizers." Quoted in Frank B. Wilderson III, *Red, White, & Black: Cinema and the Structure of U.S. Antagonisms* (Durham, NC: Duke University Press, 2010), 149.

Selected Bibliography

I list here the writings that were of the most significance when writing this book. This bibliography is not a complete record of all the sources I consulted. Instead, it shows the range of works upon which I developed my thoughts and ideas.

Adam, Barbara. "The Gendered Time Politics of Globalization: Of Shadowlands and Elusive Justice." *Feminist Review* 70 (2002): 3–29.

Adeyemi, Kemi. "The Practice of Slowness: Black Queer Women and the Right to the City." *Gay and Lesbian Quarterly* 25, no. 4 (2019): 545–67.

Ahmed, Sara. "A Phenomenology of Whiteness." *Feminist Theory* 8, no. 2 (2007): 149–68.

——. *Queer Phenomenology: Orientations, Objects, Others.* Durham, NC: Duke University Press, 2006.

Aiken, Joshua, Jessica Marion Modi, and Olivia R. Polk. "Issued by Way of 'The Issue of Blackness.'" *Transgender Studies Quarterly* 1.7, no. 3 (2020): 427–44.

Alexander, Karl, Doris Entwisle, and Linda Olson. *The Long Shadow: Family Background, Disadvantaged Urban Youth, and the Transition to Adulthood.* New York: Russell Sage Foundation, 2014.

Alexander, M. Jacqui. *Pedagogies of Crossing: Meditations on Feminism, Sexual Politics, Memory, and the Sacred.* Durham, NC: Duke University Press, 2005.

Alexander, Michelle. *The New Jim Crow: Mass Incarceration in the Age of Colorblindness.* New York: New Press, 2010.

Al-Saji, Alia. "Too Late: Racialized Time and the Closure of the Past." *Insights* 6, no. 5 (2013): 2–13.

Aminzade, Ronald. "Historical Sociology and Time." *Sociological Methods Research* 20, no. 4 (1992): 456–80.

Anderson, Elijah. *Code of the Street: Decency, Violence, and the Moral Life of the Inner City.* New York: W. W. Norton, 1999.

——. "The White Space." *Sociology of Race and Ethnicity* 1, no. 1 (2015): 10–21.

Anzaldúa, Gloria E. *Borderlands/La Frontera: The New Mestiza.* 4th ed. San Francisco: Aunt Lute Books, 2007.

Auyero, Javier. *Patients of the State: The Politics of Waiting in Argentina.* Durham, NC: Duke University Press, 2012.

Auyero, Javier, and Débora Alejandra Swistun. *Flammable: Environmental Suffering in an Argentine Shantytown.* Oxford: Oxford University Press, 2009.

Baldwin, James. *The Fire Next Time.* New York: Vintage International, 1962.

——. *The Price of the Ticket: Collected Nonfiction, 1948–1985.* London: St. Martin's, 1985.

Barthold, Bonnie J. *Black Time: Fiction of Africa, the Caribbean, and the United States.* New Haven, CT: Yale University Press, 1981.

Bederman, Gail. *Manliness and Civilization: A Cultural History of Gender and Race in the United States, 1880–1917.* Chicago: University of Chicago Press, 1995.

Benjamin, Ruha. *Race after Technology: Abolitionist Tools for the New Jim Code.* Cambridge: Polity, 2019.

Benson, Janel E., and Frank F. Furstenberg Jr. "Entry into Adulthood: Are Adult Role Transitions Meaningful Markers of Adult Identity?" *Advances in the Life Course Research* 11 (2007): 199–224.

Berlant, Lauren. "Live Sex Acts (Parental Advisory: Explicit Material)." *Feminist Studies* 21, no. 2 (1995): 379–404.

Bhabha, Homi K. "'Race,' Time and the Revision of Modernity." In *Theories of Race and Racism: A Reader,* 2nd ed., edited by Les Back and John Solomos, 422–36. New York: Routledge, 2009.

Birth, Kevin K. *Any Time Is Trinidad Time: Social Meanings and Temporal Consciousness.* Gainesville: University Press of Florida, 1999.

Blume Oeur, Freeden. *Black Boys Apart: Racial Uplift and Respectability in All-Male Public Schools.* Minneapolis: University of Minnesota Press, 2018.

Bonilla, Yarimar. *Non-sovereign Futures: French Caribbean Politics in the Wake of Disenchantment.* Chicago: University of Chicago Press, 2015.

Bonilla-Silva, Eduardo. *Racism without Racists: Color-Blind Racism and the Persistence of Racial Inequality in the United States.* Lanham, MD: Rowman & Littlefield, 2010.

——. "Rethinking Racism: Toward a Structural Interpretation." *American Sociological Review* 63, no. 3 (1997): 465–80.

——. "'This Is a White Country!' The Racial Ideology of the Western Nations of the World Systems." *Sociological Inquiry* 70, no. 2 (2000): 188–214.

Bosniak, Linda. *The Citizen and the Alien: Dilemmas of Contemporary Membership.* Princeton, NJ: Princeton University Press, 2006.

Bourdieu, Pierre. "The Abdication of the State." In *The Weight of the World: Social Suffering in Contemporary Society,* edited by Pierre Bourdieu et al., 181–88. Stanford, CA: Stanford University Press, 1993.

——. *Outline of a Theory of a Practice.* Cambridge: Cambridge University Press, 1977.

——. *Pascalian Meditations.* Stanford, CA: Stanford University Press, 1997.

——. "Time Perspectives of the Kabyle." In *The Sociology of Time,* edited by John Hassard, 219–37. New York: St. Martin's, 1990. First published 1963.

Bourdieu, Pierre et al., eds. *The Weight of the World: Social Suffering in Contemporary Society.* Stanford, CA: Stanford University Press, 1993.

Bourgois, Philippe. *In Search of Respect: Selling Crack in El Barrio.* Cambridge: Cambridge University Press, 2003.

Brand, Dionne. *A Map to the Door of No Return: Notes to Belonging.* Toronto: Random House, 2001.

Browne, Simone. *Dark Matters: On the Surveillance of Blackness.* Durham, NC: Duke University Press, 2015.

Bruce, La Marr Jurelle. *How to Go Mad without Losing Your Mind: Madness and Black Radical Creativity.* Durham, NC: Duke University Press, 2021.

——. "Interludes in Madtime: Black Music, Madness, and Metaphysical Syncopation." *Social Text* 35, no. 4 (2017): 1–31.

——. "Shore, Unsure: Loitering as a Way of Life." *GLQ: A Journal of Lesbian and Gay Studies* 25, no. 2 (2019): 352–61.

Burton, Linda M., Dawn A. Obeidallah, and Kevin Allison. "Ethnographic Insights on Social Context and Adolescent Development among Inner-City African-American Teens." In *Ethnology and Human Development: Context and Meaning in Social Inquiry,* edited by Richard Jessor, Anne Colby, and Richard A. Shweder, 395–417. Chicago: University of Chicago Press, 1996.

Burton, Linda M., and M. Belinda Tucker. "Romantic Unions in an Era of Uncertainty: A Post-Moynihan Perspective on African American Women and Marriage." *Annals of the American Academy of Political and Social Science* 621 (2009): 132–48.

Byrd, Jodi A. *Transit of Empire: Indigenous Critiques of Colonialism*. Minneapolis: University of Minnesota Press, 2011.

Cacho, Lisa M. *Social Death: Racialized Rightlessness and the Criminalization of the Unprotected*. New York: New York University Press, 2012.

Chakravartty, Paula, and Denise Ferreira da Silva. "Accumulation, Dispossession, and Debt: The Racial Logic of Global Capitalism; An Introduction." *American Quarterly* 64, no. 3 (2012): 361–85.

Chan, Kenyon S., and Shirley Hune. "Racialization and Panethnicity: From Asians in American to Asian America." In *Toward a Common Destiny: Improving Race and Ethnic Relations in America*, edited by Willis D. Hawley and Anthony W. Jackson, 205–23. San Francisco: Jossey-Bass, 1995.

Collins, Patricia Hill. *Black Feminist Thought: Knowledge, Consciousness, and the Politics of Empowerment*. New York: Routledge, 2000.

Conley, Dalton. *Being Black, Living in the Red: Race, Wealth, and Social Policy in America*. Berkeley: University of California Press, 1999.

Coontz, Stephanie. *The Way We Never Were: American Families and the Nostalgia Trap*. New York: Basic Books, 1992.

Coser, Lewis A., and Rose L. Coser. "Time Perspective and Social Structure." In *The Sociology of Time*, edited by John Hassard, 191–202. New York: St. Martin's, 1990. First published 1963.

Dalsgård, Anne Line. "Standing Apart: On Time, Affect, and Discernments in Nordeste, Brazil." In *Ethnographies of Youth and Temporality: Time Objectified*, edited by Anne Line Dalsgård, Martin Demant Frederiksen, Susanne Højlund, and Lotte Meinert, 97–116. Philadelphia: Temple University Press, 2014.

Dalsgård, Anne Line, Martin Demant Frederiksen, Susanne Højlund, and Lotte Meinert. *Ethnographies of Youth and Temporality: Time Objectified*. Philadelphia: Temple University Press, 2014.

De Vos, George. "Ethnic Pluralism: Conflict and Accommodation." In *Ethnic Identity: Cultural Continuities and Change*, edited by George De Vos and Lola Romanucci-Ross. Chicago: University of Chicago Press, 1975.

DiAquoi, Raygiene C. "Critical Race Life Course Perspective Theory: A Framework for Understanding Racism over the Life Course." *International Journal of Qualitative Studies in Education* 3, no. 1 (2018): 36–54.

Doane, Ashley W., Jr. "Dominant Group Ethnic Identity in the United States: The Role of 'Hidden' Ethnicity in Intergroup Relations." *Sociological Quarterly* 38, no. 3 (1997): 375–97.

Donald, Stephanie H., and Cristoph Lindner. *Inert Cities: Globalization, Mobility and Suspension in Visual Culture*. New York: I. B. Taurus, 2014.

Du Bois, W. E. B. "The Black Man Brings His Gifts." In *W.E.B. Du Bois: A Reader*, edited by David Levering Lewis, 453–65. New York: Henry Holt, 1995.

——. *Black Reconstruction in America, 1860–1880*. New York: Atheneum, 1998. First published 1935.

——. *Darkwater: Voices from within the Veil*. New York: Verso, 2016.

——. *The Philadelphia Negro*. Philadelphia: University of Pennsylvania Press, 1899.

——. *The Souls of Black Folk*. New York: Barnes & Noble Classics, 2003. First published 1903.

Duck, Waverly. *No Way Out: Precarious Living in the Shadow of Poverty and Drug Dealing*. Chicago: University of Chicago Press, 2015.

Duneier, Mitchell. *Slim's Table: Race, Respectability, and Masculinity*. Chicago: University of Chicago Press, 1992.

Durkheim, Émile. *The Elementary Forms of Religious Life*. Translated by Carol Cosman. Oxford: Oxford University Press, 2001. First published 1912.

Dwyer, Owen J., and John Paul Jones III. "White Socio-Spatial Epistemology." *Social & Cultural Geography* 1, no. 2 (2000): 209–22.

Edelman, Lee. *No Future: Queer Theory and the Death Drive*. Durham, NC: Duke University Press, 2004.

Edin, Kathryn, and Maria Kefalas. *Promises I Can Keep: Why Poor Women Put Motherhood before Marriage*. Berkeley: University of California Press, 2005.

Elias, Norbert. *Time: An Essay*. Cambridge: Blackwell, 1992.

Emirbayer, Mustafa, and Ann Mische. "What Is Agency?" *American Journal of Sociology* 103, no. 4 (1998): 962–1023.

Ermath, Elizabeth Deeds. "The Solitude of Women and Social Time." In *Taking Our Time: Feminist Perspectives on Temporality*, edited by Frieda Johles Forman and Caroran Sowton, 27–46. Oxford: Pergamon, 1989.

Estes, Nick. *Our History Is the Future: Standing Rock versus the Dakota Access Pipeline, and the Long Tradition of Indigenous Resistance*. New York: Verso Books, 2019.

Fabian, Johannes. *Time and the Other: How Anthropology Makes Its Object*. New York: Columbia University Press, 1983.

Fanon, Frantz. *Black Skin, White Masks*. Translated by Richard Philcox. New York: Grove, 2008. First published 1952.

——. *The Wretched of the Earth*. Translated by Richard Philcox. New York: Grove, 2004. First published 1961.

Feagin, Joe R. *The White Racial Frame: Centuries of Racial Framing and Counter-framing*. New York: Routledge, 2013.

Ferguson, Ann Arnett. *Bad Boys: Public Schools in the Making of Black Masculinity*. Ann Arbor: University of Michigan Press, 2000.

Ferguson, Roderick A. *Aberrations in Black: Toward a Queer of Color Critique*. Minneapolis: University of Minnesota Press, 2004.

Ferreira da Silva, Denise. "Reading the Dead: A Black Feminist Poethical Reading of Global Capital." In *Otherwise Worlds: Against Settler-Colonialism and Anti-Blackness*, edited by Tiffany Lethabo King, Jenell Navarro, and Andrea Smith, 38–51. Durham, NC: Duke University Press, 2020.

——. *Toward a Global Idea of Race*. Minneapolis: University of Minnesota Press, 2007.

——. "Unpayable Debt: Reading Scenes of Value against the Arrow of Time." In *The documenta 14 Reader*, edited by Quinn Latimer and Adam Szymczyk, 81–112. Munich: Prestel, 2017.

Fields, Barbara J. "Whiteness, Racism, and Identity." *International Labor and Working-Class History* 60 (2001): 48–56.

Filipcová, Blanka, and Jindřich Filipec. "Society and Concepts of Time." *International Social Science Journal* 107 (1986): 19–32.

Fisher, Celia B., Seyatta A. Wallace, and Rose E. Fenton. "Discrimination Distress during Adolescence." *Journal of Youth and Adolescence* 6 (2000): 679–95.

Flaherty, Michael G. *Textures of Time: Agency and Temporal Experience*. Philadelphia: Temple University Press, 2011.

——. *A Watched Pot: How We Experience Time*. New York: New York University Press, 1999.

Fleming, Crystal. *Resurrecting Slavery: Racial Legacies and White Supremacy in France*. Philadelphia: Temple University Press, 2017.

Foner, Philip S., and David R. Roediger. *Our Own Time: A History of American Labor and the Working Day*. New York: Verso Books, 1989.

Fordham, Signithia, and John Ogbu. "Black Students' School Success: Coping with the 'Burden of Acting White.'" *Urban Review* 18 (1986): 176–206.

Forman, Frieda Johles, and Caroran Sowton, eds. *Taking Our Time: Feminist Perspectives on Temporality*. Oxford: Pergamon, 1989.

Forman, Frieda Johles, with Caroran Sowton. "Feminizing Time: An Introduction." In *Taking Our Time: Feminist Perspectives on Temporality*, edited by Frieda Johles Forman and Caroran Sowton, 1–9. Oxford: Pergamon, 1989.

Foucault, Michel. *Discipline and Punish: The Birth of the Prison*. New York: Vintage Books, 1995.

Freeman, Elizabeth. *Time Binds: Queer Temporalities, Queer Histories*. Durham, NC: Duke University Press, 2010.

——. "Time Binds, or Erotohistoriography." *Social Text* 23, no. 3–4 (2005): 57–68.

Furstenberg, Frank, Jr., Thomas D. Cook, Jacquelynne Eccles, Glen H. Elder, and Arnold Sameroff. *Managing to Make It: Urban Families and Adolescent Success*. Chicago: University of Chicago Press, 1999.

Garbarino, James, Kathleen Kostelny, and Nancy Dubrow. "What Children Can Tell Us about Living in Danger." *American Psychologist* 46 (1991): 376–83.

Gauthier, Anne, and Frank Furstenberg Jr. "Historical Trends in Patterns of Time Use among Young Adults in Developed Countries." In *On the Frontier of Adulthood: Theory, Research and Public Policy*, edited by Richard Settersten Jr., Frank Furstenberg Jr., and Rubén G. Rumbaut, 150–76. Chicago: University of Chicago Press, 2005.

Gee, Gilbert C., Abba Hing, Selina Mohammed, Derrick C. Tabor, and David R. Williams. "Racism and the Life Course: Taking Time Seriously." *American Journal of Public Health* 109, no. 1 (2019): 43–47.

Gilmore, Ruth Wilson. *Change Everything: Racial Capitalism and the Case for Abolition*. Chicago: Haymarket Books, forthcoming.

Gilroy, Paul. *The Black Atlantic: Modernity and Double-Consciousness*. Cambridge, MA: Harvard University Press, 1993.

——. "The Dialectics of Diaspora Identification." In *Theories of Race and Racism: A Reader*, 2nd ed., edited by Les Back and John Solomos, 564–76. New York: Routledge, 2009.

Glassner, Barry. "An Essay on Iterative Social Time." *American Sociological Review* 30, no. 4 (1982): 668–81.

Glenn, Evelyn Nakano. "From Servitude to Service Work: Historical Continuities in the Racial Division of Paid Reproductive Labor." *Signs: Journal of Women in Culture and Society* 18, no. 1 (1992): 1–43.

Glissant, Édouard. *Poetics of Relation*. Ann Arbor: University of Michigan Press, 1997.

Goff, Philip A., Matthew Christian Jackson, Brooke Allison Lewis Di Leone, Carmen Marie Culotta, and Natalie Ann DiTomasso. "The Essence of Innocence: Consequences of Dehumanizing Black Children." *Journal of Personality and Social Psychology* 106, no. 4 (2014): 526–45.

Goffman, Alice. *On the Run: Fugitive Life in an American City*. Chicago: University of Chicago Press, 2014.

Goffman, Erving. *The Presentation of Self in Everyday Life*. New York: Doubleday, 1959.

Goldberg, David Theo. *Racist Culture: Philosophy and the Politics of Meaning*. Malden: Blackwell, 1993.

Goonan, Casey. "Policing and the Violence of White Being: An Interview with Dylan Rodríguez." *Black Scholar* 12 (2016): 8–18.

260   SELECTED BIBLIOGRAPHY

Gowan, Teresa. *Hobos, Hustlers, and Backsliders: Homeless in San Francisco.* Minneapolis: University of Minnesota Press, 2010.

Halberstam, J. Jack. *In a Queer Time and Place: Transgender Bodies, Subcultural Lives.* New York: New York University Press, 2005.

Hanchard, Michael. "Afro-modernity: Temporality, Politics, and the African Diaspora." *Public Culture* 11, no. 1 (1999): 245–68.

Hannerz, Ulf. *Soulside: Inquiries into Ghetto Culture and Community.* New York: Columbia University Press, 1969.

Harding, David J. *Living the Drama: Community, Conflict and Culture among Inner-City Boys.* Chicago: University of Chicago Press, 2010.

Hardt, Michael, and Antonio Negri. *Empire.* Cambridge, MA: Harvard University Press, 2000.

Harney, Stefano, and Fred Moten. *The Undercommons: Fugitive Planning and Black Study.* New York: Minor Compositions, 2013.

Harris, Cheryl. "Whiteness as Property." *Harvard Law Review* 106, no. 8 (1993): 1707–91.

Harris, Kathleen M., Greg J. Duncan, and Johanne Boisjoly. "Evaluating the Role of 'Nothing to Lose' Attitudes on Risky Behavior in Adolescence." *Social Forces* 80, no. 3 (2002): 1005–39.

Hartman, Saidiya V. "The Anarchy of Colored Girls Assembled in a Riotous Manner." *South Atlantic Quarterly* 117, no. 3 (2018): 465–90.

——. *Lose Your Mother: A Journey along the Atlantic Slave Route.* New York: Farrar, Straus & Giroux, 2007.

——. *Scenes of Subjection: Terror, Slavery, and Self-Making in Nineteenth-Century America.* New York: Oxford University Press, 1997.

——. "The Time of Slavery." *South Atlantic Quarterly* 101, no. 4 (2002): 757–77.

——. *Wayward Lives, Beautiful Experiments: Intimate Histories of Social Upheaval.* New York: W. W. Norton, 2019.

Harvey, David. *The New Imperialism.* Oxford: Oxford University Press, 2005.

Hassard, John, ed. *The Sociology of Time.* New York: St. Martin's, 1990.

Hayward, Clarissa Rile. *How Americans Make Race: Stories, Institutions, Spaces.* Cambridge: Cambridge University Press, 2013.

Hong, Grace Kyungwon. "Intersectionality and Incommensurability: Third World Feminism and Asian Decolonization." In *Asian American Feminisms and Women of Color Politics*, edited by Lynn Fujiwara and Shireen Roshanravan, 27–42. Seattle: University of Washington Press, 2018.

Hoy, David Couzens. *The Time of Our Lives: A Critical History of Temporality.* Cambridge, MA: MIT Press, 2012.

Iton, Richard. *In Search of the Black Fantastic: Politics and Popular Culture in the Post–Civil Rights Era.* Oxford: Oxford University Press, 2008.

Jackson, George L. *Blood in My Eye.* Baltimore: Black Classic Press, 1990. First published 1972.

James, Joy. *Resisting State Violence: Radicalism, Gender, and Race in U.S. Culture.* Minneapolis: University of Minnesota Press, 1996.

——. "The Womb of Western Theory: Trauma, Time Theft and the Captive Maternal." *Carceral Notebooks* 12, no. 1 (2016): 253–96.

James, Joy, and João Costa Vargas. "Refusing Blackness-as-Victimization: Trayvon Martin and the Black Cyborgs." In *Pursuing Trayvon: Historical Contexts and Contemporary Manifestations of Racial Dynamics*, edited by George Yancy and Janine Jones, 193–205. Lanham, MD: Lexington Books, 2012.

Jaques, Elliott. *The Form of Time.* London: Heinemann, 1982.

Johnson, Monica Kirkpatrick. "Social Origins, Adolescent Experiences, and Work Value Trajectories during the Transition to Adulthood." *Social Forces* 80, no. 4 (2002): 1307–40.

Johnson-Hanks, Jennifer. "Waiting for the Start: Flexibility and the Question of Convergence." In *Ethnographies of Youth and Temporality: Time Objectified*, edited by Anne Line Dalsgård, Martin Demant Frederiksen, Susanne Højlund, and Lotte Meinert, 23–40. Philadelphia: Temple University Press, 2014.

Keeling, Kara. *Queer Times, Black Futures.* New York: New York University Press, 2019.

Kelley, Robin D. G. *Freedom Dreams: The Black Radical Imagination.* Boston: Beacon, 2002.

——. *Race Rebels: Culture, Politics, and the Black Working Class.* New York: Free Press, 1994.

——. "Resistance as Revelatory." In *Youth Resistance Research and Theories of Change*, edited by Eve Tuck and K. Wayne Yang, 82–96. New York: Routledge, 2014.

——. *Yo' Mama's Disfunktional! Fighting the Culture Wars in Urban America.* Boston: Beacon, 1997.

Kidd, Celeste, Holly Palmeri, and Richard N. Aslin. "Rational Snacking: Young Children's Decision-Making on the Marshmallow Task Is Moderated by Beliefs about Environmental Reliability." *Cognition* 126 (2013): 109–14.

Kim, Claire Jean. "The Racial Triangulation of Asian Americans." *Politics and Society* 27 (1999): 105–38.

Kim, Jina B. "Toward a Crip-of-Color Critique: Thinking with Minich's 'Enabling Whom?'" *Lateral* 6, no. 1 (2017). https://csalateral.org/issue/6-1/forum-alt-humanities-critical-disability-studies-crip-of-color-critique-kim/.

King, Deborah K. "Multiple Jeopardy, Multiple Consciousness: The Context of Black Feminist Ideology." *Signs* 14, no. 1 (1988): 42–72.

King, Mike. "Aggrieved Whiteness: White Identity Politics and Modern American Racial Formation." *Abolition Journal*, May 4, 2017. https://abolitionjournal.org/aggrieved-whiteness-white-identity-politics-and-modern-american-racial-formation/.

King, Tiffany Lethabo, Jenell Navarro, and Andrea Smith. "Beyond Incommensurability: Toward an Otherwise Stance on Black and Indigenous Relationality." In *Otherwise Worlds: Against Settler Colonialism and Anti-Blackness*, edited by Tiffany Lethabo King, Jenell Navarro, and Andrea Smith, 1–23. Durham, NC: Duke University Press, 2020.

King, Tiffany Lethabo, Jenell Navarro, and Andrea Smith, eds. *Otherwise Worlds: Against Settler Colonialism and Anti-Blackness.* Durham, NC: Duke University Press, 2020.

Kotlowitz, Alex. *There Are No Children Here: The Story of Two Boys Growing Up in the Other America.* New York: Doubleday, 1991.

Ladson-Billings, Gloria. "From the Achievement Gap to the Education Debt: Understanding Achievement in U.S. Schools." *Educational Researcher* 35, no. 7 (2006): 3–12.

Lawler, Steph. "White Like Them: Whiteness and Anachronistic Space in Representations of the English Working Class." *Ethnicities* 12, no. 4 (2012): 409–26.

Laybourn, Sun Ah. "Adopting the Model Minority Myth: Korean Adoption as a Racial Project." *Social Problems* 68 (2021): 118–35.

Laymon, Kiese. *Long Division.* Chicago: Bolden Books, 2013.

Lesko, Nancy. *Act Your Age! A Cultural Construction of Adolescence.* New York: RoutledgeFalmer, 2001.

Lewis, Amanda. "'What Group?' Studying Whites and Whiteness in the Era of 'Color-Blindness.'" *Sociological Theory* 22, no. 4 (December 2004): 623–46.

Lewis, David J., and Andrew J. Weigart. "The Structures and Meanings of Social-Time." In *The Sociology of Time*, edited by John Hassard, 77–101. New York: St. Martin's, 1990.

Lewis, Oscar. *The Children of Sánchez: Autobiography of a Mexican Family*. New York: Random House, 1961.

Liebow, Elliot. *Tally's Corner: A Study of Negro Streetcorner Men*. Lanham, MD: Rowman & Littlefield, 1967.

Lipsitz, George. *How Racism Takes Place*. Philadelphia: Temple University Press, 2011.

——. *The Possessive Investment in Whiteness: How White People Profit from Identity Politics*. Philadelphia: Temple University Press, 2006.

——. *Time Passages: Collective Memory and American Popular Culture*. Minneapolis: University of Minnesota Press, 1990.

Lovelace, Earl. *The Dragon Can't Dance*. New York: Persea Books, 1979.

Lowe, Lisa. "Heterogeneity, Hybridity, Multiplicity: Marking Asian American Differences." *Diaspora* 1, no. 1 (1991): 24–44.

MacLeod, Jay. *Ain't No Makin' It: Aspirations and Attainment in a Low-Income Neighborhood*. 3rd ed. Boulder, CO: Westview, 2009.

Macmillan, Ross. "'Constructing Adulthood': Agency and Subjectivity in the Transition to Adulthood." *Advances in Life Course Research* 11 (2007): 3–29.

Mahoney, Joseph L., and Andrea E. Vest. "The Over-scheduling Hypothesis Revisited: Intensity of Organized Activity and Participation during Adolescence and Young Adult Outcomes." *Journal of Research on Adolescence* 22, no. 3 (2012): 409–18.

Maira, Sunaina Marr. *Missing: Youth, Citizenship, and Empire after 9/11*. Durham, NC: Duke University Press, 2009.

Majors, Richard, and Janet Billson. *Cool Pose: The Dilemmas of Black Manhood in America*. New York: Lexington Books, 1992.

Manzo, Kathryn A. *Creating Boundaries: The Politics of Race and Nation*. Boulder, CO: Lynne Rienner, 1996.

Marini, Margaret M. "The Transition to Adulthood: Sex Differences in Educational Attainment and Age at Marriage." *American Sociological Review* 43 (1978): 483–507.

Martinot, Steve. *The Machinery of Whiteness: Studies in the Structure of Racialization*. Philadelphia: Temple University Press, 2010.

Martinot, Steve, and Jared Sexton. "The Avant-Garde of White Supremacy." *Social Identities: Journal for the Study of Race, Nation and Culture* 9, no. 2 (2003): 169–81.

Marx, Karl. *Capital*. Vol. 1. New York: Penguin Books, 1976. First published 1867.

——. *Early Writings*. New York: Penguin, 1992.

Massey, Douglas S., and Nancy A. Denton. *American Apartheid: Segregation and the Making of the Urban Underclass*. Cambridge, MA: Harvard University Press, 1993.

Maturana, Humberto R., and Francisco J. Varela. *Autopoiesis and Cognition: The Realization of Living*. Holland: D. Reidel, 1980.

Mawani, Renisa. "Law as Temporality: Colonial Politics in Indian Settlers." *University of California Irvine Law Review* 4, no. 65 (2014): 65–96.

Mbiti, John S. *African Religions and Philosophy*. New York: Praeger, 1969.

McClintock, Anne. *Imperial Leather: Race, Gender, and Sexuality in the Colonial Contest*. New York: Routledge, 1995.

McKittrick, Katherine. *Dear Science and Other Stories*. Durham, NC: Duke University Press, 2021.

——. *Demonic Grounds: Black Women and the Cartographies of Struggle*. Minneapolis: University of Minnesota Press, 2006.

——, ed. *Sylvia Wynter: On Being Human as Praxis*. Durham, NC: Duke University Press, 2015.

Medoff, Peter, and Holly Sklar. *Streets of Hope: The Fall and Rise of an Urban Neighborhood*. Boston: South End, 1994.

Melamed, Jodi. *Represent and Destroy: Rationalizing Violence in the New Racial Capitalism*. Minneapolis: University of Minnesota Press, 2011.

Merton, Robert K. "The Matthew Effect in Science: The Reward and Communication Systems of Science Are Considered." *Science* 159, no. 3810 (1968): 56–63.

——. "Socially Expected Durations: A Case Study of Concept Formation in Sociology." In *Conflict and Consensus: A Festschrift in Honor of Lewis A. Coser*, edited by Walter W. Powell and Richard Robbins, 262–83. New York: Free Press, 1984.

Mignolo, Walter D. *The Idea of Latin America*. Oxford: Blackwell, 2005.

——. "Sylvia Wynter: What Does It Mean to Be Human?" In *Sylvia Wynter: On Being Human as Praxis*, edited by Katherine McKittrick, 106–23. Durham, NC: Duke University Press, 2015.

Miles, Tiya. "Uncle Tom Was an Indian: Tracing the Red in Black Slavery." In *Relational Formations of Race: Theory, Method, and Practice*, edited by Natalia Molina, Daniel Martinez Hosang, and Ramóna A. Gutiérrez, 121–44. Berkeley: University of California Press, 2019.

Miller, Jody. *Getting Played: African American Girls, Urban Inequality, and Gendered Violence*. New York: New York University Press, 2008.

Mills, C. Wright. *The Sociological Imagination*. Oxford: Oxford University Press, 1959.

Mills, Charles W. "The Chronopolitics of Racial Time." *Time and Society* 29, no. 2 (2020): 297–317.

——. *The Racial Contract*. Ithaca, NY: Cornell University Press, 1997.

——. "White Time: The Chronic Injustice of Ideal Theory." *Du Bois Review* 11, no. 1 (2014): 27–42.

Mischel, Walter, Yuichi Shoda, and Philip K. Peake. "The Nature of Adolescent Competencies Predicted by Preschool Delay of Gratification." *Journal of Personality and Social Psychology* 54 (1988): 687–96.

Moen, Phyllis. "The Gendered Life Course." In *Handbook of Aging and the Social Sciences*, edited by Robert H. Binstock and Linda K. George, 175–96. New York: Academic Press, 1996.

Moen, Phyllis, and Robert M. Orrange. "Careers and Lives: Socialization, Structural Lag, and Gendered Ambivalence." *Advances in Life Course Research* 7 (2002): 231–60.

Molina, Natalia, Daniel Martinez Hosang, and Ramóna A. Gutiérrez, eds. *Relational Formations of Race: Theory, Method, and Practice*. Berkeley: University of California Press, 2019.

Moore, Wendy Leo. *Reproducing Racism: White Space, Elite Law Schools, and Racial Inequality*. Lanham, MD: Rowman & Littlefield, 2008.

Morris, Aldon D. *The Scholar Denied: W. E. B. Du Bois and the Birth of Modern Sociology*. Oakland: University of California Press, 2015.

Morrison, Toni. *Playing in the Dark: Whiteness and the Literary Imagination*. New York: Vintage, 1992.

Moten, Fred. *Black and Blur: Consent Not to Be a Single Being*. Durham, NC: Duke University Press, 2017.

——. *In the Break: The Aesthetics of the Black Radical Tradition*. Minneapolis: University of Minnesota Press, 2003.

Moten, Fred, and Stefano Harney. "The University and the Undercommons: Seven Theses." *Social Text* 22, no. 2 (2004): 101–15.

Muñoz, José Esteban. *Cruising Utopia: The Then and There of Queer Futurity*. New York: New York University Press, 2009.

——. *Disidentifications: Queers of Color and the Performance of Politics*. Minneapolis: University of Minnesota Press, 1999.

Nanibush, Wanda. "Outside of Time: Salvage Ethnography, Self-Representation and Performing Culture." In *Time, Temporality and Violence in International Relations: (De)fatalizing the Present, Forging Radical Alternatives*, edited by Ann M. Agathangelou and Kyle D. Killian, 104–18. New York: Routledge, 2016.

Negri, Antonio. *Time for Revolution*. Translated by Matteo Mandarini. New York: Bloomsbury, 2003.

Newman, Katherine S. *No Shame in My Game: The Working Poor in the Inner City*. New York: Alfred A. Knopf, 1999.

Ngo, Helen. "'Get Over It'? Racialised Temporalities and Bodily Orientations in Time." *Journal of Intercultural Studies* 40, no. 2 (2019): 239–53.

——. *The Habits of Racism: A Phenomenology of Racism and Racialized Embodiment*. Lanham, MD: Lexington Books, 2017.

Nickrand, Jessica. "Minneapolis's White Lie." *The Atlantic*, February 21, 2015. https://www.theatlantic.com/business/archive/2015/02/minneapoliss-white-lie/385702/.

Nyong'o, Tavia. "Non-binary Blackness: After the End of the World with Samuel R. Delany." Art Practical, November 21, 2019. http://www.artpractical.com/feature/non-binary-blackness-after-the-end-of-the-world-with-samuel-r.-delany/.

Ogburn, William Fielding. *Social Change with Respect to Culture and Original Nature*. New York: B. W. Huebsch, 1922.

Ogle, Vanessa. "Whose Time Is It? The Pluralization of Time and the Global Condition, 1870s–1940s." *American Historical Review* 118, no. 5 (2013): 1376–402.

Oliver, Melvin L., and Thomas Shapiro. *Black Wealth/White Wealth: A New Perspective on Racial Inequality*. New York: Routledge, 1995.

Omi, Michael, and Howard Winant. *Racial Formation in the United States: From the 1960s to the 1990s*. 2nd ed. New York: Routledge, 1994.

Pager, Devah, and Lincoln Quillan. "Walking the Talk: What Employers Say versus What They Do." *American Sociological Review* 70 (2005): 355–80.

Pager, Devah, Bruce Western, and Bart Bonikowski. "Discrimination in a Low-Wage Labor Market: A Field Experiment." *American Sociological Review* 74 (2009): 777–99.

Painter, Nell Irvin. *The History of White People*. New York: W. W. Norton, 2010.

Pallas, Andrew. "Educational Transitions, Trajectories, and the Pathways." In *Handbook of the Life Course*, edited by Jeylan T. Mortimer and Michael J. Shanahan, 165–84. New York: Springer Science and Business Media, 2004.

Patterson, Orlando. *Slavery and Social Death: A Comparative Study*. Cambridge, MA: Harvard University Press, 2018. First published 1982.

Perry, Pamela. "White Means Never Having to Say You're Ethnic: White Youth and the Construction of 'Cultureless' Identities." *Journal of Contemporary Ethnography* 30, no. 1 (2001): 56–91.

Phruksachart, Melissa. "The Literature of White Liberalism." *Boston Review*, August 21, 2020. https://bostonreview.net/articles/melissa-phruksachart-literature-white-liberalism/.

Quashie, Kevin. *The Sovereignty of Quiet: Beyond Resistance in Black Culture*. New Brunswick, NJ: Rutgers University Press, 2012.

Ray, Victor E., Antonia Randolph, Megan Underhill, and David Luke. "Critical Race Theory, Afro-pessimism, and Racial Progress Narratives." *Sociology of Race and Ethnicity* 3, no. 2 (2017): 147–58.

Rich, Adrienne. "'Disloyal to Civilization': Feminism, Racism, and Gynephobia." In *On Lies, Secrets, and Silence: Selected Prose*, 275–310. New York: W.W. Norton, 1979.

Rifkin, Mark. *Beyond Settler Time: Temporal Sovereignty and Indigenous Self-Determination*. Durham, NC: Duke University Press, 2017.

Rios, Jodi. *Black Lives and Spatial Matters: Policing Blackness and Practicing Freedom in Suburban St. Louis*. Ithaca, NY: Cornell University Press, 2020.

Rios, Victor. *Punished: Policing the Lives of Black and Latino Boys*. New York: New York University Press, 2011.

Ritchie, Andrea J. *Invisible No More: Police Violence against Black Women and Women of Color*. Boston: Beacon, 2017.

Robinson, Cedric. *Black Marxism: The Making of the Black Radical Tradition*. Chapel Hill: University of North Carolina Press, 1983.

——. Preface to *Futures of Black Radicalism*, edited by Gaye Theresa Johnson and Alex Lubin, 1–18. New York: Verso, 2017.

Rodríguez, Dylan. "Inhabiting the Impasse: Racial/Racial-Colonial Power, Genocide Poetics, and the Logic of Evisceration." *Social Text* 33, no. 3 (2015): 19–44.

——. *White Reconstruction: Domestic Warfare and the Logics of Genocide*. New York: Fordham University Press, 2021.

Roediger, David R. *The Wages of Whiteness: Race and the Making of the American Working Class*. Brooklyn, NY: Verso, 1991.

Romero, Andrea J., and Robert E. Roberts. "Perception of Discrimination and Ethnocultural Variables in a Diverse Group of Adolescents." *Journal of Adolescence* 21 (1998): 641–56.

Rosaldo, Renato. *Culture and Truth: The Remaking of Social Analysis*. Boston: Beacon, 1989.

Said, Edward W. *Orientalism*. New York: Vintage Books, 1979.

Sampson, Robert J., Jeffrey D. Morenoff, and Thomas Gannon-Rowley. "Assessing Neighborhood Effects: Social Processes and New Directions in Research." Annual Review of Sociology 28 (2002): 443–78.

Sánchez-Jankowski, Martin. *Islands in the Streets: Gangs and American Urban Society*. Berkeley: University of California Press, 1991.

Sassen, Saskia. *Guests and Aliens*. New York: New Press, 1999.

Schwartz, Barry. *Waiting and Queuing: Studies in the Social Organization of Access and Delay*. Chicago: University of Chicago Press, 1975.

Scott, James C. *Domination and the Arts of Resistance: Hidden Transcripts*. New Haven, CT: Yale University Press, 1990.

Scott, Joseph. "Black Science and Nation Building." In *The Death of White Sociology: Essays on Race and Culture*, edited by Joyce A. Ladner, 289–309. Baltimore: Black Classic Press, 1973.

Seamster, Louise, and Victor Ray. "Against Teleology in the Study of Race: Toward the Abolition of the Progress Paradigm." *Sociological Theory* 36, no. 4 (2018): 315–42.

Settersten, Richard A., Jr. "Age Structuring and the Rhythm of the Life Course." In *Handbook of the Life Course*, edited by Jeylan T. Mortimer and Michael J. Shanahan, 81–98. New York: Springer Science and Business Media, 2004.

Sexton, Jared. "The Social Life of Social Death: On Afro-pessimism and Black Optimism." In *Time, Temporality and Violence in International Relations: (De)fatalizing the Present, Forging Radical Alternatives*, edited by Ann M. Agathangelou and Kyle D. Killian, 61–75. New York: Routledge, 2016.

——. "The *Vel* of Slavery: Tracking the Figure of the Unsovereign." *Critical Sociology* 42, no. 4–5 (2014): 1–15.

Shakur, Assata. *Assata: An Autobiography*. Chicago: Zed Books, 1978.

Shanahan, Michael J. "Pathways to Adulthood in Changing Societies: Variability and Mechanisms in the Life Course Perspective." *Annual Review of Sociology* 26 (2000): 667–92.

Shange, Savannah. "Black Girl Ordinary: Flesh, Carcerality and the Refusal of Ethnography." *Transforming Anthropology* 27, no. 1 (2019): 3–21.

Sharma, Nandita. "Strategic Anti-essentialism: Decolonizing Decolonization." In *Sylvia Wynter: On Being Human as Praxis*, edited by Katherine McKittrick, 164–82. Durham, NC: Duke University Press, 2015.

Sharpe, Christina. *In the Wake: On Blackness and Being*. Durham, NC: Duke University Press, 2016.

Shaw, J. Brendan. "'I Don't Wanna Time Travel No Mo': Race, Gender, and the Politics of Replacement in Erykah Badu's 'Window Seat.'" *Feminist Formations* 27, no. 2 (2015): 46–69.

Silva, Jennifer M. "Constructing Adulthood in an Age of Uncertainty." *American Sociological Review* 77, no. 4 (2012): 505–22.

Sirianni, Carmen. "Economies of Time in Social Theory: Three Approaches Compared." *Current Perspectives in Social Theory* 8 (1987): 161–95.

Smith, Andrea. *Conquest: Sexual Violence and American Indian Genocide*. Cambridge, MA: South End, 2005.

——. "Heteropatriarchy and the Three Pillars of White Supremacy: Rethinking Women of Color Organizing." In *Color of Violence: The Incite! Anthology*, edited by Incite! Women of Color against Violence, 66–73. Cambridge, MA: South End, 2006.

——. "Sovereignty as Deferred Genocide." In *Otherwise Worlds: Against Settler-Colonialism and Anti-Blackness*, edited by Tiffany Lethabo King, Jenell Navarro, and Andrea Smith, 118–32. Durham, NC: Duke University Press, 2020.

Smith, Mark M. *Mastered by the Clock: Time, Slavery, and Freedom in the American South*. Chapel Hill: University of North Carolina Press, 1997.

Sojoyner, Damien M. "Dissonance in Time: (Un)making and (Re)mapping of Blackness." In *Futures of Black Radicalism*, edited by Gaye Theresa Johnson and Alex Lubin, 59–71. New York: Verso, 2017.

——. *First Strike: Educational Enclosures in Black Los Angeles*. Minneapolis: University of Minnesota Press, 2016.

Sorokin, Pitirim, and Robert Merton. "Social-Time: A Methodological and Functional Analysis." In *The Sociology of Time*, edited by John Hassard, 56–66. New York: St. Martin's, 1990. First published 1937.

Spillers, Hortense J. "Mama's Baby, Papa's Maybe: An American Grammar Book." *Diacritics* 17, no. 2 (Summer 1987): 65–81.

Spivak, Gayatri Chakravorty. "'Can the Subaltern Speak?' In *Marxism and the Interpretation of Culture*, edited by Cary Nelson and Lawrence Grossberg, 271–313. Urbana: University of Illinois Press, 1988.

Stallings, L. H. *Funk the Erotic: Transaesthetics and Black Sexual Cultures*. Chicago: University of Illinois Press, 2015.

Tadiar, Neferti X. M. "Life-Times in Fate Playing." *South Atlantic Quarterly* 111, no. 4 (2012): 783–802.

Tang, Eric. *Unsettled: Cambodian Refugees in the New York City Hyperghetto.* Philadelphia: Temple University Press, 2015.

Thompson, Derek. "The Miracle of Minneapolis." *The Atlantic*, March 2015. https://www.theatlantic.com/magazine/archive/2015/03/the-miracle-of-minneapolis/384975/.

Thompson, E. P. "Time, Work-Discipline, and Capitalism." *Past and Present* 38 (1967): 56–97.

Thrift, Nigel. "The Making of a Capitalist Consciousness." In *The Sociology of Time*, edited by John Hassard, 105–29. New York: St. Martin's, 1990. First published 1980.

Trouillot, Michel-Rolph. *Silencing the Past: Power and the Production of History.* Boston: Beacon, 1995.

Tuck, Eve, and K. Wayne Yang. "Decolonization Is Not a Metaphor." *Decolonization: Indigeneity, Education and Society* 1, no. 1 (2012): 1–40.

Valentine, Charles. *Culture and Poverty: Critique and Counter-proposals.* Chicago: University of Chicago Press, 1968.

Wacquant, Loïc. "Inside 'the Zone': The Social Art of the Hustler in the American Ghetto." In *The Weight of the World: Social Suffering in Contemporary Society*, edited by Pierre Bourdieu et al., 140–67. Stanford, CA: Stanford University Press, 1993.

——. "Scrutinizing the Street: Poverty, Mobility, and the Pitfalls of Urban Ethnography." *American Journal of Sociology* 107, no. 6 (2002): 1468–532.

——. *Urban Outcasts: A Comparative Sociology of Advanced Marginality.* Cambridge: Polity, 2008.

Walcott, Ronald. "Ellison, Gordone, and Tolson: Some Notes on the Blues, Style and Space." *Black World* 22, no. 2 (1972): 4–29.

Walia, Harsha. *Undoing Border Imperialism.* Oakland: AK Press, 2013.

Warren, Calvin L. "Black Time: Slavery, Metaphysics, and the Logic of Wellness." In *The Psychic Hold of Slavery: Legacies in American Expressive Culture*, edited by Soyica Diggs Colbert, Robert J. Patterson, and Aida Levy-Hussen, 55–68. New Brunswick, NJ: Rutgers University Press, 2016.

——. *Ontological Terror: Blackness, Nihilism, and Emancipation.* Durham, NC: Duke University Press, 2018.

Watkins, William H. *The White Architects of Black Education.* New York: Teachers Education Press, 2000.

Waziyatawin. *What Does Justice Look Like? The Struggle for Liberation in Dakota Homeland.* St. Paul: Living Justice, 2008.

Weber, Max. *The Protestant Ethic and the "Spirit" of Capitalism, and Other Writings.* New York: Penguin Books, 2002. First published 1905.

Weheliye, Alexander G. *Habeus Viscus: Racializing Assemblages, Biopolitics, and Black Feminist Theories of the Human.* Durham, NC: Duke University Press, 2014.

——. *Phonographies: Grooves in Sonic Modernity.* Durham, NC: Duke University Press, 2005.

Whitesel, Jason. "Intersections of Multiple Oppressions: Racism, Sizeism, Ableism, and the 'Illimitable Etceteras' in Encounters with Law Enforcement." *Sociological Forum* 32, no. 2 (2017): 426–33.

Wildcat, Daniel R. "Indigenizing the Future: Why We Must Think Spatially in the Twenty-First Century." *American Studies* 46 (2005): 417–40.

Wilderson, Frank B., III. "The Black Liberation Army and the Paradox of Political Engagement." In *Postcoloniality-Decoloniality-Black Critique: Joints and Fissures*, edited by Sabine Broeck and Carsten Junker, 1–34. Chicago: University of Chicago Press, 2014.

———. *Red, White, & Black: Cinema and the Structure of U.S. Antagonisms*. Durham, NC: Duke University Press, 2010.

———. "Social Death and Narrative Aporia in *12 Years a Slave*." *Black Camera* 7, no. 1 (2015): 134–49.

Wilderson, Frank B., III, and Tiffany Lethabo King. "Staying Ready for Black Study." In *Otherwise Worlds: Against Settler-Colonialism and Anti-Blackness*, edited by Tiffany Lethabo King, Jenell Navarro, and Andrea Smith, 53–73. Durham, NC: Duke University Press, 2020.

Williamson, Terrion L., ed. *Black in the Middle: An Anthology of the Black Midwest*. Cleveland: Belt, 2020.

———. *Scandalize My Name: Black Feminist Practice and the Making of Black Social Life*. New York: Fordham University Press, 2017.

Willis, Paul. *Learning to Labor: How Working Class Kids Get Working Class Jobs*. New York: Columbia University Press, 1977.

Wilson, August. Introduction to *May All Your Fences Have Gates*, edited by Alan Nadel, 1–8. Iowa City: Iowa University Press, 1988.

Wilson, William Julius. *The Declining Significance of Race: Blacks and Changing American Institutions*. Chicago: University of Chicago Press, 1978.

———. *The Truly Disadvantaged: The Inner City, the Underclass, and Public Policy*. Chicago: University of Chicago Press, 1987.

———. *When Work Disappears: The World of the New Urban Poor*. New York: Vintage, 1996.

Wise, Tim. *Speaking Treason Fluently: Anti-racist Reflections from an Angry White Male*. Berkeley: Soft Skull, 2008.

Womack, Ytasha. *Afrofuturism: The World of Black Sci-Fi and Fantasy Culture*. Chicago: Chicago Review Press, 2013.

Wood, Geof D. "Desperately Seeking Security." *Journal of International Development* 13 (2001): 523–34.

———. "Staying Secure, Staying Poor: The Faustian Bargain." *World Development* 31 (2003): 455–71.

Woods, Clyde. *Development Arrested: The Blues and Plantation Power in the Mississippi Delta*. New York: Verso, 1998.

Wright, Michelle M. *Becoming Black: Creating Identity in the African Diaspora*. Durham, NC: Duke University Press, 2004.

———. *Physics of Blackness: Beyond the Middle Passage Epistemology*. Minneapolis: University of Minnesota Press, 2015.

Wright, Richard. *Native Son*. New York: New American Library, 1950.

Wright, Vanessa R., Joseph R. Price, Suzanne M. Bianchi, and Bijou R. Hunt. "The Time Use of Teenagers." *Social Science Research* 38 (2009): 792–809.

Wynter, Sylvia. "No Humans Involved: An Open Letter to My Colleagues." *Forum N.H.I. Knowledge for the 21st Century* 1, no. 1 (1994): 42–73.

———. "Unsettling the Coloniality of Being/Power/Being/Truth/Freedom: Towards the Human, after Man, Its Overrepresentation—an Argument." *CR: The New Centennial Review* 3, no. 3 (2003): 257–337.

Young, Alford A. *The Minds of Marginalized Black Men: Making Sense of Mobility, Opportunity, and Future Life Chances*. Princeton, NJ: Princeton University Press, 2004.

———. "White Ethnographers on the Experiences of African American Men: Then and Now." In *White Logic, White Methods: Racism and Methodology*, edited by

Tukufu Zuberi and Eduardo Bonilla-Silva, 179–200. Lanham, MD: Rowman & Littlefield, 2008.

Yu, Henry. *Thinking Orientals: Migration, Contact, Exoticism in Modern America*. New York: Oxford University Press, 2001.

Zerubavel, Eviatar. *Social Mindscapes: An Invitation to Cognitive Sociology*. Cambridge, MA: Harvard University Press, 1997.

——. "The Standardization of Time: A Sociohistorical Perspective." *American Journal of Sociology* 88, no. 1 (1982): 1–23.

——. *Time Maps: Collective Memory and the Social Shape of the Past*. Chicago: University of Chicago Press, 2003.

Zick, Cathleen D. "The Shifting Balance of Adolescent Time Use." *Youth & Society* 41, no. 4 (2010): 569–96.

Zuberi, Tukufu, and Eduardo Bonilla-Silva. *White Logic, White Methods: Racism and Methodology*. Lanham, MD: Rowman & Littlefield, 2008.

Index

ableism, 251n85

Aberrations in Black: Toward a Queer of Color Critique (Ferguson), 174

abolitionism, unlearning and, 200–201, 253nn5–6

Abu-Jamal, Mumia, 199

Adeyemi, Kemi, 52

"Adore" (Prince), 199

adulthood, Black youth transition to, 110–13, 164–65

affirmative action, 148

African Religions and Philosophy (Mbiti), 158–59

Afrofuturism, 188, 251n91

Afro-modernity, 37

Afro-pessimism, 215n26

agency, criminalization of, 86

Ahmed, Sara, 66–67, 89, 148; on whiteness, 15

a'ightness, Black excellence vs., 181–82, 249n59

Alexander, Michelle, 247n30

Alexander, M. Jacqui, 4

Allison, Kevin, 143

ambiguity: CP Time and, 44–45, 48–49; white discomfort with, 72, 157–66

American Community Survey (ACS), 93–94

American Dream, fast life and, 143–45

American Slave: A Composite Autobiography (Rawick), 39

American Time Use Survey (ATUS), 24, 80

Aminzade, Ronald, 37

ancestry tests, 96

Anderson, Elijah, 137–38, 183–84, 248n43

androcentric logic, misogynoir and, 74–79

Angélique, Marie-Joseph, 92

anthropology, time and, 214n24

anti-Blackness: ableism and, 251n85; Black youth awareness of, 111–13, 150–54, 177–84; capitalism and, 73–74; increase in, 168; loss of time and, 62–68; in Midwest, 90–99; misogynoir and, 78–79; police violence and, 86–88; racialization and, 19. *See also* race, racialization, and racism

Anti-terrorism and Effective Death Penalty Act (AEDPA), 238n19

Anzaldúa, Gloria, 126

arson, urbanized space and, 127–28

Asian community, in Twin Cities, 98–99, 233n37

assimilation: critical race theory and, 22, 218n76; immigrant resistance to, 237n13; Indigeneity and, 95–96

The Atlantic magazine, 24–25, 91–94

Australia, conquest of Indigeneity in, 95

Auyero, Javier, 10, 249n72

Badu, Erykah, 153

Baldwin, James, 104–5, 159, 190–91, 213n2

Bambara, Toni Cade, 204

Barthold, Bonnie J., 38–39, 75, 99

beauty: as cognitive labor, 76–79; racialized and gendered standards of, 54–56

Berlant, Lauren, 183

Biden, Joe, 167

Billson, Janet, 216n45

biography, *tabanca* time and, 126–36

biological time, 72

Birth, Kevin, 237nn12–13

The Black Atlantic (Gilroy), 37

Black Codes, 86

Black excellence, construction of, 181

Black history, suppression of curriculum on, 115–19

Black Lives and Spatial Matters: Policing Blackness and Practicing Freedom in Suburban St. Louis (Rios), 81–82

Black Lives Matter movement, 177

Black Midwest Initiative, 90–94, 231n7

Blackness: Black youth's embrace of, 160–66; contributions to knowledge and, 9; CP Time linked to, 41–49; crime and criminalization linked to, 42–43, 183–84, 189–93, 224n67; epiphenomenal time and, 180; fungibility of, 172–73, 243n29; futurity and, 176–84; Indigeneity and, 8, 89–90, 94–99; in Midwest, 89–99; phenomenology of, 89–94,

271

Blackness (*continued*)
232n17; physics of, 148; police response to, 84–88; qualitative collapse of, 9, 215n33, 219n78; racial time and, 37–38; relational racial identity and, 96–99; space and, 31–32, 235n68; surveillance and criminalization of, 69–74; *tabanca* time and, 126–36; time and, 31–32; white misappropriation of, 161–62

Black privilege, 156–58, 165

Black Radical Tradition, runaways and fugitives in, 7–8

Black Reconstruction in America (Du Bois), 146–47

Black's Law Dictionary, 147

Black studies scholarship: funk and, 4; urban sociology and, 174, 196; whiteness principles and, 158–66

Black Time: Fiction of Africa, the Caribbean, and the United States, 38–39, 75

Black Wealth/White Wealth (Oliver & Shapiro), 155–56

Black womanhood: black girl ordinary and, 249n59; CP Time and, 51–56; fast life and, 139–40; gender-based violence against, 239n9; gendered division of labor and, 239n8; misogynoir and, 74–79; police encounters with, 81–88; present orientation and, 170–71; reproductive labor and time theft for, 103–6; sex trafficking and, 138–39

Black youth: cool pose of, 216n45; CP Time and, 40–41; culture of, 11; demographics, 212; developmental deadlines for, 211; expendability of, 5–7; in fast life, 52–54, 137–45; future for, 27–28, 167–68, 176–84, 194–98, 201–6; innocence perceptions about, 214n17; job search and hiring process for, 119–24; life expectancy perceptions of, 149–54, 192–93, 211–12; "maybe environment" for, 25; perceptions of race, racialization, and racism by, 71–74, 210–11; perceptions of time by, 1–4, 208–10; police and, 80–88; prescience in present orientation of, 184–88, 204–6; present orientation of, 168–76; racialization and sexualization of, 71–74; relational racial identity and, 96–99; school experiences of, 43, 113–19; strategies for dealing with whiteness among, 157–66; temporalization in urban space of, 18–23, 214n16; time concepts of, 1–4, 29–37, 57–58; time theft vs. time use for, 79–88; transgressive temporalities of, 26–27, 35–37; in Twin Cities, 93–94; urban sociology and, 4–5

Blume Oeur, Freeden, 174, 178, 248n34

Bonilla, Yarimar, 13

Bonilla-Silva, Eduardo, 16, 23–24, 68–69, 148

Bosniak, Linda, 237n16

Bourdieu, Pierre, 44–49, 60–61, 148, 179

Brand, Dionne, 147, 248n31

Browne, Simone, 12, 70

Bruce, La Marr Jurelle, 74, 179–80, 187, 192–93, 203, 236n1, 244n46

Burton, Linda, 143

Butler, Octavia, 251n91

Byrd, Jodi, 252n3

Cacho, Lisa, 53, 142

Canada, Black population in, 92–93

"Can You Use That Word in a Sentence?" contest, 9

capitalism: bourgeois time and, 152–53; CP Time and, 52–54; fashion and, 163–64; racial violence and, 105–6; temporal capital and, 153–54; time theft and, 68, 99; time use and, 80–88

carceral space, time and, 42–49, 99

"Carnival Tabanca" (Bunji Garlin), 125

Center for Urban and Regional Affairs, 105

Chakravartty, Paul, 106

Chauvin, Derek, 243n27

Cheryl Johnson McCaskill Communications, 164

Chicago School, 90

childhood: Black youth experience of, 101–3, 170, 203; time theft and, 103–6

chronos, Greek concept of, 30, 54, 220n9

citizenship, immigration and, 237n16

Clark, Jamar, 85

class stratification: delayed gratification and, 145, 241nn28–29; education and, 116–19; risk/resiliency research and, 171–73

Clifton, Lucille, 191

Clinton, Hillary, 167

clocking, racism and, 152–54

code switching, job searching and, 138, 239n3

Coleman, Chris, 105

Collins, Patricia Hill, 74–75

colonialism: critiques of research on, 250n78; Indigeneity and, 95–96; Midwest and, 89–90, 94–99; racialization and, 19; settler narratives of, 243n24; time in relation to, 37, 49, 99; violence of, 67. *See also* settler time

Common (musician), 102

consistency, white framing of, 56

consumption, Black experience with, 69–74, 164–66, 245n57

INDEX 273

corporeality, space and time and, 101

Coser, Lewis, 32–33

Coser, Rose, 32–33

Council of Minnesotans of African Heritage, 94

counter-frames of whiteness, 149, 161–64

COVID-19 pandemic, 201–6

CP Time (Colored People's Time): defined, 23–24, 38; as hidden transcript, 54–56; as praxis, 49–54; productivity and subversiveness of, 57–58; racialization and, 37–41, 223n53; as resistance, 38, 40–49, 202; transnational variations on, 223n55

Crawford, Randy, 129–30

creativity, CP Time and, 40–41

crime and criminalization: anti-Blackness and structural racism and, 243n27; of Blackness, 42–43, 183–84, 189–93, 224n67; curfews and, 81–82; deportation and, 134–36, 238n18; epidermalization and, 70; fast life and, 142–45; of immigration, 131, 238nn18–19; language of, 214n16; police violence and, 81–88; present orientation and, 171–72; time and, 53–54, 60–61; of time use, 81–88; urbanized space and, 172–73; zero-tolerance policies and, 118–19

crip time, 223n55

critical race theory: racism in, 225n86; whiteness and, 22, 218n76

cubist ethnography, 10

cultural lag, 234n50

culture: a'ightness, Black excellence vs., 181–82; appropriation and misappropriation of, 162; Black culture, suppression in school of, 115–16; Black youths inversion of white culture, 159–66; CP Time and, 38–41, 43–49; Indigeneity and, 96–99; neighborhood effects and, 171; racialization and, 19–20; structure and, 101–6; time and, 32–33; in urban sociology, 173–76

cumulative dis/advantage hypothesis, 155–56, 191

curfews, time theft and, 81–82

curricular coevalness, Black students and, 113–19

dark sousveillance, 12

debt: education debt, 118–19; taken time and, 68–74

delayed gratification, 145, 241n28

Denton, Nancy, 106

deportation time, 26, 126–27, 131–36; music and, 193–94

depressive time, Bruce's concept of, 179–80

developmental deadlines: Black youth perceptions of, 211; fast life and, 141–45; risk/resiliency research and, 171; disorientation, COVID-19 pandemic and, 201–6

Donald, Stephanie, 85

double consciousness, Du Bois's concept of, 63–66, 73, 83–84, 111–13, 180–82

The Dragon Can't Dance (Lovelace), 194

drug trafficking: fast life and, 137–45, 240n13; time and, 51–54

Du Bois, W. E. B., 49, 63, 67, 134, 138, 146–47, 158, 174–75, 180–82, 225n86, 225n88

Duck, Waverly, 250n73

Durkheim, Émile, 30–31

economics: Black Midwest and, 91–94; temporal dispossession and, 155–56

Edelman, Lee, 5–6, 178, 214n21

education: class stratification and, 116–19; fast life as alternative to, 139–45; futurity orientation in, 174; myth of meritocracy and, 178; racial differences in experience of, 94, 110–13, 154–56; suppression of Blackness in, 113–19; time construction and, 152–54. *See also* school

empathy, Hartman on, 238n25

employment: Black youth experience of, 154–56; fast life as alternative to, 137–45; job search process and, 119–24; racial patterns of, 93–94, 111–13

enclosures: in education, 117–19; fast life as escape from, 143–45; racialized space as, 127–36

end of time, 199–200

enjoyment, property of, 147

Enlightenment, time and, 32, 74

epidermalization, 70–72

epiphenomenal time, 180

Ermath, Elizabeth Deeds, 74–75

Estes, Nick, 243n24

ethnographic research: cubist ethnography, 10; Midwest and, 90–94; mixed methods in, 8–14; present orientation in, 168–76, 196–98, 246n11

ethnonoir research, 231n6

Fabian, Johannes, 7, 60, 162, 168, 220n6, 246n11

families: Black youth perceptions of, 101–3; deportation time and, 131–36; incarceration impact on, 43; migrant experience of, 126–36; present orientation and, 170–71; reproductive labor and time theft for, 103–6

274 INDEX

family regulation system, 51, 225n93
Fanon, Frantz, 3, 70–73, 138
fashion trends, Black youth knowledge of, 159–66
fast life: Black youth experience in, 52–54, 137–45; defined, 137
"Fast Life" (Kool G. Rap and Nas), 143–44
Feagin, Joe, 149, 161
feminism: misogynoir and, 74–79; time and, 51–54
Ferguson, Anne Arnett, 118–19
Ferguson, Roderick, 174
Ferreira da Silva, Denise, 22, 34, 68, 78, 106, 175, 220n3, 239n3, 248n42, 250n78
Fields, Barbara, 29
The Fire Next Time (Baldwin), 190–91
Firsts (Morales art piece), 87–88
Fleming, Crystal, 34–35
Floyd, George, 90, 203, 243n27
Franklin, Benjamin, 52
Freeman, Elizabeth, 32, 153
fugitivity: criminalization of Blackness and, 86; runaways and legacy of, 7–8, 222n46; time and, 38–39, 202–3, 244n46
fungibility of Blackness, 172–73, 243n29, 247n29
funk: mixed methods research on, 8–14; time in context of, 2–4
Funk the Erotic: Transaesthetics and Black Sexual Cultures (Stallings), 3
Furstenberg, Frank, 171
future: in Black music, 188–93; Black youth views of, 27–28, 167–68, 176–84, 194–98, 201–6; deported time and, 194; prescience of Black youth about, 184–87; whiteness and perceptions of, 32–33, 159, 163–66, 243n24

Garlin, Bunji, 125
gender: CP Time and, 54–56; fluency in, 213n7; misogynoir and, 74–79; time construction and, 151–54; violence and, 239n9
gentrification, racialization and, 105–6
geopolitics of economy, Mignolo on, 33–34
G. I. Jane (film), 77
Gilroy, Paul, 33–34, 37, 144
Glenn, Evelyn Nakano, 103–4
Glissant, Édouard, 202
globalization, migration and, 98–99, 233n37, 233n39, 244n41

Goffman, Alice, 172–73, 247n29
Goffman Erving, 56
Gowan, Teresa, 231n6
Great Migration, 89
Guadeloupean labor movements, 13–14

Habeus Viscus (Weheliye), 195–96
hair care and hair styles: culture and structure and, 101–6; racialized and gendered standards of, 54–56, 76–79; resistance to whiteness and, 157–66
Halberstam, J. Jack, 53, 152–53
Hanchard, Michael, 35, 37, 61
Hannerz, Ulf, 234n50
Harding, David, 171–73
Hardt, Michael, 134
Harney, Stefano, 3, 253n6
Harris, Cheryl, 147–48
Harris, Kamala, 36–37
Hartman, Saidiya: on afterlife of slavery, 115, 144, 189–90, 203, 221n30; on Black womanhood, 174–75; on crime and survival, 134, 238n25; on economic inequality, 91; on fungibility of Blackness, 172–73, 243n29, 247n29; on life course and state terror, 140; on pain and identification, 184; on representation and violence, 220n3; on social time racialization, 84; on space and time, 126; on urbanized space, 18–23, 213n2; on whiteness and slavery, 147
Harvey, David, 60, 152–53
Hassard, John, 30–31
hauntings, Blackness and, 19, 217n57
Hayward, Clarissa, 34
Hegel, G. F. W., 252n119
heteronormative logics, queer and trans identity and, 214n21
hidden transcript, CP Time as, 54–56
higher education, racial differences in, 112–13
hiring process, time racialization and, 119–24
history, Black youth perceptions of, 188–93
Hmong American community, in Twin Cities, 98–99
Hong, Grace, 19
Hudgins v. Wright, 95–96
humor, CP Time and, 41, 46–49

Illegal Immigration Reform and Immigration Responsibility Act (IIRAIRA), 238n19
illegitimacy, Western, white constructions of, 75–79
immigration: deported time and, 131–36; globalization and, 98–99, 233n37,

233n39, 244n41; legislation involving, 238n19; time and space and, 126–36

Immigration and Customs Enforcement (ICE), 131

Immigration and Naturalization Services (INS), 131

Indigeneity and Indigenous groups: Blackness and, 8, 24–25, 89–90, 94–99; colonialism and, 252n3; in Midwest, 94–99; oppression of progress and, 37; relational racial identity and, 96–99; Spirit time of, 223n55; time and, 45–46, 243n24; in Twin Cities, 90–94. *See also* Native American youth

Industrial Revolution, temporality and, 39

Infante, Chad Benito, 173

infrapolitics: CP Time and, 40–41; racialized violence and, 72

insurgent time, 23–24, 35–37, 50–54, 57–58

integrity, racialized questioning of, 63

intergenerational wealth transmission, 111–13, 165

interlude, deported time and, 236n1

International Monetary Fund (IMF), 98

intersectionality, racialization and temporalization of Black youths and, 18–23

In the Heat of the Night (film), 42

In the Wake: On Blackness and Being (Sharpe), 185–88

Iton, Richard, 93, 217n64

Jackson, George L., 253n21

James, Joy, 75, 150, 200, 253n5

James, Rick, 199

Jim Crow of the North (PBS documentary), 108

Job Corps, 224n81

Kabat-Zinn, John, 196

kairós, Greek concept of, 30, 54

Kant, Immanuel, 78

Keeling, Kara, 152, 176, 191, 202–3

Kelley, Robin D. G., 40–41, 164, 166, 174, 202–3

killing time, racial representations of, 191–92

Kim, Jina B., 186–87

King, Deborah, 75–76

King, Mike, 22

King, Tiffany Lethabo, 202

knowledge, Black contributions to, 9

Kotlowitz, Alex, 170, 247n14

Kristeva, Julia, 74

labor: of anti-Blackness, 62–63; Black youth temporality and, 25, 154–56; CP Time and, 50–54; education for, 116–19; fast life as

alternative to, 137–45; gendered division of, 239n8; immigrant patterns of, 126–27, 236n7; processing time and, 63–68, 71–74; racial differences in, 94, 111–13; racialized hiring processes and, 119–24; time racialization and, 39–41, 165–66; whiteness and, 146–47

Ladson-Billings, Gloria, 118–19

lateness: Black youth's resistance to, 35–37, 50–54, 57–58; CP Time and, 43–49; rejection of protocols for, 2–5; transnational variations on, 223n55

Laymon, Kiese, 9

Learning to Labor (Willis), 116–17

Lesko, Nancy, 27–28, 118–19, 123–24

Lethabo, Tiffany, 94

Lewis, Oscar, 246n11

liberalism, futurity and, 177–78

Liebow, Elliot, 176

life expectancy (life course): Black youth perceptions of, 111–12, 192; fast life and, 139–45; prescience of Black youth about, 185–88; present orientation and, 170–76; white opportunity structures and, 149–54

limbo, CP Time and, 47–48

liming, 129, 237n12

Lindner, Cristoph, 85

linear temporality: Black youth awareness of, 112–13; whiteness and, 34

Lipsitz, George, 15, 105, 107, 146, 153–54, 157, 162, 188, 219n1

loitering, racialization of, 85

Long Division (Laymon), 9

loss, time and, 238n24

Lovelace, Earl, 194

lysis *(lyse)*, Fanon's concept of, 3

madtime, Bruce's concept of, 187

Majors, Richard, 216n45

Mama (television program), 162

Managing to Make It: Urban Families and Adolescent Success (Furstenberg), 171

Mann, Simone, 12

marginalization, time theft and, 152–54

Martin, Trayvon, 85–86

Martinot, Steve, 19–20, 73, 143, 218n69, 241n4

Marx, Karl, 80

Massey, Douglass, 106

mass incarceration: CP Time linked to, 42–49; drug offenses and, 238n29; racialization and, 224n68; whiteness and, 247n30. *See also* carceral space, time and

276 INDEX

"Matthew Effect," 155–56
"maybe environment": Black youth and, 25; fast life and, 139–45; in Minnesota, 99–106; origins of, 89–109; white spatial-temporal imaginaries and, 106–9
Mbiti, John, 33, 158–59, 177
McCaskill, Carl, 164
McCleskey v. Kemp, 150
McClintock, Anne, 104
McKittrick, Katherine, 10, 72, 194–95, 232n15
Medoff, Peter, 127–28
memory, misappropriation of, 162
mental health, prescience about Black life course and, 186–87
meritocracy, myth of, 178
Merton, Robert, 31, 141, 155
Midwest: Blackness and Indigeneity in, 94–99; culture and sociology in, 89–94; "maybe environment" in, 99–106
Mignolo, Walter, 33–34
migrant justice collectives, 238n18
Miles, Tiya, 97
Miller, Jody, 239n9
Mills, Charles, 61, 67–68, 99, 107, 148, 219n1
mindfulness, 196
Minnesota: "maybe environment" in, 99–106. *See also* Twin Cities
Minnesota Bureau of Criminal Apprehension, 186–87
Minnesota Compass, 105
Minnesota Homeless Study, 99
Minnesota Nice, 93–94
"The Miracle of Minneapolis" (Thompson), 24, 91–94, 108–9
misogynoir, 177–78; temporal dispossession and, 74–79
mixed methods research, 8–14
mnemonic community: Black youth and, 188–93; historical events and, 33–34
modernity: Afro-modernity and, 37–38; Blackness linked to, 159; time and, 32, 221n22; whiteness linked to, 39, 160–61
money and time: Black womanhood and, 51–56; Black youth consumption and, 163–64, 245n57; Black youth labor and employment and, 147–48; fast life and, 138–45; processing time for Blackness and, 69–74; reproductive labor and, 153–54; space racialization and, 103–6; wealth inequality and, 110–13
Morales, Ricardo Levins, 87–88
Morrison, Toni, 187–88
Moten, Fred, 3, 38, 232n17, 253n6

Movement for Family Power, 51, 225n93
Moynihan Report, 170
multiple consciousness of Black women, 75–76
Muñoz, José Esteban, 178, 183, 192
Museum of Science (Boston), 130
music: Afrofuturism and, 188–93; Blackness and, 115, 236n1; Black youth involvement in, 11, 41, 159–60, 193–94; space and, 193–94

Native American youth, 8; in Minnesota, 95–99; school experiences of, 113–19. *See also* Indigeneity and Indigenous groups
Native studies, slavery and, 94
Navarro, Jenell, 94, 202
negativity, racialization and, 20
Negri, Antonio, 134
New York Times, 164
Ngo, Helen, 21, 65, 95, 148–49
Nickrand, Jessica, 24, 91–92
No Future: Queer Theory and the Death Drive (Edelman), 5–6
No One Is Illegal (NOII) movements, 238n18
North Minneapolis (Minneapolis), 104–6
Notes of a Native Son (Baldwin), 159
nowness, power of, 194–98
Nyong'o, Tavia, 72

Obeidallah, Dawn, 143
objectivity, violence and, 126
Ogburn, William Fielding, 234n50
Ogle, Vanessa, 30
Oliver, Melvin, 155–56
Omi, Michael, 21
"On the Faith of the Fathers" (Du Bois), 63
On the Run: Fugitive Life in an American City (Goffman), 172–73
opportunity: fast life and, 144–45; race and, 119–24; rejection of Black youth from, 164; structures of, 207–8; white time and structures of, 149–54
Otherness, temporality of, 39–40, 99–100
otherwise worlds, Black youth and, 202
overstanding, 240n20

Painter, Nell Irvin, 21
pan-toting tactics, workplace resistance and, 40–41
pastness, *tabanca* time and, 125–26
pathology, in urban sociology, 173–76
Patrick, Deval, 167

penal-legal system, racialization of time and, 19, 217n63
Perry, Pamela, 190
persuasion, CP Time and, 44–45
phenomenology: of Blackness, 89–94; of whiteness, 66–67, 89
The Philadelphia Negro (Hartman), 174–75
Phillips, Susan, 45–46
Physics of Blackness, 49
Poitier, Sidney, 42
police and policing: Black youth and, 80–88, 177–78, 204; deportation time and, 135–36; prescience of Black youth about, 186–87; racialization and, 128–29, 237n9; slavery compared with, 189; in Twin Cities, 90–94; in urbanized space, 241n30. *See also* state terror
politics, time and, 167–68
positivist sociology, job search and hiring process and, 122–24
possession, whiteness and, 146
The Possessive Investment in Whiteness (Lipsitz), 146
postremoval time, families and children and, 131–36, 238n20
poverty: de-pathologization of, 174–76; risk/resiliency research and, 171; in Twin Cities, 91–94
power: time and, 38–41, 44–49, 60–61, 168–69, 223n55; whiteness and, 146–49
praxis: CP Time as, 49–54; humanness as, 195–96
presence/attendance, CP Time and indeterminacy of, 44–45
present orientation: of Black youth, 168–76, 181–84; in ethnographic research, 168–76, 196–98, 246n11; futurity and, 176–84; power of nowness and, 194–98; prescience in, 184–88, 204–6
Prince (Rogers Nelson), 199
prison-industrial complex: CP Time linked to, 42–49; deportation time and, 134–36; transgressive temporalities and, 129–30, 237n11
private property, time as, 80
processing time: job search and hiring process and, 123–24; labor and, 63–68; oppression and, 189; racialization and, 61; surveillance and criminalization of Blackness and, 69–74; as time theft, 80–88
progress: linear time linked to, 74; oppression of, 37; whiteness linked to, 32–33

punctuality: Black youth's resistance to, 35–37, 50–54, 57–58; COVID-19 disorientation and, 201–6; CP Time and, 43–49; rejection of protocols for, 2–5

Quashie, Kevin, 181–82
queer identity: Black youth and, 5–6, 73–74; funk and, 3–4; futurity and, 182–83, 192; heteronormative logics and, 214n21; misogynoir and, 74–79; runaway status and, 8; slowness and, 52–54; time and, 152–54, 243n30

race, racialization, and racism: beauty standards and, 54–56; Black youth perceptions of, 156–58; ethnography and role of, 11–14; hiring process and, 119–24; loss of time and, 62–68; in Midwest, 90–91; modernization and, 33–34; opportunity and, 119–24; prison-industrial complex and, 129–30, 237n11; relational racial identity and, 96–99; scholarship on, 34–37; in school, 113–19; space and, 99, 101–6; suppression of curriculum on, 115–19; temporalization of youths in urbanized space and, 18–23; time and, 5–7, 23–24, 32, 34–35, 37–41, 210–11; time use vs. time theft and, 60–61, 79–88, 165–66; in Twin Cities, 91–94. *See also* anti-Blackness
racial time, 61: Fleming's concept of, 34–35; social time as, 37–38
Rawick, George, 39
reflexion, definition of, 220n6
refugee temporality, 223n55, 233n37
relational racial identity: formation of, 96–99, 233n36; white spatial-temporal imaginaries and, 107–9
representation, violence of, 220n3
reproductive futurism, queer theory and, 5–6, 214n21
reproductive labor: misogynoir and, 74–79; time theft and, 103–4, 153–54
resistance: by Black womanhood, 55–56; CP Time as, 38, 40–49; deportation time and, 134–36; fashion as tool for, 163; to whiteness, 149, 162–66
Resurrecting Slavery: Racial Legacies and White Supremacy in France (Fleming), 34–35
reverse racism: affirmative action as, 148; white claims of, 156–58
Rich, Adrienne, 29–30, 220n4
Richards, Beah, 42
ridicule, inverting whiteness with, 158–66

278   INDEX

Rifkin, Mark, 25
Rios, Jodi, 81–82, 235n68, 241n30
Robinson, Cedric, 7
Rock, Chris, 77
Rodríguez, Dylan, 42, 178, 224n67
Roediger, David, 147
"Rondo Days" festival, 105
Rondo neighborhood (St. Paul), 104–6
Roof, Dylan, 251n94
Rosaldo, Renato, 11, 21, 34, 39, 46, 126
Roxbury (Boston), 127–28, 171–72
Run-a-Way (multiservice center)
    (pseudonym): emergency shelter and
    independent programs at, 16–18;
    organization and activities of, 14–18;
    research at, 7–8
runaways: Black youth as, 201–6; fugitives
    vs., 7–8

Sampson, Robert J., 171–72
Sanders, Bernie, 167
Scenes of Subjection (Hartman), 184
school: Black youth experience of, 154–56;
    CP Time and, 50–54; for Native American
    youth, 97–99; spatio-temporal locations
    of, 130; teaching biases and, 63–64; time
    racialization in, 43, 113–19; unlearning
    in, 200
Secondary Security Screening Selection, 134
self-definition/self-determination, CP Time
    and, 50–54
Settersten, Richard, 141–42
settler time, 25, 94–99
Sexton, Jared, 42–43, 94–95, 226n1
sex trafficking, Black womanhood and, 138–39
Shakur, Assata, 116–17
Shange, Savannah, 249n59
Shapiro, Thomas, 155–56
Sharma, Nandita, 20, 98
Sharpe, Christina, 185–88
Shaw, J. Brendan, 166
shopping, Black experience with, 69–74
Silko, Leslie Marmon, 232n27
Simone, Nina, 6
Sirianni, Carmen, 179
Sklar, Holly, 127–28
slavery: afterlife of, 67, 115, 144, 189, 221n30;
    Black youth perceptions of, 188–93; in
    Canada, 92–93; fashion as link to, 163;
    Indigenous groups and, 95–96; in Native
    studies, 94; in school curriculum, 115–19;
    time racialization and, 37–39, 49, 223n53;
    whiteness and, 147

slowness, Black practice of, 52–54
Smith, Andrea, 94–96, 161–62, 202
Smith, Jada Pinkett, 77
Smith, Mark, 39
smudging (Native tradition), 97
social capital, Blackness and, 99–100
social death, 142
Social Death: Racialized Rightlessness and
    the Criminalization of the Unprotected
    (Cacho), 53
social institutions, racialization and, 20,
    225n91
social time: CP Time as, 50–54; inclusion
    and exclusion and, 57–58; racialization of,
    23, 37–38, 83–84; stigmatization of Black
    sociality, 174–76; theories of, 30–37, 220n7
sociogenesis/sociogenic principle, 73
sociology: alternative methods in, 11–14; of
    education, 116–19; Midwest in, 90–94;
    risk/resiliency research in, 171; skepticism
    concerning, 9–11, 216n37; space and
    time in, 99–101; time and, 29–37, 57–58,
    175–76, 202–6
Sojoyner, Damien, 51, 117, 192
Somali migrants, in Twin Cities, 98–99
Sorokin, Pitirim, 31
sousveillance, 12
Southeast Asians, in Twin Cities, 98–99,
    233n37
sovereignty, Blackness and, 94–95
space: in Black music, 188–93; Black
    womanhood and, 55–56; carceral
    space, 42–49, 99; CP Time and, 51–54;
    criminalization and, 81–82, 235n68;
    deportation time and, 131–36; music and,
    193–94; racialization of, 99, 101–6; time
    and, 4–5, 24–26, 95–99, 129–30; urbanized
    space, 18–23, 213n2, 221n29; whiteness and,
    89–90, 106–9, 148–49, 160–66
Spillers, Hortense J., 75–77, 150
Spivak, Gayatri Chakravorty, 43
Stallings, L. H., 2, 4
state terror: life course and, 139–40; prescience
    of Black youth about, 186–87, 197–98,
    204–6. See also police and policing
stereotypes: of race and time, 43; of whiteness,
    160–61
stereotypes of whiteness, 160
Streets of Hope: The Rise and Fall of an
    Urban Neighborhood (Medoff & Sklar),
    127–28
strikethrough, 215n26
suburbanized space, race and, 241n30

INDEX   279

Sullivan, Shannon, 148–49, 158
surveillance: of Black youth, processing time and, 69–74; racialization of, 234n49
survival: deportation time and, 134–36; fast life and, 142–45
Swartz, Jeffrey, 245n57
Swistun, Débora Alejandra, 10

tabanca time, 25–26, 125–36
Tadiar, Neferti X. M., 80
taken time, debt and, 68–74
Tally's Corner: A Study of Negro Streetcorner Men (Liebow), 176
Tang, Eric, 223n55, 233n37
teaching biases, Black students, 63–64
technology, time racialization and, 39
teefing time (theft of time), 59–61
"Tell Me" (Groove Theory), 193
temporal capital, 153–54
temporal coordination, Zerubavel's concept of, 31–32
temporal dispossession: job search and hiring process and, 120–24; misogynoir, 74–79; wealth inequality and, 155–56
temporality (time): Black youth perceptions of, 1–4, 150–54, 208–10; Black youth transgressions of, 26–27; COVID-19 disorientation and, 201–6; deportation time, 131–36; end of time, 199–200; future and, 27–28; immigrant perceptions of, 129; marginalization of, 30; in music, 188–94; owning vs, borrowing of, 1–4, 80–88; queer identity and, 52–54; race and opportunity and, 119–24; racialization and, 5–7, 19–23, 34–35; role of, 23; school bell as indicator of, 113–19; settler time, 97–98; sociology of, 29–37; space and, 4–5, 24–26, 99, 129–30; *tabanca* time, 25–26, 125–36; Trinidadian perceptions of, 126–30, 237n13; violence and use of, 165–66; white manipulation of, 37–41, 179–80, 219n1; whiteness and, 26–27, 33, 37–41, 43–49, 57–58, 80, 106–9, 146–49, 219n1; of youths in urbanized space and, 18–23
temporalization, Black culture and, 162–63
tempus nullius, 95
Trouillot, Michel-Rolph, 126
terra nullius, 95
There Are No Children Here (Kotlowitz), 170
Thích Nhất Hạnh, 196
Thompson, Derek, 24, 91–94, 108–9
Thompson, E. P., 104

Timberland, 164–65, 245n57
Time and the Other (Fabian), 99–100
Time Binds: Queer Temporalities, Queer Histories (Freeman), 32
time management, 59–60
time mining, 69–74
time theft: education as, 116–19; racism and, 62–68; space racialization and, 103–6; time use vs., 79–88. *See also teefing* time (theft of time)
"To Be Young, Gifted and Black" (Nina Simone), 6
Tolle, Eckhart, 196
tone policing, 82
transformativity, CP Time, 50–54
transgender identity: funk and, 3–4; heteronormative logics and, 214n21; runaway status and, 8–9, 216n47; time and, 153–54, 243n30
transgressive temporalities, 23–28; CP Time as, 41–49; curfew violations and, 81–82; deportation time and, 134–36; fast life and, 137–45; incarceration and, 129–30; lateness and, 57–58; present orientation and, 169–76
transience, CP Time and, 47–48
trapping (drug trafficking), 137–45
Treaty of Mendota, 95
Treaty of Traverse des Sioux, 95
Trentham, Henry James, 39
truancy, fugitivity and, 36–37
Trump, Donald, 22, 167, 185
Twain, Mark, 191
Twin Cities: Black youth in, 24–25; demographics of, 93–94; economic inequality in, 24, 91–94; "maybe environment" in, 99–106, 108–9; migrant groups in, 98–99; racist real estate policies in, 108–9; Rondo and North Minneapolis neighborhoods in, 104–6; whiteness in, 89–94. *See also* North Minneapolis (Minneapolis); Rondo neighborhood (St. Paul)

"U, Black Maybe" (Common), 102
"Uncle Tom Was an Indian: Tracing the Red in Black Slavery" (Miles), 97
underclass, 106
The Undercommons: Fugitive Planning and Black Study (Harney & Moten), 3
unlearning, abolition and, 200
unquantifiable time, 66
unsettleable (unpayable) debt, 68–74, 163–64

urbanized space: ambiguity of, 102–6; Blackness and, 100–106, 234n50; Black youth racialization and, 18–23, 213n2; deportation time and, 131–36; fast life in, 143–45, 241n30; gentrification and, 127–28; inert city concept of, 85; interaction orders in, 250n73; job search and hiring process in, 120–24; present orientation in, 169–76, 183; Rondo and North Minneapolis neighborhoods, 104–6; temporalization of, 18–23, 102–6, 213n2; white spatial-temporal imaginaries and, 106–9

vagrancy laws, criminalization of Blackness and, 86
violence: Back Midwest and, 90–94; Black womanhood and, 239n9; Black youth perceptions of, 189–93; fast life and structure of, 142–45; police violence, 80–88, 250n82; processing time and, 61, 189; profitability of, 165–66; racism and, 63–68, 216n42; social organization of, 171–73; time and, 33–34, 38–39, 51–54, 68–74, 165–66; of urban renewal, 105–6

Wacquant, Loïc, 183
wages, public and psychological wage of whiteness, 146–48
waiting, CP Time and, 44–46
Walcott, Ronald, 38–39, 46
Walia, Harsha, 238n18
Warren, Calvin, 195, 215n26
Wayward Lives, Beautiful Experiments: Intimate Histories of Social Upheaval (Hartman), 84–88, 174–75
Waziyatawin, 95
wealth: Black youth perceptions of, 110–13; temporal dispossession and, 155–56
weed legalization, 238n29
Weheliye, Alexander, 4, 195–96, 225n88
white habitus, 16, 35, 41–45, 107–9, 148
White Men Can't Jump (film), 160
whiteness: accrued time and, 152–54; aggrieved whiteness concept, 218n74;

anti-Blackness and, 150–54, 161–62; Black youth perceptions of, 15–18, 156–66; CP Time as resistance to, 41–49; critical race theory and, 22, 218n76; history and, 190; Indigeneity and, 95–96; misogynoir and, 74–79; modernity linked to, 39; phenomenology of, 66–67, 89; progress linked to, 32; public and psychological wage of labor and, 146–47; racialization and, 21–22; space and, 89–90, 106–9; strategies for dealing with, 157–66; temporality of, 26–27, 29, 33, 37–41, 43–49, 57–58, 80, 106–9, 146–49, 219n1; in Twin Cities, 93–94; wackness of, 157–66
white time: Black youth and, 61; resistance to, 23; *tabanca* time and, 124–29
wigging tactics, workplace resistance and, 40–41
Wildcat, Daniel R., 223n55
Wilderson, Frank, 31–32, 82, 95, 162, 223n53, 232n27
Willis, Paul, 116–17
Wilson, August, 65
Wilson, William Julius, 99–100, 234n50
Winant, Howard, 21
Womack, Bobby, 106–7
Womack, Ytasha, 251n91
Woods, Clyde, 117
work. *See* labor
World Bank, 98
Wright, Michelle M., 9, 48–49, 93, 148–49, 159, 180, 191, 215n33, 219n78
Wright, Richard, 99
Wynter, Sylvia, 4, 21, 73, 226n106

Yo' Mama's Disfunktional! (Kelley), 174
Young, Alford, 175

zero-tolerance policies, race and, 118–19
Zerubavel, Eviatar, 31–32, 34, 189, 191, 221n22, 251n93
Zimmerman, George, 85–86

Milton Keynes UK
Ingram Content Group UK Ltd.
UKHW021101110424
440985UK00007B/184